The
Korean Road
to
Modernization
and
Development

Norman Jacobs

# THE
# KOREAN ROAD
# TO
# MODERNIZATION
# AND
# DEVELOPMENT

UNIVERSITY OF ILLINOIS PRESS

Urbana and Chicago

© 1985 by the Board of Trustees of the University of Illinois
Manufactured in the United States of America
C 5 4 3 2 1

*This book is printed on acid-free paper.*

Library of Congress Cataloging in Publication Data

Jacobs, Norman, 1924–
   The Korean road to modernization and development.

   Bibliography: p.
   Includes index.
   1. Korea—Social conditions  2. Korea—Economic
conditions—1945–      . 3. Korea—Politics and government.  4. Social structure—Korea—History.  I. Title.
HN730.5.A8J32  1985       306'.09519       84–16431
ISBN 0–252–01120–1 (alk. paper)

# Contents

# Preface

Why have the nontribal societies of mainland Asia (that is, those Asian agricultural societies other than Japan), in spite of tremendous changes and the not inconsiderable advisory and material aid which they have received from many sources, as yet not developed? The present study will attempt to provide an answer to this vital question through a case study of one such Asian society, Korea.

Reluctantly, my discussions of the post-1945 society are limited to the Republic of Korea (ROK), popularly known as South Korea, ignoring the Democratic Peoples' Republic of Korea (DPRK), popularly referred to as North Korea. The decision to do so is based on the following considerations: First, I have been unable to research or interview in, or even visit, the DPRK. Second, although excellent secondary studies of the DPRK, such as Scalapino and Lee's *Communism in Korea*, part II, and original source material in both Korean and English exist, those vital, critical-in-depth, firsthand accounts of the many facets of the development process by competent Korean and foreign scholars and participants which are available for the ROK are not similarly available for the DPRK. Third, since the present study is macroscopic as well as microscopic, theoretical as well as empirical, historical as well as contemporary, it is lengthy enough as it is.

In offering the Korean case study as a "typical" example of a mainland Asian development endeavor, I do not wish to imply that all mainland societies have identical development problems and processes, let alone that all these societies are alike. I have previously described my experiences in and observations about the development process in China (in contrast to Japan), Iran, and Thailand, and I would be hard pressed to offer still another monograph on Asian development if the Korean scenario was identical to those. And yet, at the same time, I believe that in spite of all the often significant differences among mainland Asian societies, they do share certain similarities, some of which are crucial for understanding the development process in those societies. This is one of the prime hypotheses of the present study, as it was in my previous inquiries.

Another salient hypothesis is that conversely, although Japan shares certain characteristics with its Asian mainland neighbors including Korea, certain other mainland and Japanese characteristics are qualitatively distinct, and it is these contrasting characteristics which I believe provide the clue to understanding Korean (and generally mainland Asian) and Japanese reactions to the challenge of development, which is the prime question posed in the study's opening remarks.[1]

# 1

# Introduction

## Feudalism and Patrimonialism

I wish to designate the two contrasting, qualitatively different selected sets of characteristics as a patrimonial social order in the case of the Asian mainland including Korea, and as a feudal social order in the case of Japan.

In a patrimonial, unlike a feudal, social order, (1) the primary social unit is not an organized group of warriors bound by social ties of defined rights, privileges, and obligations between superiors and inferiors, but a civil bureaucracy whose subordinate members owe open-ended obligations to superiors who may not, and usually do not, offer their subordinates reciprocated rights or privileges; and (2) the rewards for service to superiors are not stipulated access to land and its profit, termed fiefs, which must be constantly defended against political-economic rivals, but rather stipends, termed prebends, granted to public officeholders on grace by and solely at the option of superiors.

To elaborate—in a patrimonial social order as contrasted with a feudal social order (italicized terms designate social institutions and will be defined and discussed later in the chapter):

1. The right to *authority* is determined primarily by moral-intellectual considerations, monopolized by a self-asserted elite, and validated by the dissemination of morally based service (termed prebends) in the society through political means by that elite and on terms defined by that elite. This may be contrasted with a right to authority determined

1

by superior pragmatic ability to administer and coordinate the competing politically oriented groupings in the society.

2. The *economy* is manipulated in the name of public service morality by a political elite, with morality having primacy over economic objectivity. This may be contrasted with having objective economic profit as the goal of economic action.

3. The *division of labor* qualitatively distinguishes between an intellectual-moral role and other roles; contrasted with a division of labor in which all occupations are of equal moral worth, though not all roles are privileged.

4. The system of *stratification* entitles only the intellectual-moral role to formal corporate (or legal) recognition and protection of its independent rights and privileges. This may be contrasted with a system in which all legitimate roles are able to assert and strive to win corporate protection for their rights and privileges.

5. *Descent* forces the division of strategic property (normally land) among all legitimate heirs in a way that no recipient receives anywhere near the accumulation of the previous generation; contrasted with descent through one heir or the separation of property and status.

6. *Religion* is concerned primarily with man's adjustment to this social order, whose rules are determined and administered by an intellectual-moral elite. This contrasts with religious concern primarily with man's inner personal adjustment to an other-worldly order, administered by a number of competing religious associations.

7. The sanction to determine what constitutes a *legitimate social order and legitimate change* in that order is monopolized by an intellectual-moral elite. This contrasts with sanction in the hands of that element in the society which manifests the most effective ability to solve the existing problem of order.

I shall now explain and justify my choice of this particular theoretical design and contrast it with those of other observers of Asian development.

Because of the vitality of the bureaucracy in a patrimonial social order, some observers prefer to consider it a bureaucratic social order. But at least some feudal orders had highly sophisticated bureaucracies; Japan and Germany come immediately to mind. Hence I prefer to consider the patrimonial bureaucratic social order a particular kind of bureaucratic social order. Other observers have termed a patrimonial social order an Asiatic social order (some prefer the designation Asiatic Mode of Production), since it was in Asia that this kind of social order first came to their attention. But I do not consider Japan to be a patrimonial social order, although I concede that it had certain patrimonial characteristics similar to those found in both China and Korea, just as the Korean social order has had certain characteristics typical of feudal Japan. (I speculate that historically the patrimonial is attributable to the Chinese influence, while the nonpatrimonial is indigenous, emerging from a social order Korea once shared with certain of its northeast neighbors, including Japan. However, although both the patrimonial and nonpatrimonial elements have interacted symbiotically over the course of Korean history, it was the patrimonial which predominated and set the tone of the social order. This is the mirror image of the Japanese case, in which the Chinese [and Korean] patrimonial influence was and is present, but the nonpatrimonial indigenous element has dominated.) In spite of these continuities, however, certain characteristics of the two kinds of social orders are qualitatively distinctive, and I expect to demonstrate in this study that those discontinuous characteristics have been instrumental in propelling these two kinds of societies along very different development roads.

The terms patrimonial and feudal are *model* descriptions; that is, they are logically interrelated descriptions of reality, but they do not pretend to reproduce reality. For models are artificial, arbitrarily selective creations of observers, which can be useful in explaining the nature of reality. For this reason, models of the very same reality may vary from observer to observer. At first blush this may seem to be a major flaw. But to observers this is a model's virtue, since it can be made to focus upon what particular observers believe are the significant aspects of reality. Models then are not to be judged on their ability to include everything about reality, but on how well they provide a guide to understanding a particular query about a particular reality. It is pointless to criticize a model because it does not satisfy everyone's curiosity on all occasions. Provided it is logical and consistent, a model should be judged on its utility for the particular purpose at hand. Since it is the model which determines which questions will be asked as well as how these questions will be answered, no matter how logical and how enlightening a model may be in answering some questions it can be useless, or worse, misleading, in answering other questions which are outside its discourse.

The implication I wish to draw from this theoretical discussion of models is that most existing models of development, whether capitalist or socialist in inspiration, are not necessarily universally valid, though they may claim to be so, because they have emerged from western intellectual interpretations of their own feudal and subsequent Eurocentric social experience. In particular, I suggest that these models are not appropriate to illuminate the development process in patrimonial social orders such as Korea. My conclusion is not now as iconoclastic as it was when I suggested it more than two decades ago. Clearly western development models, no matter how brilliantly conceived, have failed to provide a guide to, let alone helped to solve, the development problem in the world's undeveloped, nonfeudal social orders. I believe that the present study's model is at least a step in the right direction. To be sure, the patrimonial model is not original with me. It was first formulated by eighteenth-century westerners hoping to explain in what ways and why the societies of Asia were different from their own. At that time the differences were not obviously technological and so fortunately the models focused upon social rather than material considerations. The two theoretical giants of the nineteenth century, Karl Marx and Max Weber, and their disciples in this century, notably Karl A. Wittfogel, contributed importantly to the model's elaboration, while most recently it is the Japanese who have refined the model in the light of their empirical studies of a number of Asian societies, including their own.

I freely acknowledge my debt to all my predecessors and contemporaries. However, because my study of and experiences in Asia and my theoretical and empirical interests have differed in a number of respects from those of other observers, likewise my particular patrimonial model differs in any number of respects from those of other observers. It is in order, therefore, to record briefly some of the possible fundamental differences between this and similar models.

I believe that:

1. The patrimonial is a (model) social type distinct from and parallel to a feudal-cum-successor social type, each with its own stages of social evolvement, *including the present*. This view differs from conventional Eurocentric models which assume (1) that all precapitalist or presocialist agrarian societies are feudal, or, (2) if the patrimonial concept is recognized, that patrimonialism is a stage which existed universally prior to feudalism, or (3) that patrimonialism is Asia's peculiar road to a universally shared evolutionary destiny.

2. The "traditional to transitional to modern" social process model so prevalent in contemporary development thinking need not necessarily connote the same kind of change in patrimonial social orders which it has in the feudal-cum-successor social orders of western Europe and Japan, from whose historical experience the model was derived. Thus the process of change in contemporary continental Asia—at issue, Korea—must not be considered an incompetent, in-

complete version of what happened in the transition from feudal to modern social orders in western Europe and Japan. Rather the process in continental Asia is a qualitatively different kind of experience, one consistent with patrimonially defined goals and social organization which must be studied and understood in its own terms. This view implies dissent from the prevailing "sociology of the developing areas" which argues that continental Asian societies will sooner or later have to conform to the feudal-cum-successor experience, preferably under the patronal guidance of either the capitalist West or socialist East, if they are ever to succeed in making the transition from tradition (associated with nondevelopment) to modernity (associated with development).

3. Model builders should no more limit themselves to the western European historical experience in constructing a feudal-cum-successor model than they would in constructing a patrimonial model. But they must also resist the temptation to tinker with the western European model in the light of the Asian-Japanese development experience. Rather they should attempt to construct a fresh model which combines the historical development experience of both western Europe and Japan, like the model offered earlier in this section.

4. Patrimonial social orders, now or in the past, are not static. In fairness to at least certain of the observers who described patrimonial social orders as unchanging—Marx comes to mind—it must be pointed out that they never meant to suggest that these societies were absolutely immutable, but rather that they were not dynamic in the sense that certain changes significant for the development process to succeed were not, and perhaps were not capable of, taking place under the prevailing rules of these societies. Consequently, although I regret their terminology, I am in sympathy with their point of view. I do believe that although certain not inconsequential changes are occurring in Asian patrimonial social orders, and many of these changes smack of those associated with the process of building a modern industrial order in societies which emerged from feudalism, the changes may not be those necessary and sufficient to develop patrimonial social orders successfully.[1]

## Modernization and Development: Patrimonial Modernization and Colonial Patrimonialism: Orientalism and Dependency Theory

One implication which may be drawn from the previous observation is that modernization is not necessarily the equivalent of development, although historically the two processes have been linked in feudal-cum-successor social orders. I define modernization as the introduction of novel means in order to improve a society's performance, but with the aim that those changes not challenge, and in fact reinforce, certain cherished goals and organizational procedures. Novel stimuli may come from indigenous or external sources, or a combination of the two, the mix varying from time to time in a society and from society to society. In Asia, when that stimulus has been derived, directly or indirectly, from western Europe or the United States, it usually is termed *westernization*.

Development, in contrast, I define as the maximization of the potential of a society, regardless of the society's existing goals and organizational procedures. Development thus is an open-ended commitment to accepting or rejecting innovation on the objective grounds of whether or not innovation contributes positively to maximization, and, although this may not be apparent at first, "no matter what" the consequences that change may have for existing cherished goals and ways of doing things. Following the lead of the sociologist Max Weber, this kind of objectivity is often contrasted with substantive objectivity, which accepts innovation only to the extent that it contributes to reinforcing certain existing cherished goals and tasks—which is my definition of modernization. To be sure, such a difference between objectivity and substantive objectivity is an ideal, since in the real world (which social scientists like to believe exists), no society, no matter how developed, is totally objective any more than any society, no matter how undeveloped, is totally unobjective. Nevertheless, the distinction between objectivity and substantive objectivity is defensible and I hope useful if we understand that (as in my distinction between modernity and development) reference is only to those decisions which the particular (in this case patrimonial versus feudal) model has selected for scrutiny and if those decisions are evaluated in terms of whether or not they have been made primarily on objective or substantively objective grounds. It is also pertinent to keep in mind that my distinctions of both modernization-development and objectivity-substantive objectivity are not drawn in terms of all the singular characteristics of specific individual societies, since that would be meaningless for my purposes, but rather with respect to certain model-selected considerations which I have come to believe are characteristic of two qualitatively distinctive kinds of social orders.

A significant implication of this line of reasoning is that development is a particular kind of modernization which up to now has occurred only in a particular kind of social order, the feudal-cum-successor, and that modernization is integral to the development process, but not vice versa. I am aware that most observers of development reverse this terminology, considering development as an integral part of the modernization process. But I do not view such a difference as merely semantic, since these observers consider all premodern agricultural societies as feudal and therefore ripe for development, which, though logically defensible according to their model, obviously I reject, believing as I do that such a view obscures rather than clarifies the real-life development problem in those societies I designate as patrimonial. Hence, though a member of a decided minority, I hold to my connotations of the terms development and modernization.

Turning specifically to Korea, we observe first that modernization, as I choose to define it, has occurred a number of times in Korean history, most pertinently during the nineteenth and twentieth centuries, when it coincided with external, especially western and Japanese, intrusion. Hence I suggest that the conventional question, whether or not the changes in those centuries in particular are truly modernizing innovation, ought to be rephrased to ask whether those changes were modernizing or developmental. Without denying the modern character of many of these innovations, I suggest that those changes were not simultaneously developmental, in spite of the fact that a number of them resemble in form the very changes associated with the modernizing process in developed societies, because they have been deliberately employed to reinforce developmentally counterproductive patrimonial goals!

I consider this point of view helpful in understanding why modernizing innovations which had been integral to the Japanese development process did not develop Korea during the Japanese occupation. We can similarly treat the argument that save for such foreign intervention, Korea could and would have developed as a consequence of those eighteenth- and nineteenth-century innovative internal changes which preceded foreign, especially Japanese, penetration. Although no one can logically deny such a possibility, I suggest that this conclusion need not be the only implication from the evidence. We need not assume that the indigenous Korean innovations, though necessary, were sufficient to stimulate development, if simultaneously existing Korean patrimonial goals and procedures detrimental to the development process were not altered. Economists call such modernizing innovation *selective rationality* or *selective objectivity*, using selective in the sense that (1) not all the innovations judged necessary and sufficient to stimulate development are present, or (2) the innovations resemble those of developed societies but have not operated to stimulate development because of countervailing influences. In the present study I prefer to use the appellation *patrimonial modernization* to describe such a phenomenon in patrimonial social orders.

The Japanese occupation of Korea also is useful for appreciating how a colonial power modernizes without developing a patrimonial society, not only by not changing that society's fundamental patrimonial goals and organizational procedures, but also by positively reinforcing those goals and procedures by modernizing them; for example, by providing more efficient patrimonial administrative control over the populace and prebendary access to its wealth. Moreover, in the process of revitalizing those aspects of the patrimonial inheritance which were not conducive to development change, the Japanese colonialists successfully not only stifled the Koreans' ability to adapt and maximize the developmentally potential aspects of the colonialists' nonpatrimonial social order, thus reducing the social encounter between colonialists and colonials to selective acceptance of the superficial aspects of the colonialists' society, but also established the precedent for accepting innovation as a modernizing and not necessarily a development experience. I call this kind of colonialist-colonial encounter *patrimonial colonialism* or *colonial patrimonialism*.

Although Korea certainly was not the only patrimonial society to experience this kind of colonial rule, its case is especially interesting—and damning—because the Japanese authorities, at the least through officially supported scholarship, were very much aware of the patrimonial character of Korean society, and hence knew full well what they were up to. The western colonialists, in contrast, can at least plead ignorance in those instances when, with the best of intentions, they misapplied their allegedly universal evolutionary model to guide professedly developmental programs in their colonial and ex-colonial possessions. When these innovations did not stimulate development, much to their but not our surprise, they could attribute their failings to practical, procedural difficulties, such as overcoming the weight of "tradition" in a "stagnant" society and creating better lines of communication and good human relations, and control, between the governors and the governed. By looking at the process of productive (developmental) change in the developed societies, we can see that such difficulties must be overcome if a society is to develop, but let me repeat that overcoming them is not necessarily sufficient to develop a patrimonial society such as Korea.

Which brings us to discussing two logically independent but often interrelated development concepts, namely, Orientalism and dependency. *Orientalism*, according to its critics, is the characterization of Asian societies—originally Islamic Near Eastern, but subsequently all those of the continent—as static, authoritarian, and even despotic, and wanting in autonomous urbanism and interest-group organizations. In contrast, western European societies are dynamic, progressive and even revolutionary, politically multicentered and potentially democratic, with defined legal rights. The critics consider Orientalism a Hegelian myth; an idealized construct contrasting an Orient of moral degradation mired in the undesirable (the traditional), in contrast to what the Orient should be and could be if properly modernized along European lines. *Dependency* connotes that Asia's backwardness has been due to a colonial and postcolonial discrepancy between the ability of the developed economies (the center) and the inability of the undeveloped economies (the periphery) to accumulate and invest capital productively, because the center decision-makers who command the international economic order are dictating the terms of center-periphery economic relationships to the latter's disadvantage. Dependency is contrasted with *internalism;* that is, accounting for backwardness on the basis of internal, in the present case Oriental, characteristics, which are considered in isolation from the external pressures crucial to the dependency partisans. Since a number of dependency theorists are Marxists, a sometimes expressed but more often enthymemic theorem is that the process of gaining independence from the debilitating grip of the capitalist international economic order requires establishing a socialist economy. Thus is Marxism supposed to solve the dilemma of Asian undevelopment by destroying degrading, discouraging Orientalism, which places the onus for Asian backwardness on the character faults of its decision-makers and people, while at the same time showing a way out by attacking the capitalist perpetrators of postcolonial exploitation of former Asian possessions.

We can both accept and reject these two models. I am not an Orientalist in that, first, I do not view Asian societies as static. Quite the contrary, I consider them capable of modernization today as in the past. Yet I also believe that, save for Japan, Oriental societies are qualitatively different from non-Oriental societies with respect to certain significant characteristics, and hence that the modernization process has been and will continue to be qualitatively distinct in the two kinds of societies. Second, although I expect to demonstrate in the course of the study that some of the distinctions between Asia and Europe first raised by the Orientalists are pertinent to Korea's development process, I am convinced that others are not. To wit, I do not attribute differences to race, culture, "values," or motivation, but to the fundamental character of the social orders. My reaction to dependency theory is similar. I am fully conscious of the adverse effects of Japanese colonialism, and fully support the idea that the actions of postcolonial agents of the international economic order are significant in discouraging the development of the ROK economy in particular and the society in general. Nevertheless, I also believe that this does not imply that the converse is either logically valid or empirically true; that is, that an Asian patrimonial economy such as the Korean, if it severs its links to the international (read capitalist, if you will) economic order, even if capitalist decision-makers are replaced by socialist ones, will *necessarily* develop. I believe so, not because I consider Asian decision-makers incompetent, venal, unmotivated, and, worst of all, traditional, but because of the fundamental character of the social order within which they must act and which to date they have not confronted, let alone qualitatively altered. I hasten to add that I do not expect nor do I preach that they alter these fundamentals along western or Japanese lines. And based on what we know of both the ROK and the DPRK I cannot see that infusions of either socialism or capitalism respectively—whatever these European concepts truly connote in the patrimonial Asian context—will solve the problem, since patrimonialism can thrive in both kinds of social systems, as the two Koreas attest. In sum, I am not an Orientalist, but I am a patrimonialist. I refuse to consider dependency and internalism as an either-or dichotomy, though I believe that the internal is the major variable while dependency is the contributory, albeit necessary, influence.[2]

## Social Institutions and the Format of the Study

We shall now examine the elaborated overview of the contrasts between patrimonial and feudal social orders given earlier. Those contrasts were social institutional in nature. *Social institutions* may be defined as the key foci of a social order organized into particular structures. A social institutional analysis contrasts with both expressive-cultural and motivational analyses. That is to say, although I do not suggest that these other approaches are without merit, I do believe that for the particular problem at hand, (1) the social aspect is more pertinent than expressive cultural ideas or values (I understand social as denoting the relationships between human beings and the structures which arise to define the terms of and facilitate those relationships. Social may be contrasted with cultural, which denotes the products of human beings, such as their language, their artistic and mundane material creations, the patterns of their behavior, and particularly their expressive thoughts, usually termed values), (2) organization is more relevant than interpersonal relations, and especially (3) opportunity, particularly institutional opportunity, is more apposite than individual incentive ("the achieving ethic").

Specific rosters of social institutions will vary according to particular analysts' judgments of which aspects of social orders are significant for understanding the problems they have chosen to investigate. I consider the following seven institutions as both necessary and sufficient to explain the development problem in Asian societies:

1. *Authority*, the legitimate exercise of will and power in a society

2. *Economy*, the production, distribution, and consumption of a society's subsistence

3. *Occupation*, the mode of specialization of those seeking privilege in a society

4. *Stratification*, the evaluation and relative ranking of individuals in a hierarchy which determines relative access to the society's privileges

5. *Kinship and Descent*, the biological relatedness of human beings (kinship) and the terms under which strategic property, particularly land, is transferred from one generation to the next (descent)

6. *Religion*, the role of religious beliefs in determining the legitimacy of social relationships and social actions, and the role of religious practitioners in the social order

7. *Legitimate social order and legitimate change*, the society's determination as to what this constitutes and to whom the decision is entrusted.

The present study will describe in detail how the institutional characteristics of a patrimonial social order, contrasted when appropriate to the characteristics of the feudal-cum-successor social order, influence the Korean modernization and development process; especially how those patrimonial institutional structures, goals, and procedures have facilitated modernization yet have not facilitated, and have even impeded, development.

Each institution will be discussed in turn, each discussion constituting one or more chapters. I am well aware that this format is not ideal. For example some of the discussions, those on authority, economy, and religion in particular, are lengthy, while others, kinship-descent specifically, are very brief. Second, certain topics such as administration are pertinent to the discussions of a number of different institutions, and hence must be referred to more than once, in this case under authority, economy, and religion. Third, an institutional analysis, since it treats the key foci of a society as discrete, may give the false impression that societies are fragmented and discontinuous, and may otherwise obscure vital interconnections. I have tried to remedy the first problem by dividing the discussions of authority, economy, and religion into two chapters each, the second by avoiding repetitive discussions while cross-referencing, and the third also by cross-referencing. If the reader still is not mollified, I can only point out that the popular topical approach obscures those very social characteristics that the present study wishes to highlight; that is why, with all its drawbacks, I still prefer using the discrete, institutional approach.[3]

## Chronology

Although we must be concerned with Korea's past to some extent, since I am a sociologist and not an historian my reference to that past is both cursory and theoretical. The chronology is thus limited to the following:

| | |
|---|---|
| Imperial Dynastic Korea | until 1910 |
| The last imperial dynasty | 1392-1910 |
| Japanese Occupation | 1910-45 |
| American Occupation in the south and Russian Occupation in the north | 1945-48 |
| Independent Korea: The Republic of Korea (ROK) in the south and the Democratic Peoples' Republic of Korea (DPRK) in the north | from 1948 |
| The Republic of Korea | |
| The Rhee regime—Syngman Rhee | 1948-60 |
| The Chang regime—Chang Myŏn | 1960-61 |
| The Park regime—Park Chung Hee | 1961-79 |

Thus I terminate the study with the demise of President Park in 1979, and do not discuss the succeeding Chun Doo Whan regime, primarily because the record is not yet available. Preliminary assessment, however, indicates that although Chun will develop his own distinctive ruling style, we can look forward to continuity in those institutional characteristics I shall describe in detail in the following chapters. Some examples: Chun, like Park, is a general who has surrounded himself with clients drawn from the eleventh and fifteenth military academy classes (as Park did from the eighth class), favors industrial growth in Kyŏngsang province, has stressed economic-military strength and self-sufficiency while continuing to import food grain (now predominantly wheat save for failure in the rice crop), promises economic stabilization to combat rampant inflation while simultaneously pursuing rapid economic growth linked to exports for the international economy, rules by centralized patronal guidance of a bureaucratic staff while denouncing false reporting out of fear of reprisals for not fulfilling Chun's commands and quotas, and rhetorically denounces corruption without severing those political-economic relations which encourage it.

# 2

# Authority:
# The Formal Patrimonial
# Apparatus

## The Leader and His Staff: The Titular Ruler and the Decision-Making Staff

In Korean patrimonial thinking, the foundation and rationale for a political order is its virtue and the litmus test of that virtue is the virtue of its titular ruler. For although a ruler should respond creatively to the realities of Korean politics, if he indiscriminately resorts to force or relies solely on guile, no matter how successful he appears to be at the time, history will judge him, his lineage or associates, and his political order adversely. A ruler validates and enhances his virtue primarily by protecting the people through inspiring and surveilling his subordinate officials. If he does so, or at least looks as if he is doing so, when something goes amiss—natural or political—it is the officials and not the titular ruler who are judged culpable.

The monarchs of the past were never absolute, though any number of them, by dint of a commanding personality and historical circumstance, were able to dominate officialdom, just as weak monarchs in turn could be dominated by officials. However, although these officials as aristocrats were thus able to perpetuate their authority as a group over the generations, they never institutionalized the kind of legally defined rights and privileges vis-à-vis the monarch so characteristic of a feudal aristocracy. Hence individual aristocrats found themselves depending on establishing and maintaining a particular individual patrimonial-cliental tie to a particular patronal monarch to obtain and preserve their political prerogatives. Thus the officeholding members of the aristocracy, at least, supported the ruler, as he was the source of their authority and the means to protect their prebends against both out-of-office aristocrats and ambitious commoners. The consequence was an ambiguously defined symbiosis between titular ruler and decision-making staff.

The essence of that relationship, as the aristocrats saw it, was to have the monarch reign but not rule, or at least to contain the ruler's decision-making by their input and review. The means created at various times to achieve this goal included, first and foremost, a council system. The aristocratic counselors claimed that their rights originated in an ancient South Hall where all adult males, regardless of rank or prestige, were entitled to a say in decision-making. Whether this was historically valid or not, the counselors persistently resisted a monarch's attempts to convert them into his pawns on the patrimonial grounds that any titular ruler was replaceable, whereas it was the staff which was the eternal repository of patrimonial virtue, and hence of authority. However, since over time the councils proliferated, and in accord with patrimonial principles were unspecialized, the counselors spent a good measure of their time interfering with each other's activities and discussing endlessly, especially when they preferred not to act.

Another staff limitation on ruler initiative was a Board of Censors whose responsibility it was to bring to the attention of the ruler its own and others' warnings of structural or human defects in that patrimonial virtue so vital for staff loyalty and morale, anywhere in the administrative apparatus, which included the attempts of monarchs to concentrate power in their own hands. Censors could thus either facilitate or cripple an entire administration, let alone any innovation. However, censors were formidable foes only when they worked in concert against the rulers. When they could not, which was often, they created dissension, even chaos, and at the least inertia.

A final example: Political critics, often non-officeholders, constantly offered suggestions for reform and even radical changes in existing policies. Since some of them recommended council dominance of the monarch, not surprisingly the counselors were fond of quoting such tracts in their disputes with monarchs.

In his perpetual struggle with his staff, the ruler was not without weapons of his own. First, the ruler could appoint directly to office those and their heirs who had sided with the ruler in his achieving or maintaining authority, termed merit subjects. As long as they did not join with the regular staff, perhaps to block the appointment of new merit appointees, the old merit appointees were useful to the ruler in counterbalancing antimonarchial regular appointees. Second, the ruler had the right of short-term appointment, of rotation of existing appointees, and of final decision on dismissals. If the opposition protested too vehemently, a strong ruler might dismiss them in mass. Third, the monarch could employ personal aides outside the regular administrative structure, dependent solely on his prebendary grace, such as secret censors loyal to him alone, to implement policies rebuffed by the decision-making staff. Fourth, emergencies, such as a threat of foreign intervention, sometimes enabled a ruler to concentrate power and initiative into his hands. And although a king did not have authority over the military in peaceful times, he might control royal guards who were mandated to suppress rebellion, a commission which some rulers interpreted liberally to include subduing any and all of their troublesome foes. Fifth, imaginative rulers or those who came to power under dubious circumstances created novel political organs or recast existing ones to serve their own purposes. Finally, a ruler could always count on the fierce competition for appointment to the few available positions of higher office to play off one candidate against another to the monarch's advantage.

But none of these ruler or staff prerogatives ever changed anything institutionally. Neither ruler nor staff, if either was ever so inclined, was able to alter the pattern of ruler-staff, especially council, relations. At best ruler prerogatives only defended monarchial privileges against overzealous staff initiatives. The goal, or at least the consequence, was a harmony in varying degrees of equilibrium, though never a static relationship between ruler and staff. That arrangement did not necessarily work well, save in those instances in which the threat of catastrophe for all encouraged unanimity and creative decision-making.

Contemporary Korea is a republic, and hence the titular ruler is a president. Unlike formerly, authority and political initiative are consolidated in his hands. His extensive prerogatives, especially the right of special powers in emergencies, are legitimized in a constitution. Each president enacts his own constitution, which reflects his singular vision of the presidency and his distinctive ruling style and which each ruler considers an inviolate, sacred document. The validity of the constitution, and consequently the presidential powers derived from it, are affirmed periodically but only by popular referendum.

Under Park, in theory, executive decision-making became a rationally systematic process carried out by differentiated political and administrative staffs. In addition a cabinet, which met twice a week, advised the president along specialized lines. But Park vetoed or ignored the decisions of both staff and cabinet, absented himself from

cabinet meetings, and went over cabinet heads to make his own informal contacts and decisions on an individual, personal basis both
within and without the entire formal decision-making apparatus. The
prime minister, though appointed by the legislature, required presidential approval, as did the leaders of the executive staff, who were
nominally selected by the prime minister. The multitude of executive
agencies and boards, many imitative of American decision-making,
such as the National Security Council, Audit Board, and Inspectorate,
were put under presidential control or review, serving as both buffer
and counter to any potentially independent cabinet initiative. Simultaneously, interagency bickering, so typical of patrimonial bureaucracies, dependent as they are on the grace of a patronal president for
prebends, enabled the Korean president to neutralize potentially
meaningful staff opposition to his actions. In sum, presidents, especially Park, have been able to consolidate executive initiative in their
own hands on a larger scale and more efficiently—that is, in a more
*modern* way—than was ever possible in the past.

The older conciliar and censorial review functions of the administra-
trative staff have been inherited by default by a national assembly.
The president has consistently opposed both roles. (The question of
the assembly as a force for exterior, "popular" review of the executive
will be discussed subsequently.) *Conciliar role:* The assembly is required to meet only ninety days a year, and though extraordinary sessions can be called by the president or by one-third of the assembly
members, such sessions are mandated only to review executive decisions. The president can require reconsideration of any bill, though a
two-thirds vote of the assembly can override. One-half plus one can
impeach a prime minister or state counselor, while two-thirds can impeach the president. But this and many other assembly prerogatives
are nullified in a state of emergency, which has become the political
norm. Most pertinently, the president makes policy, resisting all attempts by the assembly to do so, though Park used his cliental Revitalization Reform Political Fraternity within the legislative government party. Conversely, the assembly has no means to force its will on
a reluctant executive. When its "irresponsible elements" have refused
to endorse executive initiatives, the president has ordered the government party to ram through his program (Rhee once locked in the legislators until they agreed to do his bidding), dissolved the assembly,
or simply refused to accept its decisions.

The opposition in the assembly, because it has been well aware of
its limited contribution to policy-making and because it is not an autonomous power center,has tried to carve out a role as investigative

and judicial *censor* of the executive. The assembly believes this to be relevant, even essential, to the political modernizing process, but the executive denies this, denouncing the assemblymen as petty power-seekers thwarting the national will as defined by the executive.[1]

### The Administrative Staff: The Bureaucracy

Beyond the infinitesimal policy-making staff, the larger, though still highly selective, administrative and technical staff—the bureaucracy—prevails. In theory, once recruited, trained, and certified as patrimonialists, all bureaucrats are assumed thereafter to be so imbued with moral self-control that they can be trusted on their own consciences to fulfill their responsibilities without the necessity of resorting to any formalized norms of personal conduct or performance. However, in marked contrast to the decision-makers, the administrators and technicians have also been trained in procedure or in specific subject matter, or both, and for that very reason have been considered inferior to decision-makers.

The bureaucracy has ever attempted to establish a separate identity and power base independent of the titular ruler and his personal retainers by striving to institutionalize a universal commitment to patrimonial moral purity and virtue. Since a patrimonial bureaucracy, by definition, does not depend upon a popular power base, such a tactic has been judicious. But there have been problems. First, unlike its Chinese counterpart, loyalty to ideology in Korea was rarely able to overcome parochial communal, especially kin, loyalties and create a solidary bureaucratic identity; quite the contrary, as we shall see, because Korean ideology and kinship exacerbated existing fragmented partisanship. Second, the ruler could exploit crises to open the coveted senior civil posts to outsiders, that is, individuals not indoctrinated in the requisite moral (read, bureaucratic group) loyalty. Such appointees, though in truth more patrimonial than the regulars because they were more dependent on the patronage of the titular ruler for prebends, understandably were less than enthusiastic about supporting their regular appointee rivals' doctrine of moral purity. Third, those certified as eligible for public office at all times exceeded the number of available openings. Consequently, by being able to manipulate both the number and the character of these appointments, a titular ruler was able to prevent the rise of any solidary front against his rule.

The intense competition for office also came to corrupt the selection process. Corruption was aggravated by the penetration of a money economy, since this afforded a more convenient medium and increased the opportunity for acquiring prebends through political favor (see Chapter 5). The consequence: the ever-intensifying scramble for appointment and promotion created a perception of public office as a prebendary prize and status symbol rather than as a sacred responsibility and trust. The public and national interest suffered. Certainly, in accord with the patrimonial notion of individual self-discipline and initiative, particular bureaucrats did act otherwise. But unfortunately this was neither the impression nor the norm inherited by the Republic.

The specific character of the contemporary bureaucracy, especially in the light of its past, is as follows: First, a singular mix of external control and internal autonomy. The elite decision-makers and their aides have been able to bend the bureaucracy to their will and prevent the emergence of any independent power base within its ranks. This is symbolized by the circumstance that the power to define and maintain the civil service code is vested in the president rather than in the formal legal system. More to the point, the executive controls the higher civil servants, and through them their aides, by making the security of agency and bureau heads dependent on the patronage of their executive ministers in the cabinet. The executive neutralizes assembly control and even nominal supervision of the bureaucracy. Legislators who infiltrate the higher civil service do so as individuals, and hence are co-opted by the executive, and thus no longer are to be considered legislators (see Chapter 7).

One consequence of executive politicization of the bureaucracy is that if executive direction is reasonable and task-oriented, the administration is effective. But if it is not, which is more typical, the result is either a pontificating executive with an ineffective arm, as under Rhee, or a freewheeling bureaucracy in which individual chiefs at various levels seize the initiative and act on whim, as during the Chang regime. Under such circumstances, as long as the chiefs appear to be formally conforming to appropriate rules and regulations and do not overtly challenge the power base of superiors, they are free of restraints, frustrating the emergence of a productively autonomous bureaucracy. This is not necessarily unwelcomed by an executive and its agents in the bureaucracy more interested in dissipating a potential political threat than in creatively resolving differences on vital issues on merit.

Second, Korean bureaucratic loyalty is vertical and particular. Satisfying one's superiors takes precedence over loyalty to the organization or to a task since security and promotion are more dependent on the personal considerations of patronal approval than on objective criteria such as job performance. For the very same reason, horizontal communication and concerted action are rare. And if a superior is transferred, he will try to move his cliental associates with him.

Consequently, third, bureaucrats can be unrealistic or indifferent to problem-solving, wary of innovation, wasteful, and authoritarian toward their critics especially without but also within the system, as long as they mollify their political patron(s). Because they are reasonably free of objective task review, bureaucrats can afford to devote their efforts primarily to influence-peddling and protecting and advancing their rank and prestige. They can afford to be indifferent to a public from which they derive no material or psychological rewards, and which has become resigned to tolerating their ways and cost.

Fourth, since task performance is subordinated to bureaucratic convenience, unless tinkering with the existing organization is inescapable, it perseveres. Yet, perhaps paradoxically, new sections, bureaus, and even agencies are often created, primarily to provide employment for clients. Such organs usually are added on to, rather than articulated with, let alone integrated into, the existing structure, with little thought given as to how this will affect performance.

Fifth, Koreans at all costs strive to avoid controversial issues likely to lead to vindictive personal confrontations. Conversely, conflicts over issues are attributed, and often rightly so, to interpersonal difficulties, and resolved, or more probably sidestepped, accordingly. Thus inept and even illegal acts are ignored or covered up if they will provide an excuse for personal discord, and critical program and personal evaluations and end-use studies, especially those from cliental inferiors, must be avoided.

Sixth, for all these reasons, when prodded to do something, decision-makers prefer to rely upon formalistic proposals to provide the illusion of productive action and to substitute moral intent for accomplishment. Most typically, the decision-making leadership, accompanied by catchy sloganeering and much hoopla, piously appeals for discipline, integrity, and devotion to duty, leaving subordinates in the unenviable position of attempting to stir up the lethargic bureaucracy. Sooner or later, at some appropriate descending level in the bureaucratic hierarchy of command, the campaign is neutralized and forgotten.

Seventh, Korean administrators prefer generalists to task specialists. Responsibilities are deliberately ill-defined to enable individuals to be hired, fired, and transferred, and to adjust quickly to abrupt shifts in policy without disrupting good human relations between patrons and clients. Specialists certainly are not unknown in the Korean bureaucracy, but they tend to be isolated by their unsympathetic colleagues and denied influential positions from which they might compete with and even neutralize generalists. And since specialists are less apt to be or have a powerful patron, they are more insecure than the generalists.

Eighth, the recruitment and training of bureaucrats reinforces generalism. Pre-service training reflects the bias of the Korean educational system (see Chapter 9), namely, its penchant for abstract lecturing rather than practical training and its fancy for legal formalism rather than the social and behavioral sciences. A number of institutes of public administration now exist. Although some of these, Seoul National University in particular, are turning out creditable graduates, too many candidates are the products of diploma mills. This is critical because the bureaucratic appointment and screening process is not as selective as it could be, given the great number of candidates appointed out of patronal consideration when measured against the total actually required for mandated tasks. For although merit selection is required by statute, there are a number of exemptions which enable the civil service to accept desirable candidates without formal examination. And once they are appointed, there is only perfunctory probation and modest, if any, in-service retraining.

Ninth, jurisdiction is as vaguely defined and regulated as job specification and performance. Deliberately so or not, the statutes which establish and define the role of the many agencies, bureaus, and subcomponents of the bureaucracy have created a great deal of administrative overlap and duplication. Such confusion and conflict are not easy to resolve because no reviewing, truly coordinating, and mediating agency exists in the Korean administrative system. Programs may be assigned to agencies incapable of handling them or split up to resolve competition, even if they are better handled as units. Consequently, on the agency or subagency or even the individual level, one jurisdiction may be busy to the point of being overburdened with responsibility while another is at leisure.

Tenth, superiors may be unrealistic about the burdens they place on their staffs, and morale suffers accordingly. Since fear of not pleasing superiors militates against rational, meaningful protest by subordinates, unqualified individuals may carry out requests with mixed or even disastrous consequences.

According to public administration scholar Hahn-been Lee, all these bureaucratic characteristics are not eternal (that is, cultural) but are reflective of a three-stage, universal, unilinear process which unfolds within a predictable time span—namely, a backward-oriented ("escapist") stage, a present-focused ("exploitive") stage, and a future-directed ("developmental") stage. The concrete, measurable difference between these three stages lies in the contrasting relationship between the decision-makers, termed the political elite, and those responsible for directing the bureaucracy, termed the task elite, on the one hand, and between the task elite and the bureaucrats, especially the upper civil service, on the other hand. Lee contends that the ordinary bureaucrats, on their own, realistically cannot be expected to provide the inspirational source of disciplined, dedicated, creative, and productively innovative—that is, developed— administrative behavior. That must come from the task elite on its own or under prodding from the political elite. In the escapist period, all—the political and task elites and bureaucrats alike—are dedicated to routine and pageantry, consuming valuable and scarce personnel and materiel without productive results. In the exploitive phase, the political elite, for any number of reasons—philosophy, weakness, ineptness, or opportunism especially— allows the task elite and the bureaucracy to serve their own interests and advantage, creating widespread misappropriation of resources, popularly termed corruption. Finally, in the development phase, all three parties are united in their dedication to performance, ideologically and through the political elite's oversight of the task elite, and in turn through the task elite's surveillance of the bureaucrats. Consequently, the entire administrative system is creatively adaptive and innovative, that is, developmental. In the Korean case, Rhee is the example of the escapist, Chang the exploitive, and Park would have been the developmental, according to Professor Lee.

We now are prepared to draw conclusions. In doing so I wish to rephrase Professor Lee's suggestive observations in my own patrimonial terms. Rather than view the recent administrative history of Korea as illustrative of a series of problems associated with a universal process of nation-building, we can interpret that history as a process of patrimonializing a nonpatrimonial ("western") administrative structure to insure that it will well serve persistent patrimonial bureaucratic goals and operating procedures. For example, one of the goals of a patrimonial political elite is to control and maintain patronal relationships with a clientele dependent on it for prebends. This has been variously served in Korea by maintenance of the status quo under the last imperial dynasty (according to Lee's model a first phase), by the efficiently exploitive mechanisms of the Japanese, the American-filtered Rhee regime, and the interim Chang government (all second phase), and then by Park's realization that maximizing the resources of the existing political order can produce more prebendary dividends than the means heretofore prevailing (the third phase). In each case, each succeeding political elite has appreciated the advantage of updating (that is, modernizing) but not necessarily qualitatively changing (that is, developing) certain inherited administrative practices, for development would require certain kinds of commitments which would threaten the patron-client foundation of the administrative order. I suggest that Park's subsequent shift from concern with development to national security in part was a realization that the security of his cliental interests was being threatened by 'certain latent consequences of his development programs (to be discussed further in this and subsequent chapters).

We can also evaluate the earlier litany of apparent incompetence and skulduggery within the patrimonial context, rather than by comparing the Korean performance against what we may have been educated to expect in terms of a western, nonpatrimonial model. If comparison with the western model is the measure by which to judge the Korean performance to date, then it clearly is mixed, if not wanting. But if we observe that even though work is motivated fundamentally by having all-powerful patrons dispense prebends to loyal subordinates rather than by appealing to and rewarding task performance, those innovative, western-inspired administrative means which contribute positively to persistent patrimonial notions have been or are in the process of being accepted, as Professor Lee's study suggests they are, then we cannot dismiss the existing Korean administrative system as an inept, venal, or dysfunctional, inevitably replaceable relic. Rather I suggest the Koreans are trying to work out what they consider to be a satisfactory relationship between certain cherished patrimonial principles and those novel, especially western-inspired, administrative means which will help them to better achieve patrimonial goals. But that kind of arrangement at optimum is a signal characteristic of a modernizing, but not necessarily developing, political order.[2]

## Korean Factionalism

For many observers, local or outside, partisan political contention is one of the endemic character traits of Koreans. According to one, perhaps biased, account, the practice originated when the early patriarchal consanguineous units were being welded into kingdoms under Chinese influence. By converting ancient Korean patriarchal rights into prebends, offering compliant patriarchs seals of office, benefices, and Chinese moral and material support, but always threatening to withdraw those favors, the Chinese were able to prevail, playing off one Korean leader against another in a game of divide and rule. Whether this is true or not, indigenous Korean rulers were to use such a patrimonial design to tame the patriarchs-turned-aristocrats by attempting to bureaucratize them. The aristocrats rose to the challenge by forging consanguineous alliances in hope of capturing monopolistic access to a ruler and his closest staff in order to obtain or legitimize *prebendary* advantage, rather than trying to institutionalize access to *feudal* political rights and privileges on a regularized, defined hereditary basis.

On the surface, consanguineal contention often revolved about deciding which of the partisans was more loyal to patrimonialism, and hence by implication which was more in accord with morality, and hence more worthy to rule. The controversy was fueled by two ambiguities in patrimonial political thinking; namely (1) that while moral rectitude of a political order based upon an idealized past is essential, yet administrators disciplined by mastery of the appropriate moral tracts (in this case Confucian classics) and certified by civil sevice examination are free to adapt their generalized patrimonial education to serve the "practical" concrete concerns of the day; and (2) that no precise definition of "practicality," and hence any consensus as to what this implied, emerged, whether in Korea or any other patrimonial society. Yet many observers believe that ideology was not at the heart of the contention, rather that the quest for authority and prebends was. Certainly new factions formed most readily whenever opportunities arose to destroy the influence of prominent factional patronal leaders, and hence their ability to guarantee prebends, especially public office, to their followers.

It was the ruler who usually decided which faction was to prevail in a major, prolonged dispute, especially if merit appointees (who did not enjoy an independent power base) were involved. Since, as suggested, much more than ideological compatibility or personal sentiment went into the making of such an important judgment, and hence a decision was never obvious until it was made, factionalists had to be most careful how they went about trying to assure the ruler's patronal favor for themselves, for maneuvering could be compromised by opposition charges that it smacked of disloyalty to the ruler. Especially the line between a faction, which was legitimate, and a clique, which was by definition politically immoral and subversive, was ambiguously drawn. An opposing faction was sure to, and a ruler might, draw the line as close as possible to treason whenever possible to do so.

At least some factions, and hence their rivalries for the glittering prize of the prebends of public office, persisted over generations. This was practically facilitated by the establishment of factionally sponsored countryside academies where those not in office could go to lick their political wounds, reestablish factional discipline, replenish their ranks with new recruits, and plot a return to office. Factional viability was ideologically rooted in the Confucian Chinese *Chia-Li Chieh-Li* of Chu Hsi, minor in Chinese thought but central to aristocratic Korea with its emphasis on genealogy as the wellspring of prebendary privilege. This treatise rationalized loyalty on moral, patrimonial grounds—in the Korean context, persistent loyalty within the smaller kin unit but flexible loyalty with regard to forming larger factional units of advantage.

The effect of historical factional formation and strife on contemporary Korean political behavior is not difficult to discern. First, it made even the most upright official fearful of, and in turn capable of, engaging in moral denunciation, rumormongering, backbiting, sowing suspicion, blackmailing, and conspiring. Second, in the process individuals and even factions were driven to seek security by becoming dependents of powerful patrons, insofar and for as long as they were willing and able to protect clential interests. Third, although at first it would seem to encourage frank discussion of issues, factional disputation too often was over impracticalities which could be and were resolved on moral-patrimonial and not on objective-pragmatic grounds. Fourth, factional strife too often made contention the issue rather than contending over issues, to the extent that some have characterized that strife as the Korean national political sport. Faction leaders were seldom if ever encouraged to become effective resolvers or compromisers, instead of obstinate partisan champions of their followers' caprices. Fifth, disputation was limited to bureaucratic insiders. Outsiders, for example tradesmen, and their ideas and concerns were not considered proper subjects for serious discussion unless particular bureaucrats on their own initiative became interested, and then they filtered those interests through their own patrimonial moralism. Finally, and in sum, factions and their activities were not a potential source for the generation of viable political parties, which many, including Korean political scientists, consider key to the modernizing-cum-development process; quite the contrary, factions impede such a process.

Contention can be found throughout the contemporary structure of Korean authority, at all levels from the primary ranks through their respective components to irreducible cell units within which basic cliques align and realign. In some instances, cliques coalesce around common bonds of kinship, locality, and academic training; in the military, for example, around the graduating class. In other cases it is the fortuitous personal contact with charismatic patrons that first sparks the formation of a coterie. One survey found that over one-half the sample preferred loyalty to patron over loyalty to office, but only if and as long as a patron offered protection and prebends. Hence, there is little thought of compromise and merging among factional rivals, since that offers scant advantage, especially to leaders, and when cooperation does occur it is ephemeral, since it has been incited by opportunity and will surely end when new opportunities arise.

Political parties especially are notable for their factional strife, for parties in truth are collectivities of individuals who have banded together to enable a leader to attain and maintain power and reflective advantage for his followers. Party members do not see themselves as representatives of a constituency outside themselves, whether it be those in other parties or those outside the party system. Especially, they do not view themselves as representatives of geopolitical or class interest groups, but as representatives of their political selves, establishing at best shallow ties outside the parties and only in so far as outsiders are helpful to the party members in their personal political struggles. Or, to rephrase, parties are seekers of power and not the result of it. They are not, therefore, a force for breaking out of particular loyalties such as kin or self-interest to broader, more impersonal loyalties as they have been elsewhere; quite the contrary, they are a force for the retention of such loyalties.

Political parties recognized by the government as legitimate lack ideological conviction. One cause of this, to be sure, is that the executive has been able to monopolize ideology, leaving the parties it tolerates little ground for maneuver save over how to assist the executive in carrying out its goal of militant anti-Communism. Hence, interparty contention over issues is shallow and superficial, being but a vehicle to denounce opponents as inept and hence unworthy to exercise power, or a bargaining device to obtain a share of the available power and prebends. Indifference to ideology certainly does have the advantage of permitting rapid realignment of cliental forces with minimal disruptive aftereffects. But it encourages raiding and the formation of opportunistic cliques whose members will ally themselves to anyone willing and able to offer some advantage in return for support. These cliques can be exploited by capable leaders to capture control of a party and even government power. But since members will desert their cliques readily if they believe it to be in their interest, leaders must be strong and sagacious to the point of being devious if they are not to lose their followers to other cliques or alternative leaders, and so further fragment the party. As the prospect for achieving power rises, so does the temptation to form factions, so that ironically the closer a leader comes to actual authority, the less chance he may have to lead a united party, because individuals, sensing power and prebends, attempt to form their own base to reap the political harvest for themselves.

Once in power, the leader presents himself as a political messiah, mandated to carry out the political will as he conceives it. He considers those who lost the struggle as carping factional pariahs likely to preach needless disharmony and political immorality if they are allowed to continue to struggle. This point of view is not without justification. But the leader goes further, drawing a fine line between contention and subversion, and thus is ever ready to use force if his didactic appeal for consensus and responsibility (read, subordination) fails. This posture enables the leader to ward off any legitimate claim by his opponents to share the prebends, while internally it assures followers that their monopoly on privilege is secure, thus discouraging raiding by rivals.

Historically, one can discover the roots of the present political situation in the Japanese period, when various Korean leaders both within and without the country constructed fiercely competing resistance organizations. Since the Japanese earlier had destroyed the monarchy and its bureaucracy, and when independence came in 1945 it was not achieved as the direct result of the efforts of any Korean group, no universally accepted, united cadre of founding fathers was available to take over authority from the Japanese. The indecision of the Americans, the disruptions of the Korean War, and the Republic's persistent contention with the north have intensified the uncertainty and fluidity of the political scene, characterized especially by a bitter and prolonged tug-of-war between the government and leading opposition parties.

But analytically the strife may be attributed to a continuation of older patrimonial conditions, albeit in novel (that is, modern) form. Specifically, dynastic administrative factionalism and cliquism now envelop the political parties. The older loyalties of region, kin, and prior association also survive. Only now fortuitous administrative propinquity also is sufficient to build patrimonial, patron-client organs of advantage. But contemporary patrons must be especially alert to opportunities for acquiring prebends, given the ever-changing political scene and, particularly with such high stakes, the fact that clients are more willing to desert the apparent bonds of "natural" loyalty than they have been in the past. Beyond the ability to dispense prebends of a quality and quantity previously unknown, the present leaders also have a decided advantage in that they can use their "modern" monopoly over the levers of power to suppress their opponents and prevent factional strife among their own constituents to a degree hitherto unknown, ignoring the prodding of the opposition, save on those occasions when outside influence, such as that of an occasionally disapproving United States, seems to warrant otherwise.[3]

### Centralization and Localization of Authority

The Korean rulers first attempted to centralize authority by offering direct benefits to local notables if they participated in and supported the center polity even against their own local loyalties and interests. The effort failed. Finally, as was the case in China, the Korean center came to accept local loyalty and strength, and to depend on an emerging ability to sanction and protect existing local prebendary prerogatives to keep potentially centrifugal local political power in reasonable equilibrium with minimal center security requirements. In Korea, as in China, legitimizing prebends came to depend on locals' ability to gain the sympathy of the central monarch, but, in contrast to China, Koreans retained existing prerogatives intergenerationally. For unlike the Chinese ruling class, the Korean local political elite remained an aristocracy of birth, rooted in local patriarchal tribal chieftainship, even though it adopted the individual merit morality of China.

Thus even when the locals from time to time participated in authority at the center, they still retained their local power bases. The ideal of the locals was to use their home bases to seize preeminent power at the center, while the ideal of the center was to diminish and neutralize these bases, knowing full well that eliminating particular local centers of power was ever possible, but eliminating local power per se was not. Although consequently the center was never a truly centralized enforcer of its will, the locals were never feudators legitimately able to exercise legally recognized rights in dealing with it. Rather the locals strove to create groups—factions if you will—to represent their prebendary interests at the center court. One author has termed this system multicentered despotism; I prefer *multicentered patrimonialism*.

Because it was patrimonial, the Korean path to political consolidation and nation-building was constructed from the center in descending order out to the periphery, rather than, as in feudalism, from the local area by ascending pyramidization to the center. In retreating from an attempt to impose his authority despotically on the periphery, the Korean ruler was forced to settle for quite tenuous links to the various local centers of power.

How this was accomplished is complex and controversial, and I can only briefly outline the patrimonially relevant major contours of that process. First, the center gradually controlled or neutralized the local notables by converting them or replacing them with centrally appointed or approved local representatives who were the vital loyal bureaucratic link in a chain stretching from the center down into the vast hinterland.

Second, the center appointed supervisors, such as the sometimes secret censors, to monitor local political activity. This could be dangerous to center interests, since the supervisors could collude with locals, a typical problem in patrimonial administration. Since the supervisors could move about at will, were mandated to examine normally confidential files, commanded whatever local support was necessary to carry out their missions, and could judge and even punish on the spot, the mere rumor that supervisors might appear was often sufficient to keep officials in line and away from economic and political temptation. This technique is characteristically patrimonial; that is, it uses representatives of superior levels especially but not exclusively from the center outside the formal hierarchical chain of bureaucratic command, sometimes with special extralegal secret mandates, to enforce the center will and intimidate personnel at any and all subordinate levels. This contrasts with feudally rooted bureaucracies which rely upon predictable schedules and regulations of a formal hierarchy in which officials at each level are directly responsible only for the performance of those on the immediately descending level of command.

Third, the emerging control of the center over the periphery is reflected in the organization of the local bureaucracy, termed by Koreans the provincial system. This eventually consisted of a chain of provinces, subprovincial great regions and great counties, and districts. This system did not penetrate the village communities where most of the populace lived; the center relied on local notables to watch over its interests there informally. Because the district apparatus was so crucial to both controlling and extracting from the populace, it was as elaborate as the provincial and even the central administration, while the chain of command between district and province was understaffed, indifferently treated, and even ignored.

The military came to be charged with protecting the northern frontier, and indirectly the capital, from invasion. Maintaining the loyalty of local commanders could be difficult, especially in times of turmoil or invasion when they might cooperate with the enemy or exploit the local population for their own personal advantage. In spite of this constant threat to center control, and even sovereignty, center civil-patrimonial dominance over the local military was never institutionally challenged. One reason was that the threat of treason was used to subordinate potential centrifugal military tendencies to central civil direction. But more to the point, the mission of the military commanderies, particularly on the level equivalent to provinces, was civil-bureaucratic in that it facilitated migration into the thinly populated northern frontier provinces and provided manual labor service in support of centrally controlled, truly military garrisons.

Fourth, the dominance of the center over the periphery was assured by preserving the capital as the locus of primary political patrimonial initiative. Hence individuals had to be either physically present or represented at the capital to secure and expand their prestige, power, and prebends; yea, even to protect their local interests! Consequently, although dynastic Korea was not an urban society in the western demographic sense, a very sizable percentage of the populace always have lived in or near the capital.

Fifth, capital dominance also was secured by ranking local officials of comparable responsibility lower than those in the capital. Not surprisingly, in consequence local officials sought to obtain posts in the central administration, to the extent that by the twentieth century few truly local officials existed. Even political exile reinforced the magnetic attraction of the capital in that exile dispersed center officials intent on reversing their descent into official purgatory all over Korea, infecting the locally privileged with a vision of a heavenly capital. Finally, by offering status and prebends to all those aristocrats who qualified, the civil service examination tempted even the most enterprising local notables away from achieving their ambitions through exploitation of their local bases. Hence, although local political centers certainly survived, they acted more as revitalizing and recruiting sources for the center than as threats to it; and that perhaps is why the center tolerated them.

Sixth, the center dominated the periphery by preventing its officials from sinking institutionally recognized independent roots in the periphery. Center officials never were appointed to their home areas or where their kinsmen were influential; in fact they might very well be deliberately appointed where those opposed to their relatives or political faction were strong. Officials were appointed to posts for stipulated short terms—for example, during the last imperial dynasty, provincial governors served for a year, and most others for three— and they could be transferred at any time at the option of the center. Ironically, the only viable local political ties most officials were able to preserve were those among colleagues who came from the same geographical roots and who happened to be posted in the capital at the same time. But concerted agitation by such individuals was limited by the confines of the administrative apparatus, especially at its central heart.

Seventh, since the administrative machinery only functioned down through the distict level, few officials were required to be on duty at any one time. At the end of the imperial period, for example, there were only 332 district magistrates, the most frequent centrally posted local officials. One consequence was that it was not too difficult for the center to supervise and control its field representatives. Another consequence was that there always were many more qualified civil servants than available positions. Candidates therefore accepted, and even encouraged on their own, frequent and rapid rotations in office even if that meant no further appointment at all. For only a single appointment, no matter how humble and brief, carried with it lifetime official status and prerogatives. This was salient because after the destruction of the old aristocracy (see Chapter 7) the composition of the political aristocracy was not persistent, only the notion of an aristocracy was. Without someone in a kin group appointed to a central office over a stipulated number of generations, an individual, his kinsmen, and by extension his entire local group, reverted to commoner status. And the vital option to appoint, which determined aristocratic status, was held firmly and exclusively by the center, which could and did use it to keep locally rooted aristocrats in line.

We now are prepared to draw conclusions. In spite of the cultural unity of Korea and the neutralization of once-powerful local notables, local political loyalties persisted. And in spite of its unchallengeability, the central administration especially in the nineteenth and twentieth centuries proved to be weak and ineffective in controlling the countryside. I suggest that these apparent paradoxes can be resolved by grasping the nature of the relationship between center and periphery in historic patrimonial bureaucracies. To wit, the center's interest is in insuring the maximum extraction of prebendary tribute with a minimum of fuss while simultaneously thwarting anyone on the local level who might interfere. The center had to learn that, given the level of political technology and communications then available, it could not hope to achieve those goals by direct supervision and decision-making everywhere in the periphery. Rather it came to appreciate that, so long as no overt challenge arose from below, the center need not intervene; that it could husband its limited political capital and restrict exercise of its power, using it only when an organized local threat to the center's prerogatives arose. In other words, the center, by default, realistically was willing to accept local political initiatives as long as they were temporary and individual. In like spirit, local officials, whether rotated magistrates or permanently assigned locally recruited clerks, were permitted to serve their own interests, so long as they did not overdo the privilege and threaten the viability of the system. The center, through all these concessions, hoped to insure that no local political interest ever would be able to force the center to accept legally (that is, to institutionalize) independent local authority as a right. And the center succeeded. For even though Korea was split asunder, encouraged indirectly or directly by foreign intrigue and invasion, at most peripheral power aspired to seize the center or to establish an independent rival to the center, rather than striving to stand against the center and extract formal-legal local rights and privileges. Even the most successful of Korean rebels became only a shadow government, albeit a powerful one, behind the center but not an institutional alternative to it, as did the Japanese military clans. What I am driving at is that although historic Korean authority never created a truly centralized political apparatus, for all the political weakness, confusion, and often disunity in the country, no peripheral element, no matter how powerful, ever created the kernel of independent feudal authority. This apparent political anomaly has intrigued observers, who have characterized the Korean system as multicentered despotic or centralized feudal. I suggest that these characterizations, though sensitive to the nuances of Korean political reality, are attempting to provide an explanation within the framework of the western experience. I prefer to view historical Korea as an example of a typical patrimonial society before the advent of modern technology made formal political centralization feasible; that is, one in which central authority never institutionally renounced political centralization, though it was forced by circumstance to accept political initiative in the periphery. In political science jargon, Korean local power was *deconcentrated;* that is, the periphery was mandated to carry out centrally determined initiatives, with local decision-making limited to whatever the center offered patrimonially on grace or deemed residual to its interests. Local power thus was not decentralized; that is, the center never permitted the periphery to carry out decisions of its own making as a legal right, as was so typical of feudally rooted political authority.

The formal structure of contemporary local authority is composed of the dynastic system of tiers of descending jurisdiction from the center through the province to the county and ultimately the district, with the addition of a new lowest tier, the township, reflecting further central penetration of the countryside. The administrative organization at all levels resembles the center save for changes in nomenclature (e.g., bureaus instead of ministries) and a centralized police force not subject to the jurisdiction of any local authority. A township is defined as an urban settlement with a population of 20,000 or more. Cities are townships which have at least 50,000 residents. Two special super-cities, Seoul and Pusan, exist outside the administrative chain under direct control of the center, while all the other cities are incorporated into the regular structure at the county level, subordinating them to provincial jurisdiction in the regular command chain.

The means by which the center controls local authority are as follows: First, the local bureaucracy, like the center, acts independently of legislative review, by virtue of those vested executive powers which purport to enable the executive to translate Diet generalities into the nitty-gritty specifics of daily administrative routine. Moreover, during a political emergency, which seems to be a chronic situation of late, the executive can use administrative decree to control local as well as center affairs. The inability of outsiders to influence government policy or programs is as obvious on the local as it is on the national level.

Second, there is an often competitive dual chain of field command. One chain operates from the technical ministries in the capital to their subordinate bureaus at all field levels. The second chain, under the Ministry of Home Affairs, is charged with reviewing budgets, supervising local personnel, recommending new appointments throughout the administrative system, except in the two special cities, and, most pertinently, controlling the ubiquitous police. The provincial minister of home affairs is the critical link in this chain because he is the principal activator of the capital's wishes. The capital controls this minister carefully, for example through rapid rotation before he can entrench himself locally.

Third, virtually all local personnel of any consequence—some 17 percent of the work force—are members of the central civil service, and those of major consequence, such as provincial governors, are members of the central higher civil service. Since the security and fortune of all these individuals are dependent on the center, their goal is to satisfy the capital's interests even when those interests conflict with the interests of locals under their jurisdiction.

Fourth, a decision at a superior level in the vertical chain of administrative command automatically supersedes a possibly conflicting decision at a subordinate level. Decision-making therefore concentrates at the center and is not seriously reviewed, let alone interfered with, by those situated below the center.

Finally, jurisdiction now is being exercised over even the smallest possible administrative unit, in contrast to the older system which limited itself to concern at or above the district. This is especially characteristic of urban centers. In Seoul, for example, the mayor is appointed by the president with the prime minister's routine approval, while the two vice-mayors are similarly appointed but with mayoral certification. Seoul is divided into nine districts, which are first subdivided into two levels of neighborhoods, the lesser of which consists of 100-200 houses, and then into blocs of some 20-40 houses each. The district chiefs select the superior-neighborhood heads, who in turn pick the heads of both the subordinate-neighborhoods and blocs. All these petty officials, for long unpaid local notables, are given responsibility for carrying out center policies and controlling, reporting on, and otherwise being responsible for the behavior of those under their jurisdiction. Volunteers for such a dubious honor are hard to find; but once suggested for the posts, individuals find it difficult to refuse, since that would arouse the ire and suspicion of both the government and their neighbors. Vulnerable as they thus are, such appointees are only too willing to carry out the political will of the center.

In sum, Korean authority is highly centralized and is becoming more so all the time. Korean administration has profited, if that is the term, from the Japanese modernizing improvements in the loose imperial system and from advanced American techniques of public administration, both of which have streamlined the system and made it possible to exercise jurisdiction at local levels far beyond the reach of the older apparatus. Local penetration and control also have been facilitated by the government's modernizing programs, fueled by war rehabilitation grants, appropriated Japanese property, and foreign aid, all of which have passed through center hands on the way out to the periphery. The possibility of receiving a share of this wealth has depended on the locals cooperating with the center's wishes. Modernization, since it touches all aspects of Korean life, also has escalated administrative jurisdiction, which in turn has expanded Seoul's censorial supervision, including the auditing of local authority, especially through the Ministry of Home Affairs and such organs as provincial administrative boards. Consequently, through Seoul's carrot or stick, local authority continues to serve as local agent for center will, with little or no delegation of initiative yet with full responsibility for putting the center's programs into effect. In sum, modernization has created more perfect deconcentration but not even incipient decentralization, and truly local authority has not emerged.

Some consequences: Local bureaucrats passively await center direction or approval before they are willing to act. Local problems and interests have a low priority at the center. There is scant local input and adaptation to what the center proposes. The scramble for the center's favor discourages local horizontal coordination and cooperation, and local political loyalty and consciousness mean little save as they might serve as stepping-stones to national favor and prominence.

What I have described is the Korean version of modern patrimonial local authority. When the system works well and when programs are wisely chosen, the center can move rapidly and effectively; as, for example, in building the Seoul-Pusan superhighway. But alas, the center can as readily blunder, as in the case of Taegu's over- and ill-conceived ecological expansion, because there is no countervailing, creative input to override, amend, or even question center decisions.[4]

## Korean Village and Communal Organization

Beyond the formal administrative apparatus, which historically terminated at the district level, lay innumerable natural communities. The persistent question: how to organize these communities and articulate them with the formal system of authority so that they would serve the interests of that authority.

Rather than depend upon legally recognized local representatives and exercise direct political and military control, the Korean patrimonial center governed the countryside by depending on cooperative influential locals whose potency was derived from their patriarchal leadership of consanguineal and pseudo-consanguineal units. The patriarchs were willing to align their own, and by implication their communities', interests with those of the formal administrators, and hence of formal authority, because the administrators were recruited in part from patriarchs and because the patriarchs could use the legitimacy of formal authority to enforce their own control over and exploitation of the villagers when patriarchal-kin prerogatives were insufficient. The political system thus survived because natural village communitarianism survived, and vice versa. Such a system has been variously characterized as Asiatic feudal, Asiatic despotic, or, specific to the natural community level, as primitive Asiatic communitarian; I prefer the term *primitive patrimonial*.

When the system was perfected, the district level articulated with the natural community through an intermediary two-tier, formal but unofficial administrative chain of command of *myŏn* (superior tier) and *tong-ri* (inferior tier). Since the tong-ri encompassed some four to eight natural communities, some observers prefer to visualize the natural community as a hamlet, reserving the terms *village cluster* for tong and *village* for ri, while others use the term *natural village* for the natural community and *administrative village* for tong-ri. Whatever their equivalent terms, tong-ri were required by the formal administration to have a responsible leader selected either temporarily or for life from among the leaders of their constituent natural communities by their respective myŏn heads or by the natural communities' informal leaders with the myŏn heads' approval. The tong-ri heads saw to such supra-natural community concerns as maintaining and regulating irrigation facilities and communal land, and informing and entertaining officials of the formal administration who radiated patrimonial grace by traveling on circuit.

The myŏn heads in turn were selected from among the tong-ri heads, and hence were also commoners. But in contrast to the tong-ri heads, the myŏn heads were paid and had staffs to assist them. However, both heads and staffs were replaced (usually yearly) to prevent any abuse of authority and to induce tong-ri heads to serve. The responsibilities of myŏn heads far outweighed the advantages, since they were responsible on their level for very much what the magistrates were on their formal-district level; to wit, law and order, repair of facilities, demographics, and registration.

Another channel the formal administration could rely on to communicate with and to control the informal orbit were those members of the local gentry not holding public office, especially retirees. These gentry acted in council to advise and otherwise aid, but also to watch over, the magistrates and their staffs in their dealings in turn with informal administrative leaders and their constituents. Since the members of the gentry were physically and socially close to the locals, while magistrates were not, gentry were expected to bargain on village service obligations and tax matters in the mutual interest of both villagers and magistrates. If the gentry were passive or corrupt, siding with self-serving magistrates or members of their staffs, this made life extremely painful for villagers. Only if magistrates and gentry conflicted could villagers gain. But sooner or later, any magistrate and the gentry were sure to come to terms in order to realize their common objective of maximizing villagers' responsibilities, and hence of making the existing political system work reasonably well with minimal overt pain and fuss to all concerned. When the system worked smoothly, the villagers survived, albeit barely so, while the formal administrators received their prebendary due and the gentry maintained their prerogatives and prestige.

Certain natural community activities beyond the capacity of individuals or immediate relatives, such as defense against outsiders, rain-making worship, and water projects, have been made feasible through exploiting natural village communitarianism, if necessary under the direct command of a patrimonial patriarch or his designate. The most significant communal pursuit however has been time-consuming wet rice cultivation, especially its planting and harvesting, which has been carried out through communitywide *ture*. In contrast to the communal-customary ture, *p'umasi*, ad hoc, short-term labor exchanges between individual households, arose to handle small-scale, non-villagewide or nonvital tasks such as dry farming.

Another prominent village communal organization has been the *kye;* volunteer organizations of specific kinds of people who come together to accomplish specific goals which as individuals they find impossible due to their limited resources. Kye are autonomous of villagewide responsibilities and concerns, although originally they could have been village consanguineal organs. Early kye raised funds for recreation and progenitor veneration, while later kye specialized in welfare, cooperative self-help, and especially funding or avoiding usury debting. In the early twentieth century kye generated credit for small-scale commercial and artisan capitalism. All these kye still exist, so that we can say that kye are the most persistent and widespread Korean communal organization.

The contemporary ascending local administrative chain of command consists of *ban*, ri, and myŏn. The typical ban is composed of approximately ten families, though any number of ban are larger or smaller; the ri is an administrative collectivity of some 700 households; and the myŏn comprises 100 ri. Not by accident, the natural village of some hundred households is not included in this hierarchy.

With authority as centralized as it is today, the prime function of the myŏn office is to translate the general directives of the center into specific ri and ban requirements. For it is now at the ri level that the ruralite meaningfully confronts the wishes of the formal administrative apparatus. Prior to the military coup of 1961, the ri head was elected from among local informal leaders, but now he is appointed by the myŏn chief because, it is claimed, under the former system the various village factions and consanguineals divisively disputed over his selection. Though an appointee, the ri chief is not a civil servant, and thus is not entitled to a government stipend, continuing to be, according to rural custom, paid at harvest by the villagers. The ban chief is not a civil servant nor is he paid for most of his duties, although he has full responsibility for insuring the conformity of those under his jurisdiction to center will. Hence the office is rarely sought after, and some chiefs are elected against their will. Most recently, the ban chief's duties expanded to include monitoring the government's rural-uplift programs and the chiefs are being paid for this, thus bringing them further within the formal administrative net.

With an ever-expanding role for ri and ban chiefs, and the arrival of government agents, such as police and agricultural extension workers, in the villages, most informal leaders are being limited increasingly to their historic core role of defenders of village morals and ceremonial rectitude. But as men of middle years (average age, forty-five), with experience (some are former ri and ban chiefs) and social connections (as old notable or consanguineal influentials), or as younger men of proven ability, at least some informal leaders may be consulted by formal officials before the latter carry out their programs, or the informal leaders may serve as channels of communication, especially during an emergency, e.g., for disaster relief. Hence at least some informal leaders continue to play their age-old role of adjusting the requirements of the formal political administration to the local scene.

Many informal village associations too have been integrated directly into the formal chain of administrative command, or indirectly through carrot and stick made to serve the interests of the center. Thus, although the ture and p'umasi continue to fulfill a familiar need in a familiar way because of the very nature of agricultural work, some kye have become ri in scope, reflecting a shift in emphasis from the natural village to the bureaucratically inspired community. Irrigation associations now are highly structured, with formal agenda and assessments calculated by the authorities, and charged with carrying out bureaucratic hydraulic programs, and membership in forestry associations is compulsory with heavy penalties on those who illegally cut trees or are negligent in preventing fires.

Accompanying these accommodations is the relentless penetration of the local communities by novel local branches of the center, such as youth groups and agricultural associations. Membership is compulsory. Leaders often are recruited from the able, young, and ambitious, since it is they rather than the prestiged and those otherwise associated with the existing power structure who are most apt to support center aspirations. Novel center programs and services also threaten to break the self-sufficiency of the natural community by turning attention toward, and making survival dependent on, formal authority outside and administratively above the natural community. Thus although labor exchange and mutual aid continue at the village level, postal facilities and fertilizer distribution, for example, are at the myŏn office.

The vital informal organization of the natural community is, as always, the consanguineal unit. When consanguinity overlaps propinquity by virtue of one or a few consanguineal organizations being predominant in a community, that community can rely on consanguineal solidarity and the authority of consanguineal leaders to organize village life and activities, and, by collectively supporting a candidate for appointment as ri chief for example, insure the consanguineous community a favorable response from the bureaucracy. In those communities where no consanguineous unit is dominant or a dominant unit is weakened by factional strife, however, the tension between community and kin loyalty creates an impasse which village residents alone cannot overcome. Finally, the widening breach in the wall of natural community isolation has encouraged the emigration of consanguineals and the immigration of nonmembers, weakening solidarity at the very time the bureaucrats bearing prebends have come into the natural community, determined to circumscribe consanguineal functions. Consanguineal loyalty, however, persists in village neighborhoods which subdivide the present residents of the natural communities according to ancestry, bifurcating especially ex-aristocrats and commoners, old-timers and latecomers, and ex-landlords and tenants.

The fundamental units of neighborhoods are individual households, which interact with each other face to face on the basis of reciprocity. The heads of the households represent their residents in the outside world, for example, at village council meetings or in contacts with the bureaucrats. However, certain heads, on the strength of their personal qualities, informally make significant village decisions which the village council then formally ratifies. Household-head decision-making thus is both hierarchical and equalitarian; hierarchical in the sense that certain heads (local notables) preempt the privilege of initially screening the issues, but equalitarian in the sense that all heads finally decide communally on the basis of one vote per household. These two principles are not necessarily reconcilable. The ensuing bickering between households may only be extinguished after neighbors compel the obstinate troublemakers to desist. If a controversy is deep or persistent enough to come to the attention of formal local authority, an official may force the kind of decision on the disputants which only further alienates them from each other, and they thereafter prefer to deal with the polity as infrequently as possible. It is conventional anthropological wisdom that conflicting kin are easier to reconcile than non-kin, but this is not borne out in the Korean case. For although factional strife certainly will occur in those natural communities not under the firm hand of a dominant patriarchal clan, it also occurs within a single consanguinity if there are a number of competing branches, and even among individual households if there is no unity within the consanguineal branch. For quite in keeping with patrimonial principles, the communal prerogatives and responsibilities of hierarchical patriarchy will constantly clash with individual equalitarian competitiveness for the uncertain prebendary favor of potential patrons, intensified now with the intrusion of bureaucrats among consanguineal superiors. If this competition creates open friction rather than passive evasiveness, the aggressive ones may be forced out of the community to keep the peace.

In Japan, in contrast, ambitious communal leaders have been able to mobilize local communal sentiment and organization to bargain with formal authority for recognition of local rights, if necessary by employing force. Japanese communal organizations have been truly tightly knit solidary units whose leaders forged novel bonds based upon propinquity and objective goals which transcended those limiting affinities of kin, class, or short-term prebendal self-interest which have enabled formal Korean authority to deflect any concerted threat to itself. Thus, within the village, the Japanese five-man group became an important neighborhood mutual-aid organ, while in Korea it was a government surveillance organ to be avoided whenever possible. It is interesting to note in this regard that Korean kye which raised productive capital for constructive community cooperative action, in contrast to those which funded recreation, immediate self-interest, or usurious commercial capital, originated during the Japanese occupation and under their inspiration.

The conclusion as I see it is that an inability to maintain reasonably tolerable human relationships upon which to build and preserve true solidarity, not only between consanguinities and within natural communities, but also in all Korean face-to-face organizations which are constructed along similar lines, has militated against Korean primary groups contributing maximally to Korean development.[5]

# 3

# Authority:
# The Relationship
# between Political Authority
# and the People

### The Legal Heritage

In patrimonial thinking, law is a didactic expression of ethical rulership whose purpose is to inculcate proper conduct so that individuals will live harmonious, disciplined, productive, and, above all, virtuous lives. Consequently, the lawgiver and executor, whether a titular ruler or his aide(s), should be a model and teacher rather than a lawyer and warden. Nevertheless, humans being human, from time to time contention is sure to arise under the best of circumstances. Then, although some purists consider it to be a sign of moral failure, authority, as society's designated arm of morality, must use law to control and chastise the immoral. Much of formal law, consequently, deals with preserving the moral character of authority and with those transgressions which interfere with moral administration, such as treason, lese majesty, tax default, or counterfeiting. In contrast, defining and protecting private interests is considered marginal at best, amoral at worst, and hence not worthy of much concern; this is especially true of commercial disputation (see the succeeding chapters). For this reason, and because an official might fear being considered too poor a model to inspire his charges to be moral without the need to litigate, and hence unworthy to hold public office, officials took a stern view of those who sought redress through the courts, regardless of the merits of their cases. To discourage suits, the technicalities of the law were kept secret from the populace, lest some be tempted to use the law against their more morally worthy, less litigious fellows.

Lawyers were discouraged from appearing in court, and when they did show up were under constant suspicion and surveillance as potential troublemakers. As was the intent, the populace considered the law and the legal machinery as serving the interests of the state and not themselves, unless the two interests fortuitously coincided, and as a punishment rather than a protection. Hence, prudence dictated that the ordinary man avoid contact with the law whenever possible.

Since the law supported the ruler's authority and that authority was centralized, the law upheld the center in its conflict with local, potentially decentralizing authority by refusing to formally recognize local rights and autonomy, by enforcing codes of conduct devised at the center which could vary according to local preference, and by lodging the final decision on punishment for serious crimes in either the capital's justice or criminal departments or in the titular ruler himself.

One of the most sacred canons of patrimonial authority is loyalty to the titular ruler. To help maintain unquestioned devotion to the ruler, loyalty to *all* superiors, public and private—whether wife to husband, child to parent, servant to master, or inferior bureaucrat to chief—was legally prescribed. Any lapse in fidelity to superiors was construed as disloyalty to the ruler, the very model center of the political order.

How arbitrary is such a legal system? Certainly the ruler was restrained by the decisions of the moral lawgivers of the past and the moral legal-reviewers of the present, for example, the censors. However, strong rulers and legal administrators, since they were patrimonially certified as properly disciplined by moral training, felt justified in interpreting existing law to serve their immediate, albeit moral, interests. They could take advantage of the fact that the few legal experts who existed usually were removed from the exercise of authority and that the legal role was subsumed under the administrative role. Second, a select few not actually in authority but certified as moral were not subject to law, because they were supposed to be so sufficiently self-disciplined as not to require formal coercion. Simultaneously, the very poor and the depraved were likewise exempt, because those under extreme duress were considered beyond moral redemption.

It is useful to contrast Law, which is eternal and reflective of a perfect didactic model, with laws, which are ephemeral devices to cope with this less-than-perfect world of not-too-moral human beings. Law may be exemplified by the proclamation of a single novel code either by the founder of a new dynasty or, especially in the case of the last imperial dynasty, by an innovative ruler, which serves to legitimize the dynasty or reign as patrimonially moral. Laws, on the other hand, include administrative codicils and the decisions of magistrates and other judges who, as self-disciplined moralists, had the patrimonial right and duty to apply legal sanctions of their own to assure moral (that is, harmonious) though not necessarily just settlements. Consequently, the same judge could decide the same legal circumstance differently on two different occasions. In time, especially in a long peaceful period such as the last imperial dynasty, such confusion in the laws became overwhelming and a new comprehensive code (Law), reflecting a new moral consensus, was compiled. But the process of creating laws also began anew, since the distinction between Law and laws had to be maintained on moral grounds. Consequently Law never became a universal guide for specific decision-making, while the laws never became more than a series of concrete particulars. This dilemma was resolved through unwritten legal codes; namely, memorials and discourses among judges which reflected their consensus, but which could not, on patrimonial legal grounds, be translated into universal, impersonal, abstract legal guides. And since these unwritten codes could not be revealed to those who came before the judges, they never guided popular legal conduct nor were the resulting decisions regarded by the public as other than capricious.

Since as long as general peace and harmony prevailed among commoners the formal legal system treated them and their concerns indifferently, private interests were forced to seek their own legal recourse. Unlike in the West, however, this did not encourage the creation of a corpus of common law which in time was incorporated into formal law, because in patrimonial societies non-formal law a priori is considered amoral, irrelevant, and unenforceable. Consequently, when authority did intervene in private disputes it did so on terms reflecting its own interests, which did not necessarily resolve the quarrels but only dampened overt dissension. Accordingly, popular conflicts usually were arbitrated by local notables and consanguineal leaders, in the expectation that the affect of kin or community would enforce the decision and reduce any surviving tension and the community could return to normal. Moreover, since those notables and leaders did not have any institutionalized right to use force, it was often difficult for the community to enforce its will, and those who were not satisfied with the decision could resist and even refuse to participate in arbitration if they felt the decision was likely to go against them. For all these reasons, popular justice was as unpredictable and could be as personally and socially unrewarding as formal justice.

The formal and informal legal paths did cross whenever formal authority decided that it was useful to redress popular grievance, lest failure to do so encourage widespread dissatisfaction with authority and even spark rebellion. For all its romantic representation in the popular opera, the system operated under strict ground rules so as to insure that it would serve the interests of a patrimonial authority with minimal effort and risk to itself. First, as an act of patrimonial grace, the agents of formal law responded to cases they chose, typically those which could be disposed of most readily on a non-precedent-setting basis and hence would not alter the legal corpus or machinery. Second, the means to gain judicial attention were petitions for the ordinary and memorials for officials, but going out of channels over a social (ordinary) or political (official) superior's head, not to speak of using false charges, was punished severely. Third, in a society without regularized channels of public information, petitions and memorials enabled authority to learn who its potential foes—especially unproductive and venal officials—might be, what they were up to, and thus to act against them before they had the chance to disrupt the political system. Finally, such information could be referred to appropriate agents or used to alter existing programs without recognizing any legitimate popular right of access to or pressure on formal political decision-making.

Another example of patrimonial grace was the dispatch of legal agents to protect the people in general and encourage uprightness among officials in particular, by spot-checking the local administrative process. But agents varied greatly in zeal and ability, their decisions were singular and hence set no legal precedent, their judgments depended on fortuitous visits, and they could be neutralized if locals were clever in concealing guilt or were able to coerce or collude with the agents.

Any legal entanglement implied culpability of some sort, perhaps because authority, kin, and community were embarrassed by the fact that personal charm and informal pressure were not sufficient to dampen conflict. Hence it was morally proper to harass the accused even before he was judged. Once convicted the prisoner became an immoral outcast, totally at the mercy of those carrying out the sentence for, in patrimonial legal thinking, the legal code (Law) could be interpreted by judicial moralists who were free to improvise beyond the code as they saw fit, subject only to their disciplined moral imagination and personal whim.

Since guilt was collective, punishment might require exile not only for oneself but for one's kin and reduction of one's community to lower political status, involving humiliating labor service in the salt fields or mines. Similarly, the stigma of incarceration remained and ex-prisoners were shunned lest their associates be suspect. Hence, even though the officials-aristocrats were given special legal privileges such as freedom until judged and, if convicted, possible incarceration rather than death, they were as determined as commoners to avoid contact with the formal legal system.

On a broader scale, the open-ended moral mandate of authority to punish included the right to use institutional violence against its enemies, in the name of upholding a moral rectitude considered synonymous with the political welfare of the particular regime in power.

The fact that formal law was imposed on Korea from without, either against its will or as a choice without any viable alternative, is pertinent to understanding both the Korean image of law and its application in the society. From the establishment of the early bureaucratic states to the end of the nineteenth century, imported Chinese law predominated. Each Korean dynasty adopted the prevailing Chinese legal code of the time, primarily to legitimize the dynasty as patrimonially moral and hence acceptable to its stronger neighbor. However, the extent to which the Chinese codes were concretely applied in organizing Korean administration and dispensing justice is uncertain. Some scholars see the Korean "supplements" to these codes as attempts to translate Chinese principles into Korean specifics, such as the Korean code of filial piety which stressed sharper class distinctions of legal privilege and liability than did its Chinese model. Be that as it may, both Chinese and Korean law were valid in theory, even though in fact discrepancies between them existed and could not be resolved simply by limiting the application of the Chinese code to dynastic legitimacy as Law and the Korean statutes to practical administrative laws. Perhaps this discrepancy contributed to the contemporary confusion between formal sham and objective reality and between what legally is enforceable and what is not.

Modern law came to Korea under circumstances similar to Chinese law, in this case through Korea's other stronger neighbor, Japan. Japan exploited the fact that Korean law then was ill-suited to the needs of a modern society by judging and punishing Koreans according to Japanese standards, such as considering the felling of trees on communal land as criminal. The Japanese also further intensified fear and disrespect for law because they used it, as did those in the past, as an instrument of repression and control. They were aided in this by those Koreans who were cynically prepared to take advantage of their countrymen as police agents or informers or to falsely accuse others of crimes in order to settle personal scores or to blackmail, thus exacerbating existing social fissions rather than healing the wounds of the society. Since, as in the past, bribery and expedient cooperation primarily assured that the system would work in one's favor, formal law continued to be avoided whenever possible.[1]

## The Contemporary Legal System

Japanese legal personnel departed in 1945, being replaced by their Korean counterparts and subordinates who were used to, and not unsympathetic to, their predecessors' legal thinking and administrative procedures. True, the American occupation forces tinkered with the existing legal machinery, eliminating many of the flagrant abuses of Japanese legalized violence (for example, summary police justice) and were an inspiration for those Koreans who were to revamp the judicial administration and legal education. Nevertheless, because they accepted and built upon a fundamentally imperial and especially Japanese legal milieu and machinery, the Americans were instrumental in providing both continuity and the imprimatur of "democracy" and "modernity" for many imperial and Japanese legal concepts and practices (such as the use of law to threaten the weak, indifference to due process and individual rights, and the use of trials to wear down the accused) in the subsequent "truly Korean" legal system. Likewise, although the polity has enacted many countervailing legal statutes, no one, least of all the government itself, expects such statutes to be enforced, especially since most of them are inconvenient to the government! In sum, Koreans continue to be uneasy about formal law, many considering it a fraud which the imaginative and the powerful still have the means to avoid.

For this reason, a Korean legal scholar has suggested a reevaluation of existing formal law, either adapting the people to the statutes or, more feasibly, retaining only those statutes which can be enforced. Otherwise too many Koreans will never respect rule by formal law or consider law to be a useful catalyst for productive change. At first blush, this appears to be a realistic reaction to the existing legal culture. But I believe that this posture sidesteps the crucial institutional role of law; namely that since law, now as in the past, serves the interest of authority— especially to facilitate ruler and staff maintenance of political morality, as they define that morality—and hence not even subsidiarily either outside interests or those who disagree with the state, then the Korean populace by responding accordingly *is* acting legally rational. My conclusion: as long as authority is as patrimonial as ever, so will be the law, and the popular reaction to it.

A specific illustration of my reasoning: Although the courts and their mentors were cut loose formally from executive dominance under the Republic, in fact each president has made every effort to co-opt the legal machinery and thwart legislative and interadministrative judicial review of his decisions. To do this the executive relies on ad hoc regulation through ordinance in times of emergency, chronically proclaimed, without even perfunctory ex post facto legislative review. Park especially pressed the docile legislature to whittle away in fact what the constitution guaranteed in theory. And lest even the constitution itself stand in his way, he established a 1972 constitutional committee independent of the courts to review cases involving constitutional questions like, for example, the legality of political parties. He used military courts and the chief justice of the Supreme Court in treason trials against his radical opponents, the former because those courts do not allow effective appeal, the latter because this assures that decisions cannot be overturned on "technicalities." The executive does not allow itself to be sued by ordinary, and hence by patrimonial definition morally inferior, Koreans, unless it is certain it can win the case, thus risking nothing while appearing to appease. And even if someone somehow wins, his victory is of dubious value, since winners are considered to be troublemakers who must be watched carefully for any possible legal infraction which, when discovered, will bring the full weight of moral authority against them. Preventive detention, warrantless arrest, and rearrest on suspicion of resumption of unwelcome political activity or the fortuitous appearance of new evidence on old charges are the norm. Since the modern executive is thus efficiently using modern legal forms to serve time-honored patrimonial goals and values, the populace reacts in its time-honored fashion of overt passivity, evasion, and contempt for formal law. So much for the argument of adjusting Korean law to the legal culture in order to *preserve* popular respect for the law!

The modern legal profession is ill-equipped to resist that prevailing legal culture, if it is ever so inclined. For one, the profession is a segment of the patrimonial political establishment by virtue of the fact that the few who are allowed to pass the bar annually almost to the individual enter government service and not private practice. Second, all those legally trained are organized into a bar association under the Justice Ministry which insures that their profession cannot become a potential source of active resistance to authority, although isolated individuals do raise their voices in futile protest from time to time. Third, legal specialists are not prepared through training or socialization to become protectors of the nonbureaucratic social will, let alone civil rights. They are educated to pass the difficult bar examination, which stresses formal legal theory and political science to the detriment of the humanities and especially the social relevance of law. Certainly, this is not without logic, for only those few are passed for whom the state has vacancies, and thus the competition to qualify is very fierce. Recent educational innovation stressing the needs of a contemporary society has been paralleled by increasing limitation of legal autonomy and therefore it is doubtful that the reforms can contribute to substantive legal development.

The judicial administration conforms formally to modern legal practice. It is a unified, centralized system of district courts, with attached family courts since 1963, representing the eight provincial capitals, plus Seoul; of branch courts, bringing legal services to the rural areas; of a high court of initial appeal; and of a Supreme Court of final appeal. Trials are either open or closed and without jury, decisions being made by majority judgment of *judges* who have the right to intervene in the proceedings to assure a fair and adequate process. Chief judges at all levels have the right to rotate and reassign judges under their respective jurisdictions and to set court calendars. The Supreme Court is also the brain of the judicial system, determining court practice and the character of judicial administration through its housekeeping, investigatory, and disciplinary committees. Operationally, however, the executive has increasingly come to dominate the judiciary and erode its autonomy. The Committee of Chief Justices charged with identifying judicial problems and proposing solutions has been abolished. The president of the Republic now appoints the chief judges, and has limited their role to advisory review and settlement of cases of executive interest and to presiding over trials of constitutional cases involving the executive. Because it has never broken new philosophical, especially constitutional, ground through the appeal process (since almost all its cases are routine, technical reviews of lower court decisions), the Supreme Court has not developed into a countervailing force for judicial restraint of the increasingly arbitrary executive. On the contrary, the court has provided legal justification both before and after the fact for executive initiatives, and stood aside on grave political questions. Ordinary judges are even less prone to rock the executive's boat. Relatively inexperienced and overworked, few of them have the time to reflect hard on the social impact of their cases. Though judges may be removed for discipline and not solely for constitutional violation, that rule seems designed more for political control than to insure judicial purity. And surely, with executive eclipse of the legislature, judicial standards of conduct and qualification which are constitutionally prescribed by the assembly are not effective.

More so than judges, *public prosecutors* confront the ordinary public, which both fears and respects them and strives to appease them by hastening to settle out of court. For though in theory only an administrative arm of the Ministry of Justice, prosecutors have wide latitude whether to prosecute or not; they control their own (judicial) police, investigations, and sanctions; operate anywhere in the Republic; assign cases to themselves or those they designate; and especially focus their attention on political and social issues of significance to the state, including civil liberties—in brief, see themselves and are seen by the public as modern censors.

*Court aides*—clerks, bailiffs, marshals—have special impact on the populace's legal image because they are the members of the legal system that the unsophisticated and powerless must initially contact. Unfortunately, as patrimonial bureaucrats, their sensitivity to public relations and the social impact of the law leaves something to be desired. The attitude of clerks is especially important because, on retirement, they can become scriveners, that is, general "honest" legal advisers and preparers of legal documents who provide guidance through the thicket of the legal bureaucracy for a populace which only becomes enmeshed when it cannot informally conciliate and settle its disputes out of court.

*Attorneys* are consulted only when formal litigation is inevitable. They are selected by clients not on the basis of either chance or reputation, but through personal recommendation. Consequently, if a case is lost clients feel personally betrayed, as if by a kinsman, projecting that hatred and mistrust on the legal system itself. Since attorneys, like judges and prosecutors, are carefully certified, there are fewer than a thousand in all Korea. Hence, they consider themselves members of the privileged elite entitled to the society's advantages, rather than as crusaders for social causes or morality. They are passive in court, since it is the judge who directs and develops the trial. They are not specialists because there is little incentive, legally or financially, to become so. And because they act alone and not in firms, since they trust their fellows no more than those in the general society trust each other, attorneys are often overworked, spread thin, and ill-prepared in court. Consequently, they prefer to settle out of court with opposing attorneys or to go before judges they know, which even more than bribery may determine a decision in this, a society revolving about personal affect. For all these reasons, attorneys are held in low esteem, especially by clients, who are reluctant to trust and cooperate with them. Authority in turn takes a dim view of attorneys who are reluctant to serve its interests because it considers them court assistants, and hence instruments of its will. The 1973 constitution went further in defining the attorney's role as that of defender of the constitution, a clear warning against those who might be tempted to represent unacceptable political causes and clients. The idea of attorneys acting as representatives of private interest groups, such as the business community, is a recent and as yet not widely accepted notion.

Another arm of the law that the populace directly confronts is the *police*. The fundamental assumption that the police are the fist of the central state has survived the many political vicissitudes of Korean history. For example, the short-lived Chang government learned to its sorrow that, when it reined in the police, power and prestige began to melt away, since the regime's supporters and foes alike saw this policy as a sign of weakness and ineptness and, quite correctly, of inevitable disaster. At present the police are used primarily to enforce the government's version of "national security" and otherwise prevent unauthorized congregation, protest, or discord by rivals or critics. Unrestrained as they are by any concept of civil liberty, policemen are accustomed to apply torture and force confession rather than follow hard evidence. The overwhelming number of popular petitions submitted to the authorities complain of police abuse. The government, though conceding that a problem exists, has pleaded for understanding, citing an understaffed, undertrained, and underpaid police force trying to cope with increasing crime in an unsettled era of rapid change. The government has also asked that the people appreciate that much of the petty extortion that goes on raises funds necessary to carry on legitimate police activities, such as purchasing equipment. Certainly this is unorthodox by modern standards, but it is consistent with the time-honored patrimonial concept of farming the people for administrative sustenance. How much of what the police glean goes for public use, and how much is passed on to the executive for political purposes as widely charged, must be pure conjecture.

In sum, the populace, now as in the past and with good reason, distrusts or fears all organs of formal law, preferring to avoid at any cost legal entanglement even in a private, purely civil capacity. The populace is convinced that law can never be counted on to serve its interests, especially if its interests conflict with those of the authorities. Or, to rephrase for our purposes, because contemporary Korean law is patrimonial, that is, arbitrary, capricious, irrational, and the punitive moral arm of authority, it is not conducive to establishing the rational rules of the political game in a developing institutional order.[2]

## Patrimonial Democracy

The Park regime often defended the legitimacy and legality of its actions on grounds that liberal political democracy had failed in, and hence was inappropriate for, Korea, especially as that system was practiced by his predecessor, Chang Myŏn. Although in our terms the Chang regime was not "liberal democratic" but rather was old patrimonial wine in a newly labeled bottle, clearly it was not as repressive as either its Rhee predecessor or its Park successor. Park associated liberal democracy with Chang's license to demonstrate and his inability to enforce order, in part because he alienated both army and police, which in Park's military eyes opened the Republic to infiltration by its Communist enemies. Consequently, when the military, and ultimately Park, came to power, they felt fully justified in imposing a strong centralized executive, excluding legislators from effective decision-making on the grounds that they were venal opportunists and that party government was inappropriate for Korea for the indefinite time being.

The dream of Korean political democracy, however, has never been renounced. At the least it has been treasured as the Republic's talisman in its struggle with the DPRK for control of the peninsula. But, the argument goes, democracy must be adapted to the realities of the Korean present. These realities require that the president respond "flexibly" to the needs of a society considered to be under chronic crisis, for only the president truly understands what the people need in their present unenlightened (patrimonially speaking, morally wanting) state. Without such guidance, Korean society is sure to degenerate into factionally ridden congeries, if not a mob. Above all, Koreans need unity under a strong leader, for only with unity can the people resolutely eliminate waste and corruption, progress, and develop. Such democracy contrasts with the imitative western democracy of sloganeering and idle chatter about liberty and rights characteristic of pre-coup Korea.

The Park government made much of the point that its authority was absolutely legal because, unlike the Rhee regime which acted contrary to its constitution, when the Park regime became dissatisfied it replaced the existing constitution with the Revitalizing one which gave it more flexibility and more freedom from the carping of dissenting legislators. But even more serviceable to Park's "Korean-style democracy" was the ordinance tradition which concretely fleshes the bare constitutional bones. A typical Park ordinance was No. 9, which made it a crime to advocate disloyalty by agitating for repeal of or maligning his sacred constitution. The regime also used the compliant judiciary and periodic popular referenda to refurbish its morally righteous legal image and ratify its version of Korean democracy. Each referendum was considered a mandate for mounting a fresh campaign against organized dissidence, especially in the opposition parties, and against those individuals who would question the right of authority to demand unqualified loyalty. Referenda also enabled the executive to denounce agitation for civil rights as a licentious ploy to thwart majority will. Clearly Korean democratic rights and the scope of participation in decision-making have been what the executive wants them to be, and it is debatable whether it wants them to be conducive to political development.[3]

### Control of the Media

The media as a form of popular communication and as an expression of political grievance rather than solely a source of entertainment have a long history in Korea. The availability of movable type and high-quality paper were to facilitate the widespread circulation of government and private journals at the end of the nineteenth century. At first these were written in Chinese for an elite audience, but soon the nongovernment papers contained articles in Korean, the Protestant press using the phonetic alphabet to open the press to a wider audience. Then, as later, the private press's principal themes were support for Korean national identity, human dignity and rights, and exposure of corruption and political abuse. This crusade did not flag even under the repressive Japanese, who first temporarily and then in 1940 permanently outlawed the Korean language press. The Japanese were ever alert to any slight, intervening at will in editorial policies, suspending publication, and purging those personnel they distrusted. To minimize harassment, the papers avoided direct political confrontation, but ever defended the Korean cultural identity against all Japanese attempts to submerge it. After national liberation in 1945, the press revived with more enthusiasm than strength, but in a free atmosphere of energetic political criticism. The American occupiers, soon vexed by the leftist press, purged it, a precedent which was expanded to all shades of opinion under Rhee by the simple expedient of not renewing press licenses, or more typically through laws which equated press criticism with treason. The more liberal attitude toward

the press of the Chang regime was followed by a return to press surveillance and even suppression under the military and its successor
government. In sum, the press, save for government-controlled and
house organs, has a long history of irreverence for authority, while
authority in turn has viewed such unsolicited criticism from outsiders
with typical patrimonial distaste, feeling itself fully justified in denouncing and suppressing such advice as detrimental to national security and interests. (The other branches of the media—journals,
magazines, and books since the turn of the century; radio and film
since the Japanese occupation; and finally television under the Republic—may be similarly characterized, and thus we shall not review
them separately.)

To those in authority, now as in the past, the people have the right,
yea the responsibility, to be informed, but not to be unduly agitated
and morally misled, while those in the media have no institutional
right to inform the people, but only a graceful patrimonial privilege,
grantable and withdrawable by authority at any time. Authority carries out its self-appointed mission to supervise media messages and
personnel through two channels, namely, (1) the Ministry of Culture
and Information, and (2) various media associations which all personnel are required to join.

The *ministry* examines all publications whether before the fact, as
school texts, or after the fact, as broadcast and TV tapes which must
be held for one year, subject to review at any time. Anything whatever going back to the founding of the Republic—in the government's
view 1945—is subject to review and punishment, even if, typically,
the transgression is ex post facto. Those devices used to control the
populace in general, such as emergency decree No. 9, are used to
suppress media "pseudo-reports" and uncomplimentary editorials.
Complaint letters to the editor are investigated by the police, on ministry suggestion. The ministry has established special screening committees and holds periodic conferences with media officials to insure
that they all understand and conform to the government's views on
controversial matters, preferably through self-policing. But, just to be
sure, the Korean Central Intelligence Agency (KCIA) is authorized to
investigate and remove what the ministry considers potential Communist subversives from the media. The government has entrusted
the ethics committee of *media associations* to inculcate sufficient responsibility (read, hesitation) in individuals so that they will desist
from expressing "provocative" ideas. Under the hoary principle of
collective guilt, the committees' officers themselves are held responsible and can be purged for their members' activities. Similarly, those

who, even innocently, transmit or receive condemned material, such as book wholesalers and retailers who do not return objectionable items to publishers, can be punished.

A fascinating example of media harassment was the 1975 campaign against the *Tong'a-Ilbo*, a newspaper with magazine and TV affiliates. The paper was a leader, and hence a symbol to Koreans, of their struggle for national identity and dignity under the Japanese and for basic freedoms under the Americans and the Republic. What particularly seems to have irked the government was the paper's reprinting of statements by dissidents in the political parties and church organizations. *Tong'a-Ilbo* personnel were subjected to violence by parties unknown, its papers stolen at distribution centers, its staff surveilled by uniformed police and plainclothesmen, and certain of its managers, editors, and reporters pressured to resign. But the authorities especially hoped to bankrupt the paper by pressuring its advertisers to terminate their notices, while the Ministry of Culture and Information was assuring the curious that this was but a natural reaction to the prevailing economic recession. The government was prepared for the usual outcry from the opposition party, the media, and the intellectuals, all within the orbit of acceptable, though unwelcomed, critics. But it did not anticipate a popular reaction which took the form of personal-support advertising from individuals in all walks of life. Some advertisers were anonymous out of justified fear of retaliation, but a surprising number were willing to identify themselves. At the same time advance subscriptions were sold and special funds raised to support those dismissed. Although to no one's surprise the government prevailed in purging those on the paper it disliked, many saw the incident as indicative that the government would go to any length rather than respond to the issues raised in *Tong'a-Ilbo*. For to do otherwise, I suggest, would violate one of the cardinal tenets of political patrimonialism, traditional or modern, namely, that the less-than-moral outside the political pale have no right to offer unsolicited political advice to the moralists within.

Instead, authority prefers to communicate directly with the populace as in the past through, for example, didactic enlightenment lectures by the titular ruler before a captive audience surveilled by the police. As of old, the titular ruler also goes on circuit among the people to radiate his patrimonial charisma. Park especially enthusiastically embraced what became an annual opportunity to travel and focus the country's attention on his concerns, to press for diligence, discipline, and study, and to warn against irresponsibility and discord. Another modern version of an old ploy is the dispatch of anonymous agents from the capital to ascertain how the modernizing projects in the countryside are faring. Finally, in contrast to the case of *Tong'a-Ilbo*, the polity expects businesses and associations to place revenue-producing advertisements in those organs willing to agitate for support of government policies, including confrontations with the DPRK.

It is not easy to gauge how effective the media, whether pro- or anti-authority, are in the political process and, by implication, in the development process. First, even without political pressure, and thus within the government organs as well, the media are plagued by the usual Korean internecine strife. Broadcasting is notorious for rapid turnover of personnel, especially in patrimonial patronal fashion, if a director is replaced. Second, although the media are and can be useful in such modernizing endeavors as mass education directed to such special target audiences as women and ruralites, too often they offer only politically safe entertainment. Third, the government's ability and willingness to turn off credit for those it dislikes, and help those it does like with such prebendary plums as the textbook market, does much to discourage publishers from being responsibly independent, not to speak of taking an antigovernment stand. Hence some 70 percent of the books and magazines published are (in descending order of importance) comics, politically innocent reference material, and literature, which characterizes much of Korean publishing as being of dubious reading value or escapist pap. Nonetheless, as the *Tong'a-Ilbo* incident shows, the people will respond to a media offering more than authority is willing to concede.[4]

### Control of the Populace

*The Politically Unorganized Community*

A census and an identity tag system were the primary tools which imperial authority came to rely upon to control wanderers, those avoiding political surveillance or conscription, those who abused the bondage regulations, and all those who might otherwise pose a danger to the authorities, as well as to insure that the general populace met its economic responsibilities.

Mandatory identification to facilitate surveillance survives in contemporary Korea in the form of family registers, individual identity papers, permanent and temporary domicile records, and especially highly detailed dossiers, all of which data computers and the other paraphernalia of modern technology make instantly available to any interested government agency, a situation not unique to Korea of course. The dossier system, a Japanese innovation, was resuscitated and expanded by the American military government's Public Information Section, which found it useful in keeping tabs on those it considered subversive. The Japanese and American files were inherited by the KCIA, an organ which has profited from continued access to modern American technological know-how in collecting and exploiting data. The KCIA has extended its influence abroad, especially watching over Koreans living in the United States and those foreigners, notably Americans, working for research and international agencies concerned with or dealing with Korea; all this presumably with reciprocal agreement allowing their foreign counterparts similar privileges in Korea.

The KCIA's mandate to surveil and, especially under Park, to act against the populace if necessary has been based on the premise that all criticism of, let alone opposition to, authority is subversive of the nation in its life-and-death moral struggle with the DPRK. Although authority does offer positive incentives for political neutrality if not cooperation, such as advancing salary payments to government workers in the urban areas and prebendal uplift programs in the rural areas, authority favors relying on negative sanctions to control those whom it considers are slandering (read, criticizing) its policies or personnel. Of particular interest is what the government media has termed in English "the flunky law," which makes any Korean living inside or outside Korea who defames either his country or government to foreigners, especially newsmen, subject to seven years' imprisonment and/or a ten-year suspension of civil rights. Those convicted of this or similar transgressions, when released, can be reimprisoned unless they desist. And those who question the right of the government to act so, on whatever grounds but especially by crying for civil rights, are judged just as disloyal. Consequently, protestors and petition signers are automatically investigated and usually arrested by the KCIA. Clearly, as far as authority is concerned, a politically innocent populace is inactive, not the least because of the degree of surveillance and the number of regulations in the urban centers and the informal pressures and fear of collective suspicion in the rural areas.

Ruralites also have been kept in line for a long time by prohibiting them from holding weapons, even for village self-defense against outside predators, human or animal. Ruralites have had even fewer formal channels to express their resentments than urbanites, and ruralites must be more circumspect because they are more easily dis-covered and punished, especially these days by witholding such vital prebends as fertilizer. And yet villagers have been no less resistant to government pressure than urbanites. However, rural protestors have focused their attention on ri chiefs, the intermediate flash point be-tween informal and formal authority. This is because ruralites, more than urbanites, have learned that it is more fruitful to resist individual officials who can be replaced, rather than try to change the structure of authority, which is never negotiable. For the government can be made to accept the inevitability of granting a graceful favor which en-hances its image of popular benevolence, but will never concede dimi-nution of its patrimonial prerogatives, certainly not through popular protest. [5]

### The Politically Organized Community—the Parties and the Legislature

The politically sensitive organized community consists of political parties and the national assembly on the one hand, and intellectuals and academics on the other hand. *Parties* are rooted in the sporadic modernizing efforts of a small group of late nineteenth- and early twentieth-century nationalists-intellectuals who were vainly trying to become the vanguard of a Korea that never was to be. The Japanese, who were to occupy Korea for half a century, proscribed organized Korean political activity. Thus, although a political underground, in-cluding leftist parties, did exist in Korea throughout the occupation, by default overt politics was restricted to émigrés, particularly those in China and the Soviet Union. With the end of Japanese rule those diverse elements at home and abroad surfaced on the political scene.

But in time Rhee, with American concurrence and sometimes ac-tive support, established a highly centralized, autocratic authority, which in the name of anti-Communist nationalism harassed his oppo-nents within and without the polity. Although a non-Communist lib-eral left was technically legitimate, it was under Rhee's constant suspi-cion of being a front for the outlawed extremist left. During the brief Chang interlude, various reformist parties from moderate to radical flowered. But they bickered among themselves over affiliation, tac-tics, and especially prebends, and were unable to gain any potent support outside the organized political circle, and hence were unable to control the prevailing unrest or prevent their temporary ally, the military, from seizing power in the 1961 coup.

In command ever since, the military has confined party politics to a very narrow band of professionals of unquestionable anti-Communist credentials, no longer tolerating mere non-Communists. The government is thus able to restrict opposition criticism to rebuking its modernizing program and its tactics of confrontation with the DPRK on grounds of error in judgment or, more typically, patrimonial moral fault (corruption). Even so the opposition parties are denounced as carping opportunists who would rather bring down the nation than give up political ambition. In contrast, the public, viewing executive hostility, is fearful of being closely associated with party programs or ideology. Isolating the populace from the political process allows the executive to regard the constitutional guarantees of popular political participation as symbolic and of no matter in limiting the executive's political freedom of action. Thus neither the government nor the opposition have an active popular constituency which could provide significant input in determining policy or tactics. The government party is a public relations chorus that can be called upon to ratify prior decisions of the executive, coming to life only when the executive senses a threat to its policies. Popular political participation— voting—occurs under very restrictive circumstances, most typically during a crisis, especially one of the regime's perception, in which the government can count on the people appreciating that only traitors would react negatively and vote against it.

Once its decisions are ritually ratified, the executive is assured that most of those in the opposition parties will desert their causes, not out of an ideological change of heart, given the narrow range of tolerated political dissent, but out of hope that their leaders will guide them to the government's prebendary trough, if not into the government itself. Similarly, within the government party, cliques group and regroup behind the scenes in hopes of retaining or gaining executive favor. In this sense, Korean parties are not sustained, unified interest groups, but are modernized factions which are formed and reformed quickly and opportunistically for patrimonial advantage.

Where an opposition can articulate its views and confront the government is in the *national assembly*. Since legally the assembly cannot be abolished, the executive has strived to minimize the opposition's freedom of action and destroy its credibility. First, the government has exploited the fundamental character of assembly politics; to wit, it is the executive which initiates legislation and carries it out, reducing the assembly, especially the opposition, to a censorial role. The government thus can often characterize the assembly as an irritant standing in the way of the "true" public interest espoused by the government. Second, the government has tried to limit the assembly's activities to discussing how best to carry out policies which the executive already has decided and such matters as budgeting rather than exploring fundamental controversial questions such as executive prerogatives, civil rights, and free political expression. The opposition, to be sure, regards the government claim that freedom of expression would only tempt the Republic's enemies to destroy it as self-serving and a ploy to perpetuate executive autocracy. Third, the executive has cleverly varied its prebendary carrot and punitive stick to keep its adversaries off guard and divided, which has the further advantage of confusing the public and reinforcing the image of assembly irresolution. Fourth, the government does not pressure when it will appear to be an obvious bully or when it believes it will lose the argument. Fifth, it especially tries to avoid giving the legislators the opportunity to create a rumpus within the assembly which can spill out in the street, where it is sure to come to the attention of the media, especially the foreign media. Because it controls the domestic media, the government has the advantage in appealing through it directly to the populace over the assembly's head to neutralize any legislative resolution the executive opposes. The government prosecutes publishers who report opposition statements too fully or favorably. And the government has arrested articulate opposition spokesmen inside and outside the chamber and held them for secret trial under a news blackout, so that their cases cannot be used to spread the opposition's point of view to the public. Finally, the executive has deliberately downgraded the assembly by suspending sessions periodically under martial law and emergency decree, by using referenda to ratify its decisions, and by permanently shifting legislative responsibility to an executive organ, the National Council of Unification.

In spite of all these advantages, the executive cannot always have its way with the legislature, especially if the executive pushes to the point of endangering the regime's stability and credibility. Both Rhee and Park were brought down by this, Park paying with his life for his rashness. Assuming American tolerance because of the geopolitics of the peninsula, Park embarked on a three-month campaign against the opposition party by using riot police to raid its headquarters, expelling the opposition leader from the assembly, and trying to isolate him and his supporters from what were assumed to be pliant legislators. But much to Park's surprise and chagrin, all the opposition legislators resigned and sympathy demonstrations by students and others had to be quelled by martial law; all reminiscent of the 1960 agitation which toppled Rhee. Park's actions soured the army and particularly the KCIA, whose chief lured Park to its headquarters and murdered him, ending an eighteen-year regime.[6]

*The Politically Sophisticated Academic Community*

Student political involvement has an honored, even heroic and romantic, tradition in Korea. Students were among those who rose up against the Japanese in 1919 and who continued resisting when other patriotic elements were repressed. Students were part of the revolutionary underground which surfaced in 1945, augmented in time with recruits from the ever-expanding educational system. Like their contemporary counterparts in the political parties, students have been split into left and right partisans and within these broad categories into contentious factions. The right under Rhee was organized into a compulsory National Defense Corps, in theory an autonomous association but in truth controlled by the executive through an obliging Minister of Education. The left, suffering the same suppression as the left parties, strives to hold on through various ostensibly innocuous study groups and clubs in the leading universities. But any student who criticized Rhee's harsh rule was denounced as subversive, surveilled by the police, and subjected to institutional violence whenever actively protesting. Rhee was finally toppled over a confrontation between students and authority in 1960. This primarily spontaneous outpouring of rage and grief by the student community well illustrates the paradoxical political strength and weakness of the student movement and its tenuous ties to the populace at large. Idealistic, issue-oriented, nationalistic, and freer of the pressures and restraints on both the other politicized elements of the society and the apolitical populace, students resent and more openly express political dissatisfaction. But they offer no coherent practical program of their own, nor an organization capable of putting a program into effect. In 1960 they overestimated the importance of their role and underestimated the benevolent neutrality of the military in overthrowing Rhee. They were unprepared for the inability and unwillingness of the Chang regime to materialize their views on political reform and were unable to prevent the military coup of the next year.

The military revived and even intensified student repression, given the more modern technology available to a military and its greater fear of protest and unsolicited suggestions for political freedom, which it regards as only encouraging license and political impotency. The new regime moved quickly to control the student problem at the source by regulating the nature and number of those in school, especially those in the humanities and social sciences, which specialize in training future bureaucratic decision-makers. However, entrance ceilings and liberal arts quotas were evaded, and campus unrest increased as political repression in the society escalated. The government then moved more forcefully. Campuses have since been relocated from where agitation was most contagious to more remote locations, where it was said the more tranquil atmosphere was conducive to rational reflection; the exodus of Seoul National University from the center of the city is an example. The police have striven to confine demonstrations to the particular campuses at which they originate, if necessary by using the army to occupy those schools under emergency ordinances, as at Korea University in 1975. The authorities have been particularly wary of coordinated, intercampus protest, especially students from the prestigious universities inflaming even those attending middle schools. The police warn parents to convince their student offspring to refrain from political protest or the family collectively will suffer. Similarly students are expected to report campus agitators or the authorities will judge the students likewise delinquent. Student protestors are arrested and their subsequent release made conditional on their good behavior. Those who have been expelled from the universities can only be reinstated by the gracious individual act of the minister of education; if an institution reinstates without prior ministry approval, the institution is punished. Plainclothes agents initiate staff or student purges, often without formal charges or the opportunity to defend oneself. Student clubs and organizations have been abolished, partly to sever any linkage between the opposition parties and students, a tie which earlier enabled students to earn future party credentials by serving as campus clients of prominent politicians. Positively, the authorities have expanded campus recreation in the belief that this dissipates the youthful zest for excitement which motivates political agitation, have saturated the academic media with appeals for hard work, have required lectures in moral guidance, and have regularly mobilized students to demonstrate for government programs.

A key constituent of the government's efforts to politically neutralize the campus is the administrative and professional staff. Administrators are expected to spy and report on professors, and professors on students. Professors lecture on morality and preach active anti-Communism, and visit parents in order to persuade them to press their youngsters to conform politically and comply with government campus regulations, or the professors face the consequence of having their tenure nullified on grounds of incompetence or idleness.

As in the case of student agitators, no formal charges need ever be presented, and hence no defense or appeal is feasible. Some professors learn of their severance only by removal or clearing out of their desks. As in Japanese times, unsigned resignations, usable at any time at the option of higher authority, may be required of professors before appointment.

And yet, for all the government fury, the professorial political role is ambiguous, some would say compromisable. This is because, although academics view themselves as critics of existing political policies, they also consider themselves as a potent source of shaping those policies. Hence many academics, termed *patronized scholars*, have welcomed the opportunity to serve as counselors or as employees of government agencies. These individuals enjoy special privileges such as subsidized overseas travel, and some have become well-compensated confidants of high officials. But they are viewed with mistrust by colleagues, though just how compromised such individuals are and to what degree they have helped to erode a potentially viable source of critical review of executive policy is much debated.

In sum, by either carrot or stick, the authorities have succeeded in neutralizing professors, administrators, and students as potentially countervailing elements in Korean politics and thus as positive contributors to the Korean political development process. Individuals of great courage and fortitude certainly do speak out, but too often they are silenced by intimidation, denial of privileges, incarceration, and even exile and execution.[7]

## The Dearth of Countervailing Political Interest Groups

Although Koreans often manifest a strong loyalty and responsibility to primary affiliates based on kin and locality, they have not shown the same interest or ability in creating viable secondary (i.e., intermediate) community affiliations. Secondary groups lack discipline, stability, ideological commitment, and, unless (and sometimes even if) they are small, are both factional and fractional. Consequently, the political elite, with justification, has claimed that secondary association members are bumblers, opportunists, and more a thorn than an aid to the elite in modernizing the society, and hence unworthy to share in decision-making. Yet that elite has done little constructively to remedy the situation. Contrariwise, authority has exacerbated the problem by interfering in, demoralizing, and weakening secondary organizations in the process of subordinating them to the political will. This scares away the populace from joining and productively participating in any secondary associational activities, even those which might carry on a dialogue with, if not pressure or bargain with, authority or stand as a buffer between polity and individual. I do not consider that this is pathological and due to some fault in the Korean national political character, but rather that it is a rational response to the patrimonial facts of Korean political life. Since I argue that Korea is not a western feudal-postfeudal social order, we cannot expect to find associations with nonpatrimonial characteristics within Korean society. Thus I agree with the critics of Gregory Henderson's seminal "mass society" thesis that his use of that western typology is neither valid nor fruitful when applied to Korea. However, simultaneously, I do not agree that, because of this, Henderson's fundamental insights on Korean associations must be rejected, though I prefer my own vocabulary.

Thus I utilize (though sometimes rephrase) Henderson's thesis that Korean individuals are politically isolated—in Henderson's terminology, atomized—once they step out of the protected cocoons of their primary associations (which have limited jurisdiction in the larger society) unless those individuals have vital political connections, which even for the privileged minority who have them are tenuous indeed. Most individuals are co-opted by authority and organized into associations of authority's choosing to serve its patrimonial interests through either exploitation of authority's virtual monopoly of access to the society's prebends or coercion. Rhee preferred to use armed bullies, Park preferred the KCIA (whose leader ironically was his undoing), and both, as the Japanese before them, depended routinely on the police to bring the hesitant into line, much as the dynasts used outcast gilds and private guards to express "popular" discontent with associations which stood against authority's will. The captive associations are made to serve as conduits for instructing and mobilizing the membership to actively support official policy, especially through mass rallies, since they both provide a feeling of involvement without allowing the associations' leadership to participate in decision-making and focus and energize the moral wrath of the in-group against the polity's enemies, internal or external. Rallies are most intimidating when they appear to be spontaneous, so that care must be taken to insure satisfactory attendance either directly, by secret communication from authority to the leaders of the front associations instructing them to assemble their members, or indirectly, for example, by commandeering public transport which will not only move the faithful to attend but also encourage the lukewarm, who might otherwise go to work or on personal errands. The associations also are encouraged and even subsidized to place newspaper advertisements sponsoring the rallies and appealing for financial and material support for the cause. The noisy displays of unity and harmony between polity and populace in this, a patrimonial social order, are considered most important because volunteer secondary associations are virtually nonexistent and the front associations are incapable on their own, or the government is unwilling to chance their working up much membership élan for polity policies outside the rally process.

Since the redefinition of the role and reorganization of student associations in the twilight of Park's power well illustrates my observations on front secondary associations, I have chosen to discuss them here rather than in the previous section. When all student organizations—political, religious, or whatever—were abolished, most were incorporated directly into the student defense corps, which all middle- to college-level students were required to join. The corps were organized hierarchically with the president (Park) as commander-in-chief, the education minister as his deputy, the provincial governors and local officials as subordinates, and deans and faculty as the final link in the chain of command. Corps members (students, that is) were expected to avoid what was termed the "excessive social participation" and divisive conduct of the past, that is, political activity embarrassing to authority. Positively, the students were expected to support the polity's goals of national unity by actively working in rural development programs and by mass rallying, at which time they swore to be ever diligent in their studies. All this certainly is a far cry from the political role the students conceived for themselves and their secondary associations in the heady days of their 1960 revolt.[8]

## A Profile of the Korean Patrimonial Political Man

Perhaps because they have survived a history of turmoil with their identity and integrity intact, Koreans are ever optimistic about an uncertain, undefined future. Simultaneously, they accept the often-harsh reality of the present because, as they put it, if you must eat bitter fruit, do it now. One of the signal characteristics of that present to which all must be reconciled is this world's capriciousness. The observers who attribute the source of national character to nature point to Korean geography to explain this belief; to wit, a temperate climate of great potential but ever subject to nature's whim, such as the inadequate and uncertain rainfall. Others provide a religious ("value") explanation in the Korean Buddhist belief of a world in constant flux.

Whatever the explanation—and I will suggest still another in due course—capriciousness is most evident socially in Koreans' inability to rely absolutely on associates to fulfill their obligations, especially in secondary groups, but in a crunch even within primary groups based on kin and geography. Individuals learn early that they can only truly rely on themselves, or more precisely their wits, and be ever ready to respond quickly to opportunity, free of the confining ties and encumbering pledges made in good faith at the time but under differing circumstances, a situation which must be expected in this capricious world. Especially when survival is at stake, individuals must be pragmatic. Without the survival of individuals, Koreans reason, of what value is the survival of groups; or as it is put, without Koreans, how can a Korea exist? Hence, loyalty can be a sometime quality in all social relationships, but especially in those relationships dependent on an impersonal, intangible standard, such as public consciousness. Although Koreans do respect those who keep their word and put feelings and rapport before self-seeking, especially under prevailing capricious circumstances, they expect tolerance of those who do not, and above all they expect that individuals will never be backed up against a wall of immutable duty and responsibility.

Although accordingly regarded both by others and themselves as egocentric, Koreans nevertheless believe they are productive achievers because they are pragmatic risk-takers who rely on luck, ever willing to go ahead, if necessary without careful preparation and with scant regard for the consequences of failure. For of what value are abstract reasoning or ideological conviction in responding to this capricious, irrational world? Thus, alas, most profound thinkers of Korean history, of which the nation can be justly proud, are known more for their seminal contributions to the philosophy of China and Japan than to Korea!

For all their faith in compulsive ego expression, Koreans nevertheless expect those individuals who somehow can make sense out of, and control, this capricious environment to provide stern, even authoritarian, discipline to keep in check the harmful, individual egotism of most, whether those individuals be parents, reference group members, or political representatives. Yet, while Koreans thus see the struggle of life as one between individual, egotistic passion and the demands of one or more reference groups, because of the very capriciousness of the social order, they cannot be assured that society's demands can or should be regularized. Consequently, response to authority is often formalistic and minimal, sufficient to repress egotistic emotions and behavior which could antagonize those in authority, but not so great that conformity will interfere with taking advantage of capricious opportunity. Hence, although Koreans are fatalistic and formally passive toward authority, they occasionally act violently against those in authority who thwart their will, though significantly not against authority itself.

I now wish to discuss the implications of the psychosocial observations for patrimonial formal authority and decision-making. An awareness of and apparent compliance with patrimonial authority is manifest. It is unlikely that any Korean can escape either knowledge or jurisdiction of formal authority, with all its regulations, ever-present visibility via modern education and media, mechanisms of control, and mass mobilization apparatuses. But beyond this obvious fact, it is more difficult to gauge accurately how positive political support really is, for no other reason than that the patrimonial rules of the game preclude any meaningful expression of the popular will. Surveys suggest that although institutional authority as such continues to be accepted with the same awe as of yore, perceptions of political effectiveness—that is, belief by individuals that they can creatively contribute, even very modestly, to decision-making—are low; and the higher the educational level, the greater the feeling of helplessness. Those who are members of or expect to join the elite, not surprisingly, have the highest hopes, while those with little chance or desire to do so have limited confidence about influencing even local officials. Those aware of, but not in sympathy with, the elite are ambiguous and frustrated, caught between their optimism for the future and their realistic sense of the here and now. They "optimistically" support democracy, but for a vague tomorrow. For today they believe it is not achievable, save for voting, which is but ratifying the decisions of a patrimonial authority, a symbolic act of compliance from dutiful cliental subjects, who are expected to be content with what political prerogatives their mentors gracefully grant them. Korean patrimonial democracy thus is an exercise in free will only to the extent that one either conforms or faces punishment from an often-vindictive moral avenger. Although few Koreans, being realists, dare to face such willful authority directly, most wherever possible do evade the capriciously enforced rules and regulations of their patrimonial masters in the hope that luck or fate will somehow enable them to persevere until that tomorrow when inevitably the current regime will disappear from the stage, as all past regimes have, and the opportunity to satisfy individual egos will be realizable. By evading true compliance while formalistically conforming, Koreans assure their own survival and psychologically soothe those in authority. But justified or not, such dissimulation does not contribute positively to mobilizing the population to confront the critical development challenges of today productively (to this point we will return, especially in the next two chapters).[9]

## The Japanese Contribution: How to Modernize a Patrimonial Polity

We already have argued (in Chapter 1) that what the Japanese and then the Americans did or did not do when they occupied Korea, and the ways in which their policies and social values subsequently influenced Korean institutional thinking, is vital to understanding the modernizing process not only in Korea, but in Asian patrimonial societies in general. The Japanese, in contrast to the Americans, always were sensitive to Korean patrimonialism because of the awareness of the influence of Chinese patrimonial institutions on Japanese society for over a millennium. The Japanese were convinced that since they had mastered simultaneously the secret of the Asian modernizing process and of Korean patrimonialism, of those on the Korean scene Japan alone was capable of altering Korean society for the better.

The primary political medium of Japanese-directed change in Korea was the government general, which replaced a resident generalship that had introduced basic Japanese legal, administrative, and economic principles and forms during the brief protectorate of 1906-10. After the reorganization of the 1920s, the government general consisted of a governor general and a civil administrator-assistant, appointed by the Japanese prime minister, who supervised a bureaucracy and coordinated a ministerial policymaking secretariat. The entire central executive was organized along Japanese functional lines and staffed by Japanese, although it did include a central advisory council of Korean elders who were willing to serve. But those counselors advised only on request, which was infrequent indeed, and on ceremonial rather than practical matters.

The governor was responsible formally solely to the Emperor, and not to the Japanese Diet, so that he was immune to legislative oversight. Since the governor held prime-ministerial rank, the stipulation that he report to the minister of colonies, and in wartime to the home minister, was not likely to be more than a ritualistic formality of filing annual reports, depicting an ever-expanding Korean paradise under Japanese benevolence meant for international media distribution. Although the governorship was opened to civilians after the 1919 uprising, only military officers of command rank were ever appointed, under the notion, soon to be accepted within Japan itself, that only such individuals were above the partisan politics and strife of civil self-interest, and hence worthy both to represent Japan and to achieve its noble mission in Korea. In sum, the governor was an absolute military ruler, unencumbered by restraints as long as he did not bring down the social order or disgrace Japan before the international community, who was mandated to exploit fully that freedom of action to redirect Korea according to the Japanese grand design which, I suggest, was to retain fundamental Korean patrimonial institutional principles while introducing novel, Japanese-designed, more efficient means to achieve those time-honored ends.

To this end, the Japanese reorganized—in our terms, modernized—the Korean administrative apparatus along the following lines: First, they centralized the chain of command by restricting all primary decision-making to the capital. Local authority was allowed only those prerogatives expressly mandated to it, usually designed to carry out the center's objectives. The governor general selected the provincial governors, who in turn chose most of the local officials at their or lower echelons. All these officials were made members of the central civil service, terminating the older system of separating the capital from local rosters.

Second, the Japanese elaborated and professionalized the provincial and district administrators, especially by attaching secretariat staffs to province and district governments and creating provincial advisory councils. The membership of these councils were one-third appointed and two-thirds elected, with the former predominantly Japanese and the latter Korean. Counselors were restricted to those men of means and property, either Japanese or Korean, who were dependent on the continuing patrimonial grace of Japanese authority, and thus sympathetic to Japanese interests.

Third, although the Japanese continued to focus vitally on the province and the district, they expanded their formal chain of command to include lower, more remote levels, especially for the first time in the rural hinterland. Some of the reformers of the late imperial period had suggested this, but it was the Japanese who actually terminated the long-standing compact that as long as locals did not unduly irritate a remote formal authority and met their obligations, they would be left to their own devices. The Japanese achieved their goal primarily through creation of special urban communities where Japanese congregated and enjoyed special privileges and rural townships for Koreans. As they had earlier in their own country, the Japanese tried to make the township, rather than the natural village community, the focus of local rural loyalty and participation. The primary instrument, as in Japan, was to provide modern services, such as education and health, in the township, eclipsing the local headman's role of dispenser of supravillage prebends. The township headmen were Koreans to be sure, but they were appointed by Japanese to supervise Japanese laws, and thus, like it or not, were the agents of the Japanese physical and ideological penetration and control of rural Korea.

Fourth, the executive clearly dominated the political apparatus. There was no national legislature, and councils on the local level were completely advisory and met only at the grace of the executive. A judiciary existed and, as in Japan, could be embarrassingly assertive, but its decisions could be neutralized by executive decree.

All these measures were designed to enable the center to move more quickly and effectively than had any previous national Korean administration, whose directives had been ever diluted and compromised once they left the capital. This was significant because, fifth and foremost, and in sum, as the government general came to be the virtual arbiter of Korean life, intervening at will and making the major decisions in the society, it became the primary agent for initiating and determining the design of Korea's modernization in general. Korean conformity to that design was insured through both positive incentive and coercion.

*Incentive:* The Korean elite was co-opted by the Japanese policy of granting titles to the surviving aristocracy and prebends, such as suffrage, to the elite and to those enterprising commoners who themselves facilitated or persuaded their fellow Koreans to accept Japanese rule. During the early period of occupation, those Koreans who cooperated were considered traitors by Koreans. But after the 1919 protests failed, and certainly by the 1930s when it was clear that no viable alternative to Japanese rule was in the offing, most Koreans decided, as had their forebears in the face of oppressive indigenous rulers or foreign invaders, to make the most of the inevitability and pragmatically exploit whatever opportunities the Japanese offered. The privileged or would-be privileged learned the Japanese language, adopted Japanese dress, and sent their children to be indoctrinated in Japanese schools, in Japan proper if schooling was unavailable because of restrictive quotas. Ordinary Koreans were brought into the Japanese stream through employment in modernizing projects, especially in the 1930s. Although their opportunities were more limited than those of the elite, at least some ordinary Koreans became lower-level administrators, especially in those politically sensitive positions the Japanese felt were essential for contact and even rapport with the general populace, such as in the police and eventually in the military. The government, as back home, used all the paraphernalia of social identification and the pulpit of the schools to mobilize support for itself and its policies. For many Koreans this was the first time any authority had ever tried to involve them either as individuals or en masse in politically generated social action.

*Coercion:* It must be mentioned immediately that overt coercion, even violence, to insure conformity was an ever-present threat in Japan itself, and Japanese authority in Korea was unlikely to act with restraint in a colony when it was unwilling to do so at home, especially since even the very limited restrictions on executive license which existed in Japan were absent in Korea. Similarly, the governor general was even more free than his Korean predecessors to coerce by fiat and because he had modern means to do so. At first the Japanese relied primarily on their army to force conformity and put down rebellion. But after 1920 it was considered better public relations to use the civil police, in greater and greater numbers as time went on; by 1941, one of every 400 Koreans and Japanese residing in Korea was in one way or another a policeman! In addition, as in Japan, a secret police was created to constitute a separate force charged specially with investigating and extirpating "subversion." The provincial governors were authorized to dispatch the police expeditiously even to the lowly township level with a blanket mandate to gain entry anywhere at will, to arrest without warrant, to interrogate and torture, and to punish summarily (including the time-honored humiliating public whipping)—all without any restraining judicial review. The police were also authorized to suppress "dangerous thoughts." Intellectuals the government did not like were forced out of the capital into exiled silence and foreign missionaries who denigrated Japanese rule were harassed. The police surveilled, and if necessary infiltrated, any Korean organization, intimidating or bribing to prevent antigovernment demonstrations. Police dossiers were kept on all potential troublemakers. Before any offender or even suspect was released from custody, the police required a signed letter of apology for causing the government trouble and thanking the police for its benevolent, graceful compassion. Confessions were routinely extracted, usually by torture, and individuals were blackmailed into betraying colleagues.

Although exposure to this aspect of Japanese political culture acquainted Koreans with modern methods of repression, it also showed Koreans how to combat such restraints. Koreans living in Japan contacted Japanese radicals, who taught them how to resist underground, form front groups with those difficult to bully (farmers, for example), and organize strikes and demonstrations under the very noses of the police. But radical resistance was soon dissipated by factional strife which alienated popular support. The Korean penchant to organize through reference groups rather than through isolated individuals made relatives and close friends vulnerable to betrayal whenever anyone was apprehended by the police. Isolated and dispirited, some radicals apostatized and were released, conditional upon surveilled good behavior, while others were forced to flee abroad. In consequence, the less militant and more poorly organized protestors against Japanese rule became convinced that it was wiser to retreat into the protective confines of their primary groups and await a better day.

Japanese modernizing authority, for all its transforming, especially formal administrative innovations, thus reinforced the ordinary Koreans' existing fear and suspicion of repressive civil and now military patrimonial decision-making. This in turn reinforced their conviction that now, even more than in the past, opportunism, connivance, nepotism, and self-interest were essential to security and survival, unless somehow one was lucky enough to become a member of the polity and exploit that opportunity for all it was worth. And those who came to authority after 1945, Rhee and Park and all those individuals who had been reared by and were privileged by association with the Japanese, accepted as modern and legitimately Korean not only the trappings of the government general such as state ceremonies and official and school uniforms, but also much of the institutional substance and political style which I have described as contemporary—to the extent that many younger Koreans are unaware that the source is Japanese. Hence, what is most remarkable about contemporary Korean society is that it is a museum of Japanese colonial (especially patrimonial) practice and ethos, while its decision-makers who accept those patrimonial practices and that ethos as their own are ever proclaiming that they are anti-Japanese leaders.[10]

### The Contribution of the United States: Retaining and Further Modernizing Political Patrimonialism

The American occupation made a number of what hindsight indicates were bad political decisions. First, although the commanding general on the spot in Korea would soon be given carte blanche to act, Korea remained for too long under the nominal authority of a supreme commander for the Allied powers in Tokyo, whose initial, primary mandate was to preserve law and order over a defeated enemy, including its former colonial possession, Korea. Precious few of the best and the brightest of the American administrators and technical experts who arrived in northeast Asia for occupation duty, especially in that critical initial period, willingly accepted assignment to or even temporary duty in less comfortable, and what they considered peripheral, Korea.

Second, because after years of Japanese discrimination few Korean administrators were trained adequately by American standards, the Americans felt initially they must rely on Japanese willing or forced to stay on; or at least the Americans rationalized their decision thusly. These ex-bureaucrats were permitted, and in some cases encouraged, to use existing Japanese government general policies and methods, with only minor modification in those instances of flagrant authoritarianism. In doing so the Americans seemed oblivious to the fact that they were perpetuating, and in the eyes of some zealous Korean bureaucrats legitimizing, the Japanese autocratic political style. It is especially ironic that the Americans mistakenly believed, and some Koreans claimed, that all they were doing was adapting "traditional" Korean, rather than Japanese, structures and procedures to democratic ends.

Third, the Americans threw away a valuable opportunity to restructure the existing bureaucracy or build a new one from scratch. By not purging the bureaucracy of those Koreans who had collaborated with the Japanese, in Korean eyes the United States seemed to be suggesting that it wished to sanction and legitimize any number of past practices, which angered and bewildered many Koreans of all political persuasions. The members of the Korean advisory council which screened new bureaucratic appointments were selected from the old elite, who used this fortuitous opportunity to appoint like-minded friends and purge their potential enemies, especially those who were more sympathetic to the very productive administrative changes the Americans finally became aware were important, but alas too late in the game. Especially, the new bureaucrats revived the notion of exploiting public office for prebends, if not for outright bribery. The ensuing naked struggle for personal advantage, termed a "descent into chaos" by Henderson, was exacerbated by the absence of any towering national leader whom the Koreans respected and the Americans were willing to back, and by a left-right cleavage which the bureaucratic establishment used to suppress its critics.

Fourth, when the Americans abandoned the universally unwanted trusteeship and created the independent Republic, they opportunistically supported those Koreans who were willing to maintain the status quo, even if they were neither democratic nor competent. For the cold war had begun, and the Americans were more than willing to listen to those who preached repression of all but the anti-Communist right. The radical threat was real enough, but the right saw to it that the American-supported counteraction encompassed many more dissidents than radical extremists, establishing the precedent, if one was needed, for repression of all political opposition in the nominally democratic Republic-of-Korea-to-be.

Fifth, the Americans never were in a position to appreciate, let alone influence, the Korea that existed outside the few larger urban centers, since at best the American military government and civil affairs field teams were stationed in the provincial capitals, and even there jurisdiction was very limited. Moreover, the first teams were not knowledgeable about the country, including the language, and hence found it difficult to make independent judgments without being dependent on censoring interpreters or limiting their local contacts to English speakers. (Additionally the teams duplicated the chain of command, were ill coordinated, and were even rivals.) Hence there was little if any real contact between the Americans and Koreans, especially nonbureaucratic ruralites, and consequently few Americans truly understood how the vast majority of Koreans lived and thought. Most of the locals the Americans did interact with were landlords or ex-bureaucrats from the Japanese period, anxious to make contact with Americans to maintain respectively their economic privileges and authority.

Sixth, when the Americans opted for an occupation, they retained the skeleton of the Japanese government general with its civil secretariat, its staff under a military governor (in this case, an American commanding general), and its specific functional departments and related specialized agencies. Hence, for example, the education department continued to propagandize for support of authority, newspapers either were government organs or were surveilled to insure neutrality at least, and paramilitary youth groups and the numerous public safety and police agencies, including their secret and peace preservation subunits, were not only retained but refurbished, though to the Americans' credit the thought control police was abolished as blatantly undemocratic. Most pertinently, even after a recruitment and screening process, half the Korean police force, especially the key leaders and advisors, had served during the Japanese period, when they had earned a justified reputation for equaling the cruelty of their masters. Even the most archconservative Koreans resented this policy.

Seventh, the Americans introduced reforms which, based on their home experience, they considered democratically progressive, but which often backfired in this alien environment which the Americans neither understood nor controlled. For example, they terminated the Japanese policy of subordinating the police to the military. This move made sense in the context of American postwar democratization of Japanese society, and in Korea because the military were unreliable. But it enabled those Korean factions who could control the police through co-optation of the police chief to expand their numbers and entrench themselves in the force, and thus exploit the police for prebendary self-interest in the bureaucracy and in the society at large.

Eighth, one of the most fascinating latent consequences of the American administration was an *increase* in political centralization when compared to the Japanese design. The Japanese had left operational command of the political apparatus, especially the police and local appointments, to the provincial governors. But the Americans, after a year of local improvization, based on their own decentralized political model which they believed had failed in Korea, reconcentrated decision-making and administrative control in the provincial centers, and subsequently in the capital, Seoul, where the Americans gathered. Especially the Korean executive secretariat in the capital, with American blessing, was able to reassert control over its bureaucracy through a provincial affairs section which reviewed *all*, not only political, local activities, such as budgets. And by applying newly introduced, modern American techniques of public administration in the bureaucracy, the secretariat was able to extend the range of its jurisdiction and control over the local society to an extent earlier executives were unable to realize.

In sum, by building on rather than destroying or otherwise qualitatively changing the Japanese political style, the Americans provided the Korean decision-makers who inherited the political apparatus with a still more "modern" version of their patrimonial political past than the Japanese had created. The Koreans thus inherited the worst of *both* the Japanese patrimonial colonial institutions and of those earlier, developmentally counterproductive, patrimonial Korean ones the Japanese deliberately had preserved, albeit in "modernized" form. I suggest this in spite of the apparent counterevidence that the superstructure of American-inspired, nonpatrimonial authority ("democracy") has been implanted in Korea's constitution and all Korean Republic rulers have firmly proclaimed, and may have believed, that they are helping to create a Korean version of American authority and politics. I make no judgment of the potential viability or desirability of American political institutions in Korea. Rather I have tried in this and the preceding chapter to understand how and why the Koreans act as they do politically, especially how and why they are guided by patrimonial principles and procedures long since established as reasonable, legitimate, and morally desirable. Nevertheless, I do not wish to suggest that these choices are either inevitable or immutable, and more to the point, are justifiable in the very terms of what the Koreans themselves claim they want for their society, simply because they are consistent with historical or existing political institutions. That, I suggest, is to confuse political modernization with political development.[11]

# 4

# The Agricultural Economy

## Landed Power and Its Role in Patrimonial Finance

Land, or more accurately the administrative control and exploitation of agricultural cultivators, has been the primary means until most recently through which Korean authority, as authority in all historical agricultural societies, has financed itself. However, since I view Korea as patrimonial, I do not wish to interpret Korean society and its land pattern in terms of the prevailing, western-inspired model which postulates a universal, unilinear metamorphosis from primitive antiquity to feudalism. Consequently, I believe the following about the historical character of Korean land tenure:

First, I consider whether or not private land tenure existed before the twentieth century a nonissue. The maxim that titular rulers own all the land in patrimonial Asian societies only has meaning within the context of an other-than-modern concept of property and ownership in which no one truly *owns* land. Rather individuals have proprietary rights as cultivators, controllers, or exploiters of many kinds. A ruler's preeminent right to land is symbolic, signifying his, and his polity's, right to at least a portion of the land's increment, and his right to a say in the cultivators' activities to secure his increment. The ability of particular individuals to buy, sell, mortgage, and inherit land, therefore, does not necessarily confound the ruler, unless this otherwise challenges the ruler's share of production.

Second, in patrimonial reasoning, the right to the land's increment is a graceful prebend granted by a titular ruler to an official. Although in Korea office and aristocratic rank tended to go in the same direction and often were blurred, the right to a benefice never became a feudal vassal's personal grant (a fief) from a lord's personal landholdings. Rather the cultivators owed public due in both produce and labor service, and therefore the classic and much-debated issue as to whether that due was public tax or private rent, I suggest, is another nonissue. Ultimately the distinction is only whether the government agents come in person to collect the patrimonial leader's share of "his" property, or whether that share is passed through prebendally appointed hands which could be and often were sticky, a constant functional problem in this kind of system.

The primary significance of these two characteristics is that the ability of a patrimonial aristocracy like Korea's to frustrate rulers' attempts to convert land benefices into temporary, exclusively officeholding prebends did not pose an *institutional* threat to center authority. This was so because these "lords of the land" neither mobilized cultivators and aides to oppose central authority, nor concerted among themselves to convert fiscal advantage to formally recognized economic, political, and class rights; but rather validated their fiscal depredations through existing claims to officeholding. Legally only a titular ruler could grant and protect landed prebends against all possible rival claimants, and thus it was the ruler's favor rather than feudal military-political sagacity which was vital in collecting and protecting the landed surplus. This was especially true in eras of chronic instability and rapid change in fortune and even during the period of military ascendancy which occurred in Korea during the twelfth and thirteenth centuries—all periods in which, according to conventional wisdom, feudalism is supposed to arise.

Two further contrasting characteristics of patrimonial and feudal tenure: Cultivator military service in a patrimonial economy like Korea's is not considered to be a byproduct of the aristocrats' military obligation, as it is under feudalism, but is a specialized labor service— typically earthwork construction, but also husbandry on land whose income has been reserved to support the military.

Finally, since adequate labor is the key to land's value, what labor cannot be procured voluntarily must be assured by draft. Nevertheless, I believe that the Korean agricultural laborer was neither a slave nor a serf. On the one hand, the peasant was free to cultivate and reside on his own land, yet he enjoyed this privilege on prebendary grace, that is, insofar and for as long as it suited the interests of those who controlled him. Thus he could be moved about at will, although this was not usual save in periods of national peril, such as invasion.

On the other hand, all this vitally differs from a feudal (manorial) economy in which the lord rather than the cultivator was usually moved, and if the cultivator was moved it was as an individual, and not as a member of a community, as in a patrimonial economy.

The cultivators' burdens, nonetheless, were onerous in patrimonial Korea. In theory, peasants surrendered on average one-half of their crops to those who held the land's prebend, part of which on privately granted land constituted the government's tax. However, those in charge of overseeing royal and government-reserved land also had the right, not given to private grantees, of conscripting labor from cultivators of the surrounding countryside to service those lands. And since, at least at first, virtually all the grantees, whether government or private, were absentee "lords of the land," they had to employ overseers, enforcers, and even tax farmers recruited from personal bondservants, petty officials, and local merchants to manage and collect the lords' share of the crops. This further added to the cultivators' burden, since these intermediaries flagrantly abused their fiscal authority. By the last few centuries of the imperial era, local landed gentry had reduced their commoner cultivating neighbors to tenants and even sharecroppers. The problem was exacerbated by a rising population which increased competition for and reduced the size of individual holdings of available land. However, cultivators most resented official collusion which protected illegal land-grabbing, inflated taxes, and imposed abusive and unwarranted labor service. Hence, when cultivators rose in defiance, it often was the abusive officials rather than the landlords whom the peasants attacked. At the end of the last century, entrepreneurial cultivators and usurious lenders, even hated outside merchants, had obtained and increased holdings at the expense of those very petty officials and local gentry who earlier had co-opted land held by individual cultivators.

As fluid as land possession had become, the system was not "modern" in the legal sense. For one, tenurial rights were vaguely defined, although ten years' squatting normally assured a cultivator's claim. An owner's formal document only certified the original grant, and the courts only recognized jurisdiction when fraud was charged. Land claims, as other claims in this patrimonial society, often depended not so much on informal community acceptance as on a claimant's ability to gain a magistrate's favor, especially since neither custom nor consensus was necessarily enough to resolve serious disputes of any kind.

Proposals to reform and regenerate the land tenure system were not lacking, but these suggestions either went unheeded, or if they were seriously considered—as for example an 1894 edict to register land transfers— were not enforced. It devolved upon the Japanese occupiers to alter the existing land system drastically. In 1906, even before formal annexation, Japanese nationals were given the right to buy, sell, and mortgage land. In the same year the Korean government was pressured into "requesting" the Japanese to undertake a modern cadastral survey, an effort which went on for more than a decade and hence into the actual occupation, and which along with the commercialization of land was to have a profound effect on existing Korean land patterns and ownership. The model for the new system was the Japanese land act of 1873, which required cultivators who wished to be owners to register their surveyed land, since modern ownership was a formally recognized legal right. The effect in Korea, not unanticipated by the Japanese in the light of their own experience, was to reduce most "independent" cultivators to tenants or agricultural laborers, partly out of ignorance or force and fraud in the registration process, and partly out of the cultivators' inability to compete in the emerging money economy and hence acquire the specie to pay the land tax now required of all landowners. The survivors became the core of a new elite underclass to the Japanese, who, as in Japan, were sophisticated, comparatively well-to-do conservatives whom the government could count upon to help keep the peace and otherwise rally the rural countryside to support Japanese policies. This elite became increasingly important to the Japanese as they relentlessly pursued their goal of transferring the choicest Korean land directly or indirectly to their countrymen, arousing the ire of most rural Koreans.

The medium the Japanese created to do so was the Oriental Development Company (ODC), a quasi-government organ which predated the annexation, and in which the old Korean government was a shareholder because of its land rather than a monetary contribution, like the Japanese. Through control of nationalized palace and common pasture, and unregistered and tax-defaulted land, the company came to own and manage the choicest and largest tracts in the country. One of its earliest agricultural projects was to resettle Japanese cultivators in Korea on very favorable terms, that is, on already highly productive, developed land where Korean farmers had to be dispossessed, and on tracts larger than those Korean cultivators—or Japanese farmers back home for that matter—were privileged to husband. However, the resettlement projects never succeeded, partly because of Korean resistance, but mostly because the Japanese preferred to be landlords rather than cultivators, since as landlords the Japanese could exploit Korean labor through high rents and tap sources of productive loan capital unavailable to their Korean counterparts. Under such terms, the bigger the landlord, the greater the profit. And the biggest, and hence richest, landlord of them all was the ODC, which hired thousands of Koreans as wageworkers or sharecroppers to cultivate the land that once was their own!

Whether private Japanese, ODC Japanese, or Korean, 3.4 percent of those resident in Korea came to own half the cultivated land, while 75 percent of the populace were either full or partial tenants. Most landlords were absentee, using ruthless intermediaries who had ready access to the equally ruthless Japanese police or their Korean lackeys to help collect high rents (50-60 percent of the estimated yield) or dispossess defaulters. As elsewhere in Asia, rents usually were collected in kind—in Korea 93 percent so—at a conversion rate determined by the landlord. As burdensome as rents were, there were many additional, often hidden, levies, such as advanced seed loans, capital tool costs, free labor service for landlords, and, to rub salt in the wound, the owners' land taxes passed on to the cultivators. Moreover, the government, directly via ODC or indirectly through Japanese or Korean landlords, charged the cultivators for the cost of introducing and then maintaining a commercial agriculture, e.g., expenditures for irrigation and fertilizer. All these obligations, so typical of Asian patrimonial peasant economies, might add up to 90 percent of the cultivators' crop. A 1925 survey indicated that half the farmers were in a perpetual debt trap. Unlike even the shabbily treated peasantry of pre-World War II Japan, Korean cultivators could not sell or lease their land without bureaucratic approval, were limited in the choice of what crops to grow and how to grow them, and were even more at the mercy of usurious and profiteering middlemen than were their Japanese counterparts.

The consequences? Widespread rural misery and out-migration to neighboring lands, for example to Manchuria. Whatever limited rural capital most Korean farmers had accumulated earlier in the century was dissipated in the course of sheer survival. Although a few prebendally favored Korean landlords prospered, and a small number of entrepreneurial individual cultivator-owners somehow held their own, the Japanese policy of deliberately destroying viable small producers succeeded. Finally, the Korean tenure system was one means by which the Japanese were able to raise the food, fiber, and capital they required for their own economy at the expense of the Koran rural economy. This bias plus the resort to police coercion to enforce landlord-tenant relations, paternal government interference into land management, and commodity price fixing to the advantage of non-ruralites, were all precedents which the Japanese bequeathed to republican Korea.

Could such a land system be modern? The simple, unitary, formal-legal determination of ownership and rights and obligations; the concept of land as a marketable commodity in a commercial economy; a tax system based on land value and not on the vagaries of the harvest; taxes paid in specie and not in kind, enabling a government to calculate its budgets rationally; a rural economy in which profit is not equivalent to rent; the potential alienation of cultivators from the land they husband—all smack of modernity, at least from the western economic standpoint. Yet, in contrast, older landlord-tenant (or laborer) rent and managerial relationships, enforced, albeit now legally, by often unsubtle coercion rather than free contract, persisted. Thus we can but conclude that the system in 1945 was neither "traditional" nor "modern" but had significant elements of both; or to rephrase for our purposes, the system and the Japanese role in shaping it were but another example of *modernized patrimonialism*—a system in which certain fundamental institutional relationships deliberately were not changed, only their formal expressions were, in order to take advantage of up-to-date, effective (rational?) means to achieve persistent patrimonial goals. In other words, I suggest that the Japanese began the process of *modernizing* the Korean land system, but they deliberately chose not to *develop* it. They left that as well as their notion of what properly constitutes modernizing a land system as their contribution to an independent Korea.[1]

### Land Tenure and Reform in Contemporary Korea

In October 1945, the American occupation authority prohibited landlords from unilaterally cancelling land contracts, legalized rent in cash rather than in kind if the tenants so desired, and limited annual rent to one-third of the value of the harvest. And in February 1946, the Americans created the New Korea Co. (NKC) to collect rent on land over which they had inherited "vested" jurisdiction, namely, on the Japanese land holdings of the ODC (some 15 percent of the country's farmland) and on some 102,000 privately owned Japanese plots, and to collect service fees on certain collateral ODC facilities, for example warehousing and irrigation. Not surprisingly, the economically afflicted Korean populace came to regard NKC as a prime patrimonial plum. Being appointed to it offered not only bureaucratic status and assured remuneration in a chaotic economy, but also access to prebendary favors dispensable to relatives, potential political allies, and those able and willing to offer bribes and kickbacks to insure company indulgence.

But, alas, in 1948 the Americans decided to distribute NKC land holdings for fifteen yearly payments of thrice the annual rent (equivalent to 20 percent of value per year) through the medium of a newly created heir of NKC, the National Land Administration. Since a new cadastre was considered impossible to carry out, the old Japanese land survey, in spite of its obvious biases and obsolescence, was retained, though subject to the "interpretation" of Korean assessors who were surveilled by obviously suspicious Americans. Preference was given to the tillers and toilers on the spot, but those living nearby, refugees from the DPRK, and returnees from abroad were also eligible. Resale was prohibited for a minimum of ten years, and title could be revoked only for nonpayment. Ninety-one percent of the vested land was disposed of; what remained was orchard and disputed land. The Korean bureaucrats, patrimonial to the quick, insisted on "morally" screening all the potential buyers, ostensibly to weed out pro-Communist tenants, much to the dismay of at least some Americans who wanted the pragmatic "land to the tiller" principle of the successful Japanese land reform to prevail. Conservative bureaucrats also tried to stall the transfers, claiming that only a truly independent Korea should have the authority to institute such a reform. This argument found some favor in Washington, and so, although the Koreans were unsuccessful in preventing the transfers from taking place, they were able to keep those concerned Americans from pressuring the Koreans to follow suit on land under their jurisdiction.

To no one's surprise, the Koreans continued to procrastinate after achieving their independence. Serious consideration was finally to come just prior to the DPRK invasion of 1950, but the reform was not consummated until after the North Koreans had instituted Communist-revolutionary land redistribution in the areas they overran and in the process eliminated many formerly resisting landlords, thus providing the ROK with a public relations challenge and an opportunity. The government also stood to gain materially, because cultivators' payments were made to the government in grain, while landlords' reimbursements could be made in ever-inflating paper money doled out at the government's pace. At first sight, the terms of transfer seem more generous to tenants than the American initiative; to wit, land was sold at one and one-half times the annual rent—actually only one and one-fourth times, given a government subsidy—on a five-year payment schedule (and thus at 30 percent of the value per year), with a three-*chŏngbo* (approximately 7.4 acre) ceiling and the same restrictions on resale as the American plan. However, there were many exceptions, such as gardens, land held by schools, public organizations, and farm research agencies, and land reserved for consanguineal duties and care, thus pruning the eligible share of the targeted land to 69 percent. Nonetheless the result was striking. The large holders who once owned 90 percent of the land were all but eliminated, while the number of small and medium holders increased dramatically. In 1970, for example, 69 percent of Korean farmers were full operator-owners, 24 percent part owners and renters, and only 7 percent still tenants; alternatively, 83 percent of the land was legally in operator-owner hands. When the reform became inevitable, many landlords sold out at distress prices, rather than accept what from their standpoint was virtual confiscation, and the value of the bonds which the landlords received in compensation from the government for their land diminished rapidly in the raging inflation.

However, as dramatic as the transfer was for tenurial modernization, certain formal stipulations in the reform and the way in which it was carried out left standing old difficulties and created new ones for the new landowners, paradoxically leading to an increase in tenancy. First, in the eyes of some critics at least, the three-chŏngbo ceiling, beyond which land had to be transferred, was set too high by Korean though not by American standards. Hence the amount of especially good eligible land to transfer was considerably diminished. Second, half the members of local distribution boards were landlords who, in concert with the local-official members, were able to insure that any decision or dispute which came before the boards would be decided in the landlords' favor. Third, many landlords jacked up rents just prior to transfer to justify a high selling price. Intended or not, this created a larger repayment debt, and hence greater hardship for the ex-tenants. Fourth, landlords were permitted to sell or otherwise divide their property among their relatives and clients, thus further reducing the pool of available land. In these cases, the ex-landlords were able to continue controlling their former holdings through operating agreements with such new owners. Fifth, tenancy continued in disguise through secret oral contracts for the new owners to continue paying rent, sometimes as advanced loans or labor dues, to their ex-landlords. Sixth, reminiscent of the Japanese land reform in Korea decades earlier, only one-half the new owners ever registered and hence legalized their rights, in spite of the widespread publicity this time. Such land could be legally reclaimed by its former owners and the cultivators returned to tenancy. Interestingly, some tenancy is still legal—for example, on clan land where indigent relatives could earn a livelihood for a 30 percent rent fee if they also maintained the clan tombs and ancestor halls—but more pertinently, about half of tenant land has been held illegally. Much of this has been innocent; for example, holding out land to protect relatives "temporarily" absent from the village who, if they were judged to be absentee landowners, could lose their tenurial rights. But some such individuals in fact are urbanites, investing capital in rural real estate and employing cultivators and using overseers to protect investor interests. For all these reasons, a 1970 survey estimated that tenancy rose 31.8 percent in the 1960s.

But perhaps the major source of persistent tenancy is that the reform in truth was but a land redistribution program in that the government did not finance the land's development or provide the technical services to enable the new title holders, representing one-third of the farm families in Korea, to increase their productivity to keep up with constantly inflating costs and taxes. Small farmers, even though they consume most of their production, find themselves at the mercy of the commercial economy for such commodities as fertilizer. Such smaller and less efficient cultivators are vulnerable to being squeezed out by entreprenurial medium-sized holders who are eager to add to their farms. All holders, regardless of their diligence and thrift, are confronted from time to time with emergencies beyond the capacity of limited budgets to remedy. But when farmers fall into debt, they have no recourse other than to turn to usurious money lenders because the reform, under American prodding, made the mortgage of land illegal, at least for the first ten years, heavily fining violators and threatening to confiscate their property. Once in default, such cultivators become tenants once again, usually covertly so in order not to rouse the ire of the authorities, or join the increasing rural exodus.

The government has responded by offering to raise the ceilings on holdings in order to better accommodate, or according to some observers create, a trend to commercial agriculture—in truth, agribusiness—say to ten or twenty chŏngbo. Critics consider this proposal an attempt to revive the plantation overseer agriculture of the Japanese ODC, or at least provide a golden opportunity for real estate speculators to increase their rural holdings legally. The polity has replied that if the land is used improperly, the government will force the land's resale. An alternate suggestion is that the government help form cooperative farming units by consolidating the small holdings and otherwise prepare the land for mechanization, hopefully creating the incentive for cultivators to stay put.

In sum, the Korean Republic has continued the process of formally modernizing land tenure first inaugurated by the Japanese, but has not qualitatively altered, that is, developed, certain long-standing patrimonial tenurial characteristics.[2]

## Exacting Authority's Economic Due from the Peasantry

Authority has derived its revenue from the land primarily by extracting (1) a share of the produce (a) essentially grain but also (b) local specialized products, termed *tribute;* (2) labor service, termed *corvée;* (3) military service, which to some observers is but a specialized form of labor service; and (4) miscellaneous dues.

*The produce or land tax:* Until the twentieth century the bounty of the land financed both central and local authority, whether collected directly on government-administered land as a tax, or indirectly on privately exploited land as a portion of the rent. As in all patrimonial economies, the authority's share of the land's surplus was set and reset at the graceful whim of the ruler. Examples: Even though tax rates were universal, deviations were permitted, supposedly to take into account differences in regional and individual productivity as such and over time. Such a system, even with the best of intentions, enables government assessors and collectors to exact a bargainable, extralegal impost from the cultivators by allowing assessors to threaten to increase the prevailing rate and collectors to extract higher than legal rate while pocketing the difference. Cultivators were forced to store, process, and then transport tax crops. Levies were exacted at the discretion of the collectors, often at times disadvantageous to the cultivators, such as when crops were in short supply just before harvest.

Connivance between government agents and land managers removed existing holdings and kept newly cleared land off tax registers, decreasing the pool of taxable land and intensifying the tax burden on the land still on the rolls. Cultivators did not necessarily benefit from working nontaxed land since the managers exacted their dues free of official review, and were ever tempted to increase the levies to cover the bribes necessary to keep the land off the rolls. If the practice became widespread, not only did the polity's revenue decline, but independent islands of illicit wealth could arise, shaking the very economic foundations of the patrimonial order, even threatening the dynasty's viability. Consequently, it behooved a ruler from time to time, and certainly at the initiation of a novel polity (dynasty), to rectify existing abuses, if necessary by altering statutes. But in time the extra dues and illegalities reappeared and the new system proved to be as onerous as ever.

*Tribute:* In addition to the universal offering of grain, certain rare or choice local tributary specialties were reserved for the ruler. The tribute system suffered from the same sort of assessment and collection abuses and exploitation as the grain tax, especially the custom of allowing local officials patrimonially to set the levy at whatever they thought proper. This was particularly insidious in the case of tribute because if the assessed was unable to fill the quota, he was obliged to obtain the required commodity wherever it could be found and at whatever cost, even in those cases when the local area no longer produced the item (if it ever had), yet that product was listed on the local area's tribute roster!

Perhaps the worst tribute abuse was farming, that is, contracting for tribute's collection and forwarding to merchant intermediaries favored by the authorities. Certain officials, aristocrats, and even Buddhist priests received tribute as a prebend from the ruler. These individuals then sold the privilege, sometimes by competitive bidding, enabling them both to secure their prebends in income in advance and to leave the unsavory business of actually squeezing the commodities out of the producers to others more adept at it—individuals, we can be assured, who were not about to lose a whit of their investment. So lucrative was tribute farming, and so politically well connected the practitioners, that even monarchial reformers found it difficult to rectify such an obviously abusive system. When private contractors finally were eliminated, this only enabled bureaucrats and their allies to exploit the prebend directly.

*Corvée labor service:* Unlike its feudal counterpart, patrimonial labor service was not restricted to obligees' free time or to projects of mutual value to obligees and superiors. The obligees or their kin or cohorts were required to meet their own expenses and, if appropriate, provide their own tools. Like the other obligations, corvée was levied at a rate set patrimonially by local officials, in this case by magistrate clerks, within the broad outlines laid down by central authority.

Corvée has been classified both by Korean scholars and by the government in many ways. We can briefly review one scheme by way of illustration, without claiming it is superior to any of the others. First category: basic agricultural labor. This was an obligation on residents or neighbors to cultivate official land. Each local official had the patrimonial right to decide whether to rely on corvée, tenancy, or bound labor to cultivate any particular official tract, and hence agricultural corvée could vary by locality and over time. This, by the way, illustrates that the universal, unilinear theory that labor evolved from bondage through corvée to freedom is not valid, especially in patrimonial societies.

The second category of corvée comprises specialist, primarily artisan, tasks. Most typically the obligation was levied on those already so engaged, but it could be forced on those employed otherwise who happened to be residing in an area where certain specialized tribute tasks were performed but for which labor secured through other means was inadequate. For this reason the quality of the work varied greatly, but then the corvée cost the government little or nothing. Some typical examples include salt-farming, fishing, and mining.

The third category, public labor, usually devolved on the unskilled. Sometimes great numbers were drawn widely from the surrounding countryside and even from afar; in early Korea in order to construct irrigation systems, the classic patrimonial corvée, and later to build new capitals in record-breaking time. But most typically this corvée provided local community services using local material and manpower, such as clearing land and maintaining magistrates' offices and domiciles. Although originally only aged and infirm parents were excused, others, particularly the rich, came to buy off the service for a prebendary gratuity, and thus the corvée fell more heavily on those (usually the poor) who remained on the rolls. Also local officials were ever tempted to exploit the corvée for their own personal benefit. Even when central authority formally phased out corvée by converting the obligation to grain, and then to specie, local beneficiaries resisted, and the due survived in substance if not in form, the obligation being added on to, rather than replaced by, new taxes.

*The military obligation:* Some observers consider the military obligation a specialized corvée in that males from age 16 to 60 were liable; those in service were sustained by reservists who also cultivated the land of those on duty; and, most pertinently, in contrast to feudal military drafts, the corvée obligees were used in manual tasks often only marginally related to a fighting role, such as building fortifications. Other observers liken the service to a tax, since neither the aristocracy nor the deprivileged and bound were obligated, while certain of the deprivileged performed alternative duty; and the due could be bought off by finding a substitute or providing two bolts of cloth for each year of service. For these very reasons, the military roster, unless periodically rectified, diminished over the life of a dynasty, and once again the additional burden increasingly fell on those unlucky enough to remain on the rolls.

*Miscellaneous dues:* These obligations were the principal source of peasant irritation since local officials more arbitrarily set rates and more flagrantly abused their prerogative in collecting than they did in the case of the primary obligations, sometimes drastically diminishing the meager margin of economic safety between peasant survival and disaster. Some miscellaneous dues were fees for the right to use essentials which had been declared state monopolies, such as salt, or the right to engage in particular occupations, such as fishing in restricted waters. Others were levies which originally were temporary measures to raise emergency funds, but which subsequently were converted into permanent fees at the whim of patrimonial official fiat.

The ability of authority to enforce all these four categories of obligations was dependent on maintaining a relible, up-to-date census roster and identity tag system. Conversely the ability of the populace to survive was dependent on falsifying rosters and credentials, in spite of severe penalties for doing so, since for most the alternative of fulfilling the dues was considered to be more onerous. Cynics claim that the very reason that these obligations were set as excessively high as they were was because bargaining enabled the center to get its reasonable due while simultaneously providing prebends for its conniving local officials. Since, unlike in a feudal order of defined obligations, the institutional line between an economically illegal act and a patrimonially justified benevolent act was hard to draw, a twilight area existed within which bargaining, but also fraud and exploitation, flourished.

Contemporary authority has many modern instruments at its disposal to extract its due from ruralites, a subject we shall discuss in detail subsequently in this and the next chapter. Suffice it to observe here by way of illustration, with respect to taxes: First, ruralites pay approximately three-eights of the national levy in spite of the fact that their income is lower than that of urbanites while many of their costs are higher. Second, the multiplicity and severity of many impositions assure at least partial survival of the old game of local officials either bargaining with the assessed for a gratuity or illegally setting higher rates and pocketing the difference. Finally, new levies do not replace but only supplement older dues. For example, miscellaneous dues now include "volunteer" donations to such novel causes as police benefits, school support, village improvements, military and veterans' relief (after the Korean War), anti-DPRK preparedness campaigns, and international fetes such as the Olympics in which Korean prestige is on the line. Some of these funds do go to the causes for which they are supposed to be raised, but others do not. Some are one-time levies, but others, as in the past, become permanent dues with only the names to remind anyone of long-forgotten justifications.[3]

### The Basic Relationship between Authority and Agriculture

Korea has not been blessed with a sufficient or reliable source of water for agriculture; specifically, water is unevenly distributed in the peninsula and is universally short in the late spring and hot summer months, when it is very critical for rice cultivation. Drought is not uncommon. Consequently, Korean authority has been vitally involved with irrigation since ancient times, a role some claim is at the very foundation of all patrimonial orders. For this, central authority provided the experts and drafted corvée peasant labor on both public and private land, and soldiers on military land, in order to construct, maintain, and repair hydraulic works. But it was the local official who typically carried out the actual work, with the provincial governor mandated to verify that the system functioned properly and that it was not abused, especially that labor was not misemployed to enhance the value of privately exploited land. But local notables were able to appropriate ancient hamlet and interhamlet communal water rights on land they were clearing, often with the connivance of local magistrates who were doing the same on publicly owned property; all to the detriment of the cultivators, who found their rent and taxes rising for the use of the water and to whom hydraulic innovation was therefore a mixed blessing.

Irrigation has been but one aspect of authority's concern with improving agricultural technology. A Korean scholar has examined the various agricultural handbooks of the last imperial dynasty, which were most often government-inspired or sponsored in the hopes of propagandizing polity policies as well as diffusing useful peasant innovations. The contents of the books, whether directly attributable to government policy or not, demonstrate that by the late nineteenth century significant agricultural innovation did occur and that agriculture was ripe for modernization and even development in that (1) productivity had greatly increased following the diffusion of rice transplanting and the double-cropping of barley as an alternative to rice, (2) innovative cultivators were growing marketable crops such as ginseng, tobacco, and cotton, thus fueling an emerging commercial agricultural economy characterized by class and land differentiation and contract labor, and (3) rational land management was being increasingly practiced not only by educated notables, but also by talented and ambitious commoners, who because of their limited education and class status were ineligible to hold public office.

And yet, in spite of such appropriate technology, individual entrepreneurial talent, and innovative spirit, the agricultural revolution of the West or Japan did not occur in Korea. The primary impediments, I believe, were institutional. First, although agriculture definitely was not stagnant and in fact was very innovative, it suffered from the heavy hand of an authority which not only pounced on the very surplus it encouraged through confiscatory tax levies but also permitted fraud by local officials and the exploitation of cultivators through, for example, seed and consumption loans at usurious rates, postures not likely to increase productivity beyond the bare minimum required for sheer survival. Second, although the handbooks as well as certain statutes extolled creativity, such earnest suggestions too often were only moral preachments which in practice were either ignored or misapplied out of the malice or indifference of individual bureaucrats who, in patrimonial thinking, were free to accept, adapt, or finesse all such pronouncements to their own predilections. Third, because in fact the Korean bureaucracy was not the instrument of a centralized despotism, in spite of what some patrimonial theorists have claimed, even with the best of intentions the center was not able either to provide the service and direction the cultivators wished, or to force those local officials who were unwilling to stop, for example, the indiscriminate cutting of forests or the inequitable distribution of precious water. Perhaps for the same reason, the center, for all its formal concern with irrigation, never devised a comprehensive flood control scheme, let alone put one into practice. But most to the point, fourth, authority limited its response to palliation for problems which required structural reform. This was only too evident in a famous rural seminar held in the waning days of imperial Korea, at which approximately seventy knowledgeable individuals—mostly nonofficial intellectuals, including some commoners—were requested to offer suggestions to the monarch on overcoming the rural malaise. The institutionally sensitive suggestions—namely, land redistribution, national management of government land then being abused locally, tax redistribution to end the privilege of the idle elite, reorganization of village cooperative labor, and reduction of cultivator indebtedness—either were ignored by the king and his ministers or, if accepted, were forwarded for local review, which insured that the proposals would be conveniently weakened if not forgotten. Authority was positively responsive only to those "realistic" programs, such as diffusing agri-

cultural knowledge, which were expected to increase agricultural production and dampen rural unrest as well as replenish the government
treasury.

The consequence? It would be primarily though not exclusively the
Japanese who would be the initial instrument for modernizing Korean
agriculture.[4]

### The Persistence of Mini-Agriculture in Modern Korea

Korean agriculture, under the best of circumstances, is a difficult
undertaking. Cropping must be pushed to the very limits of the growing season, especially in the frigid north. All usable land is intensely
cultivated, some two-thirds of it double-cropped. Upland agriculture
exists, but Koreans clearly prefer irrigated cultivation in the plains.
Consequently water is the crucial but uncertain variable. Hence competition for water is fierce; if those nearest the service take more than
the allotted share, then the others will suffer as much as if the drought
were natural. And since drainage often is poor, fields freeze in winter,
rendering them useless or most difficult to work.

Even with, or because of, land reform, most holdings are minuscule, being under one chŏngbo (approximately 2.5 acres, that is)
with the typical plot a scant one-half to one chŏngbo, and are, as always, deliberately fragmented to share the diversely fertile soil as
equitably as possible. Each holding is an individual enterprise utilizing predominantly immediate kin on the smaller units and additional
hands, especially for planting and harvesting, on the larger units.
Large farms, that is those few over two chŏngbo, are four-and-a-half
times as productive as smaller ones, because they use more labor and
require less time per hand to complete the same amount of work. But
alas, most cultivators do not have such large units and hence cannot
take advantage of the economy of scale.

Since labor is very intense in spite of recent mechanization, especially in tillers, perhaps the better term to use to describe Korean agriculture is gardening. Labor, which is required especially during
planting and harvesting, can be otherwise inactive the rest of the
year. Thus 90 percent of rural income comes from farming, second
jobs being considered only to supplement income during the slack
season, and livestock raising but a recent innovation. For too long the
very poor have survived through the winter by poaching on the forest
reserves to collect firewood for sale. In brief, peasants are not operating at their maximum potential, and insofar as they are not, they are
underemployed. But this is not the disguised unemployment of the

classical economist since the marginal cultivators in particular would not be employed elsewhere.

Although their produce is eagerly awaited by urbanites, including the tax collectors, and the cultivators have responded to the demands of that market to the economic advantage of all concerned, too many cultivators are not truly modern farmers, but rather still peasants surviving precariously from season to season as best they can. For example, during the bleak spring before the harvest, some are not able to consume their own grain because they must sell it or loan it to others, and hence cannot survive from harvest to harvest without a grain grant against an advance pledge of the next harvest. Though, as we shall see, the polity has remedied at least some cultivator disabilities, the rural economy, save for the 1970s, is a net exporter of capital to the urban communities.

In sum, most cultivators are ever at the mercy of adverse natural and institutional forces, burdened with debt and inadequate capitalization and services. If all this is apparent to us, it is likewise obvious to the farmers themselves. They are not unproductive, economically "irrational"—traditional, if you wish—beings because they choose to be so, but rather they have learned through bitter experience that survival demands that they follow a set of rules in an economic game which is determined by others than themselves. To this we now turn.[5]

## The Formulation and Administration of Contemporary Agricultural Policy

The rationale for formulating agricultural policy is derived from the patrimonial principle that morally superior urban authority has the right to determine what is in the best interest of the morally inferior, nonbureaucratic rural populace, without drawing that populace into the decision-making process; therefore, what authority decides does not necessarily have to coincide with what rural recipients consider necessary and appropriate. The farmers' reaction? As one cultivator put it to me, "I often receive from the government what I do not want, yet I am unable to obtain what I truly need and want." The specific character of Korean patrimonial public administration has been examined in the previous two chapters and need not be described anew. We need only provide agricultural examples and discuss some consequences.

*Formulation:* Since research restricts moral patrimonial decision-making, it is often ignored or used after the fact, especially to nonpatrimonial foreigners who subsidize the projects. This cavalier attitude may lead to unanticipated or unfavorable consequences. For example, the expressway building program, for all its value in advancing agricultural commercialization (1) interfered with local irrigation systems and contributed to extensive flood damage; (2) encouraged speculative land fever astride the roadways, which removed vital farm land from production and spawned disputes which raised social tensions; (3) made wage labor more attractive than farm work, driving up farm costs; and (4) polluted neighboring farms. Similarly the program to metalize farmhouse roofs usually provided only a cosmetic change, though at times the metal proved to be a poor substitute for time-tested natural materials. Likewise, objective economic cost analysis is slighted because it can doom a politically attractive patrimonial scheme such as turning marginal lands into grain fields because it proves that overcoming the soil's high acidity is prohibitively costly.

*Administration:* First, the rural development system, since it is patrimonially deconcentrated, is accorded little or no leeway to adapt center policy and priorities to local needs and potential. Hence the staff may have to meet Seoul's unrealistic "rule by model" demands by scrimping on quality or quantity or by falsifying the record. Second, though its activities are many, the system is incredibly understaffed. This is a prime example of a patrimonial bureaucracy arrogating all possible decision-making lest it go to others by default, rather than husbanding its limited resources and allowing outsiders willing and able to do so to share the responsibility—as, for example, by encouraging those companies who can supply the farm tools to train farmers in the tools' productive use, as is the case even in very bureaucratic Japan. Third, bickering rivalry over access to prebendary plums goes on between different administrative levels, especially between province and district, and among the many different agencies, all of which may become involved in the same rural projects, creating unnecessary, wasteful duplication and unaccountability. Fourth, face-to-face working contact between administrators and farmers is not necessarily the norm; interaction may be limited to occasional didactic, inspirational lectures by visiting bureaucrats who expect village leaders to carry out government programs. Consequently, cultivators are not necessarily cooperative, since they resent being treated like children. Moreover, fifth, farmers are disillusioned by false promises, such as fertilizer shipments which arrive too late to use but well after the farmers have been cajoled or forced into shifting their cropping pattern, and a program of pig-raising which creates surpluses that add to cultivator indebtedness rather than to income. Programs and promises often reflect the whim of a particular bureaucrat and hence will be disregarded if that individual is replaced or if his, or his superior's, interest changes, most typically on other than "rational" economic grounds. Sixth, "ardent farmers" entitled to government support are more often patrimonial political clients of officials than agricultural innovators. In like spirit, grants may be inadequate for the economic task, because they are political prebends which must be dispensed as widely as possible for political effect rather than for economic feasibility. And since the rural areas, regardless of economic need, are far from the center's patrimonial view and concern, they can be more safely slighted than the urban economy, which consequently is more productive than the rural economy. Seventh, no reliable neutral source exists on which the farmers can rely to supply data to evaluate the projects which the government requires they physically and financially support. Rural statistics are considered state secrets by the agencies which collect them, data which must be kept from morally wanting nonpatrimonialists who might use such knowledge to their own selfish advantage against the economically unsophisticiated or, especially, to become economically independent of their morally superior bureaucratic decision-makers, a patrimonial nightmare. Eighth, and finally, the farmers consider many projects as but a modern form of exploitive corvée, since the project directors prebendally skim or extort from the cultivators when allocations are decided and while the projects are being carried out. For all these reasons, most farmers are reluctant indeed to invest their capital, time, and labor in projects which come to them from above and afar.[6]

## The Dilemma of a Patrimonial Economy: The Grain Purchase Policy

Self-sufficiency in food grains, especially in rice but also in barley, and most recently in wheat, is an essential element in the polity's goal to create a self-reliant, independent, and economically viable ROK, and a cornerstone of that goal is the managed purchase and pricing policy. The required amount of rice is gathered by the government either as taxes collected in kind, an honored "tributary" tradition as we have seen, or as partial payment for government-distributed fertilizer. At one time the polity also provided lien loans against rice, but this has been abandoned.

The Japanese during World War II were the first to institute modern grain control through quotas, in exchange for seed and fertilizer, and consumer rationing. After that war the Americans set the market free, on principle and because they assumed that rice would be plentiful, since the huge amounts previously exported to Japan would henceforth go exclusively into domestic channels. But the population surge, the propensity in a "free" society to consume at more than subsistence levels, and a disrupted transport system, all combined to create shortages. The Americans then returned to government collections and urban rationing and initiated a policy of importing grain to make up deficits. Because data were poor and scanty and the postwar bureaucratic management was in a state of confusion, anticipated and unanticipated grain shortages and deficit imports persisted throughout the American occupation and into the Republic. Although the new government made a determined effort to collect all grain not actually consumed by producers, it failed to meet even half its collection goal. So in 1949 the authorities reestablished a free market with priority rationing to the polity's prebendary clients, but this did not work either. Hence, the next year the government introduced grain management, which is essentially still the program. Under this plan, the government co-opts a portion—on the average one-third, though in 1975 it was as high as one-half—of the annual rice crop, permitting the remainder to enter the open market. The precise percentage is set annually by government fiat. Since that decision is made at a time in the growing cycle too late for the producers to plan the next year's production, and since the government is not always able to predict the food grain demand, shortages do occur, which the polity seeks to remedy not by internal rationalization but through imports.

*Prices:* The grain management system is supposed to stabilize not only supply but also prices, both for cultivators and for consumers. The government is especially fearful that unless urbanites are guaranteed reasonable and constant food prices, they will escalate their wage demands, both fueling inflation and boosting industrial costs, and hence raise export prices on Korean manufactures (subsequently discussed). But supply and price variability is built into grain production and marketing under any circumstance, and in the Korean agricultural economy that volatility works to the disadvantage of producers. This is because, unlike wage earners in manufacturing, no matter how economically well-off producers may be theoretically, they have little or nothing to sell and hence are cash-short and debt-prone except at harvest. But for that very reason prices then are at their lowest, since grain is most plentiful while producers must sell to pay off past indebtedness. Grain becomes scarce, and in market terms the price rises, as the agricultural year progresses, while simultaneously producer debt rises. Perhaps the annual cycle is broken by a second crop—by rice, or more typically by barley—but in any case, by late spring or summer, supply is at its lowest and price is critically high. Ironically, at this time most of the producers themselves have to buy or otherwise obtain grain to prevent starvation, a long-standing fear in rural Korea. The government's collection and price/supply stabilization program is supposed to smooth out this cycle. The key, of course, is the government's offering price for its grain at harvest time, whether that grain be taxes in kind, levies, or fertilizer barter. The price is set by the National Assembly, and it is set lower than the price on the open grain market, a policy first decided by the Japanese, but followed by all succeeding polities. In the later 1970s the government did make an effort to refurbish its popular *political* image in rural Korea by substantially increasing the rice purchase price to approximately twice the world price at considerable expense to itself, since the government has to resort to overdrafts from the Bank of Korea to finance such purchases, a situation which helps feed inflation; for example, the 1975 purchases increased the money supply close to 100 percent. However, simultaneously the polity was stimulating increased productivity through inputs dependent on imported diesel fuel and chemicals, which escalated farm costs substantially after the second oil shock of 1978. Thus, even in the best of times, the price magnanimously increased as an act of patrimonial grace always has been lower than rapidly escalating producer costs. Moreover, it is only the very few large-scale commercial farmers and the middlemen, who can afford to hold on to grain, who profit at all by escalating prices in the cyclic year, and even their opportunities are circumscribed, since few are able to raise the necessary capital at equitable interest rates to hold stock for other than rapid turnover profit. The vast majority of cultivators who have no grain to offer, on the other hand, must purchase their subsistence grain at this time on the exorbitantly priced open market, because they are prohibited from access to released government stocks at depressed lower prices which are available only to urban consumers! Clearly it is the cultivators who are shouldering the burden of grain price inflation, and it is the government and its prebendary urban clients who are profiting by the government's grain program—a modern example of the long-standing exploitation of ruralites by the bureaucratic-urban community.

*Supply:* The grain self-sufficiency program has not succeeded. On the one hand, the exploited cultivators, although they have increased production significantly since the later 1970s, cannot or will not meet the government's production goal as long as the grain-grasping polity rails against cultivators raising, in theory illegally, cash-crop vegetables while refusing to face realistically producer cost problems in the increasingly agricommercial economy of Korea. On the other hand, urban consumers are not cutting consumption; and why should they when they can buy rice at bargain prices— sometimes at half the international rate, because the government is willing to import whatever rice is needed to make up a deficit at international prices and if necessary sell the rice at administered, deliberately depressed internal prices in order to keep its urban clients happy. Imports further discourage producers from increasing their yields, since that depresses the rice price. In 1975, Korea was only two-thirds self-sufficient in rice, whereas a decade earlier it was 90 percent. And yet even with its obvious bias, some observers believe that the government program is not truly helping itself or urban consumers. First, when the gap between their costs and the forced sale price is high, the desperate but wily farmers provide inferior rice, which only the urban poor, not the vital clientele the polity wishes to mollify, will buy. Second, the cost of rice is an ever-decreasing percentage of urban budgets. Third, government stocks are but a minority of those available to the market, and hence their release does not always dampen prices. Finally, when deficits occur in its food management budget, which as noted is frequent, the government cannot always release its grain at an attractive price. Some experts suggest that if the government is intent on continuing a managed grain policy, then either the two-tiered pricing system it now uses for barley should be extended to rice, so that the interests of both producers and consumers, presently incompatible, can be satisfied, or the funds used to subsidize the rice price be used otherwise, say on research. Such a proposal is realistic and rational. But it does not serve the long-standing patrimonial interests of an authority supervising the economy to provide prebends to worthy clients. Hence, even though talent is short and overextended, data are scarce and often false, waste and fraud permeate both collection and distribution, yet because the prebendary tribute is so large, so all-encompassing, so easily mined, and grain-importing is a farmed monopoly making the politically favored few so very rich, as occasional disclosures attest, the grain management system is too valuable a patrimonial tool to be discarded.[7]

## Contemporary Rural Taxes, Banking, and Credit

The structure and operation of the rural financial infrastructure, that is, taxation, banking, and credit, frustrate rather than contribute to the development of the farm economy. The problem begins with the land tax, the primary source of local rural revenue. Although farm equipment is exempt, and the entering taxable level excludes small holders, the urban salaried have more favorable immunities and ruralites are more easily subjected to illegal "voluntary" levies, such as contributions for police and military welfare and fraudulent over-assessments which are pocketed by local officials. But the prime disability of rural producers is their inability to acquire adequate credit. The core of the problem, to belabor the point, is that cultivators are captives of a commercial agricultural economy in which they are not its principal decision-makers and are otherwise unable to compete on equitable terms. They must take all the risks of production with, save for the blessed few, only marginal resources in land and capital, and with minimal positive support from authority. They too often cannot meet their routine, let alone emergency, obligations out of the fruits of the harvest, and hence become indebted, a state from which they rarely extricate themselves. If they cannot refinance those debts for any reason, they lose their land and become tenants or, now especially, day laborers or other than farmers.

The rural debt and credit structure is as follows (as derived from a number of surveys which are not always compatible in time or scope): Farmers are able to self-finance approximately three-fourths of their operations, half from savings alone. But since more than half of the loans must be used for consumption, farmers are not forming capital but merely sustaining livelihood. About one-third of farmer credit comes from institutions, the rest from private sources, which are predominantly other farmers or relatives, though advanced sales to traders contribute a significant minority share. Professional moneylenders are also an important source of funds. Their rates are very high, say 50 percent interest per year. Although the pressure of institutional credit more recently has helped to decrease this rate, that credit has not done so by much, and such loans remain the very symbol of the rural credit malaise. Interestingly, half the farmers are both lenders and beneficiaries, especially as far as their fellow villagers and relatives are concerned. This is because Koreans believe that those who have the resources are morally obligated to help their associates in need, entitling today's recipients to the same consideration in time. Loans for small cultivators are in kind, while those for the larger producers are in cash. This is because larger farms are more productive and the owners need cash to purchase inputs and to pay extra labor. Contrary to popular wisdom, only a minority ever borrow for luxuries, including ceremonies. And two-thirds pay their debts when due (a higher percentage than for urbanites!), in part because most borrowing in the private sector is personal—more than half the loans are contracted without security—and in part because more than half the loans are for vital fertilizer and if the borrowers default they lose their chance to obtain any the next time around. Most loans are for no more than a year, and over half of these are for less than six months, reflective of the planting-to-harvest, debt-to-cash cycle.

A source of credit midway between informal dependence on one's fellows and access to formal institutional channels is the kye, an autonomous organization which raises money through member contributions for some common objective. That objective may be as causal as a social affair or as purposeful as a grain loan. But many kye are formed solely to make money by loaning out the principal to members at usurious interest rates, each member receiving a share of the increment according to his particular contribution; those who do not borrow at all or who borrow late obtain the best return on the original investment. The hypothetical average village household belongs to three kye, and the average kye contains thirty members. Half of the kye are over ten years old, but some last only long enough to fulfill a single purpose. Office is formal: The head at least is elected, office is rotated among the members, and meetings are regular. Kye loans are competitive with institutional credit; where one thrives, the other wanes. Although the kye cannot compete with institutional assets or management, more favorable interest rates, and especially prebendary tie-ins for fertilizer and irrigational technical aid, yet the kye clearly has the edge in those instances in which institutional credit either is confounded with excessive red tape and corruption or is unavailable.

The Japanese introduced modern institutional rural credit to Korea, both to support their redesign of the rural economy and society and in a vain attempt to destroy the autonomous kye. Thus finance associations, dating from 1907, provided government loans primarily to prebendary-favored cooperating landlords. The Republic has inherited the associations' structure and goals, providing credit only for government objectives such as fertilizer purchase and for a fraction— one estimate has it 10 percent— of farmers' needs, while ever being tempted to make money by granting loans to noncultivating ruralites and even (as under the Japanese) urbanites! In 1956, in part through American prodding, the associations were reorganized into a truly agricultural banking system, and in 1961 merged with cooperative associations to become the National Agricultural Cooperative Federation (NACF).

I wish to comment only on certain characteristics of NACF's credit; whether NACF in truth as well as in name is a cooperative will be discussed in the next section. First, in spite of its name and formal mandate, NACF, as its predecessor, also finances nonagricultural rural activities. However, since it taps nonrural resources, such as the fertilizer subsidy, NACF does help to offset the rural-to-urban capital outflow associated with the previously discussed grain purchase program.

Second, virtually all NACF loans are short-term. Hence NACF is more a rural-commercial than a development bank, save for certain special circumstances, such as irrigation loans to cooperatives. Medium and long-term loans are not unknown, but they usually require Seoul's approval, which implies having to cope with the all-too-familiar bureaucratic red tape and prebendary petty corruption. On balance, however, since "city" banks are uninterested in providing rural credit because it is both costly and difficult to administer to countless minifarmers, and because urban speculative investment (especially in real estate) offers the banks much greater return, NACF does provide a vital, albeit not ideal, service.

Third, loaning rate schedules are unduly complex. They are based on the source and type of funding rather than on the purpose of the loan and the creditability of the borrower. They are not set by market conditions but by government fiat, fortunately below the open usury market. Some loans, termed mutual credit loans, require recipients to have a deposit account. Since such an account pays interest at a rate considerably below the loan rate, it discourages deposits, further contributing to the dearth of rural mobilizable capital.

Fourth, some loans, such as the fertilizer loan, are tied to government-sponsored programs. Unfortunately, this does not guarantee that such programs will be adequately financed, and hence the loans may be wasted. Fifth, regardless of all the justifiable as well as questionable NACF formal regulations, those who receive loans are primarily the patrimonial favorites of those who dispense the loans, whether that prebendary distributor is the cooperative itself or a village leader. Finally the small farmers, those who operate one-half to one chŏngbo sized farms, as marginal producers, critically need adequate productive credit. Although they are in fact NACF's primary borrowers, since large farmers do not need credit or can secure it elsewhere, small farmers cannot secure enough loans or those of a kind to increase productivity. This is so because the patrimonial dispensers prefer to distribute the prebendary loan plum as widely, and hence as thinly, as possible in order to maximize their political client profit, to succor symbolic edifice projects, or to indulge their ever-changing patrimonial whims.

In sum and in conclusion, contemporary Korea does not have productive *developmental* rural credit—that is, credit responding to the realities of the farm cycle; harmonizing with rationally determined rural economic goals, free of personal whim or favor; providing adequate technical services to insure productive use; utilizing simplified rate schedules based on loan function; flexibly accounting for rising labor costs and mechanization; concentrating on the medium- to long-term, leaving the short-term to commercial banking; stimulating revolving-credit funding by providing realistic interest rates on deposits; and, above all, tendering focused, adequate credit where it is truly required, since at this point in the modernizing process there is no hope of furnishing sufficient credit to all who need and want it (only 10 percent of those interviewed say they have sufficient credit). Accordingly, farmers must turn to the open credit market, at rates which are usurious even by Korean standards, to do what they, rather than a harassing, paternalistic polity without necessarily economically "rational" concerns, have in mind. A 1961 government attempt to eliminate rural usury—a negative symbol to the military, some of whom were ruralites—whereby NACF assumed debts amounting to over 20 percent per year and bought off creditors at 20 percent per year for four years while debtors repaid NACF for five years at a controlled 12 percent was a failure because open market debting, and hence usury, reappeared. And such a counterproductive credit situation will persist in spite of farmer dissatisfaction and scholarly criticism, I suggest, unless the polity is willing to subordinate its, albeit modern, patrimonial goals to developmental requirements.[8]

### The Economic Relationship between Authority and the Farmer: The Case of the National Agricultural Cooperative Federation (NACF)

Although Korean authority has persistently argued that bona fide autonomous, popular-generated cooperatives responding to farmer-defined wishes have been the source for NACF and its Japanese and Korean predecessors, in truth all those formal organizations have been government-established, directed, energized, and financed in order to carry out center-devised programs and policies. Not surprisingly then, the organization of NACF which emerged in 1961 parallels the bureaucracy; that is, it reaches from the national center in Seoul down through the province to the district or city, though certain affiliated "special product" organs are attached to the federation irrespective of bureaucratic level. The president of the Republic, under Ministry of Agriculture and Forestry guidance, appoints the president of the national federation, who is assisted by both an assembly that is mandated to make policy decisions and also an administrative board on which sit representives of the Ministries of Agriculture-Forestry and Finance and of the Bank of Korea. Assemblies and administrative boards are duplicated down the line. A staff of operational officers at each level carry on NACF's daily activities. In contrast to this purely bureaucratic organization, there are local cooperatives which farmers may join by subscribing their own capital. But they are so structured to reinforce the bureaucratic NACF organization rather than to serve popularly percolated rural concerns and interests. For example, local cooperatives are organized at the bureaucratic myŏn rather than at the natural community level. Members can be disciplined, even expelled, if they fail to live up to cooperative rules, which are determined by the government and not by the membership.

NACF and its affiliates provide a great number of rural services, such as farm inputs and supplies (all of the fertilizer and three-fourths of the tools), institutional credit (discussed in the previous section), insurance, marketing, education and technical aid and advice, export crop promotion, imported agricultural-input distribution, and rural industrial support. By constantly expanding the range of its existing programs and adding new ones, NACF has become the largest single enterprise in Korea. And since it is also the basic, sometimes the only, link between farmer and bureaucracy, most farmers have come to consider NACF, not the often-remote formal administration, as *the* Korean government. Hence, when NACF succeeds, authority in general profits. When NACF fails, it is the government and not only NACF which is blamed, regardless of the circumstances. Since the NACF leadership has little if anything to say about determining the programs which the government charges NACF with carrying out, the farmers' attitude is not unjustified.

Because of NACF's vital role in the rural economy, its policies and operations are constantly reviewed. Much of the consequent criticism includes technicalities beyond the scope of the present study. However, I believe that the following findings are pertinent. First, NACF has been faulted for endeavoring to do too much with its limited administrative staff, thus wasting resources and even courting failure and thus projecting a negative image of government effectiveness. Especially it has undertaken programs which are unduly costly, provided subsidies to marginal farmers which are in truth welfare handouts, and otherwise distributed funds without much thought to either cost effectiveness or, given NACF's limited resources, priorities. But since such activity is especially brisk at election time, clearly any number of such programs are designed to earn not rational economic profit but rather political advantage—in our argot, to dispense prebends and otherwise validate the moral worthiness of patrimonial authority.

Second, although farmers have little or no input into determining NACF policies and programs which vitally affect their livelihood, still they must deal with NACF on its own terms. This is because (1) although since 1969 local organs are supposed to review policies before they become operational, there are not sufficient elected officials anywhere in NACF, much less adequate farmer representation on the assemblies and boards at the various bureaucratic levels, to countervail NACF's centralized directives; because (2) NACF has almost monopolistic control over the economic relationship between farmers and those outside the villages; and because (3) the Ministry of Agriculture and Forestry can judge and nullify any NACF decision. In consequence, farmers have little bargaining power in determining what and in what quantity they will produce or market. Even how to care for their crops, such as whether or when to spray, is determined by NACF, regardless of whether or not the farmers believe they can afford the costs. But any economic criticism of NACF's stringent controls has come to naught, I suggest, because authority, which even today does not formally penetrate the natural village, considers such an opportunity to oversee and control farmers too valuable to surrender.

Third, American observers in particular have found that a number of economic difficulties in NACF are directly traceable to (what I see as patrimonial) public administrative malpractices. For example, the national organization deals too much in macroeconomic policies without offering any clear direction as to how to translate these lofty goals into administrative practice at the lower echelons; in our terms, rule by model. Yet the lower levels, thus left to shift for themselves without specific leadership, are not free to ignore the center's vaguely defined "general will" and are held accountable for any misbehavior; in our terms the lower levels are deconcentrated, not decentralized. Some consequences: Rules and red tape become convenient smoke screens until locals are absolutely sure their actions will not create problems in their relationships with superiors. Failures occur which might be avoided, or at least not continued after they turn sour, if the center were more willing to listen to input from below. The center, however, considers failure the consequence of foot-dragging local saboteurs or blames the incapacity of the farmer audience to take direction, a view few local bureaucrats, fearful of their superiors' wrath, seek to disabuse them of.

Fourth, since NACF units are not created nor operated according to function, those in charge of units compete for, and duplicate effort on, the more prebendally politically attractive and economically lucrative projects, while difficult and distasteful tasks are left undone.

Fifth, translating model policy into practice is complicated by the fact that the NACF administrative staff at all levels, but especially those at the flash point of contact with the farmers, primarily are patrimonial generalists. Such people managers are ill-trained and ill-motivated to be concerned with humdrum technical problems; their guidance more often than not is morally didactic, rather than demonstrative and practical; and their relationships with farmers are casual indeed after the initial contact.

Sixth, as patrimonial administrators, NACF personnel, especially decision-makers, are frequently rotated, adversely affecting office morale and project continuity and further confusing the already cynical farmers.

Clearly, and in conclusion, NACF, one of the authority's key means to control and exploit the rural economy and population, is an undeveloped though very modern patrimonial institution.[9]

### Rural Patrimonial Modernization: From Guidance to Mobilization—4-H to Saemaŭl

An archetypical example of Korean patrimonial modernization is the change from popular political passivity and polity indifference (as long as ruralites met their prebendary obligations) to authority's active mobilization of farmers' support for government rural projects. All early republican rural programs under Rhee were American-inspired. Rhee considered the 4-H clubs, the first of these, as the youth wing of his Liberal party, which he could manipulate to consolidate his political hold on the countryside, rather than as the apolitical, autonomous uplift organizations which they have been in rural America. But the Korean 4-H leaders rarely strayed from their offices, the members were not asked to do much beyond rallying for political sloganeering and to denounce Rhee's enemies, and thus ruralites, young and old, treated the movement indifferently. Then, since the clubs were so closely identified with Rhee, when he was ousted the 4-H was downgraded to youth offices in various government agencies. In contrast, extension, operative from 1957, gained the confidence of farmers, probably because the program was correctly perceived by them as fundamentally an apolitical instrument. But alas, that was the very measure of its weakness to Korean authority, which treated it indifferently, save as a means through which to deliver the wherewithal of other rural projects.

Rhee saw more political promise in the community development (CD) program, which began in 1958. The stated goal of CD is "to help villagers to help themselves" by inspiring them to carry out feasible self-improvement projects of their own devising, government aid being restricted to supplying vital but unavailable materials and technical advice. To this end, village-level agents live and work with household heads and help them to establish village CD councils which propose, plan, execute, and maintain CD projects. Our interest is in certain CD problems which may have patrimonial origins. First, Korea is unusual in that its CD village workers originally were college-educated, in part the consequence of a surplus of graduates unable to find suitable urban, particularly bureaucratic, employment. This proved to be a mixed boon, in that Korea could boast the most sophisticated, prestigious CD workers in all of Asia, but it made more difficult the chronic problem of keeping such individuals full-time residents in the villages so that the farmers could get to know, trust, and cooperate with the workers. Second, a patrimonial polity's penchant for selecting and directing village projects, contrary to CD philosophy, made the villagers reluctant to contribute their own labor, time, and meager resources to projects often of grandiose design and low priority to themselves, in the villagers' thinking devised less to serve their economic interest than to enable the polity to penetrate, interfere in, and otherwise control natural village activities and decision-making, by offering prebends to the politically cooperative.

Although these Rhee-initiated programs never lived up to their economic potential, they were helpful in establishing the political principle that those who lived at the formal village level at least were henceforth to be included within the orbit of interest and jurisdiction of center formal authority, thus extending the formal reach of the center beyond the customary district level. The military coupists and their civil successors exploited this opportunity. Soon after coming to power, they launched the National Reconstruction Movement, creating reconstruction councils not only at all the usual bureaucratic levels but also in the ri-dong, where the formal village chiefs became the local heads of the movement. The new organization consolidated under its wing all the existing, often independent and competitive, government agencies, including extension and CD. The following year the movement was renamed the Office of Rural Development

(ORD). Its stated goal was rural progress through cultivator moral uplift, energized since 1966 through ORD's Rural Guidance program.

Various evaluations of ORD suggest that it suffered from the same
kinds of patrimonial disabilities as its predecessors. First, its goals
were set by national economic politics, which in the 1960s meant increasing food production at the expense of more pressing rural requirements. Second, programs were drawn up in Seoul with little local input. Third, real farmers were rarely if ever allowed to direct or
even carry out most projects if they expected financial or technical
support. Apparently the polity considered agriculture to be too important to be left to producers. Fourth, the education level and preparation of ORD technicians and guidance workers were lower than
their CD predecessors, since by then employment opportunities for
college graduates especially in the bureaucracy had greatly improved.
Formal training took place in large lecture halls without benefit of
practical demonstration, library facilities and assignments were minimal, and farmers were never called upon to contribute; all that would
have been a patrimonial insult to the educated, even students. Fifth,
the center was rarely attentive to the human and material resources
required to carry out its plans (rule by model). And since power and
prestige reside at the center of moral authority, as one went down the
bureaucratic ladder of ORD the quantity and quality of the staff became less and less adequate. Thus, by the time plans reached the end
of the line in the villages, there was little talent and less enthusiasm to
bring the projects into being. Sixth, ORD's channels of communication and control, though centralized, were confused. Especially, the
provincial governors were (and still are) as powerful as they ever were
under the last imperial dynasts and the Japanese, and it was they
rather than the national organization who controlled the ORD staff at
the provincial level. Seventh, provincial-level research was located at
poorly equipped, urban agricultural institutes and degree colleges
which have only tenuous ties to the real rural world. Eighth, guidance
workers were constantly pressured to produce physical results of interest to the government, if necessary on their own or by coercion,
rather than inspiring farmers to help themselves to carry out projects
of their own choosing. Ninth, the youth program, inherited from 4-H
and CD, continued to be primarily a prebendary-dispensing medium
through which the ruling party tried to assure itself of a rural political
constituency, rather than a means to inspire youth to attack the society's rural problems rationally. Tenth, programs were changed or
dropped before they had a chance to succeed because of political
changes beyond village control.

President Park's new focus upon political revitalization included the New Community Movement—*Saemaŭl*—a predominantly but not exclusively rural program whose professed aim was to narrow the rural-urban economic gap (1) by mobilizing off-season farm labor to beautify and otherwise transform the villages into better places in which to live and work and thus improve farmer morale, and (2) by nurturing support for the third and fourth Five-Year Economic Plans to eliminate rural poverty and increase discretionary income. Park's motivation was both political and economic. On the one hand, he wished to shore up rural political support, which the 1971 election revealed had seriously eroded, and on the other hand, he hoped to increase agricultural production since the hitherto free American grain imports were now repayable, thus depleting the vital foreign exchange he preferred to spend on urban industry. Saemaŭl evolved in three stages, namely, (1) 1970-74, operating in 2100 villages, focused on training and immediate living improvement, symbolized by government gifts of surplus cement, (2) 1974-76, involving 14,500 villages, centered on infrastructure and developing thrift, and (3) 1977-81, involving a final 18,500 villages, stressed productive self-sufficiency. At its height, 22 percent of the rural budget was devoted to building or updating roads, home improvements, irrigation, sewerage, community halls, forest rehabilitation, tourism, reclamation, and small industry. The government offered land, materials, technical aid and "guidance" on mutual savings and cooperation. Existing agencies—ORD and NACF especially—were required to actively support Saemaŭl; a Central Consultative Council was created in the capital to insure interagency cooperation at the national level and, through the Ministry of Home Affairs, to coordinate provincial and especially county and local operations. In theory, projects were to be carried out by voluntary labor and donated funds, relying on local initiative and responsibility under village leadership. But if this was not forthcoming to the polity's satisfaction, Saemaŭl personnel were instructed, certainly at first, to strike out on their own, trusting that their successes would convince ever-wary peasants to cooperate. Likewise, selected urban officials and students were induced to provide symbolic moral models by working in the rural areas on their free weekend time, at least in front of the media.

There is little doubt that Saemaŭl was the most ambitious scheme of the Park era to mobilize villagers to participate actively in center economic programs. Some of Saemaŭl's material results are very obvious to the eye, such as the farmhouse metal roofing project, the new roads, the irrigated fields, mechanization, and new cropping patterns. Korean farmers have become as productive as Japanese and rural worker income was comparable to urban worker income in the later 1970s which, though not quite what it seems at first blush, still was no mean achievement. But what of Park's essential goal, namely, a spiritual, revitalizing revolution which would create independently responsible but cooperative farmers with new hearts and minds, termed *Saemaŭm?* There are doubts.

For one, Saemaŭl, even more than the earlier rural uplift programs, has been a top-down, patrimonially paternal program which, for all the commendable discussion of individual farmer input, actually leaves little to villager discretion. If the villagers do not cooperate in carrying out government schemes, Saemaŭl bureaucrats with the moral-political mandate to fill quotas or face retaliation from superiors have done so in the villagers' name (deconcentration).

Quotas also are relevant in that, second, as in the past, project success is measured in terms of the amount of real estate on the ground rather than in the degree to which the farmers participate in planning choices and execution. Also those projects which use exotic materials or tools and which offer quick results and flashy show—such as the much-publicized farmhouse metal roofing project—have been stressed to give the movement the cachet of modernity and success, while the harder-to-achieve and more vital changes—such as in sanitary habits—have been downplayed or avoided.

Third, for much the same goal of demonstrating quick, visible success, projects have been often hastily drawn up and executed. The farmers, as always, have been ready to accept prebendary handouts, but they are reluctant to commit their own resources, including their precious labor time, unless forced to do so, as a modern corvée. Contrary to popular patrimonial wisdom, there certainly is a rural work ethic, to wit, the peasant proverb, "what one does will profit not only oneself, but also ancestors and descendants." But such pragmatism requires that what one does be both worthwhile and feasible—economically rational if you will—which in the case of many Saemaŭl projects has never been conclusively demonstrated to farmer satisfaction. Most damning, individuals coerced to participate neither maintain properly what they have done nor have they been inspired to initiate similar projects on their own, one of the claimed key purposes of Saemaŭl.

Fourth, the promise of a bountiful future and some short-term improvement has whetted the appetite of the young who, impatient with the gap between reality and blueprint, are further encouraged to leave the rural scene. New cropping patterns which cannot be, or by choice are not being, handled mechanically have placed further labor burdens on resentful women. It is perhaps pertinent for the study that the truly enthused supporters of Saemaŭl are village leaders who see their moral (read, patrimonial) authority enhanced by the projects, a true indication of how deeply and widely the center now has come to politically penetrate and mobilize the natural community in the center's interests.

Thus, fifth, the feverish activity of Saemaŭl has made ruralites more aware of and uneasy about the lack of control over their lives. In the name of extension—not unimportantly termed "guidance" in Korea—ORD representatives are on circuit seven days a week to surveil and interfere into cultivator activities. It is they and similar officials who continue to be the primary extra-village contacts of ruralites. Cultivators are well aware that Saemaŭl serves national (and hence fundamentally urban) and not primarily local (rural) goals, such as the call for exotic crops and for rural industry, which caters to the export market; policies which may profit ruralites one day but not another—to wit, when imported inputs of energy and fertilizer outpace the returns on the new crops the government insisted farmers grow or when crops which grow well under experimental conditions are not productive in everyday cultivation. Especially this is the case whenever center authority, exploiting its control of initiative, media, finance, and coercion, leads the cultivators to disaster, as recently happened with the "Unification" (note the political implication of the name) rice campaign. Throwing caution to the wind, the polity insisted on substituting a high-yield, "miracle" strain for existing seed. At first all went well. Coordinated with improvements in irrigation, mechanization and novel tools, pest control, and fertilizer inputs on the one hand, and cultivator-energizing through Saemaŭl and its allied "guidance" organs on the other hand, production and rural income rose dramatically. But then the second oil shock and its effect on fertilizer prices, and even more seriously the time factor and adverse weather conditions (drought) which subjected the rice to a debilitating blast disease, drastically reduced rural GNP (down 24 percent in 1980); sent the government scrambling in the international market to make up the deficit to the tune of 17 percent of the world's rice imports during 1979-80; required rural subsidies and relief, free seeds, and mobile water pumps; and forced replacement of three-quarters of the fields devoted to the new rice with old rice strains—a prime example of what a determined, administratively sophisticated, centralized patrimonial authority can accomplish, but fraught with latent danger because that authority is free of meaningful review and potential modification by outsiders.

Consequently, farmers for good reason have been as skeptical of Saemaŭl's professed intent, projects, and instruments as they have been of past programs. In sum, increasingly more frequent clarion calls for rural modernizing and government efforts to involve farmers actively have not shaken the farmers' conviction that ever since ancient times the polity's intent has been to serve its own rather than cultivators' interests. Farmers take comfort in the knowledge that they have survived, albeit as marginal cultivators on miniplots, in spite of and not because of patrimonial urban authority, whose programs have waxed and waned over the generations as have the seasons, while the cultivators, like the very soil they attend, have persevered. [10]

# 5

# The Commercial and Industrial Economy

### The Relationship between Authority and the Commercial and Industrial Economy: The Patrimonial Mandate to Supervise and Intervene in That Economy and Its Consequences

The particular mandate of Korean authority to supervise and intervene in the commercial and industrial economy is derived from the general mandate of patrimonial authority to supervise and intervene at will in the society in the interest of morality. In doing so, authority is expected to insure that commercial and industrial profit not only will not run counter to but will positively contribute to the realization of moral profit throughout the society, at least that profit will help provide the economic wherewithal for authority to carry out its moral political responsibilities in the society at large.

Over the course of Korean history, a variety of means have been devised to maximize the commercial and artisan contribution to moral profit. First among these has been direct political control of the means of production, most typically through government monopolies, such as in salt and mining. Second has been sponsorship of commercial and artisan activity by subsidizing production, providing facilities and technical advice, and setting standards and goals; all in return for a tax or government's direct receipt or control over the disposition of the product, as in the cotton industry during the last imperial dynasty. Third has been combining taxation with official usury; that is, lending some of the state's revenue, in some cases to the very sources from which it had been collected, at exorbitant interest in a market largely devoid of private capital. Such official usury has flourished in spite of the theoretical patrimonial contempt for official pursuit of crass economic profit. A fourth tactic, analogous to usury, has been for officials to buy up commodities to create scarcities and then resell the products to merchants at a profit.

The Japanese, although they vigorously went about modernizing the commercial and artisan-industrial infrastructure, did not alter these patrimonial economic ground rules. They continued the practice of publicly owning the significant means of production and enlisted the cooperation of private Korean commercialists and artisans (later industrialists) in government programs by offering such prebendary favors as government contracts, monopolistic access to scarce commodities and markets, and subsidies and loans—a fact of economic life they passed on to an accepting Republic.

At first glance, no distinctive, coherent fundamental economic philosophy has emerged in republican Korea. Although the ROK is formally committed to "free enterprise" and a market economy, it simultaneously believes that (1) Korean commerce and industry as yet are too fragile to stand on their own and compete internationally, (2) special interests are ever ready to exploit the economically naive and helpless, and (3) there is a dearth of cooperative, productive economic actors. Thus the guiding principle is that a completely free economy is temporarily impractical, and hence authority must benevolently guide the commercial and industrial economy for some time to come. The government's tolerated opponents have never questioned these premises, though they are ever ready to criticize the way the government has managed its mandate. For example, the left dissenters, when they have been allowed to dissent, preach a European-like social welfare philosophy, disputing who should profit from the government's relationship to the economy. The radicals call for nationalization of basic industries, but since many of these industries already are government-owned—to a greater degree than in theoretically socialist India, it should be observed—this is not as radical a proposal as it is made out to appear by the government.

Consequently, regardless of free-market rhetoric to the contrary, patrimonial moral supervision of, and intervention in, the contemporary commercial and industrial economy is expected to be conducted within the parameters of a mixed economy, one which has a publicly owned and operated sector but also a private sector within which the economic initiative is left to those outside authority, although authority reserves the right to supervise and intervene when it is "necessary" to do so in the interests of morality. This form of economy is advantageous to the government because, unless authority by itself is willing and able to operate efficiently at least the significant economic

activities in the society, it stands to gain more politically and economically by allowing those outside the bureaucracy to assume the burden
of costs and risks and to produce results which authority can then tax
and otherwise exploit, while still regulating the actors to insure conformity with authority's exclusively defined "moral" goals. From the
standpoint of control, however, whether an economy is state-owned
or not is irrelevant, since economic initiative in *both* the public and
private sectors is subject to surveillance and, if deemed necessary, active intervention at a time and on terms defined by authority.

Whether or not such an attitude is conducive to maximizing the
economy's potential is a key question. One can certainly argue that
when supervisory control is assured, authority will feel secure enough
to allow and even facilitate productive economic action. And Park, for
one, often used the "modern" western argument that without political stability there could not be any viable economic modernization to
justify his control over the Korean economy and society. However,
simultaneously, one can argue that control is a *political* concern, and
that if a choice must be made between control and productive economic action (a choice not necessarily welcomed by a modernized
patrimonial polity), economic performance may suffer if political concerns dominate.

We shall explore the propositions of this section in detail in this
chapter.[1]

### The Relationship between Authority and the Contemporary
### Commercial and Industrial Economy: Government Enterprise

The modern Korean commercial and industrial economy is overwhelmingly the consequence of imperial Japanese public and private
initiative. The Japanese government general prevailed in banking,
shipping, irrigation, mining, utilities, cooperatives, cigarette manufacturing, and after 1930 in certain heavy and chemical industries.
Those properties which were located in the south after 1945 were inherited first by the American military government and then by the
ROK as "vested property." It was not until some eight months after
they arrived in Korea that the Americans named a property custo-
dian; until then Korean provincial authorities were allowed to make
policy and run the enterprises as they pleased. But their ineptness
and chicanery, such as overstaffing the administration with friends,
relatives, and clients, and allowing personal favorites to acquire, exploit, and even steal property, finally forced the hesitant Americans to
act. The Americans, to their credit, tried to introduce rational ac-

counting, management, and disposal procedures, but the patrimonial urge to abuse was not overcome, for no other reason than that some 90 percent of the commercial and industrial economy was vested and hence was the key to wealth during this period of extreme economic deprivation.

The vested portion of commercial and industrial enterprise, quantitatively and qualitatively, has continued to be predominant under the Republic. On the one hand, the public sector's share of industrial investment under Park expanded at an annual rate of 10.8 percent while the general industrial economy grew by 9.3 percent, and, on the other hand, the number of public enterprises at the end of the Park era was three times what it was when he came to power. This is so because, although existing government enterprises are periodically divested, new enterprises replace them, primarily through the impetus of the various Five-Year Economic Plans, which are capitalized by an ever-expanding Special Government Accounts, and because the actual government share in any specific activity may be enhanced at any time to compensate for diminished interest elsewhere. At first government ownership was concentrated in finance, infrastructure, and especially manufacturing, but in the 1970s the focus shifted to support of the export strategy, especially in intermediate manufacturers, and most recently to steel and petrochemicals. However, interest has been persistent in banking and insurance (on average, 77 percent of these enterprises are government-owned) and large capital intensive activities. Hence, although the polity's share is some 30 percent of industrial capital investment, the government uses only 5 percent of the economy's investment in labor.

The structure of public enterprise is highly differentiated. Some enterprises, e.g., the railroads, are "autonomous" government departments, while others, such as airports, are "integrated" agencies. Both of these categories are directly held by the government, while others, such as the Korea Development Bank, are indirectly controlled through government holding companies. Although the enterprises most significant in value are government monopolies, the majority numerically, forty-nine out of eighty-nine at last count, are joint stock. (If the government holds more than 50 percent of their shares, joint stock corporations are termed "government invested enterprises.") The government need not own a majority of shares to get its way, however, and pertinently without the onus of day-to-day management, because it can limit the voting rights of private holders to a minority.

The 1948 constitution legitimized a vital role for government enterprise as a matter of social conscience, but the Korean War and an ever-escalating tide of anti-Communism was reflected in the 1954 constitution proscribing nationalization unless the society's "vital interests" were involved. The practical consequence of the new policy was not to eliminate public enterprise but to shift the polity's argument to "rational" economic grounds, namely, the need to modernize and expand what was inherited from the Japanese, the dearth of private capital, the obligation to create the infrastructure called for in the Five-Year Economic Plans, and the necessity to provide social services and employment opportunities in those areas which could not be left to the vagaries of the market. Thus has the polity mined modern, internationally acceptable economic reasoning to continue to justify both a supervisory grasp and a prebendal exploitation of a commerce and industry ever expanding into novel "modern" activities.

Although the administrative and financial performance of Korean government enterprise overall compares favorably with the achievements of other modernizing economies, and although certain enterprises, such as the electrical industry, pass muster on any standard, a pertinent fact we shall return to subsequently, most enterprises leave something to be desired, as even the polity admits. Since in Korea public enterprises are controlled and run by career civil servants or ex-military officers and not professional managers (a fact in and of itself patrimonially significant), the administrative problems these enterprises evidence are those of the Korean bureaucracy in general, described in Chapter 3. However, I do wish to reiterate that since considerations of insuring control and providing prebends for clients may outweigh considerations of maximizing the economic potential of any enterprise to a degree beyond that of "selectively rational" tolerance (see Chapter 1) granted gracefully to all organizations everywhere, I believe that one must look to other than formally "reforming" administrative practices for remedy. One illustration of my reasoning: Government enterprises operate under a mandate tinged with paradox. On the one hand, the National Assembly statutes which create enterprises are much too vague in defining their missions or how to go about accomplishing them. But this fits well the patrimonial stipulation that leaders create programs to fit their inclinations, rather than vice versa. Boards of directors, which decide, not only advise on, policy, are composed on generalists whose technical qualifications are vaguely defined and often found wanting, who can be hired and fired on grounds which are technically equally vague, and who hence are responsive to patrimonial-moral political considerations. Yet, on the other hand, for all this encouragement of an apparently freewheeling leadership, as in the past administrative procedures are extremely formalized and complex. The paradox has been exacerbated, in accord with modern patrimonial principles, by a rapid expansion of the bureaucracy, especially on the local level, while direction and supervision are becoming more, not less, centralized. The consequence: Jurisdictional lines, reports, and audits are multiplying. Most enterprises are simultaneously subject not only to a number of ministries, the Audit Department, and the Economic Planning Board, all of which usually are in open competition, but also to the provincial governors, who can interpose their authority between any ministry and its field representatives. For all these reasons, few enterprise bureaucrats are prepared to take risks which might cause them to displease their many patronal superiors, especially when it is unclear who precisely might be displeased. Thus is irresolution justified by legalisms.

A second characteristic of government enterprise is that, as in all patrimonial orders, resolute leadership from above can and has dramatically overcome even the most formidable bureaucratic inertia to lead to economic expansion, but this has its own problems, because in all patrimonial economies such pressure can be selective as to place and time and subject to extra-economic patrimonial political goals, and hence is reversible when the leader's interests change. Consequently, exploiting the circumstance that he personally approved all key public enterprise managers and that the others were civil servants he controlled through his cliental aides, and that he could divest those enterprises whose performance he disapproved and thus terminate employment of non-civil servants, Park was able to increase productivity dramatically. However, at the same time his policies increased sales for example, they did not increase the economy of scale. Wage costs were left too high. Government enterprise, even today, is tax-exempt, and, though dividends in joint enterprises are often disappointing by Korean usurious standards, they still are reckoned as too high a percentage of income by international standards. Save for those enterprises such as the Korea Electric Company which is cost-conscious and responsible for setting its own rates, at least some enterprise rates are deliberately set below cost by government fiat. Although this can and has been justified economically as "stabilizing," I prefer to view it also as a political ploy to provide prebends to mollify consumer clients which might otherwise become socially restless. Managers of "vital" enterprises, regardless of their financial performance, are assured by the polity that it will not allow failure. To be sure, rescuing ailing enterprises always can be "rationally" justified as underwriting essential economic functions, irrespective of profitability. But, I suggest, authority also is considering that, if nothing else, any government enterprise provides prebendal employment to worthy clients. Since the government concedes that its largesse contributes to inflation and a shortage of capital, more recently authority raised prices on some of its enterprises' products and tried to sell its minority shares in troubled enterprises to private parties—a far from easy task unless the authorities guarantee the purchasers high dividends. But guarantees imply that the government is continuing to subsidize those enterprises as if the polity were still the owner, and hence the government's problem of raising investment capital is not ameliorated. Moreover, since new government ventures more than make up for divestitures, and those enterprises most useful for prebendary purposes and hence apt to be the most economically wasteful are not willingly sold off nor are they the ones desired by private parties, the problem is far from being resolved.

Another government enterprise characteristic I wish to mention is the incompatibility between Korean patrimonial (political) goals and the role that the government's commercial and industrial enterprises *could* play in Korea's economic development. Korean authority, as morally didactic as it is, is not interested in patiently educating the populace to appreciate and support what it is trying to do by way of modernizing the economy. Rather the polity prefers to get its way either through direct control and intervention or prebendal subsidy, whether or not those the government controls or subsidizes truly understand the government's goals. As we have observed (Chapter 3), public feedback is not encouraged and is even resented because it comes from patrimonially moral inferiors. Privately generated groups, such as certain cooperatives, are ignored out of the conviction that the general public cannot organize on its own without bureaucratic inspiration, direction, or control. What I am suggesting is that a golden opportunity to use government enterprise as a stimulus to productive economic change, as was the case in nineteenth-century Japan, is being lost, and that this is not due to correctable ignorance, as western unilinear, evolutionary economists would have us believe, but rather to persistent institutional assumptions which are not conducive to the development process.[2]

## The Polity and the Economy

### Corruption

Gift-giving is a long-cherished practice in Korea, and is considered morally acceptable and maximally potent when it establishes a favorable climate between individuals before they have to confront each other in the market. In gift-giving relationships it is the social inferior who entreats the superior for graceful favor, since an inferior would never expect to be rewarded for facilitating the desires of his superior; that is taken for granted. If the superior does not wish to accept the relationship, he will not return the gift, for that would be an insult. Rather he passes it on as a gesture of his graceful charity.

It is gift-giving to officials by laypersons which is of interest to the present study; that is, the attempt of individual economic actors to provide certainty in their market relationships with an ever-present but capricious patrimonial authority by offering sacerdotal fees to individual members of that authority willing and able to offer security in return. This kind of gift-giving has been facilitated by the patrimonial tendency to blur the distinction between public and private exploitation of office. Thus in theory such gift-giving is justifiable in the interest of facilitating a patrimonial authority's mandate to spread morality in the society, while in practice accepting gifts from laypersons to pay attention to their economic concerns has been the prime means through which officials expect to recoup their investment in their positions, often after long years of sacrifice and professional preparation. Hence, while coming to office without wealth has not been a disgrace, nor even a handicap, leaving office a pauper has been both. Wealth is supposed to follow authority in a patrimonial economy, rather than the reverse, as usually is the case in a nonpatrimonial economy. Thus, paradoxically, public office has provided a primary means to pursue economic profit in the very name of moral profit! A line however is drawn at officials mining lay wealth too greedily, especially when it causes major popular suffering or turns official attention away from carrying out prescribed duties. An extreme example: An official of the last dynasty is supposed to have sold an island to the Japanese after receiving gifts from them; as partial punishment he was forced to buy it back at his own expense.

In the contemporary Korean patrimonial democracy, the need to finance periodic elections or plebiscites and to buy votes has intensified official gift-giving and the gesture of passing on the gifts by officials to the government party as acts of graceful charity. The Liberal party in authority under Rhee was especially notorious for demanding contributions from banks and government enterprises, and even for diverting funds earmarked for fertilizer purchases for the party's use. But just as significant are such exactions as the police regularly receiving gifts from the public they serve not only to supplement their personal income but also to facilitate investigations and other legitimate police functions, which I suggest thus are deliberately not adequately funded. The government, by assuming that its budget will be augmented through private gift-giving, can take lower salaries for granted, enabling authority both to hire more potentially loyal prebendary clients and to whittle down the number of well-educated, politically sophisticated unemployed who might take to the streets or conspire against the regime. The escalating price inflation has exacerbated the temptation of officials to expect and even demand gifts from laymen. At the least such gift-giving has siphoned off potential entrepreneurial investment capital and has discouraged the kind of economic activity that depends on low profit margins to survive—in short potentially developmental enterprise.

Korea's linkage to the international economy has expanded the opportunities for such gift-giving. Perhaps the most publicized example has been the American Gulf Oil Corporation's contributions to Korean officials and businessmen. Gulf pleaded that if it was expected to do business with Koreans, which the American government encouraged, then Korean economic customs had to be respected. Among these "customs" were outright payments, usually kickbacks to the Korean government, which used the funds for political action against its opponents, and donations of transport and supplies to government-favored Korean corporations with which Gulf was forced to deal, seemingly to enable those Korean firms to fulfill their end of the contract. Gulf also was required to purchase at a high price some of the stock of a Korean company which President Park favored, to make that company a nonrepayable "loan," and to sell it tankers which Gulf then had to lease back at a management fee. Some of these payments were funneled to the coffers of the government, in return for the polity's allowing the Korean company to prebendally bilk Gulf. Gulf capitulated because it feared that unanticipated, capricious government harassment and red tape would interfere with continuous operations. The gifts were regarded by Gulf as business costs that were carried on its books as "entertainment" to mollify its American shareholders and for American tax purposes.

But it does not require such spectacular disclosures to create Korean public dissatisfaction with official gift-giving; routine contacts between populace and bureaucrats are sufficient. The polity has responded periodically with investigations of official conduct, personnel purges, and self-purification campaigns, fearful that unless it does so from time to time it will be viewed as morally wanting, indifferent to its popular cliental wards, incompetent, and incapable of acting decisively, and in the process lose political face and even legitimacy. Most officials react paralytically rather than feverishly actively, waiting out the anti-corruption campaigns by postponing decisions whenever possible, and certainly by not making any decision that might possibly suggest hanky-panky.

But such political exorcism does not confront any substantive patrimonial procedures and problems, let alone institutional concerns. What I am implying is that for a number of reasons we should not overemphasize the significance of political corruption in determining the character of the Korean economy. First, that confuses symptom with patrimonial cause. Second, on the statistical evidence, corruption has not prevented the Korean economy from achieving one of the world's most impressive growth rates, especially when compared to other patrimonial economies. Third, corruption is no more a pervading characteristic of the Korean economy than is inefficiency, and Korea cannot hold a candle to the corruption found in certain other "modernizing" patrimonial economies.

I now am prepared to provide my explanation, promised in the previous section, of why the Korea Electric Company is productive and efficient whereas certain other government enterprises are not. In my view, *selected* economic operations are considered too vital to be left to the vagaries of individual bargaining and reward for services rendered, patron-client empire-building, or the dissipation of valuable capital investment. In these cases the opportunities for chicanery are reduced or even eliminated. What I am driving at is that both corruption and inefficiency are neither universal to particular stages of undeveloped economies, as some western economists would have us believe, nor are they chance occurrences as others have claimed. Rather, in the case of patrimonial economies anyway, they are the consequences of deliberately conscious—"selectively rational" to use the argot of certain economists—political decisions that certain economic action will provide economic benefits for vital prebendary clients within and without the polity, even if economic rationality (development if you prefer) suffers in the process, but that others which are not designated as prebendary must be run productively and without corruption. The trick of course is not to allow too many economic endeavors to be designated as prebendal, nor to allow those that are to be so looted that they fail, lest one kill the proverbial goose laying the golden patrimonial egg. The ability to do so successfully is one measure of the effectiveness of a "modern," though ipso facto undeveloped, patrimonial polity and economy.[3]

*Economic Planning*

National economic planning predates the Republic. The Japanese, especially in the 1930s, went about the modernization of the Korean economy with increasing determination and calculation. Although the Korean staff was not allowed to do more than carry out Japanese decisions, a number of future republican bureaucrats were thus exposed to modern planning. The loss of most of the country's heavy industry and power resources to the north, and the subsequent devastation of civil war, made the task of planned economic regeneration in South Korea imperative. In fact in 1948, even before the Korean War, a planning director was appointed to the State Council, but he had no vote or influence. True planning probably dates from creation of a Ministry of Reconstruction in 1955. This ministry, as the name implies, was mandated to reconstruct the prewar infrastructure. But it was not granted jurisdiction over the often-conflicting, independent, old-line ministries, a problem only partially remedied by a Council of Economic Development in 1958. As serious as such administrative stumbling blocks were, the fact that Rhee was more interested in patrimonial political manipulation than he was in productive economic action, treating his planning aides with bored condescension, was more weighty. Centrally directed and supported planning had to await the military coup of 1961.

Symbolic of the new attitude, the Ministry of Reconstruction was renamed the Economic Planning Board (EPB), whose function in the economy as a catalyst between polity and economy in a number of ways resembles the Japanese Ministry of International Trade and Industry (MITI). More substantively, EPB's chair is the deputy prime minister and its vice-chair sits in the cabinet reviewing budgets and fighting for attention and a share of the nation's resources. EPB requests all government ministries-agencies and private enterprises to submit appropriate data on all proposed projects, whose feasibility EPB then evaluates in terms of an overall blueprint—the plan. Requests normally are pruned, but occasionally are amplified if EPB considers them light or insufficient in certain project areas the plan designates as essential.

EPB depends on advisory committees drawn from both the bureaucracy and the business community to provide basic economic data, to pass on the desirability and feasibility of the projects submitted for EPB review, and to build a favorable consensus for implementing the projects which are approved, a factor which the government thinks essential in the Korean mixed economy. Perhaps the most interesting and controversial of all these advisory committees is the Professors' Corps for Evaluation, composed of some ninety members, 20 percent of whom are economists and the rest specialists in such fields as political science, law, public administration, and education. In addition, the Economic and Science Council, half of whose members are economists and a third academics, and, especially more recently (for the Fourth Plan of 1977-81), the Korea Development Institute (KDI) also contribute technically and help to determine planning goals and strategies. Projects favored by the advisory committees are reviewed by EPB in the light of both available finances and physical resources (which are determined by the national budget and foreign imports) and the projects' secondary benefits (such as reducing recession unemployment). EPB coordinates and provides the wherewithal to implement the projects it approves, subsequently monitoring and suggesting changes due to shifting priorities as a particular plan unfolds and as one plan replaces another. In sum, EPB has a strategic role in deciding the course of the Korean economy from design to execution.

The technically economic characteristics of the various Five-Year Economic Plans do not concern us; the planning ethos and process do. Most particularly, although the Korean economic performance has been quantitatively impressive, the Korean economy has not overcome certain persistent problems attributable to, or associated with, the planning *process*. I wish to review some of the problems which I believe are patrimonially relevant:

First, according to classic development theory, the growth increment of both the public and private sectors is supposed to be reinvested productively. But although Koreans are among the world's high savers, to say the least there is a great deal of investment slippage as attested by the conspicuous consuming patterns of those clientally selected, privileged economic actors within and without the polity who are directly profiting from the plan's economic growth. Park often expressed concern that the vulgar display of wealth by the privileged was encouraging cynicism, apathy, and antagonism among the vast majority of Koreans outside the government's charmed circle of patronage who were being asked to sacrifice now for eventual benefit to themselves and Korea. Yet the government does not move to limit such consumption or otherwise insure a more thorough mobilization of domestic capital, preferring rather to depend on foreign loan capital whose availability is volatile and which might dry up overnight from causes beyond the Republic's control, leaving the government unable to make up the deficit.

Second, Korean industrial growth, unlike the Japanese experience for example, has been highly urbanized. Urbanites have benefited unequally, and too often even at the expense of ruralites. The consequence: regional imbalance, rural out-migration, urban overcrowding, and a demand for urban services the government cannot or will not meet.

Third, Korean planning suffers from the same administrative deficiencies that Korean decision-making and management in general do. Most serious, too many programs are but pious declamations of center rule-by-model intent, whose enforcement declines rapidly as one descends the bureaucratic hierarchy. Yet the center, although it fears decentralizing decision-making, prefers to prod its lower echelons for assurances that they are conforming to the center's inflexible and sometimes unpromising sacred blueprints, rather than having the executive, for all its authoritarian ways, make clear-cut policy decisions and press private and public enterprise directors to conform to the expressed goals of the plans. Consequently, EPB is more a compromiser between conflicting interests than a resolute leader and executor.

Fourth, the ROK's *political* contest with the DPRK has encouraged heavy military expenditures, according to some observers inordinately high disbursements, given the reality rather than the rhetoric on both sides. Some of these costs have been met with American resources, which only puts off facing the issue of what is truly required and what is wasteful of resources better invested elsewhere in the economy.

Fifth, a decision about the proper trade-off between stabilization against inflation and rapid economic growth, especially in costly show projects, continues to vex. The government, under foreign creditor pressure, has reacted by periodically decreeing "practical," that is, moderate, domestic price rises. Although these rises are ineffective stimulants during recessions unless they are accompanied by sufficient infusions of capital, which of course threatens to refuel the inflation spiral, they do cover up economic inefficiencies which then need not be passed on to the all-important export market nor translated into wage increases commensurate with higher prices.

Sixth, it is difficult to evaluate the contribution of planning to Korea's economic growth because of a general lack of interest in research, feasibility, and end-use follow-up studies, and, until the last decade, even reliable statistics. Before then, and in some cases even today, obsolete statistics have been used, sometimes from the Japanese period, for no other reason than that later ones are not available or, interestingly, are not considered trustworthy! And although there have been great strides recently in appreciating the value and improving the caliber of sampling and data processing, there still is the long-standing patrimonial reluctance to make those findings public. Even worse than the absence of data has been its falsification to insure verbal conformity with planning agency goals and orders from superiors, or to cover fraud. Hence outsiders rarely, if ever, know what truly is going on behind the administrative curtains of either public or private enterprises, cutting off productive outsider participation and even review input in the executives' plans. Among such outsiders is the vital EPB, which thus cannot ascertain whether or not its original proposals are being distorted so it can realistically readjust the ongoing plan or use the current effort as a learning experience for subsequent plans.

The Korean Development Institute, chaired by an official of a relevant ministry and receiving data and contributions of personnel from banks, business associations, and government agencies (including EPB itself) as well as drawing on its own, was established in part to remedy such defects and is perhaps the most competent and sophisticated economic research institute in contemporary Korea. Although its work is extremely creditable and credible, since it is intimately involved in both policy-making and implementation it cannot always be relied upon as a neutral, constructive observer and critic of a plan or the planning process, especially under such a demanding patrimonial autocrat as Park. Critically, academics who are not among the "government professors" view appointments to KDI and the other agencies unfavorably, as co-optation of souls and not just of expertise, casting further doubt on their reliability.

Seventh, a key factor in Korea's rapid growth has been exploitation of its comparative advantage of an abundant, educated, and disciplined commercial and industrial manpower working for wages not in keeping with a constant price rise inflation. Hence in real terms per capita GNP is low. The problem is aggravated (or justified) by concentrating on exports to the detriment of the domestic market, especially the rural market, though a concerted effort was made in the 1970s to remedy this discrepancy.

Eighth, Korea is more highly dependent on the export market than were the classic success models, England and Japan, for example, at comparable stages of their economic growth. Consequently, the Korean economy was especially hard hit by the mid-'70s disappearance of plentiful cheap oil and food grains, which foreign advisors had told them to count on, and by the decline in foreign funding caused by an adverse balance of payments when the sale of Korean textiles and plywood declined on the recessional world market. However, the Korean economy recovered more quickly than most, because of such measures as (1) the export of construction expertise to the oil economies of the Middle East in return for energy and (2) joint economic ventures with foreigners both at home and abroad. As a result of this recovery, suggestions for encouraging import substitution in such high value-added, labor intensive enterprises as light industry were ignored, despite the fact that they could provide employment and dampen inflation better than the increasingly capital intensive export industries could ever hope to do, especially during export slumps.

We can now draw some basic conclusions. Korea's growth strategy and planning process have been strongly tied to dependency on exports and interdependence with the international market. (The question of economic dependency as such will be discussed later in the chapter.) This has not, contrary to Marxist conventional thinking, made Korea a pliant client of American, and more recently Japanese, economic interests. The relationship between the Americans and Rhee was especially stormy. Rhee regarded planning as a cross Korea had to bear to insure vital American (prebendary) assistance. He considered the planning proposals of Tosca and Nathan for post-Korean War reconstruction as an inadequate expression of American economic recompense toward a faithful and valued wartime ally, and hence he treated the projects the plan stimulated indifferently and even sabotaged some of them. Park, however, committed as he was to economic growth, was much more sympathetic to the American grand design of integrating Korea into the world trading system and to American suggestions as to how to achieve high growth rates through systematic planning. By then, sufficient numbers of Korean economists and administrators trained in the United States had found their way into responsible positions in both public and private enterprise, and were willing, even eager, to support the new approach. Consequently, American planners, directly or indirectly, were able to help determine the essential contours of the Korean economy which emerged in the 1960s; especially that it be a mixed economy in which government directs, if not operates, but that market incentives stimulate the creation of an entrepreneurial class.

I suggest, however, that in spite of the American influence, and though such an economy is not socialist in the European political-economic sense, this does not necessarily imply that the ROK is striving to create a developed capitalist market or postcapitalist market economy on the American model, whatever its partisans or critics claim. Rather ROK authority is trying to create a modern patrimonial economy, by *selectively* utilizing those aspects of the planning strategies of the developed, nonsocialist economies which will enable the ROK to maximize economic growth, *within* the limits set by patrimonial principles of control and prebendary advantage. Obviously, this is a far cry from the stagnant prebendary exploitation of a Rhee, but this is not the open-ended commitment to productive economic change characteristics of a truly development-planning ethos. Two implications: First, I wish to reverse the usual argument that the Korean economy is what it is because of its choice of its capitalist planning strategy, to argue rather that the planning strategy is what it is because of the economy's (and society's) patrimonial character. Hence, second, many Korean planning problems and their possible solutions involve accounting for variables not necessarily existent in the planning experience of the nonpatrimonial economies, although the symptoms may appear comparable, if not identical, to the nonpatrimonial planning advisors working in Korea.[4]

*Officially Sponsored Population Control*

Perhaps the most successful of the ROK's national planning programs has been family planning. Both the Japanese and Rhee discouraged such planning because they wished to maintain and even increase Korea's existing manpower; the former to provide a plentitude of cheap labor, and the latter to create strength for what he believed would be an inevitable military confrontation with the DPRK. The Chang government, typically, discussed the matter but did not act. American officialdom in Korea was inert out of fear of religious repercussions at home, though certain churches acted on their own; for example, the Methodists opened a clinic in 1957, offering both advice and materials, but only to a sophisticated urban minority.

The Park regime, committed as it was to economic growth, was more receptive to the argument that family management would facilitate economic progress. At first, the government moved cautiously, out of fear of offending prevailing sensibilities in a male chauvinistic society. But the planners were pleasantly surprised by the enthusiastically favorable response. Apparently, concern for promoting family prestige by educating fewer children had overcome the existing prejudice and become the "modern" Confucian ethic! The government then launched a major program, clearly demonstrating what a highly centralized patrimonial authority can accomplish when it sets its will to it, and when the populace is supportive. Strong national leadership, especially presidential endorsement, assured an activist bureaucracy and interagency cooperation. The program, which initially was limited to the Ministry of Health and Social Affairs (MHSA), sponsored clinics in all urban centers, including district seats, and was escalated into a politically energized mass movement incorporated into the Five-Year Economic Plans with EPB budgeting and individual ministerial assignments and responsibilities. The mass media constantly propagandized for and provided information on the program, while the schools, and eventually the military, spread the official line of "small families for a prosperous Korea." The vital key to the success of the program, however, was an operationally effective cadre of mobile workers, clinicians, and physicians. The workers were especially crucial because they penetrated the most remote areas of the country, bringing the new gospel and adapting the program realistically to local conditions. In time MHSA restricted its role to external relations, budget procurement, and personnel matters, turning over media and demonstration chores and advising the government on improving the program to a semi-official Planned Parenthood Federation of Korea, which enjoys foreign support. Program research was taken up by the Korean Institute for Family Planning (succeeded by the National Family Planning Center established with Swedish help) and by numerous specially commissioned studies and reviews, some with foreign sponsorship. The program has more recently shifted its attention from the rural to the urban, and from females to males.

The Planned Parenthood Program, by and large, has been a resounding success as measured by the dramatic decline in the birth rate. However, factors other than the program also have contributed. Among these were an expanding economy which accompanied a rise in the age of marriage, and an increase in wedlock abortion, which was conspicuously avoided in the program. Conversely, the birthrate declined in spite of critical shortcomings in the program. Among those relevant to the study is that while Park's firm support and energizing tactics assured attention and overt conformity, as all patrimonial hoopla does, such tactics were sometimes counterproductive. Quotas were not always met, but data were falsified out of fear of displeasing superiors. Indoctrination, in person or in print, was confused with understanding and consent; consequently there was little if any follow-up to insure compliance. Supplies were not necessarily available when promised. Some technicians, even physicians, fearing personal blame if anything went wrong, evaded participation as if it was a corvée. Local bureaucratic support from either busy or jealous colleagues was not always forthcoming, especially since MHSA controlled the purse strings and favored its own potential clients. In the haste to get the program moving, the training and even the selection of the critical field personnel left much to be desired, though in fairness, given the pool of potential recruits, primarily the young and educated females, and the nebulous civil service security of those accepted in this kind of special program, perhaps the original requirements and expectations were set too high. Finally, in-service training, supervision, record-keeping, and critical follow-up were resented by the moral bureaucracy and either sabotaged or ignored.

Another primary source of population control is emigration. Personal choice migration was widespread during the Japanese occupation because of political repression and economic exploitation at home, and employment opportunities for menial labor in Japan proper. Out-migration continued in the postindependence economic travail, and continues even now, when a labor surplus and the government's low wage policy attract the unskilled to Japan and the professionals to western Europe and the United States. One estimate has it that 120,000 have left the ROK in the last fifteen years. Far from discouraging such migration, the government has sponsored the departure of some 80,000 to relieve the job market, earn vital foreign exchange, ensure vital imports of oil especially, and train workers in desirable skills; the classic example is the ubiquitous Korean construction teams. In the mid-1970s the government also discussed settling 30,000 on the land in Latin America.

Emigration, however, has been tainted with illegality and fraud. Especially irritating to authority are the rich and powerful, including ex-officials, who retire abroad, carrying with them smuggled wealth which they have accumulated under suspicious circumstances. In the government's view, too many of these individuals commute between their new homes and Korea, devoid of any sense of responsibility for using their acquired skills and wealth to contribute economically and morally to achieving the government's dream of a new Korea. Their profligate habits create a negative image of Koreans abroad, and spark hatred and envy among Koreans at home. Nor can they easily be controlled. Many emigrants, rich or poor and powerful or not, get to go abroad on forged documents or through bribery of willing prebend-seeking officials, in collusion with unscrupulous travel agents. For all these reasons, authority has made the apprehension, exposure, and confiscation of the wealth of such emigrants a symbol of more than one of its campaigns against moral decadence and enervating divisiveness in the society.[5]

## Authority and the Commercial-Industrial Economy: Private and Public Enterprise in a Patrimonial Economy

One must not assume from previous discussions that the basic enterprise problems which bedevil the public sector of the Korean economy are absent from its private sector, for in the Korean mixed economy those problems are endemic to both. Among these, first, is enterprise's indifference, even antagonism, toward its consuming public, even in those instances in which the enterprise's prosperity, if not survival, depend on good public relations. Goodwill is assumed if the product is selling, even if the fabricator is a monopolist. It is commonly believed that any enterprise which actively seeks public goodwill probably has a suspect product to sell or some sort of administrative hanky-panky to cover up.

Second, enterprise leaders lack social responsibility, and formal authority, for all its professed regulative interest and moral responsibility, seems unwilling to control their behavior. Especially noticeable are substandard, fraudulent, even dangerous, products and pollution.

A third problem is unethical practices. It is no exaggeration to state that most enterprise managers survive by their wits. They not only loot the enterprise's capital, they hoard, speculate, evade taxes, manipulate prices and the market, and again and again risk all in a desperate gamble to reap quick, sizable profits or go bust. Most seem willing to do so because, just like public entrepreneurs, they can count on government-financed bailouts and protection against legal sanctions for their conduct in return for a gratuity. Periodic moral cleansing campaigns are mounted by authority to purge the most obvious and abusive of such tycoons in the hopes that such actions will allay the rage of critics and a consuming public aroused by the inflated prices that kind of conduct encourages.

Korean enterprise ethics has been variously explained and excused. Some attribute it to the Japanese practice in Korea, which set an exploitive and opportunistic tone for modern economic action. Others, more psychologically bent, point to Koreans' reckless willingness to take chances and test the limits of possibility and their overconfidence in their ability to do anything, as illustrated by the popular proverb, "if you try and don't succeed on your own, you can always read the instructions." Koreans prize luck more than they do experience; if you succeed once, perhaps you can do so again and again. Thus they are incautious and bold as long as they believe there is a chance of success. Fortunes are expected to rise and fall as ultimate destiny is tested and retested. In truth, Koreans can point to their history as vindication of the phoenixlike ability to rise again and again no matter how badly defeated they are and no matter how great the odds against their doing so.

I must point out that although Korean enterprise behavior and its roots are not the textbook-prescribed stuff out of which the routine and discipline of economic development is supposed to be achieved, in historical practice the nonpatrimonial, developed economies, including the much-admired Japanese, have had, and in a number of cases still have, their own share of economic chicanery, speculative recklessness, and corrupt relationships with their polities. Rather, what is significant about such behavior in patrimonial economies—and this is my conclusion—is that if this is singled out for special disapprobation, one must appreciate the behavior exists in both the public and private sectors of all, including "modern," patrimonial economies, whether they be market, socialist, or, as in Korea, mixed. Perhaps this is so because the demarcation line between public and private enterprise is porous, given the right of patrimonial authority to surveil and interfere readily in the private sector. Especially is this true in the case of the "strong" Korean polity which manipulates investment, production, pricing, and manpower levers, as symbolized by the aforementioned "government-invested enterprises," to get its way. Consequently, as far as patrimonial economies such as the Korean are concerned, I believe that, contrary to the dreams of ideological partisans on both sides, to favor one sector over the other does not offer a palliative for the excesses and deficiencies of the other.[6]

### The Korean Commercial Economy: The Fundamental Character of the Market

The Korean economy of the closing years of the nineteenth century in many ways was highly sophisticated commercially but it definitely was not commercial-capitalist in the institutional sense of being capable of facilitating the emergence of a *developed* commercial-cum-industrial economy. In fact the Korean case is an excellent example of the kind of commercialization which, as it becomes more expansive and successful, becomes less conducive to generating truly productive commercialization. I offer the following observations to support this hypothesis.

First, for all its acknowledged complexity, the economy in many ways was severely deficient. Transport was extremely primitive; in fact there were no land vehicles. The communication system was primarily elaborated for, and hence limited to, official requirements such as facilitating tax-grain collecting, and was left to corrupt officials and corvée labor to construct and maintain. Private commercial movement, by default, had to depend on peddlers, especially their T-frame backpacks, which, in spite of their legendary loads, was both costly and inefficient for large and heavy commodities.

Second, peddlers symbolized the transient character of most commercial transactions. Retail sellers predominantly were (illegal) squatters who were obliged to compete daily or periodically for favored market locations from which to hawk their wares, since they were regarded by the government as interlopers challenging the monopolistic privileges of the few officially patronized permanent shopkeepers and marketers. Factors existed but, for all their vitality, held no stock of their own, being but intermediaries between buyer and seller, since they too were unable to establish retail outlets to serve the public. For this reason, the factors ever strove to control their retail associates financially, in the process subordinating retailing to middleman commercial interests. In fact it was not until after independence in 1945 that true retailing finally became a legitimate function of Korean commerce. Yet it must be noted in passing that both peddlers and factors have survived to the present; the former because they are trusted by the (especially rural) populace (see also Chapter 6). After Korea was opened to foreign economic penetration, factors played the vital role of intermediary between the commercialists of the treaty ports and those of the interior. In 1895, many factor organizations were "modernized" as Chambers of Commerce. Today, factors number about 750, two-thirds of whom work in Seoul. They are strong in rice, grain, seafood, and paper trading. They continue to finance their own operations, competing with modern commercial banking.

Third, for all its monetarization, the overtaxed and otherwise officially abused commercial economy was undercapitalized and serviced by unreliable opportunists exploiting immediate advantage rather than by potential professionals devoted to the long term. The notable exceptions were certain provincial urban merchants whose organization resembled the Japanese commercial associations of the time. But unlike their Japanese counterparts, the Korean managers were unsalaried, were not autonomous of the center when sent out as branch representatives, and were recruited primarily from kinsmen, whether qualified or not. Also unlike the Japanese practice, commercial transactions were dissolvable when inconvenient to any party and cooperative alliances between firms, especially small ones, were virtually unknown.

Fourth, the Korean commercial economy was characterized by its usury funding. Originally designed to provide succor at a reasonable fee to needy farmers between harvests, such loans were expanded to raise funds for worthy causes like Buddhist projects. Finally, clerical and then secular pawnshops raised capital for peddlers and factors. All these financial organs could have contributed positively to the emergence of a productive commercial economy, had it not been for the loans' exorbitant interest charges, which drastically diminished borrowers' profit margins and drove up their costs, sometimes exceeding the income from the loans and thus encouraging high-return speculation rather than long-term productive investment. This became especially evident in farming when landlords came to use usurious private loans to supplement high rents in order to further alienate the peasants' surplus, to the point where agriculture stagnated for lack of investment capital and farmers grew restless and resentful, deserting the land or openly rebelling. But urban intermediaries, such as the factors, also exploited usurious loans to subordinate producers and retailers, threatening not only their solvency but also their ability to control and expand their market operations. Officials were usuriously investing government funds, sometimes so heavily that too little was left over for military equipment or peasant relief. Most serious, if a polity came to rely primarily on usury to meet its mounting deficits, rather than facing up to remedying existing deficiencies in the economy in the interest of increasing productivity and efficiency, usury could be and was a leading cause of that regime's demise. Legislation to curb usury, such as the 1744 edict limiting grain loans to 20 percent and pawnbroker loans to 20 percent in commodities and 50 percent in coin, was typical of the many rule-by-model edicts proclaimed but ignored for no other reason than that too many powerful interests were profiting too handsomely from usury to give it up. The increasing monetarization of the economy only exacerbated the problem, since this both facilitated and provided additional incentives for usurious lending, especially involving bureaucrats; to wit, exorbitant illicit profiteering loans now were easier to handle and hide. By offering usurious loans, but at cheaper rates than indigenous lenders, the Japanese of the nineteenth century raised the capital they needed to effectively penetrate the Korean economy, while further impoverishing local farmers and merchants. In sum, by the twentieth century commercial capital indeed was beginning to accumulate, but primarily with those in the economy least interested in productive profit; namely, those content to exploit existing modes of what has been termed in the economic-historical literature as parasitic ("booty") commercialization. Their activities certainly helped to modernize the existing economy, especially the rural one, but they did not contribute to, and in fact they thwarted, the emergence of a productive, developed economic order.

Fifth, commercialization of the economy was stimulated and directed primarily by an authority whose policies too often countered the requirements of productive commercialization. A singular source of the problem was a dilemma of authority's own making; authority viewed private, independent commercial activity as disruptive of patrimonial control of the economy, yet the polity was very conscious of the lucrative prebendal potential of exploiting a private sector market. The polity tried to escape from the horns of this dilemma by requiring government sanction for private commercialists to act, while exacting its fee for the privilege, typically by granting monopolies. By manipulating the supply of commodities made available to the monopolists and by threatening to rotate the graceful privileges it bestowed, the polity tried to assure that commercialists would be both politically inactive and economically cooperative in accepting official demands for formalized levies and capricious exactions, and for such cost-free services as building and repairing palaces. At the same time, the polity was not above actively competing with private commercialists, including monopolists, by such practices as dumping taxes-in-kind on the Seoul market without prior consultation, thus depressing prices and playing havoc with the private market. Local authority in turn was given free license to meet its expenses by extracting what it could from the local market, which, like the national market, could never free itself from moral political supervision and hence patrimonial prebendal exploitation.

An additional problem with commercialization of the economy lay in the monetarization which accompanies such change. The Korean government was attentive, but the purist elite, by emphasizing agriculture, helped to limit the circulation of coins, and sometimes even was able to force the polity to curb minting, at the very times market growth was most promising. And the government was never above debasing the coinage to try to make up for chronic deficits.

In sum, at the critical late nineteenth-century point in Korea's commercial history, authority was appropriating the major part—some estimate 80 percent—of the economy's surplus, which it was not investing productively, while it was actively discouraging others from doing so by refusing to change and even reinforcing those characteristics of the economy which were commercially exploitive (parasitic). Consequently, the commercial economy was unable to resist, let alone compete with, foreign (especially Japanese) commercial capital when it penetrated Korea at that time. However, the Japanese, as the successor patrimonial exploitive authority, deliberately chose to maintain certain existing features (e.g., usury lending) or to tinker selectively (e.g., improving the transport) but not to develop that market.

I therefore feel justified in concluding that, in spite of the existence of certain formal *technical* preconditions for the emergence of a modern productive commercial capital economy, to give the optimists the benefit of all doubt, the *institutional* means to create such an economy was absent. Or to rephrase, the Korean commercial economy was capable of helping to destroy and even reconstruct (i.e., modernize) the old agrarian economy, but not of helping to transform (i.e., develop) it.[7]

## The Commercial Economy: The Contemporary Market

In spite of the many formal changes in the Korean commercial economy, the contemporary market is as institutionally patrimonial in character, and as ill adapted to serve the needs of a developing commercial and industrial economy, as ever. This is aptly exemplified by the private agricultural produce, especially the rice market. (The government grain purchase system and its effect on the contemporary market was discussed in Chapter 4.)

The first detrimental attribute of the rice market is its structure. For example, the cultivators themselves do not actively participate in the marketing of their own produce. Although the Japanese created an effective network to collect and distribute farm produce, especially for those items they exported to Japan, and the Republic has built superhighways which have profited those fortunate enough to be situated nearby, most cultivators remain as dependent as ever on deficient local access roads which effectively isolate the producers from direct physical and informational contact with the urban market. Rather, the agricultural market is dominated by those wholesalers who can finance the collection (from minuscule, fragmented farms) and forwarding (through a multiplicity of intermediaries) of the rural surplus, and then set sale prices, if necessary by hoarding and speculating. Most retailers, in contrast, are "mama and papa" operated at home or close by, exploiting "free" kin labor without capital reserves, quickly turning over meager stocks for marginal gain. If too many customers do not pay their bills on time or decide to take their trade elsewhere, such retailers fail. They are poorly equipped, are not scientifically managed, cannot take advantage of the economy of scale, and their owners either are reluctant to or cannot risk increasing their market share, even in the local neighborhood. In short, retailing is as precarious as it ever was. But then so is most wholesaling, because wholesalers are ever tempted to tie up their free capital in loans on the lucrative usury market, and hence are unable to survive the often sudden, violent swings in prices on hoarded and speculated goods. Consequently commodity contracts, unprotected by a futures market, may have to be broken whenever prices deviate drastically from the agreed terms. The few large, centralized urban markets, in contrast, offer excellent facilities, adequate capitalization, and reasonable assurance that a fair price has been set on the commodities gathered there for wholesale or retail. But since handling is poor, costs are high, quality uncertain, and the wealthy and prominent marketers collude and cartelize, many collectors and forwarders bypass these markets, and hence they do not contribute to rationalizing prices, nor do they insure the ready availability of many commodities, including vital rice.

The second discouraging characteristic of the contemporary market is the often-paradoxical behavior of authority, specifically its capricious intervention, regulation, and competition, coupled with stubborn refusal to provide productive services when required. For example: Private marketers especially resent ubiquitous inspectors who add to cost, because they must be bribed to avoid petty harassment on technicalities. Yet these inspectors do not guarantee standardized measurements or quality control, protect against the collusion of the crafty and powerful, insure adequate storage and reserve stocks, or otherwise help to rationalize the existing market. Government stores compete with private retailers, claiming to stabilize prices. But since these stores are not cost accountable, they help to depress the private retail market in the interest of authority's prebendary clients. Heavy-handed tax assessing in the central markets drives away small-scale operators, preventing those markets from rationally determining fair commodity prices. Finally, too many officials, whether administrators or those who provide service, are patrimonial generalists who are not knowledgeable of either commodities or marketing. Yet they arrogantly insist on making crucial market and operational decisions to validate patrimonial authority's prerogatives and graceful concern.

Patrimonial thinking also bedevils the polity's use of commodity price control to dampen price inflation, stabilize livelihood, and encourage productive investment. That control over the private market has been selectively applied, aggravating price disparities, and poorly administered, subject to pressures from cliental favorites or those willing to bribe. Prices are determined in a vacuum, without any guarantee that price-controlled commodities (such as fertilizer) will be available on the market, and ever subject to instant repeal on political rather than economic grounds (as was the case during the winter of 1974-75 with coal briquettes used for home heating). Government ineptness is just as evident in its own market operations—witness the Korea Monopoly Office—perhaps more so than in the private market, since the polity can cover up its failures by restricting production and otherwise ignoring negative consumer reactions to its decisions.

The consequence is a market in which participants seek windfall, "booty" commercial profits through manipulating prices, speculating, and hoarding commodities, rather than a market in which those actors rely on the orderly accumulation of commercial profit through productive investment; in brief, a market which is unconducive to the emergence of a developed commercial, and in turn industrial, economy.[8]

## The Contemporary Commercial Economy: Credit and Public Finance

The contemporary Korean public and private financial system is vexed by high consumption and speculation, especially real-estate lending at high, even usurious, rates of return; governmental (-international) capital formation and credit rather than self-generating or equity financing; insufficient mobilization of capital and inadequate management of what capital is mobilized; overcentralization; control by policy rather than by financial decision-makers; government policies which are erratically enforced and open to abuse through bribery, as typified by the income tax; and incomplete, misleading, though overly secretive, financial information which frustrates rational decision-making. We can review some of these characteristics in more detail.

*Capital Mobilization:* The woeful government capital mobilization of 4 percent in the Rhee period was gradually increased to a very respectable 16 percent of GNP by the 1970s, though the goal was 25 percent for that decade and 30 percent for the 1980s. However, this proved to be insufficient. Household, in contrast to government, savings have been consistently poor, even dropping as the GNP rose, primarily due to persistent inflation and the desire to invest in consumption, including education (see Chapter 9). This was as true for entrepreneurs and sophisticated urbanites as for ruralites. Moreover, by relying on loans rather than self-generating funds, enterprises squeezed capital and drove up interest rates, encouraging high-risk but high-potential speculation, rather than investment for productive profit, at the least to insure that principal and interest costs were covered. Speculative profiteering was encouraged by the ability to purchase land or fixed assets whose value inflated (in the case of land in the capital spectacularly, some 2000 percent in a decade) solely by holding. The government for too long exacerbated the problem by its reluctance to tax assets, allowing loan costs to be deducted from taxes and permitting heavy lending in the foreign market (to be discussed subsequently). In consequence, the Korean economy became a "minus" saver, rather than a self-generator of its own investment capital.

The constant heavy demand for speculative capital turned most banks' attention away from savings to lending. Recent polities have attempted to remedy this, especially for themselves, by repressing their own consumption as a rule-by-model example to the commercial and industrial community and by taking various measures to encourage savings—increasing the number of banks, urging all banks to encourage depositors by increasing interest, and offering bonuses, to be split between bank and depositor, to cooperating banks. However, by setting the interest rates by fiat, the government has determined where its loan capital will flow. In this patrimonial economy this is a neutral act, since whether government-sponsored or -encouraged lending contributes to productive economic action depends on whether a particular government allocator happens to be committed to productive action. Hence, if we apply Keynesian reasoning, we see that the primary problem of the Korean commercial economy is not the lack of available capital, as serious as that is, but the fact that too much of what is available is wasted on other than productive, self-generating capital mobilization, an issue a patrimonial authority does not seem fit to address.

*The Stock Exchange and the Corporation:* The government has been unable to replace loan-capital financing with a stock exchange raising equity capital or to induce private enterprises to go public against their will. An exchange created by the Japanese was closed and resuscitated many times. In one sense, this is not surprising given the preeminent credit position and capital formation by the polity and key banks rather than through private capital, a matter which I will discuss shortly. But I believe it is of at least equal pertinence that the exchange has served primarily to raise speculative commercial, rather than productive investment, capital. Park tried to force the larger enterprises to sell shares to the public by offering the enterprises the carrot of tax benefits and the stick of boards of examiners and inspectors empowered to review enterprise financing, and by refusing further government subsidies and loans to those enterprises which the polity disapproved. The enterprises strongly resisted, seemingly preferring to fund through high-interest lending, even though in an emergency such loans have forced many enterprises into bankruptcy unless the polity bails them out with salvation loans. Some observers attribute this obdurate spirit to Korean culture; that is, to Koreans' wish to work with as small a circle of trusted personal acquaintances as possible, preferably a circle of kin. But from the economic standpoint, such a grouping of owners and operators insures control and better hides those questionable business tactics which are used to keep on top of the irrational uncertainties of the patrimonial market, such as tax evasion, speculative profit-seeking, overpayment of dividends to privileged intimates, and, in the extreme, looting firms' capital and even bankrupting them for the intimates' personal gain unless the government comes to the rescue.

*Commercial Banking:* The original modern commercial bank was a branch of the Japanese First Bank established in the treaty port of Pusan in 1876. Thereafter, the Korean banking system was to reflect either Japanese colonial financial interests—such as over one-half the bank loans in 1945 being made to Japanese public and private enterprises—or Japanese banking norms and regulations—such as nationwide branching subordinated to central headquarters in the capital city (termed "city banking"), a close connection between the government central bank and commercial banking, short-term lending, and proliferation of special banks to fund government projects. For although the indigenous banks which preceded the Japanese penetration of Korea survived and new ones emerged throughout the colonial period, they were undercapitalized and were benignly neglected, if not discriminated against, by the Japanese, who were determined that such institutions play only a minor role in the colonial economy. Consequently it was the pre-World War II Japanese system of city, special, and central banks and their structures, operating procedures, and functions which the Republic inherited as the frame of its commercial banking system, a system which, even as elaborated by the Koreans, has been proved to be ill adapted to the capital formation and mobilization requisites of the contemporary Korean economy.

Briefly, first, the system is needlessly competitive with overlapping jurisdictions. Government special banks have expanded dramatically in direct competition with regular commercial banks, offering short- as well as long-term credit for industry, agriculture, export, and housing, especially in financing government programs. New special banks are founded whenever a new program is created, rather than improving (rationalizing) and expanding existing facilities to cater to new functions. Local banks in the provincial capitals, primarily private institutions, both trap and provide local capital, but they must compete with the great number of branch offices of the capital's city banks, the key to Korea's organized credit, since the Korean economy is fueled by short-term lending and not equity capital. City banks in turn compete for business and savings among themselves, with the special banks, and, until 1972, with the unorganized money market.

Second, many banks, especially city banks, are precariously solvent, not only because their profits are driven down through competition, but because, probably in consequence, they are too liberal and unselective in their loans in hopes of attracting business. Banks also are too eager to turn over their customary short-term, largely speculative, unproductive loans, thus creating similar long-term loans, in order to sustain the high interest premiums. Third, bank loan rates are not determined by the creditability of the borrower but by an elaborate system of loan schedules, justified on grounds that the borrower's solvency and the suitability of his loan are too difficult to determine in a volatile, speculative economy. Fourth, and most crucial, the polity considers the commercial banking system as primarily a means to control and allocate investment rather than to mobilize capital. Thus for all its formal elaboration, the banking system is not as modern as the other East Asian systems.

Consequently, everyone agrees that the commercial banking system needs reforming. Koreans believe that the remedy lies in structural reform, while outsiders, especially Americans, consider the nostrum to be procedural—but then Americans usually believe that if problems are not motivational, they are procedural. Consequently, while Koreans have concentrated on creating new banks and writing new regulations, the Americans have suggested improvement in management and training; better liaison between head offices and branches, which suffer simultaneously from poor supervision and inadequate discipline, and overregulation; cost account effectiveness; reduction, simplification, and unification, rather than proliferation in the number of banks to take advantage of the economy of scale and eliminate the highly unprofitable and wastefully overlapping competition which now lowers the ratio between assets and loans; and, above all, facing up to problems rather than relying on the ploy of shuffling personnel and depending on the government to salvage them whenever the banks run into financial difficulty because of their own misjudgments. Need I suggest that all these American solutions strike at the heart of patrimonial economic verities and hence Koreans prefer to look elsewhere for amelioration?

*The Central Bank—Bank of Korea (BOK)—and Government Control of Commercial Banking:* The BOK is the successor, in design and substance, to the Japanese occupation period Bank of Chōsen, which in most ways imitated the Bank of Japan. Thus, the BOK is the prime instrument of government financial policy, since BOK is a banker's bank which holds reserves and is the loaner of last resort. Simultaneously, it is the sole note issuer and its Monetary Board is responsible for overseeing commercial banking. The board in turn is controlled by the president of the Republic in that, although since 1962 its activities have been reviewable by the Finance Ministry, all the board's representatives, except the ex officio governor of the BOK and the minister of finance, come from the Economic Planning Board, the special banks, the Ministry of Agriculture and Forestry, and the Commercial and Industrial Bank and are appointed by, and serve at the pleasure of, the president. Presidential control of commercial banking also is assured by having the superintendent of banks, who is responsible for overseeing bank regulations and policies, align many of his decisions with those of the board—as, for example, on interest rates. Yet, for all his centralizing control, the president and his staff seem unable or unwilling to solve certain recurrent problems in the commercial banking system. These include not enforcing Monetary Board regulations, especially against risky overloaning; not placing the special government banks under the superintendent's office but under the Ministry of Finance, thus setting up a dual system of banking control, policy, and funding which is confusing, not always compatible, and wasteful of precious material resources and talent; and setting interest rates by fiat and borrowing from the BOK virtually whenever and whatever the government wishes, thus casting doubt on the polity's claim that it is seriously interested in stabilizing prices.

Commercial bankers do have their own associations which set interest rates, determine their specific lending strategies, and regulate competition. But these associations have little input in determining government banking policies; for example, the *range* of interest rates is set by the government, while bankers are only allowed to set the concrete point. But perhaps more pertinently, the polity has leverage to make the associations and the banks they represent serve as still another means for government to control private banking. For the government is most banks' key shareholder—typically the proprietor of 30 to 45 percent of the assets—and their prime loaner and depositor; the government special banks are at least competitive with the commercial banks, while some, such as the Bank of Seoul, deliberately are intimidating; and banking regulations are vaguely defined, such as those on "qualified" and "exceptional" loans, and thus can be capriciously enforced. Further, the government has used its leverage not only to determine commercial banking policy, but also to exact tribute for political funding.

Foreign advisors, especially the Americans, have reacted against all this, particularly against what they consider to be too much government regulation, certainly for the size of the Korean banking community; too many unenforced and unenforceable regulations which nevertheless intimidate, whereas fewer and more restrictive rules would have a positive effect; and the proliferation of detrimental regulations such as those on interest rates while salutary regulations to police the unorganized money market for too long were nonexistent. As theoretically reasonable as these suggestions may be, they reflect nonpatrimonial market monetary thinking, whereas Korean authority and economy, and hence commercial banking, are patrimonial. Consequently, the Americans have found the Koreans amazingly difficult to convert.

*The Unorganized Money Market:* A government monetary policy characterized by low interest rates on savings, by tax regulations which promote lending rather than equity financing, by a shortage of short-term capital because the government forces the commercial banks to finance its long-term projects, and by politically motivated loans especially to the favored cliental few (yet to be discussed), has encouraged the perseverance and even expansion of an unorganized money market; that is, a residual money market outside the formal, government-controlled banking system. Since over one-half of Korea's economic actors turn to this market at one time or another, at the least to supplement the organized market's inadequate funding, the market proffers a greater percentage of available credit than in most economies, especially in those with as sophisticated a financial system as Korea's. The unorganized market is very rational in that, in contrast to the organized market, it responds readily to the economic community's requirements and its charges are amazingly sensitive to prevailing rates of return. But it is economically irrational in that it offers credit at rates which seem usurious when compared to those of the organized market, even when the organized market's extremely low rates on politically generated loans are ignored. Consequently, the unorganized money market helps to drive up costs in an economy in which the actors believe that a net profit of 50 percent is not unreasonable, a profit more often than not realizable through commercial capital speculation rather than through productive investment. Usurious rates also siphon mobilizable capital from the organized market, especially savings. The government, finding itself powerless to move against these usurious rates and otherwise enforce its fiscal policies because the unorganized market operates beyond the pale of its regulations, decided in 1972 to mount a major effort to terminate the unorganized markets by requiring the reporting and rescheduling of all its loans at lower interest rates and totally repayable within eight years at the maximum. This edict radically reduced the market's viability, but could not put it out of business. For as long as the organized market is imperfect in the terms discussed in this and the previous sections, the unorganized market fills a significant role, I suggest especially as a rational safety valve for the economically irrational, politically motivated decision-making which exists in the Korean patrimonial commercial economy.

*Public Finance:* Ministerial and agency budgeting suggestions are screened by an executive state council which relies on the assembly, if and when it is allowed to meet, to rubber-stamp its decisions, a pattern reminiscent of the imperial Japanese past. Such a budget process formally legitimizes executive control over and access to the capital market, forcing it to support elaborate government programs and priorities which create deficits and do not necessarily reflect the most productive allocation of limited capital resources. The executive's ability to get its way is facilitated also by the accounting method employed, one which obscures its operations and defers objective review by critics in and out of the government. Although double-entry bookkeeping may have been invented by Koreans, it is not universally followed in its original homeland; schedules and functions are complex and numerous, standards for cost accounting are nebulous, and data are incomplete, tardily reported, and ill-coordinated and confused, because they are not centrally collected. There certainly is a rational intent behind all this apparent irrationality, for through it the government can spend first as it wishes and justify later by postbudgeting, so to speak, and thus further bend the patrimonial economy to the patrimonial political will, no matter how all this worries and horrifies nonpatrimonial certified accountants.

*Taxation:* Observers see the tax system as laboring under two major difficulties. First, the structure is unduly complex and confusing. Rates are set very high, but exemptions and deductions proliferate, supposedly to soften the impact of the high rates. Collectors are given wide discretionary powers to enforce the tax code, and although threats against those who do not pay are frequent, they are rarely carried out (rule by model) unless quotas are forced on collectors when total returns are lower than expected. Consequently, taxation becomes a game of wits between collector and assessed. Enterprisers are notorious for evading tax rosters, registering under fictitious names, claiming fantasy functions to obtain special tax concessions, and then disappearing at tax time. Certainly one of the reasons for the reluctance of firms to go public is to prevent disclosure not only of their speculative "booty" capitalist activities, but also of their abuse of the tax system.

Second, Korean tax schedules, like schedules everywhere, are biased to favor certain kinds of payers. In the Korean case those payers are urbanites, especially those who engage in urban speculative booty capitalism and who generate a major source of the polity's prebends. For example, the property tax for too long did not distinguish between productive and speculative land use; whatever property the government holds is exempt from assessment, regardless of use; and urbanites make out better than ruralites in spite of the fact that farm costs are higher and income lower.

To be sure the polity is as aware of both these defects as its critics are. Yet the system persists. I suggest that one reason is that the existing system is consistent with the patrimonial notion that authority should never be straitjacketed by defined rules but should be free to adjust rules according to the polity's notion of how best to spread morality in the economic order, and the rules of taxation are no exception. Another and more cynical determinant is that the existing structure enables authority to exact prebendary tribute in return for gracefully exempting or lightening the burden of those authority deems worthy. (As I have argued previously, the two motives are not incompatible.) Whatever the source, as long as doubt exists that assessments as originally determined and levied will be collected, the taxed feel free to attempt to modify, if not avoid, their obligations. It is such doubt, rather than the severity of taxes, that many economists believe is so ruinous to productive economic calculation.

*The Favored Enterprise Policy:* Favored enterprises, termed *chaebŏl* (literally, financial clans), are those private sector firms which authority considers vital in creating the image of a modern Korean economy. Neither small industry nor especially agriculture, which conjures up a vision of backwardness, can contribute to building such an image. At the end of the Park era the chaebŏl constituted the forty-six largest firms, creating 13 percent of the GNP and 37 percent of the value added in manufacturing. Some are created by government prodding, such as Hyundai, a world competitive shipbuilding giant. Most are the work of individual entrepreneurs, some going back to the Japanese occupation days, who set themselves up as directors and their relatives as managers, and who, having survived the high attrition rate befalling most new enterprises in their early years, at a critical point in their qualitative development are recognized and encouraged by the government as patrimonially worthy to receive prebendal aid. The especially crucial aid is credit, and that is why I discuss the chaebŏl here, because these enterprises, unlike the prewar Japanese Zaibatsu with whom they are often compared and whose Chinese ideographs are identical, do not own their own banks (recall here that few Korean enterprises rely on equity capital to finance their operations). Also, although chaebŏl, with their close governmental links and employee paternalism, resemble contemporary Japanese combines, in Korea the polity is clearly the senior partner, and thus the chaebŏl do not necessarily have sufficient leverage to protect their economic interests. The consequence for economic modernization and development is ambiguous, as always in a patrimonial economy. On the one hand the Park government did exert its prebendal carrot and stick to induce the chaebŏl to reinvest productively whatever percentage of their surplus the government considers necessary or to face stringent auditing and confiscation of (patrimonially immoral) illicit profiteering. On the other hand, under Rhee especially most government-favored enterprises were large show projects whose physical presence (numbers) was more important than their quality; whose objective economic contribution need not have been vital; and whose managers need not have been held financially accountable for their economic judgments, since they were assured of prebendary access to (formerly Japanese-owned) vested property, the windfall profits from foreign trade, and bail-out loans at preferential interest rates to keep the firms afloat. The waste and irresponsible speculative profit-seeking which such a policy certainly did not discourage, and even positively encouraged, was ever justified by the polity as the unfortunate but perhaps necessary by-product of modernization. Valid or not, such reasoning contributed to generating booty-commercial profit at the expense of productive profit. That Park can be given credit for refurbishing the image and function of the chaebŏl cannot be denied. Nevertheless, his failed cathartic anti-conspicuous consumption campaigns and his patrimonial mining of private wealth for political funding and lucrative employment for ex-military clients also cannot be overlooked, though we probaly will never be able to know and judge the extent in quantitative terms.[9]

## The Fundamental Character of the Korean Industrial Economy

The imperial capital court long employed workshops under the control of designated bureaucrats to fabricate its weapons and service its commodities. Over the centuries, this system had become highly differentiated into more than two thousand specialized services under some twenty government agencies, employing a complex labor force from unskilled bound workers to skilled wageworkers who were allowed to work on their own, albeit under strict guidelines, whenever they were not serving the court. Local authorities also encouraged artisan craftsmanship, giving rise to highly sought-after local specialties. In addition, the state itself, or its designated agents, monopolistically managed and exploited certain large-scale or vital artisan activities, such as paper making.

The status of this artisan technology is perplexing. For example, first, although the authorities vigorously exploited the three key state-supervised enterprises—mining, salt, and cotton—they relied primarily upon unmotivated and often unskilled corvée and tribute labor and were benignly indifferent to productivity (salt), to conserving an exhaustible resource (mining), or to nurturing the earthly source of the bounty (cotton). Second, Korea was scientifically the equal of her neighbors. She was respected for her singular contributions to astronomy, bell technology, printing and metal typing, meteorology, and the practical crafts. Chinese and Japanese scientific discoveries and techniques were readily imported and adapted to Korean needs without prejudice. Nevertheless, there were serious deficiencies. For all the skills in bell metallurgy, mining technology was primitive. For even though it was obvious that dividends would be greater if the readily available advanced technology were applied, Korean mining continued to depend on maximally exploiting corvée labor and minimally investing capital. Further, science was predominantly government-inspired and controlled, and hence applied narrowly according to authority's design. Most pertinent, it was not applied to increasing artisan productivity, especially not to improving tools, in marked contrast to western European and Japanese rural tinker contributions to the development of machinery first in agriculture and then in general.

Certainly, agriculture had made startling advances by the twentieth century, at first through new techniques of transplanting and dry farming, new seeds, and new cropping (such as silk and upland), and novel irrigation technology expanded output greatly. Then, practical-minded court philosophers (see Chapter 11) inspired the compilation of promising agricultural techniques into popular texts which were disseminated all over rural Korea. But these texts also discussed how to cope with the social and economic dislocations of an increasingly commercial agriculture which were undermining authority's control over the agricultural surplus at the very time that the polity was becoming more and more dependent on increasing that surplus to make ends meet. This irreconcilable dilemma led the polity to equivocate; to wit, the government accepted technological innovation but kept it below its full potential, a classic example of the distinction between modernization and development. Government policy was especially detrimental in the case of irrigation, which is costly and ultimately requires rational management, but the impact was felt throughout agriculture. The gap between government policy and necessity was partially filled by individual entrepreneurs who hired workers to apply the latest agricultural technology to prepare and work the soil. But they were few and could not by themselves stimulate a technological agricultural revolution. In contrast, nineteenth-century Japanese were exploiting a significant breakthrough in tool technology to radically increase agricultural productivity, while most Korean farmers were still using the tools and related techniques of earlier centuries.

Korean artisan professionalism however did exist in manual industry shops, especially those engaged in brass and iron technology. However, first, their proprietors usually were not only the ones who provided the raw materials and marketed the product, but also were the managers, so they controlled both the industrial and commercial aspects of production. Since these proprietors primarily were commercialists, the industrial shops were thus subordinated to commercial interests, which, given the booty character of Korean commercialism, could not but have a negative impact on the industrial developmental potential of the shops. Second, these shops did not employ contract labor, and the state rather than the shops enforced labor discipline and required low wages regardless of productivity. That is, in the technical economic sense, the manual industry shops were not incipient (latent) industrial capital establishments, but in the *manufaktur* stage. Third, although they were private enterprises, manual industry shops were required to operate on state property, were subject to state standards and regulations with regard to what was fabricated and to whom it was disposed (mostly to the aristocracy), and were prebendally taxed for the very right to exist. In sum, the manual industry shops, for all their technological sophistication, were not qualitatively different from the other, more typical manual industries of the period.

By the twentieth century, government-operated manual industry had become significantly privatized. Managers were recruited from outside the bureaucracy, and their operations progressively freed from supervision, although they continued to be treated as state agents under state charter privileges, and hence eligible for prebendary state favors, such as tax privileges and exemptions, market monopolies, and access to the state police to discipline workers. Many of these managers were able to accumulate sufficient capital to expand their operations within their respective industries, then to other industries, and finally outside the capital area, to the rural hinterland.

Rural artisanship, however, remained more technologically and managerially primitive than urban industry. Village artisanship, though free of government restraints, was small-scale, because managers and (skilled) workers were wont to keep their activities as inconspicuous as possible, lest what they were doing come to the attention of the authorities who would punitively tax them or force the artisans to relocate in the capital. Then, ruralites regarded manual industry as but an income supplement to vital agriculture—an activity worthy of women—an attitude which the polity did not discourage. Consequently, when state-supported urban industry penetrated the rural areas, (private) rural artisanship was unable to compete, which contrasts sharply with the experiences of the subsequently developed economies of both western Europe and Japan.

We can now draw some conclusions. First, although it cannot thus be denied that at least the roots of a Korean industrial technology and organization, especially in the metal fields, existed by the turn of the twentieth century, yet I cannot agree with the claim that this demonstrates that the Korean economy would have evolved inevitably into a developed industrial one had not foreign, especially Japanese, capitalism intruded at an inappropriate time. I certainly concede that the Japanese destroyed certain Korean manual crafts and unfairly competed with others to insure Japanese industrial domination. But the Korean artisanship which the Japanese destroyed or frustrated, on the one hand, was too intimately involved with, and even subordinated to, a patrimonial commercial economy that did not, and I have argued could not, generate productive investment capital, and on the other hand, was subjected to an authority whose policy it was either

to integrate partisanship with, or keep it subordinate to, a not necessarily technologically progressive agriculture (see the next chapter),
or to exploit artisanship narrowly in a fashion inimical to maximizing
its potential; for example, to provide for the consumptive pleasures of
a social elite. Paradoxically, it was the foreigner, especially the Japanese imperial monopolist, who provided the necessary industrial investment capital and organization to build a modern industry, but of
course to Japan's specifications and exploitive advantage. The consequence is that the artisan crafts of dynastic Korea became the ancestors of contemporary small and medium, especially rural, industry, while the larger, state-sponsored urban establishments, in spirit if
not in form, became the ancestors of the modern industry of the Japanese, and ultimately of the contemporary Republic.

Second, in the process of freeing artisanship from direct state operation, patrimonial authority learned to its pleasure that it need not
own the means of production or bind the craftsmen to effectively control and economically exploit; the right of supervision and the cornucopia of prebendally granted privilege to fabricate sufficed to guarantee both objectives without the state having to invest its own time,
personnel, and capital. This principle too was reinforced by the Japanese and passed on to the Republic.[10]

## The Contemporary Industrial Economy: Some Characteristics and Problems

The growth of the Korean industrial economy since the military
coup of 1961 as measured by GNP has been spectacular; to many, one
of the few "success stories of the developing world." The Korean
economy at the end of the Park era was a far cry from the resource-
poor, overpopulated, civil-war-devastated, and recently colonial economy which Park inherited, with industry clearly the engine of that impressive structural transformation. For although the general economy
grew on the average a respectable 6.9 percent annually during that
period, industry increased 17 percent per annum, one of the world's
highest growth rates. Equally impressive is that the Korean economy
is modern, since the industrial share of the total economy is over one-
third and industry is highly differentiated into producing, consumer,
intermediate, and capital goods and hence has been able to respond
flexibly to sometimes dramatic changes in market opportunity.

Viewed closely, however, industrial performance has been marred
by a number of maladjustments which I choose to discuss at this point
in terms of the patrimonial artisan-industrial character of the imperial

and Japanese periods. (See also the next two sections for my view of the structuring effects of Korea's role in the international economy.) First, industrial progress *has been uneven;* to wit, only certain industries, especially those associated with export, have carried the flag. Such an industrial economy is termed *dual.* That is, the ROK polity, much like the late imperial and the Japanese, has singled out certain, primarily large-scale industrial activities like the chaebŏl for special attention. In return for being prebendally exploited, these enterprises are subsidized and provided with preferential credit and transport rates; with monopolistic and oligopolistic access to raw materials, production facilities, and especially markets; and, most recently, with government-financed research; thus assuring these enterprises of survival and even prosperity, sometimes, as in the past, in spite of their performance. In contrast, small or medium-sized industries find it very difficult to take advantage of market opportunity, since without government favor they must depend upon high-cost private usury loans even for their day-to-day operations; cater to a narrow domestic market; and normally enter the lucrative export market only as subcontractors of the large enterprises which squeeze them mercilessly in the best of times and drive them to bankruptcy during recession (two-thirds of small-medium industry failed in the oil crisis of 1974–75). To survive, small-medium industrialists must cut corners on quality, employ low-skilled workers at low recompense, and overlook those expensive but vital managerial and mechanical innovations which the polity routinely offers, sometimes without cost, to the favored large enterprises.

Second, *regional maladjustments* are significant. Industry is concentrated in and around two super cities, the national capital of Seoul and Pusan, and to a lesser extent in the regional provincial capital of Taegu and foreign-industry-dominated Masan. In Taegu, however, although over one-third of the gainfully employed are in industry, that industry predominantly is small or medium-sized and in textiles, rather than in such fields as electronics and petrochemicals, where preeminent wealth and the economic power of the future lie. This suggests that the key regional imbalance in the Korean case is between the major centralized urban area of Seoul-Pusan and the rest of the country, urban or rural, rather than between rural and urban areas. This is attested by the fact that in spite of rapid urbanization under Park—by the mid 1970s half the population lived in cities (that is, urban centers of more than 50,000 residents)—a number of urban centers, notably those small ports ill situated in relation to international trade and communication with Japan, lost population, while

Seoul alone held 40 percent of the urban population. A subsidiary imbalance, long practiced in Korea, is to favor the particular region of the country from which the titular ruler comes or derives a major source of cliental support; in Park's case this has meant primarily Kyŏngsang and, to a lesser extent, Kyŏnggi. (And, as noted in Chapter 1, Kyŏngsang continues to be the apple of Chun Doo-whan's eye.)

Third, an *accelerating urbanization* is rapidly reducing Korea's agricultural population, which has dwindled as ruralites have moved to the cities. But urbanization is not new in Korea, nor is it the consequence of modern industrialization. Rather, the premier urban centers—the capital and its satellites—have always attracted the politically and socially ambitious, for that is where patrimonial central authority has resided, where its officials have been educated, and from which its prebendary favors have flowed. Nowadays, those favors increasingly focus upon industry, since that is the most lucrative source of potential prebendal wealth for both polity patron and entrepreneurial client. Consequently, although EPB and the many Five-Year Economic Plans have paid lip service to reducing rural-urban disparities, when it comes down to actually allocating resources and energy, not only is scant attention paid to ameliorating existing discrepancies but, in fact, current industrial policies are widening existing differences in wealth. For example, the export-related industries which are fueling Korea's growth do not use local raw materials or the kind of labor which would exploit rural specialties. And although EPB recently turned its attention to local village industry, that effort is so designed that it will not threaten, and will even positively serve, center (especially urban) economic interests; for example, what is being encouraged are arts and crafts suitable for export and their production, as of old, is integrated into the existing farm economy as a supplemental, rather than a principal, source of income.

Most urban migrants will end up economically marginal, often isolated from kin and friends, without adequate housing (due especially to inflation, the scarcity of land, and the unavailability of residential mortgage credit), health care, or proper transport, and exploited as cheap, unsophisticated labor of scant concern to a polity which prefers to invest its resources elsewhere. And yet, because rural labor is underutilized and hence undercompensated; because it is tapped only seasonally during planting and harvesting; because peddling and shopkeeping have failed to supplement meager cultivator income adequately; and because much of rural industry is not of export quality, the urban alternative, for all its risks, is for many too difficult to resist. Local urban centers like Taegu, because they are integrated into the local agricultural economy, do employ and hence retain some local manpower and capital; but this is scant compensation for the way Seoul and Pusan (and other way stations on the economic road to Seoul or Pusan) strip the regional economy in general and the rural economy in particular of human and capital resources, thus driving up farm labor costs and otherwise binding the hinterland to the premier urban orbit—to the latter's economic advantage. In 1977, the mounting malaise and authority's fear of potential *political* unrest, especially within Seoul because it is so near to the border of the DPRK, inspired a long-range urban plan, with a watchdog committee under the prime minister, to deflect *future* growth from existing urban centers by restricting new construction there and providing tax incentives for pilot industries in virgin areas. But since the program focuses on future urban growth, and the polity has made it clear that it places a low priority on improving urban life, especially when such improvement conflicts with maximizing industrial growth, this new urban vision has proved to be only another example of patrimonial rule-by-model window dressing.

Fourth, since the Korean industrial economy is so dependent on the export demand of the international economy and does not use local factors except as cheap labor, the Korean economy is *volatile* because the domestic market is unable to take up slack in the international economy.

Fifth, in spite of the ever-increasing GNP which all Koreans have shared, and although that increase has not been as inequitably distributed as in most nondeveloped economies, yet serious *inequalities* exist and are even widening between ruralites and urbanites and within the urban community. The dislocations of the early years of the Republic leveled most of the predominantly rural populace. Then the industrial growth strategy of the 1960s and 1970s enhanced the income of both, and narrowed the income gap between the urban and rural working class since subsidization of the grain purchase programs enabled farmers to purchase what urban workers produced and thus contributed to industrial wage rises in turn. However the hard-core rural and urban poor, most notably the rural landless and the urban unskilled, were virtually untouched by this and by government prebendal poverty aid, which benefited principally the middle-income groups. Perhaps more pertinent, the international price rise in raw materials since 1974, especially in oil and machinery, over which Koreans have no control, reversed the trend of income equalization by exacerbating the gap between urban and rural costs and income; and the government's strategy of prebendally rewarding those in heavy and chemical industry and the chaebŏl in general widened the income gap between urban white-collar and highly skilled workers and blue-collar unskilled workers on the one hand, and between most of the populace, especially ruralites, and the favored entrepreneurs and managers on the other hand. Again, the government's inability to control the money supply, in part because of the all-out growth strategy and the international cost structure, has made a mockery of the much-publicized stabilization programs of the 1970s,a failure which hurt the poor and even those of middle income more than the wealthy and favored few able to take advantage of the situation.

Inequality also is a consequence of an imperfect industrial labor market, which is characterized by a great number of self-employed, by an oversupply of hands, by the practice of finding unskilled work through relatives or personal connections, by conditions of employment and wages which differ widely from industry to industry and from firm to firm, and, most critically, by the widespread use of "temporary" employees who are not privy to the perquisites, and especially the job security, of permanent workers. The term "temporary" is somewhat misleading, since time on the job is not crucial in determining promotion to permanent status, although in theory that is supposed to happen after three months; in fact, some temporary workers have been with their firms for more than twenty years. But the term is accurate in that temporaries can be dismissed quickly during recessions without severance allowances and even with their wages in arrears; thus the temporaries bear the brunt of any industrial dislocation. But the industrial group universally discriminated against is women. Females receive only half the pay of males doing the same job, work longer hours and under more primitive conditions, and are more subject to the whims of employers under the guise of protecting family morality.

Sixth, and finally, much of urban labor's woe stems from the government's policy of keeping wages behind, or rarely consistent with, productivity, and subsidiarily not enforcing labor standards on safety, sanitation, and fair play in meeting wages when due. This is because the Korean economy is labor rather than capital intensive and geared to the export market, and the government believes it must keep Korean goods internationally competitive by squeezing labor as the source of capital accumulation and by not antagonizing the export-oriented favored industrialists, whether they be domestic or foreign. But since Korea imports its oil energy and most raw materials, which it then processes and exports, it is especially vulnerable to sudden escalation of import costs, as was the case in 1974 and thereafter. At such times many firms, especially the small and marginal, failed, while the survivors cut back their employment rosters and used the occasion to hold the line on wages even as their windfall inventory profits were soaring. Some of the workers dismissed did not receive the bonuses or severance allowances to which they were entitled, and the authorities refused to enforce the pertinent labor codes. Even in the best of economic times, it is difficult for workers, even the skilled and well-paid, to keep up with inflation in an economy in which wages average a quarter of those received by American workers, while Korean costs run about half those in the United States. Almost all the income of Korean workers is consumed, approximately half being allocated for food, while employers, with the polity's benign neglect, cut labor costs rather than pay the economic piper for their managements' ineffectiveness and bad judgments.

This litany of maladjustments in the Korean industrial economy is reminiscent of the pre-World War II Japanese economy at home and in Korea. Although this fact could account for initial existence of those problems in a "modern" Korea, prewar Japanese roots cannot be blamed for their stubborn persistence, given the influx of postwar Japanese and American influence. I suggest rather that the present situation is attributable to the desire of industrial decision-makers within and without the polity to use time-tested patrimonial techniques of controlling and prebendally exploiting an industrial economy, as earlier Koreans controlled and exploited the agricultural and then the commercial economies. [11]

### Establishing Ground Rules for International Trade

Korea had been a participant in an international economy long before the mid-nineteenth century, most noticeably first with China and then with Japan. Trade with China was termed *tribute*, symbolizing a mutual adherence to patrimonial-Confucian institutional canons by way of earning Chinese patronal acceptance of Korean authority as morally legitimate. Tribute exchange, however, was more than political ritual. At the least, the members of tribute missions were allowed to engage in private trade, and whether it was formally sanctioned or not, those officials who surveilled the missions exercised their patrimonial prerogative to tax and exact bribes from the tribute traders. Tribute interchange stimulated both the variety and quantity of certain indigenous Korean commodities such as textiles and printed books. For all the Korean official patrimonial rhetoric downplaying its economic potential, and the rationalization that it was carried on to mollify a fierce neighbor who would raid if he could not trade, commerce with Japan was also stimulative to the Korean economy. The Koreans exchanged rice, textiles, printed books, and ginseng for Japanese copper, out of which they fashioned coins and the Confucian ritual goblets which they exported to China. The Japanese also provided Korea with products of south and southeast Asia, thus integrating Korea into an international commercial economy of considerable magnitude.

Modern international trading was inaugurated with the unequal Treaty of Kanghwa in 1876, by which Japan, playing well the new game of international diplomacy at gunpoint, forced Korea to permit duty-free economic interchange in the port town of Pusan, far from the patrimonial moral center of, and hence uncontaminating to, the capital. In return for subsequently revising the treaty to sanction a modest Korean tariff on Japanese goods, the Japanese were allowed to extend their trading throughout Korea, including the capital sanctuary, and then to enjoy extraterritorial privileges, which ultimately included Japanese legal and economic rights over Koreans under Japanese jurisdiction, enforced by Japanese courts and by the immediately hated Japanese police. The Japanese exploited these concessions to insure the dominance of Japanese commercial capital in Korea by competing unfairly and ruthlessly with indigenous traders and by buying up urban and rural real estate through unredeemed usurious loans with land as security. The primary instrument of Japanese penetration was its commercial banking system, especially the Korean branches of the First Bank (DIGK), which, though privately owned, issued banknotes that soon became the standard Korean paper currency. These banks offered cheap and virtually unlimited loans to Japanese to finance their increasing control over the internationally relevant sector of the Korean commercial economy. The Japanese grand design was facilitated by an initial pro-Japanese policy within the Korean government, which was reversed too late to enable Korea to stand up to the Japanese economic juggernaut. The Japanese success was soon imitated by Europeans, who claimed and received similar government-to-government commercial and then industrial concessions, while the Chinese were content to exploit a growing anti-Japanese sentiment to penetrate the indigenous retail market. In addition, individuals, especially Americans, obtained personal concessions which also amounted to sovereign rights over Korean personnel and the chance to expand a foothold in other ventures.

In sum, one way or the other, the nineteenth-century Korean economy was being linked to an emerging modern international economy, a link which was to have both positive and negative consequences for the indigenous economy. On the positive side, imported foreign machinery helped establish a modern textile industry. Producers, especially farmers, on their own initiative increased their output, showing that, contrary to conventional patrimonial wisdom, they were ready to respond to market incentives if given the opportunity. Local marketers offered imported goods and collected Korean products for export. Commission agents were especially active as vital go-betweens for foreigners and locals, mobilizing peddlers and other itinerants to collect exportables from, and deliver imports to, the remote areas; thus they linked all of Korea to the international market and in the process created a truly national Korean market for the first time. Foreigners technically trained and advised; for example, the United States Department of Agriculture's demonstration farm project near Seoul offered seed and breeding information to one and all. Finally, certain novel institutions and reorganizations often forced on a reluctant bureaucracy, such as the Customs Service, showed how an efficient and reasonably honest administration could help to improve the economy.

Negatively, the foreigners, for all their contribution to increasing the trade volume—twentyfold in the 1870s alone—and the GNP, were clearly doing so at best according to their own vision of what the Korean economy should be like and at worst in a way that promoted their own interests. Hence what economic activities the foreigners were not interested in were left as they were, and those which they did not approve of were either disrupted or destroyed. Especially this was the case with indigenous industry and commerce which were not provided with access to the loan capital and supportive services available to foreign and foreign-sponsored activities, and hence were unable to withstand the destructive impact of foreign competition. But also the mad scramble to meet the demands of the new external market, for example in vital rice, created shortages, internal economic dislocations, and inflation on the one hand, and wide fluctuations in demand and hence in price on the other hand, in both cases due to ad hoc decisions which were made outside Korea if they were not stipulated by treaty, and hence which the Koreans had little or no control over and were powerless to remedy. The Korean polity, for all its rhetoric to the contrary, aided and abetted the new economic order. Sometimes the government did so out of conscious design, as when officials were only too willing to accept bribes or a share in the profits of railroads, mines, or textile plants in return for granting a free economic hand to foreigners instead of to locals. Sometimes the polity did so out of subliminal institutional design, as when officials let the foreigners carry out certain activities which they dare not do themselves or in a way the foreigners demanded which would compromise the patrimonial character of the economy.

In brief, a pattern for helping to modernize the Korean economy by linking it to the international economy was established before the end of the ninteenth century, when Korea still was dynastic. The specific ground rules of that pattern insured that the modernizing economy would be compatible with long-standing patrimonial institutional requirements. The full implication of all this was to become manifest after the development drive of the 1960s under an independent republic. [12]

## Contemporary Foreign Aid, the International Economy, and Economic Dependency

During the Rhee period, the United States aid program suffered from American policy vacillation—in 1945 relief, productive investment and structural reform in 1948, again relief and enhancing the military establishment during and after the Korean War—and Korea's resolve to go its own way. Especially, the Americans were anxious to cut expenses and increase revenue, while Rhee (according to the American view out of cussedness and with United Nations connivance via its Reconstruction Agency [UNKRA]) was equally determined to force the Americans to invest in capital projects which the Americans considered both inflationary and unnecessarily burdensome. After the military coup of 1961, Americans and Koreans finally came to agree on a common economic goal; namely, that Korea's viability depended on a productive economy supporting a military establishment strong enough to face the rival DPRK. To help achieve that goal, the Americans offered considerable military and civil assistance, technical and material.

That American and then Japanese assistance has been a mixed blessing to the Korean economy. On the one hand, whether as grants or loans, such aid has accounted for a small but vital fraction of the GNP. It has provided capital investment, essential goods, technical help, and modern productive machinery, which, with tie-in stipulations, have pressured Korean managers to improve their efficiency. On the other hand, even if it has not generated them, certainly that aid has contributed to many of the problems we have been exploring in the present study. First, under Rhee especially, foreign aid fueled the existing unproductive commercial capitalism by providing prebendal windfall profits to the politically privileged who were licensed to import commodities to often ridiculously undervalued exchange rates. These foreign goods encouraged the rich and the not-so-rich to consume luxuriously, rather than to save, invest, and otherwise stabilize the economy as the Americans assumed would happen if the Koreans were given the opportunity to accumulate wealth. Second, imports competed with and discouraged domestic production. They helped to widen the dual-economic gap, on the one hand between large, modern factories intimately associated with the export-import market and smaller firms increasingly associated with a stagnating indigenous economy, and on the other hand between industry and an agriculture which by and large did not profit from commodity assistance. Third, some assistance has been carefully measured so as not to compete with the donor; this has been true especially of Japanese technical aid. Or the Koreans have been forced to accept commodities rather than capital, commodities from designated sources, commodities the donor believes the Koreans should have, or items the donor wants to unload; this has been especially true of American aid. Finally, even with the best of intentions on both sides, there never was certainty that massive government-to-government aid would be properly handled and invested as originally designed, whether failure to do so would occur through corruption, maladministration, incompetence, or the indifference of either donor or recipient or both. To be sure, none of these problems is peculiar to Korea.

In addition to encouraging foreign assistance, Park progressively tied Korean fortunes to the international market economy. The strategy has been to exploit the potential of that economy to fuel quantitative and qualitative growth, in part to legitimize and popularize the regime at home and enhance the regime's and Korea's political power and prestige abroad. Korea's role in the international economy has been determined by its comparative advantage; namely, by its large population, dearth of natural resources, high unemployment, and underutilization of those employed—all of which is considered remediable through labor intensive exploitation of imported capital goods and technology that converts imported raw materials to semi-finished and finished products for exports, the added value being applied to repay import costs and create profit for both management and labor in both the government and private sectors. The industrial export sector, the key to this economic game plan, consequently has been specially favored with subsidies, tax incentives, preferential loans, prior access to scarce investment capital, periodic devaluation of the currency to keep Korean goods competitive in the international market, and a labor social policy which insures peace, productivity, and wages which lag behind productivity. International investors have been offered special banking privileges and duty-free production and export zones within which they have enjoyed a virtual extra-territorial privilege of making their own economic, particular labor, decisions free of Korean legal review and interference. More recently Korean firms, supported by aggressive government promotion and subsidies, have entered the international market by investing abroad, especially in construction. The government also has tried to induce Korean overseas residents to invest in Korea.

Observers, other than ideological partisans, do not agree as to how desirable that international growth strategy has been. On the one hand, there is little doubt that the Park strategy, by eliminating the stagnant import substitution policy of Rhee—which fortunately was not in place strongly or long enough to become a permanent feature of Korean economic life—vitally transformed the Korean economy from an agricultural to a significantly manufacturing one and, within the export-pertinent manufacturing sector, from one primarily focused on textiles and plywood to one focused on electronics, synthetics, and most recently chemical and heavy industries. Manufactures now account for 83 percent of Korean exports, approximately a quarter of its GNP, and between 5 and 10 percent of its annual growth. It has also stimulated the modernization of social overhead, such as transport, both internal (roads) and external (shipping). And foreign trade has provided the incentive and wherewithal for rapid modernization of such domestic industries as textiles and electricals, and created a sizable pool of educated, productive workers and sophisticated managers and planners in both the public and private sectors. It has encouraged authority to allocate national resources effectively, mobilize capital, and enlist the productive cooperation of the business community.

This game plan, however, has many critics. They claim, first, that it has exacerbated the duality of the economy, in spite of such recent ameliorative measures for small-medium industry as creating trading companies on the Japanese model to pool investment capital and collecting-processing export commodities to take advantage of the economy of scale. A second criticism is that the cheap wage policy has depressed the domestic consumer market for goods and services, and hence has hurt the small-medium firms which cater to that market. In addition, the rich, since they have preferred the prestigious western consumer goods which have become readily available in Korea's increasingly international economy, are parasites on rather than contributors to the local economy. Critics also claim that while private foreign investments, which have been encouraged to facilitate the growth of the Korean economy, have been a major channel for importing technology, for providing skilled on-the-job training, and for upgrading marketing, they do not necessarily import the most advanced technology, since they are encouraged to exploit Korea's inexpensive labor intense potential, they control the pricing and reexport of their products, and, with the polity's blessing, they are able to distribute an exceedingly high percentage (by international standards) of their profits as dividends. Also, they offer no educative spillover for local firms in similar or related fields and have access to the government's financial trough, which some believe could better be devoted to Korean-owned enterprises. Another criticism is that although the long-range Korean international debt has been well managed, it is nevertheless very sizable and its fate is crucial to the Korean economy, since it is the primary engine of economic growth. Finally, critics point out that Korea, like other high-growth economies, suffers from serious pollution problems.

Overall, Korea's international economic strategy is often defended as reminiscent of nineteenth-century Japan's. In that case, however, exports did not compete with domestic industry, the desire of the populace and even the elite for foreign consumer goods was negligible, and the nonpatrimonial character of the social order diminished, though it did not eliminate, unproductive official favoritism and corruption, and hence the strategy facilitated Japan's economic development.

The most controversial feature of Korea's participation in the international economy is Korea's dependency; that is, the ways in which, and the degree to which, foreigners can adversely determine Korean economic policy and prosperity, and profit from the Korean economy directly through investment and indirectly through supplying what the foreigners want. Clearly an economy which imports virtually all its oil energy and such essentials as cotton, rubber, and most of its iron ore and scrap iron, and one which helps to fuel production with loans from alien governments and international agencies, is virtually subject to the political and economic whims of outsiders. The Korean polity at least has been willing to pay that price, not only for the prosperity it has generated, but because the government believes that American investment in particular commits the United States to Korea's political and military security. The Park regime was well aware that the American disenchantment with, and hence diminution of, economic and political support for Rhee hastened his demise, and was determined not to let that happen again. Consequently, the Park regime mounted a major public relations campaign, especially directed at American officials, sometimes tinged with bribery, to counter the American distaste for its political repression. Unfortunately for the Koreans the bribery became public knowledge—popularly known in the United States as Koreagate—but fortunately for the Koreans the publicity did not end though it did temporarily disrupt the Korean-American tie, primarily because of continuing American strategic interest in the peninsula.

However, the Koreans were unable to prevent a simultaneous end to cheap fuel and raw materials and the consequent world recession and lower international growth rates of the 1970s, which hit the dependent economy of Korea with special fury. The indebted were driven out of the market, laborers lost their jobs, imports were cut, and costs rose for producers and consumers competing for scarce imported goods at inflated prices. All Koreans were thus made aware of how vulnerable their prosperity was to forces beyond their shores and control. Some economists demanded that Korea henceforth depend on its own resources, create its own capital formation, produce for the domestic market, and achieve food grain independence. But the government, fearing lower growth, not to speak of withdrawal of foreign political and military support, balked. Rather than seizing an opportunity to overhaul (rationalize) the existing industrial structure, the polity resorted to its usual pattern of bailing out politically favored ailing export industries, aggressively promoting Korean products abroad, and exporting its capital potential in construction. Since growth soon resumed, the regime and its supporters considered the decision to continue hitching the "modernizing" economic star to (that is, to remain dependent on) the international market economy vindicated.

Having acknowledged all this, I still cannot concur with the popular, particularly left, view that conversely either severing the link or replacing the existing government will *necessarily* cause a qualitative change in the economy's development potential. In other (technical) terms, I am an unreconstructed "internalist," and of a particular school at that, because I locate the source of many Korean development problems in the persistent patrimonial institutional character of the social order which, since it predates Korea's dependency on the international market economy, is autonomous of that dependency and will not disappear automatically after the link is severed. I believe this would be so even if the ROK were to join the Communist common market economy; in that case Korea would only express its patrimonial character and consequent economic problems differently—as witness the economy of the DPRK.[13]

## The Japanese (and American) Contribution: How To Modernize a Patrimonial Economy

The Japanese initiated Korean commercial urbanization; modern shipping and ports, railroads, and vehicular roads; a true banking system, including a central bank and specialized rural and urban monetary facilities; modern national-internal and external trading; a unified, sound currency; multipurpose cooperatives; a unified and systematically assessed and collected tax system; an agricultural extension program which promoted new (e.g., American cotton) and improved (e.g., Japanese rice) crops, model farms and fairs, rural education, and irrigational, reclamational, and forest management; a modernized mining exploited through ministries rather than foreign concessions; novel fishing techniques and a managed, licensed catching; business codes and the modern corporation; permanent and supervised urban markets; industrial, especially manufacturing, enterprise and the training of skilled industrial workers. In brief, the Korean economy the Japanese left behind in 1945 was a far cry from the one they found on their entrance into Korea in the late nineteenth century; in fact, that economy, save for Japan proper and possibly Manchukuo, was the most advanced and integrated in east Asia.

But, in my view, that economy had two singular but interrelated negative characteristics; namely, it was modernized but not developed, and it was patrimonially modernized. It is the quality of these characteristics rather than the impressive quantity of modern infrastructure and the like which Japan bequeathed to the Koreans in 1945, I believe, that is the true measure of the Japanese legacy, a legacy the Koreans still are grappling with today, regardless of their similarly impressive GNP.

The first major feature of the Japanese occupation was that it produced *a modernized but undeveloped economy.* Koreans attribute the character of their economy in 1945 to Japanese perniciousness; that is, like any colonial master, the Japanese, whatever they claimed to the contrary, organized their possessions' economies to serve the mother country's interests. Korea accordingly provided the Japanese economy with raw materials and a market for Japanese finished goods; capital formation for Japanese enterprise in Korea and back home; a dampening on Japanese industrial product and wage costs by arbitrarily keeping down the cost of goods and services imported from Korea; a dumping ground for Japan's surplus population and those restless at home—the urban unemployed, radical intellectuals, and disaffected military; a forward base for Japan's penetration of continental Asia, especially Manchuria; and finally, when Japan went to war, a significant supplemental source for industrial goods and manpower. Paradoxically, but not surprisingly, as the Japanese were modernizing Korea to serve Japan's advantage, Koreans were being forced to migrate to Japan proper or to Manchuria in sizable numbers, to working conditions which were often harsh, though better than those at home. Conversely, the Japanese in Korea not only lived better than Koreans did, they lived better than their countrymen did in Japan.

And so we must be very cautious how we judge the obvious quantitative improvement in Korea's physical economic environment under the Japanese. If we focus on how the system worked in fact, we soon discover many characteristics which worked to the advantage of the Japanese and the disadvantage of the Koreans. Among those economic advantages for the Japanese we may note that half the capital formation in Korea was Japanese. Japanese entrepreneurs received tax advantages, loans and subsidies, and technical aid unavailable to Koreans. From 1911 to 1920 government licensing was required of all Korean enterprises, a policy supposedly designed to protect investors from incompetent Korean businessmen, but which actually eliminated serious Korean industrial competition. By 1920 the law had worked so well in discouraging Koreans and giving the Japanese an advantage that it could be repealed as a graceful gesture of Japanese reconciliation toward Koreans and as a symbol of success in Japan's reform of allegedly unscrupulous Korean business practice.

Ninety percent of the industrial or residential utility customers were Japanese. In marked contrast to Japan, rural Korea, where the Japanese were rarely found, had virtually no electricity. When forests, which had been nationalized, were subsequently turned over to private hands, the better ones were given to Japanese.

Among those economic factors which worked to the disadvantage of the Koreans was the fact that Korean laborers were paid one-third to one-half what Japanese received for the same work. By virtue of superior preparation and prior exposure to an industrial culture, and by deliberately reserving certain positions for their own, the Japanese predominated in managerial and skilled jobs, even in the labor-scarce wartime economy of the 1930s. A sizable part of the Korean labor force, particularly in the textile industry, was women and children, whom the Japanese were used to exploiting at minimum wages back home. During World War II, some one million Korean laborers were forced to serve outside Korea, especially in the Japanese home islands.

In addition, there were a number of contributing disabilities which the Japanese placed on Koreans hoping to compete with their imperial masters in their own country. First, education: Academic research projects were selected and funded because the Japanese found them useful, or at least interesting. Almost all Japanese in Korea were at school at state expense, neither of which was true for Koreans, who were basically educated to be loyal, productive hands. Those few Koreans who were allowed to pursue advanced education, especially in the liberal arts, were indoctrinated in the superiority of things Japanese and were expected to support Japan's colonial mission in Korea.

Second, the very structure of the economy was distorted to serve Japan's home island and not Korea's requirements. The transport infrastructure was laid out for Japanese military use; for example, railways were concentrated in the north where only a minority of the population resided. Mines were exploited for immediate gain; gold for the Japanese treasury, coal for the Japanese navy, and ultimately all metals for Japan's war adventures. The fishing industry was expanded and modernized, but under Japanese directors who depleted the grounds and sent the catch back to Japan. Korean foreign trade primarily was with Japan or elsewhere through its designated agents, and on terms unfavorable to Koreans, especially within a duty-free Japanese common market in which Koreans were unable to compete with more advanced and better capitalized Japanese production and distribution. The impressive industrial expansion of the 1930s was in response to Japan's needs, for example, producing a chemical industry which could not feasibly be established in Japan proper.

The third contributory disability was social. For example, the Japanese received either the major share (e.g., pensions) or exclusive benefit (e.g., grants to build and maintain Japanese religious shrines) from the government's social expenditures, while the Koreans' problems (e.g., poverty and prostitution) were considered a way of life among depraved colonial inferiors and appropriately ignored.

In spite of all these built-in disabilities, and without government protection or subsidy, Korean enterprise somehow persevered. But that enterprise was concentrated in consumer industries, such as rubber goods, textiles, and food processing, or in petty commerce, such as peddling and usurious money lending, none of which threatened the Japanese, who tolerated these activities as economic safety valves.

A number of Korean enterprises were tied to Japanese firms as sub-contractors or collecting agents, and even were managed or financed by Japanese. In brief, during the Japanese period, Korean entrepreneurs, whether they acted in the older or the modern sector of the economy, were a minority discriminated against in their own land, who contributed only marginally to the Japanese-sponsored economic modernization of Korea. Yet those Korean entrepreneurs who went abroad, especially to Manchuria, were successful economic innovators; clearly the problem was neither genetic nor cultural, but political.

The second major feature of the Japanese occupation economy was its *patrimonial character*, both with respect to what the Japanese contributed and to what they left standing from the dynastic period. For one, the power to determine and carry out Japan's economic policies in Korea was vested in a governor general, who was authorized to do so free from review of both the Japanese government at home and the Korean people. As the director, organizer, and financier of the modern, that is, Japanese, sector of the economy, the governor general was the preeminent economic actor and monopolist in Korea. Thus he could decide patrimonially the basic structure of Korean modernization; especially, who would receive economic favor and who would be ignored and harassed, and hence which elements of the economy would prosper and which would lag. It was he who decided to nurture the viable Japanese modern economy while deliberately leaving the older Korean economy, whose commercial and industrial sectors were primarily concerned with patrimonially exploited parasitic commercial capital, to survive on its own meager resources. Consequently, third, although the governor general proliferated formal, very modern commercial and industrial codes and regulations, he did nothing to shake the conviction of those Korean entrepreneurs who were emerging on the scene that the way to protect one's economic interests and survive, and perhaps prosper, was still to be opportunistically self-serving and somehow come to terms with a dangerously capricious and heartless bureaucracy, if possible by becoming a member of that bureaucracy, even as a menial.

The quintessential Japanese ploy to modernize yet maintain the patrimonial character of the Korean economy, however, was the land reform. First, by official manipulation of the registration process, most cultivators became tenants, responsible not only for continuing to pay rent in kind to Korean and then Japanese landlords at an exorbitant rate, but also now for satisfying the land's taxes in specie. This policy forced the cultivators into the commercial economy on disadvantageous terms, so that they could be further parted from what was left of their meager surplus after meeting their rent and tax obligations. Second, tenants were obliged to accept tenurial contracts which were so worded that landlords periodically and unilaterally (and hence patrimonially) determined the terms. This was not new to Korea, especially on royal and bureaucratically held land where the threat of unilateral expulsion had always existed, but the thoroughness and the facade of rational, legal legitimacy of it all was "modern." Third, tenants were obliged to bear the costs of their overlords' modernizing managerial decisions—such as more intense use of fertilizer and irrigation inputs, and growing rice where it was marginally cultivable—even though the tenants profited little from any increased productivity because of the official policy to depress rice prices to provide cheap food for urban Korea and Japan, and to raise rents collectible in that cheap rice to enable the cliental landlords to reap windfall profit from increased yields. To rub salt in the wound, fourth, landlords lent out part of the profit to their tenants at usurious rates, the return on which was reinvested in land purchases. Fifth, some tenants who could not meet their debts were forced to become wage laborers on the land, or they and their families were forced off the land into the overstaffed, and hence perpetually cheap, urban labor market. Sixth, patrimonial communitarian village agriculture survived because both the authorities and the landlords found it too convenient a means to control and discipline rural labor, especially to force on it tenant dues and taxes and such extra levies as corvée and local expenditures. Consequently, no truly modern commercial agriculture with a mobile "alienated" rural labor force emerged. The peasantry continued to be subordinated within the confines of an old social economy with the full blessing of a "modern" Japanese governor general. Seventh, the few, but not insignificant, viable small proprietary holdings that had emerged in the late imperial period, which some observers believe might have become the source of a modern productive Korean agriculture, were destroyed by nationalizing and incorporating them into the Oriental Development Company's holdings, which were turned over to Japanese landlords. Since those tracts were in already developed areas and larger than Koreans were accustomed to cultivate, other Korean farmers were squeezed into ever smaller holdings and improverishment, all of which the Japanese justified on the modern, rational economic ground of profitability, claiming such hardships to be inevitable consequence of Korean "sloth."

In time, catalyzed by an upsurge in Korean nationalism and the introduction of Marxist ideology into the countryside by urban intellectuals, the Korean cultivators came to protest the injustice of it all. Tenant strikes, media advertisements, and noisy demonstrations at landlord residences were common in the 1920s. The depression of the 1930s was most devastating, since rice prices fell while tenant rents did not. The government offered some palliatives, such as guidance in self-help, a few model village programs, and limited opportunities for farm women to earn extra income, but precious little was appropriated for rural improvement. In fact, the *total* amount spent on agriculture through all of Japanese rule was equivalent to one year's war chest levy of the 1940s! Clearly, the Japanese had decided that Korean cultivators, primarily tenants, must carry the burden of capitalizing not only Korean agriculture but the urban commercial and industrial infrastructure as well, and must do so through rent and taxes rather than through increasing the soil's productivity. But in the war economy of the 1940s, the governor general abruptly changed course, largely sidestepping the landlords by imposing his own grain collection, rationing farm inputs, imposing a labor draft, and setting contractual terms, sometimes in the tenants' favor; all to encourage the cultivators' compliance with Japanese military requirements. And since most landlords were Japanese and left Korea in 1945, the Republic's land reform of the 1950s was anticipated and feasible.

All this is crucial because, although within six months after the 1945 surrender the colonial government was no more, leaving behind a vacuum in all fields (for example, in agriculture half the technicians and most of the key administrators had been Japanese) and hence the Japanese role in Korean economic history seemed a closed book, the Americans were not only to retain but also to refine and build upon the Japanese design, passing that along as the American contribution to the emergent Republic, in the process bridging a vital gap between the prior Korean-Japanese and contemporary economies. First, the Americans encapsulated—vested—all former Japanese public and private property in government, and consequently patrimonial, hands. Second, the Americans *added* to patrimonial political control of the economy by retaining the ODC and giving it jurisdiction over activities and property never under government control during the colonial period, such as grain collecting. Third the Americans, assuming that the *Japanese* patrimonial administrative structure was a *Korean* given, trained Koreans to fill slots and perform functions vacated by departing Japanese rather than overhauling or at least seriously restructuring the existing administration, as the Americans were then doing in Japan proper. Fourth, the Americans completed Japanese schemes, such as irrigation projects, without ever questioning the way in which those projects were originally drawn up, financed, carried out, and in whose interest they had been initiated. Fifth, although to their credit the Americans did try to act responsibly by rationalizing the inventory and then the disposal of ODC-vested property as a lesson to Koreans, they soon gave up in the face of what was termed the "slow learning" of Koreans. I suggest that, to the contrary, the Koreans were quick to seize upon a golden, once-in-a-lifetime opportunity of gaining access to what was then the greatest prebendal cornucopia in Korean history. The emerging politicians were eager to provide rewards for themselves after being cut out of economic spoils and public office by the Japanese for over half a century, as well as to offer a share to those willing to become their clients. Nonpoliticans were only too willing to gain access to ODC wealth by subverting American procedures and restraints by bribery, and even when they obtained the privilege legally, they abused the trust by plundering the property. For all these reasons I conclude that, like the Japanese before them, a nonpatrimonial United States paradoxically was instrumental in further refurbishing (modernizing) the time-honored Korean patrimonial notion of how to organize and exploit an economy.[14]

## Some Final Comments on Patrimonialism and Economic Development

Economists are aware of similarities between late nineteenth- and early twentieth-century Korea and certain western societies on the eve of the great Industrial Revolution which are considered prerequisite for the emergence of a modern, developed economy; namely, a burgeoning monetarization; the commercialization of craft industry; local private challenges to state-sponsored monopolies; a proficiency in mathematics and mechanics which was being applied creatively and practically, especially in agriculture; a well-educated bureaucracy experienced in management, record keeping, and tax collecting; international trading; and especially vanguard entrepreneurs, that is, those who, often against great odds, brought people and resources together creatively at a critical point in economic time to add to, and even to redirect, the existing economy.

In the Korean case, such entrepreneurs emerged especially during the Japanese occupation at the very time that Korea's imperial masters were quite unsympathetic toward indigenous economic innovation. Without benefit of connections or education, yet through thrift and seizing opportunity, these individuals accumulated capital and produced for the domestic market, competing with and even replacing their Japanese rivals. The most notable were those who concentrated in the north; the prime example, a textile company whose proprietors were technologically efficient, aggressive marketers even overseas, ever willing to improve existing or introduce novel production and management techniques, intensive in-trainers of their labor, exploiters of Korea's natural advantage of labor intensity yet willing to automate to increase productivity, and ever responsive to consumer needs, including the Japanese military. Many of these entrepreneurs fled south in 1945 to reestablish in the ROK, and to contribute significantly to the industrialization of the ROK. Similarly, contrary to the stereotype as lazy conservatives, Korean farmers have been creative risk-takers, especially in the past two decades. They are increasingly reacting positively to the expanding market, improving productivity through novel cropping and such innovations as vinyl canopies, all on their own initiative or through self-generated cooperatives, government recognition and support coming only after the fact.

Yet in spite of these very positive contributions, certain other characteristics, ones which economists consider counterproductive to development, have prevailed. For example, classical Korean science and technology, for all its sophistication, was concrete and specific. Thus it did not inspire an integrated scientific scheme or methodology, especially not a scientific view of the world nor a positive, empirical revolution in knowledge-gathering comparable to the European Renaissance. The prevailing scientific wisdom took a dim view of experimenting, because the primary purpose of data collecting was to justify deductively derived, morally acceptable conclusions which in most cases already had appropriate illustrations. Alchemy, for example, is more than the parent of modern chemistry, it is the symbol of scientists' desire to transform nature; in Korea it was of minor interest. Yet, in spite of all these adverse influences, Korea did produce its share of creative scientific pragmatists. But they were separated both by philosophy and by class from meaningful contact with manual, potentially industrial, actors who might have objectified their ideas and sparked a true industrial revolution in Korea.

Another example is that Korean economic organization, even today, predominantly is small-scale, dependent primarily on bonds of kin and locality both to recruit and to maintain solidarity and discipline. Such bonds are considered so important that they can take precedence over skill, which not surprisingly is resented by those outside the charmed circle. Hence, productive cooperation among economic organizations has been both rare and very limited in scope, in contrast to the more prevalent collegiality, in which members unrelated by blood or geography are highly suspicious of each other. It was the Japanese who brought the joint corporate economic idea to Korea, but with only limited success and almost exclusively in the export-related modern commercial and industrial sectors. Today, individuals join chambers of commerce and similar organizations more for social prestige than to promote their economic interests.

Those economists who stress the positive similarities between the Korean and western economic experiences consider such counter characteristics as problems—bottlenecks—solvable through transplantation of universally valid technical and intellectual experience of the western developed economies. In the process, the local culture— the quirks of the Korean character—somehow must be reworked to serve rather than work against the development process. For example, since Koreans seem to work better in groups than as individuals, we should stress group rather than individual work incentives so as to generate the kind of productive behavior necessary to "break through" existing economic barriers.

I have grave misgivings about depending primarily on such an approach. An essential thesis of the present study is that western economic theory, market or Marxist, when applied to certain economies such as the Korean, is wanting. I do not believe so out of respect for the idiosyncratic differences between Korean and western culture, which I cannot deny, nor because of differences between "traditional" and "modern" economies, but rather because of differences between particular *kinds* of economies. That is, I see as crucial that Korea now, as in the past, is a patrimonial economy; one that is *qualitatively* (institutionally) different from the presently developed, once-feudal economies, even though the Korean economy was and is similar in certain *formal* particulars to the developed economies. I believe that it is on the theoretical scale of such institutional difference that the developmentally favorable and unfavorable characteristics of the Korean economy must be weighed before remedial programs are proffered, if development is to have any chance of success. [15]

# 6

# Occupation

## The Secular Learned and the Bureaucracy

I wish to discriminate heuristically between certain occupations termed primary and others termed secondary, and to analyze the goals, interests, and standards of the Korean patrimonial occupational structure on the basis of such a distinction. The primary occupations, historically, are agricultural hand labor befitting the masses and secular, formal learning intimately associated with administrative statecraft for the worthy few. (See also Chapter 2.) In this reasoning, the secular learned (I deliberately leave discussion of the religious learned to Chapter 9) stand apart as a discrete occupational grouping. In Korea, unlike China, the members of this privileged grouping have been a nonroyal but hereditary aristocracy.

A minority in that aristocracy was able to survive the Korean colonial period by serving the Japanese as clerks and flunkies. At independence they moved into the senior administrative and even decision-making positions once held by their Japanese superiors, commanding the national and local governments, the courts, the police, and the new government corporations. The significance of this occupational metamorphosis is that these individuals' values and operational procedures survived to motivate and guide the succeeding generation of planners, decision-makers, and managers recruited to carry out Park's development programs.

The administrators' vitality has been challenged by others, but not very successfully. For example, because the administrators are rooted in the executive, they view themselves and are viewed as the prime antagonists of the *legislators*. Within the executive itself, the president ever attempts to co-opt the administrative upper echelon and alienate it from its subordinates in order to subordinate the bureaucracy to presidential patrimonial whim. Finally the administrators are not beyond the review of their natural allies, that is, their future colleagues (students in higher institutes of learning) and the members of the learned community not in government service (the academic and nonacademic intellectuals).

Criticism of officials by *intellectuals* not in authority is a venerable tradition, legitimized by the Chinese patrimonial model and intensified by the Korean penchant for factional disputation. During the Japanese period, intellectuals played a vital role both in preserving the national literate culture, including the Korean language, and the sense of national identity against persistent Japanese attempts to dilute and even exterminate them, and also in renovating the cultural heritage so it could better serve the needs of an emerging modern society. Although few in number, these resisters and innovators struck a responsive chord in the general populace, which fashioned some of them into national folk heroes. Those contemporary intellectuals who now are shut out of participation in the political process by design or choice have kept alive this spirit of fidelity to principle and resistance to arbitrary authority. Thus, although some intellectuals have been willing to offer their technical expertise to the government, for example helping to draw up the Five-Year Economic Plans, most are critical of Korea's modernizing programs, believing that they serve the materialist goals of the favored few rather than the needs of the vast majority of Koreans. These intellectuals denounce those among them who do serve as traitors to the nation and to their occupational responsibilities and cause. Rather like their out-of-power forebears, such intellectuals see themselves as cultivators of their inner selves, awaiting the day when virtue will triumph and they will be called upon to reassert their historic role in defining and applying the society's ethos through statecraft.

*Students* straddle two roles, one which they share with intellectuals and one which defines them as patrimonial bureaucrats in embryo. The critical intellectual role reflects the idealism of Koreans of any age who are learned, but especially her young people, who see themselves as the only element in the division of labor free enough to be able to express the true aspirations of the Korean soul. But that expression must take into account the realities of having to compete to enter, and then to maintain a satisfactory record at, the prestigious

Seoul universities in particular, from which the polity's administrative elite is selected. That record requires that students not be blackballed and expelled as political troublemakers by an authority which cannot understand why the vision of future rewards does not make the students more peaceful and devoted to preparing themselves for their adult, especially bureaucratic, roles. Yet government's surveillance and petty harassment, and the constant frustrations of campus life—the overcrowding and inadequate facilities especially, which the polity does not remedy—ever tempt any number of students to overcome their realistic reticence and actively join those critical of existing authority and the society in general. The same quandary exists after graduation, particularly if the students go abroad. Should they return to Korea and contribute their skills, or join the "brain drain" in protest or frustration against a society from which they feel alienated? The authorities are just as ambiguous in deciding how to react. They need the talent and are embarrassed by the students' often-articulate attacks, yet out of Korea the carping critics pose less of a threat to authority's mobilization and control of the populace than they do at home.

*Professionals* are another component of the learned. In older Korea they were ambiguously located between the learned and unlearned, unworthy to serve as administrators yet obviously superior to the unlettered masses. However, professionals did not constitute a distinctive occupational grouping in that they were expected to align their interests with the rest of the learned since they served as administrative aides, either as clerks or technicians, for example, as interpreters. Nevertheless, since, in patrimonial reasoning, administrators were generalists who specialized only in human nature and were alone judged worthy to command (see Chapter 2), the qualitative distinction between them and the professionals was never obscure. The very symbol of the convergence yet divergence of these two occupational categories was the two-track civil service examination and appointment system. The Japanese modernized this distinction when they introduced into Korea their own civil service differentiation between a higher and a regular (temporary) service with virtually no upward mobility from the lower to the higher service. In Japanese times the distinction was fundamentally ethnic, in that very few Koreans were ever appointed to the higher civil service, while the reverse was true for the Japanese. As was true of many features of Japanese modernization, the Republic accepted this cleavage between higher and ordinary appointees when it established its own civil service. The significance of the distinction is that the modern equivalents of the old

professionals have had to fight against a legacy of occupational dep-
recation and discrimination. For example, physicians of late imperial
Korea predominantly were women who were primarily entertainers
of varying degrees of moral integrity. Consequently, the first modern
hospitals found it difficult to recruit females as nurses, or to interest
either sex in becoming modern physicians, since the existing folk
medicine was considered a craft for only the society's lowly. Although
medicine is becoming more attractive these days, in part because of
the high income in a period of constant inflation, in part because of
the insecurities of political employment, some one-third of the physicians and some one-half of the nurses are practicing abroad, constituting the most critical element in the brain drain, in part because
of lingering prejudice in Korea.

*Attorneys-at-law* are professionals worthy of special attention because of having been considered self-serving, and thus being subject
to the watchful eye of the moral administrators who have been charged
with making the society's key legal decisions. The Japanese intensified the distinction between administrative lawgiver and private attorney by applying a nonpatrimonial German principle of their own
modern legal system to the existing Korean patrimonial milieu; to
wit, the Japanese recognized as legal professionals only those who
had received a basic higher education in an approved legal curriculum—significantly, not an advanced professional legal education—
and who had passed a very vigorous screening equivalent to the civil
service examination. Most of those very few who did qualify were appointed as judges or public prosecutors as the punitive occupational
arm of authority. In contrast, by default, the populace's legal interests
were entrusted to those attorneys who were in private practice because they had not passed the bar, or who were self-educated and
even uneducated, yet who felt themselves resourceful (and to some
foolish) enough to try to manipulate the legal system in their clients'
behalf. Although some were committed to justice, especially in the
national cause against the Japanese, most attorneys were accepting of
alien rule, for no other reason than that they were powerless to resist
their occupier's rule by ordinance and police edict.

The consequent image of the private attorney as a morally devious
character ever to be watched by populace and polity alike, and the
feeling that the official administrative (including military) patrimonial
law has primacy over civil law, was carried over into the Republic. The
Korean polity, like its Japanese predecessor, admits to the bar each
year only the number of candidates whose services are required by
the state, although in greater numbers than under the Japanese be-

cause of the escalating development programs. The candidates now are professionally and liberally educated. But their professors are prohibited from practicing law, and they, their students, and attorneys who once were their students, are positively discouraged from legally reviewing the actions of their administrative moral betters, specifically by taking a too liberal, legalistic approach to the polity's penchant for "emergency" decision-making. Private practice is also expanding, including into such new, specialized fields as real estate, investment, and commerce. But attorneys still are not noted for being outspoken champions of the rule of law or human rights. Part of this may derive from the fact that any number of them apprentice in government service before going into practice, where they are duly socialized in what they can and cannot do within the limits of existing patrimonial political reality.[1]

## Farmers

Until most recently, farming has been the normative secular occupation of the formally unlearned. Land is considered a national asset and trust. Consequently, on the one hand, regardless of the specifications of tenure, the polity, as the self-appointed patrimonial guardian of the national interest, has supervised and, if necessary, intervened into and directed such activities as crop selection and irrigation, or has forcibly relocated the cultivators. On the other hand, cultivators are expected to serve that national (moral) interest by providing sustenance and capital resources for the patrimonial society in general and for the polity and its learned administrators in particular, in the form of both regularly exacted dues in kind or in labor and special emergency levies. Hence, on both counts, although farmers are idealized and even glorified by the learned, who usually never come in contact with cultivators, few in the society wish to become farmers if other occupational opportunities exist.

Those who have administered the cultivators and collected their dues, whether state agents or prebend-holding landlords, most typically have been rural absentees who employ local resident administrators and intermediaries, all of whom occupationally identified with the learned and not with the cultivators. The Japanese reinforced that mode by broadening the ranks of the exploiters, especially to include themselves, and by introducing a more exacting (that is, modern) system of extracting cultivator dues. Republican authority, although it further modernized rural Korea, notably by eliminating the debilitating absentee landlord system, simultaneously strengthened the old pattern of supervising and exploiting farmers in the interest of morally superior outsiders, increasingly the polity itself. [2]

## The Military

The military, although considered a secondary occupation, always has contributed vitally to the Korean division of labor by protecting the patrimonial social order, especially its agricultural surplus, from external predators—which, given the realities of Korea's geography and the restlessness of Korea's neighbors, has been no mean feat. And yet the more necessary and efficient the military has been in fulfilling its historic role, the more a quandary has arisen. For a patrimonial division of labor requires that as many males as possible be either bureaucrats or farmers. But a large standing army diverts individuals from either of these two occupations, in the process both diminishing agricultural productivity and, through military consumption, deflecting a sometimes significant portion of the surplus rightfully due the civil administrators. With their resources thus curtailed, the administrators' effectiveness declines, and with it their ability to spread morality in the society, the very rationale of their right to rule. At such time the military is well able to exploit a co-optation of the cultivators and their surplus to destroy the patrimonial social order and replace it with a feudal order.

The classic patrimonial means to escape from this dilemma is to have the cultivators assume the role of ordinary soldiery and the civil administrators assume the role of military officialdom for limited periods during military emergencies, after which time all resume their primary roles. In this way, agriculture will not suffer, and a professional military with distinctive occupational interests will not arise. This arrangement seems to have been challenged in a major way only once, during a twelfth-thirteenth century interlude when military aristocrats rose up and established their own authority, which some Korean and Japanese scholars have likened to its contemporary counterpart in Japan. Certainly there are striking parallels in administrative organization, military-civil relations, and the petty aristocratic background of the military officials. But there are significant differences. Especially in patrimonial Korea, unlike emerging feudal Japan, the civil administrators were not sidestepped and politically enfeebled by a feudal military seeking only legitimacy from civil authority. Rather the Korean military reinvigorated the floundering civilian machinery with its own superior discipline and organization, contenting itself with exploiting its occupational advantage only to insure that the choicest prebends went to the military rather than to civilians. Thus was Korea's major chance to institutionalize a feudal occupational order, if it ever was feasible, irretrievably lost.

The subsequent, last imperial dynasts resubordinated the military to civil rule. A bona fide army was established, but it was civilly controlled and centralized through co-optation of the key elements of the then-existing autonomous provincial military. Civilian provincial governors held the military and police commands in their individual bailiwicks. Military officials were separately tracked from civil officials, and the military's education so designed to induce them to identify occupationally with, and never challenge, civil bureaucratic interests.

On the other hand, the ordinary military was primarily recruited from the ranks of farmers who were forced to serve as a corvée for two or three years, unless they were able to buy out the (tax) duty. Pertinently, as corvée draftees such soldiers served even in time of war as military-support laborers rather than as professional soldiers, and in peace as transport aides or cultivators on militarily granted prebendary land turned over to the military commanderies to make them self-supporting. In brief, and in sum, ordinary military service had been successively downgraded over the ages from a privilege to a responsibility, and finally to a corvée and tax obligation which was to be avoided if at all possible.

Unfortunately, this kind of military establishment, although it served well enough the patrimonial occupational interests of an administrative-agricultural institutional order in prolonged periods of peace, was unable to cope with military adversity, especially foreign invasion. At such time the civil bureaucrats were forced to raise additional manpower outside the peasant corvée dragnet. These newcomers were organized into Righteous Armies, which harassed an enemy either in cooperation with regulars or on their own. Nevertheless, the recruits, like the regulars, were officered by civil bureaucrats, and once the crisis was over were returned to their primary occupation, farming. When the foreigner penetrated Korea in the nineteenth and twentieth centuries, the spirit of earlier Righteous Armies was evoked anew to defend sacred Korea, but alas this time in vain. The ineffective, almost comical bureaucratic standing army suffered the ultimate indignity of being abolished by the fiat of the Japanese overlord.

The contemporary Korean military owes its origins to two major sources, both of Japanese colonial inspiration; namely, those officers and men who trained and served under the Japanese and the guerrillas who operated against the Japanese on both sides of the northern frontier. The former are of special interest since they constitute the core of the ROK's modern, professional military occupational grouping. This core expanded with American support and training during and after the crucible of the Korean War, which converted an inept glorified constabulary into one of the most efficient professional fighting machines in the world. Like all truly modern armies, Korea's became skilled not only in combat but also in administrative organization, decision-making, and control. In contrast, civil authority, though adept in obtaining independence, became increasingly unable to control constant factional infighting over prebends, not to speak of solving the society's fundamental problems, and hence steadily lost the popular confidence. The military, comparing its own success with the bumbling performance of the civilians, came to view itself as the sole hope of the nation's survival. It rose up in 1961 to replace the civilians, in substance if not in form—that is, in civil garb, and has ruled Korea ever since.

That element in the military which engineered the coup, established itself, and continues in authority is the modern administrative staff and not the barracks command; that is, that element most capable of achieving the patrimonial military goal, ever glimmering since the twelfth century, of co-opting the civil administration to insure that the military rather than civilians receives the social order's major prebends. Thus ultimate occupational success in the military came to imply civil decision-maker and senior administrator rather than military commander and, for key retainers on the active or retired lists, headships of government enterprises or private corporations. Likewise the path to bureaucratic success henceforth came as readily through a military education and career as through a civil university and service.[3]

### Artisans and Workers

*Artisanship* constitutes the next subcategory of secondary occupations, because historically, like the military, though it is vital to the division of labor, it has diverted attention and manpower from agriculture, the primary mass occupation. Consequently, whenever possible artisanship was integrated with agriculture, preferably by being performed during the slack work season when it would not compete with cultivation. In those instances when artisanship was severed from agriculture, especially when it was urbanized, it had to be politically supervised and so organized to insure that it strengthened rather than challenged the patrimonial division of labor in particular and the moral institutional order in general. Thus, specific crafts were judged, and hence rewarded or discouraged, according to how well they contributed to the patrimonial blueprint. For example, blacksmithing and carpentry were rated highly because they built and embellished the palaces and monuments of the state, while artisanship which catered to consumer whim, dissipating part of the surplus rightly due to the moral administrators, was frowned upon.

The initial means authority used to insure that artisanship positively served patrimonial interests was to bind the craftsmen in official service. But in time it was considered more efficient and economical to exploit free commoner corvée craftsmen to overlap and then replace the bound artisans. For example, many of the routine clerical and maintenance jobs of local civil administrative outposts depended on such daily corvée drafts. In those instances compensatory lunch was served, a custom maintained today in many government bureaus. Those not formally called up, but on the corvée roster, might have to provide certain services in their spare time; for example, male cultivators fashioned armaments while their wives and children wove textiles, and others were forced to provide maintenance support for those on active service. Finally, authority came to believe that it had more to gain occupationally by regulating and taxing free artisans than binding them in corvée, since a growing complexity in the division of labor made it difficult to properly supervise and control artisans, and especially since countryside local merchants on contract, using their own resources and hiring free labor, were better able to fill the government's requirements in, for example, coinage, arms, and paper than were artisan monopolists under political patronage.

Though ultimately in certain respects freer of retraints in patrimonial Korea than in feudal Europe, dynastic Korean artisans, unlike feudal free manual labor, were forced to serve court or bureaucracy on its own work and wage terms, since often as not it supplied the buildings, tools, and even raw materials (or the right of access to them); official fees and bribes had to be paid to obtain government artisan contracts; and the government competed with independent manual entrepreneurship to the latter's disadvantage because the polity exploited its natural advantage of unpaid corvée labor and impressed into corvée service the most enterprising and competent artisans (even though in theory they were exempt from corvée). Above all, whether bound, corvée-obligated, or free, artisan labor was ever subject to patrimonial rather than feudal regulation by officials, usually local magistrates or their proxy, whom the free artisans in particular were required to bargain with or bribe to pursue their legitmate occupational interests. Perhaps worse than the cost burden, which could be taken into account, was the ever-present possibility that a particular official suddenly would repudiate a substantive agreement which he had made with a particular artisan, thus abusing the artisan's trust—for example, by converting a public corvée to private advantage; by increasing a service obligation, sometimes only to increase the bribe for exemption, particularly for the most skilled and competent; or by refusing to honor an exempted or reduced obligation—any of which decisions the artisans, as ordinary men, were powerless to review.

I infer from this that by submerging manual artisanship with other occupations, at first agriculture and then commerce, by treating artisanship as a temporary, peripheral activity, by forcing menial obligations (such as cleaning urban streets) on those who potentially might have developed specialized skills, by permitting artisan professionalization only among those who could not convert their skills into occupational advantage (the Buddhist clergy comes immediately to mind), or by restricting certain crafts to bureaucratic aides, the administrators of dynastic Korea deliberately prevented the emergence of such manual professional pride as occurred in the feudal occupational orders.

All these occupational disabilities provided the context for the Japanese-created modern Korean *laborer*. As they had earlier at home, the Japanese deliberately destroyed the older rural handicrafts in Korea to open a market for cheap Japanese manufactures. The land reform and the consequent rural exodus provided a large pool of unskilled hands which could be employed in urban industry cheaply and on work terms set by the colonial master. Women played a key role in the Japanese industrial design. Some imperial Korean women had been skilled artisans, for example, weavers. But the Japanese, as at home, were more interested in exploiting women as grossly underpaid, docile, unskilled workers, particularly as farm wives raising silkworms in their spare time, as servants (for Japanese especially), and most notably as urban textile workers intimidated by close supervision and iron discipline. Since most textile workers were single youngsters working for dowry money, they could be treated shabbily as temporary employees.

Although the Japanese discouraged Koreans from obtaining more than a rudimentary education, the Japanese could not prevent Koreans from learning modern industrial techniques and values on the job, at first in textiles and then in the complex heavy and chemical industries. Yet in spite of such exposure to and acceptance of industrialism before independence and the devotion to industrial growth and modern technological training since independence, certain older, patrimonially related negative attitudes toward and exploitation of labor persists. For example: As under the Japanese, the rural exodus goes on in a quantity and of a distressed quality which enables the government to keep wages below productivity; and women working because they have to are compensated at a fraction of men's wages because it is claimed that they are only collecting dowry money. And to recall still an earlier age, regardless of the rhetoric, the government exacts corvée to carry out its rural uplift and community development programs. Although many Korean workers are highly skilled and professionalized these days, as befitting a modern industrial order, and labor has contributed vitally to Korea's present economic "miracle" and modern image, most Koreans still regard those who work with their hands, even well-compensated construction engineers or laboratory scientists, as socially inferior to those who administer others. [4]

## Merchants and Industrialists

At first blush the Korean patrimonial occupational order is paradoxical. On the one hand, commerce is judged secondary and deprecated as a potential threat to the primary bureaucratic-agricultural occupational axis, because commerce both taps the cultivator surplus due the bureaucrat and tempts both cultivator and bureaucrat into debt, extracting in compensation potentially patrimonially dangerous concessions from the bureaucrat and alienating the cultivator from the land. Yet, on the other hand, imperial Korean commerce was highly organized and differentiated, technically specialized in such operations as factoring, sophisticated in such procedures as double-entry bookkeeping, and a major contributor to the economy's wealth.

The paradox disappears however with appreciation that commerce is tolerated, and even encouraged, but only as long as it does not directly challenge and can even be made to strengthen the primary occupational nexus. That goal has been diversely achieved. In brief (please review Chapter 5 for details of some of the following observations), in the imperial period, first, since significant commercial activity was bureaucratically owned or controlled, it gave priority to bureaucratic desires, public or personal. Second, private traders who leased public facilities were supervised directly, their working time, pricing, and quality and variety of wares all being decided by political fiat. Third, successful trade was highly taxed, subject to official extortion (bribery), and otherwise periodically mined, as both a legitimate fiscal privilege and a morally justified harassment of a potentially dangerous secondary occupation. Only that commerce escaped government fiscal or political interest which was small-scale and impermanent, such as the Seoul morning and rural periodic markets, hinterland peddling, and the part-time village stores. Fourth, the commercial transport and communications infrastructure was situated and organized to serve bureaucratic and not private needs. Since that structure was constructed and maintained through corvée, it was poorly serviced. Fifth, as sophisticated as were certain commercial features, others such as vehicular transport and, with the penetration of the money economy, coinage remained primitive. Finally, modern commercial innovation, when it did occur, especially in the closing days of imperial rule, came primarily from official initiatives in response to *political* considerations, especially the fear that Chinese or Japanese commercial penetration would be the cutting edge of colonial subservience.

The implication I wish to draw from the discussions of this and the previous section is that Korean modern industralists inherited the older negative occupational evaluation and vexing occupational ground rules of both manual artisans (whether workers or entrepreneurs) and commercialists. The Japanese, who introduced the modern industrial division of labor into Korea, certainly did not alter the prevailing dynastic ethos; in fact they reinforced it. They required industrial entrepreneurs to beg for a prebendarily granted privilege to act in the division of labor, and then to submit their actions to the regulations and review of an unsympathetic bureaucracy. Industrialists, consequently, learned to survive by circumventing surveillance, by bribery, and by guile; that is, by any means fair or foul, which, to be sure, did little to create a mature (that is, developed) industrial image in the eyes of either the authorities or the Korean people. And none of this has fundamentally changed under republican rule, in spite of the fact that industrialism has become the very talisman of contemporary political charisma. The Korean circumstance is in marked contrast to the Japanese, for example, in which a novel, prestigious term, *Jitsugyōka*—literally, "men who undertake a real task"—was coined to give homage to those industrialists who were being encouraged by the government to spearhead the drive to economic development and political independence; but then, in spite of many patrimonial influences enculturated from China and Korea, Japan has never been a patrimonial society.[5]

## The Articulation, Organization, and Pursuit of Occupational Interests in Patrimonial Korea

Save for intellectuals-bureaucrats, the articulation, organization, and pursuit of occupational interests are legitimate only when those interests are coordinated, if not integrated, with and ideally are subordinated to intellectual-bureaucratic occupational interests. Patrimonialists argue that this is just, because intellectuals-bureaucrats, a priori, are morally superior to all others existing or potentially existing in the division of labor, and thus have an eternal mandate to watch over the division of labor to perpetuate its patrimonial moral character. And the intellectuals-bureaucrats have diligently strived to fulfill that mandate against any and all opposition throughout the span of Korean history.

The *cultivators* of dynastic Korea protested and even rebelled against their bureaucratic oppressors, even helping to topple dynasties. But they never succeeded in, if they ever thought of, altering the patrimonial ground rules under which they were forced to pursue their occupational interests. Rather they sought only to remedy their immediate grievances. It has been suggested that this was due to the farmers' inability to organize effectively, given Korea's poor rural transport and natural communications facilities, which also encouraged parochial interests and loyalties, and thus factional bickering. Be that as it may, once appeased by graceful (prebendary) amelioration, the cultivators were willing to return to passive acceptance of the patrimonial status quo of bearable exploitation.

In contrast to the organizations which the Japanese overlords created for farmers, their own were never legitimized, and cultivator self-articulated grievances were never considered worthy of formal, that is, judicial, consideration. Cultivator efforts to express their interests and redress their grievances were judged politically subversive, and hence, if the farmers were not willing to temporize by the arbitration of the rural police, they were ruthlessly put down. Especially this was true of those who were organized into associations by outside urban intellectuals who articulated the ruralites' grievances as one constituent in an anticolonial national program. As under the Japanese, the Republic's rural organizations have been created and managed by, and in the occupational interest of, outsiders, especially bureaucrats intent on insuring that a sufficiency of the cultivators' surplus goes to the cities and into export. Farmers rarely if ever participate in the decision-making of their own organizations, e.g., the cooperatives, whose membership may be prescribed by government fiat (see Chapter 4).

At first sight, *mercantile* and *artisan-industrial* occupationalists seem to have clearly articulated goals which they have pursued with great gusto through elaborately organized associations throughout Korea. But on closer inspection we observe that private mercantilists and artisans were never able to gain legal recognition for their right to organize and pursue their occupational interests free of bureaucratic patronal supervision and interference. The gilds exemplify this. They were few in number; were highly dispersed and locally rooted, encouraging parochial opportunism rather than, like the textile gilds of Italy and the Low Countries, stimulating national and even supranational pursuit and protection of vital occupational interests; were individually, internally disciplined and organized through solidary dependence on personal ties of kin and locality rather than, as in Europe, on impersonal, commonly shared occupational interests which might cut across kin and locality; and were forced to recruit universally by occupation, rather than, as in Europe, being allowed to determine selectively their own membership (e.g., separating rich and poor), and hence were prevented from excluding those who were deemed detrimental to the gild members' maximizing their occupational advantage. This last is especially important in Korea because mercantilists and artisans (-industrialists in embryo) too were not separately organized, insuring the subordination of industrial occupational interests to nondevelopmental mercantile interests. To add insult to occupational injury, the polity forced the gilds to collect taxes on their members, to serve as spies at such communication centers as inns, and to carry out government policies, such as the forced circulation of often-bad coins. In brief, the Korean gilds were mutual aid welfare organizations and social clubs and not interest groups. Chambers of Commerce are the modern counterparts of gilds. As their forebears, the chambers too accept government articulation of their interests and prefer to pursue those interests wherever possible through the bribed purchase of monopolistic privilege.

An oft-cited apparent exception to this pattern was the itinerant peddler gilds. They were strongly bonded internally through a strict code of common responsibility and trust, and their officers were democratically elected and hence positively supported by the members. They divided up jurisdiction over the market, thus avoiding the debilitating factional strife so characteristic of other mercantile and artisan organizations, while enabling the peddlers to function nationally through intergild agreements. In fact, the peddler gilds were the only nongovernment, national organs in precontemporary Korea. With such organization behind them, the peddlers were able to resist exploitation and interference into their occupational activities by local officials and country gentry. But central authority, rather than opposing, not only tolerated but even encouraged the peddler gilds, providing them with prebendary monopolistic privileges for fees and with working capital loans. In return the peddlers were always good taxpayers and active supporters of central authority and its interests, in the closing years of imperial rule especially by serving as spies and aiding the police to break up meetings of political opponents. This cozy arrangement between peddler and polity continued under the Japanese, although it must be stated that some peddlers gave up their lives in the cause of Korean nationalism; but this too was a political and not an occupational gesture.

Contemporary nonbureaucratic *intellectuals* are very wary of being accused of political subversion, which can amount to no more than foot-dragging on actively supporting the polity's articulation of the society's interests and how to pursue them, or not enthusiastically joining government-generated intellectual organizations. Professors are proscribed from forming their own interest groups as are students; even politically innocent university religious and social clubs are forbidden.

The *military* has always had its own organization the better to pursue its vital occupational responsibility (and interest) of preserving the Korean identity and polity from enemies. But at the height of its occupational vitality in the twelfth century, and now since 1961, the military never chose the path of setting up a discrete authority to pursue and achieve potentially distinctive occupational interests. Rather, whether politically subordinate to civil authority or singularly powerful, and now whether in or out of uniform, the military has always seen fit to serve the occupational interests of civil patrimonial authority instead of striking out on its own.

However, the one occupational grouping whose organization and conduct best exemplifies the subordination of nonbureaucratic to bureaucratic occupational interests is *modern labor*. First and foremost, the labor movement was founded on and has always been associated with politics. During the Japanese occupation, but especially after the labor movement was forced to go underground in the 1930s, laborers were organized and their aspirations articulated by those who, although not exclusively leftists, still were ever trying to integrate workers into an all-embracing political struggle against Japanese colonial rule. These secret cells surfaced in 1945 as enterprise Workers Committees. Unions, now legal for the first time, were molded into an all-Korea General Council of Korean Trade Unions (GCKTU), which clamored for such political objectives as the repatriation of Japanese consultants and industrial managers, punishment of collaborators, and American support for the liberal-left government. The political right under Rhee was not idle. It encouraged political factional strife within GCKTU, creating a rival General Federation of Korean Labor Unions with those laborers sympathetic to the right. As the leftist unions became politically more extreme, the rightists, with covert police support, seized the opportunity to attack physically, and prevailed on the Americans to outlaw the leftist unions. After independence, Rhee brought the surviving unions under his firm control by seeing to it that his clients were the ones elected to the unions' significant positions of leadership. In 1953 he restructured the unions into a monolithic Federation of Korean Trade Unions, designating it as one of the five appendages of his Liberal party, and appointing its president as minister of health and social affairs. In recompense, the federation's leaders mobilized the members to agitate, and at election time gathered votes for the ruling Liberal party. Park, for all his criticism of Rhee's high-handed tactics, followed Rhee's lead in using unions to rally workers "spontaneously" in support of the regime's political programs.

Second, the polity controls the unions and determines labor policy as it sees fit by applying both stick and carrot. As the stick, the polity has claimed that any kind of union agitation only encourages the DPRK to believe its own propaganda that the ROK is ripe for internal revolution. Hence, ever since the Korean War, save for a brief period between the Rhee and Park hegemonies, strikers have been treated as traitors. All labor unions must be approved of beforehand by the government, which also has the right to dissolve them at any time if their behavior does not meet with its approval. The union chain of command is centralized to insure effective control over union policymaking, not only by the unions' chief executives but through them by the Korean chief executive(s) as well. As the carrot, the polity is the prime employer in Korea, and hence its willingness to maintain if not in-

crease prebendal funding for public projects vitally affects the livelihood of many workers.

Besides political passivity what the government desires is that
unions focus upon increasing their workers' diligence and productivity at wages and under conditions conducive to strengthening the
export economy and to encouraging foreign investment in Korea,
leaving the issue of determining those wages and working conditions
to the patrimonial benevolence of the polity. To this end, since strikes
are illegal and there is precious little opportunity for labor and management to discuss, let alone bargain over, festering disputes, the patronal authority can step in as it wishes to reconcile the parties on the
polity's terms (see also the upcoming sixth observation). Labor standards do exist, in part the legacy of the American occupation, but
they are rarely enforced (rule by model), and most small plants are
not covered unless the polity so chooses. Korea is not a member of the
International Labor Organization, and thus Korea is not obligated,
even on paper, to conform to international labor standards or rules;
again providing the polity with a patrimonial mandate to act or not as
it wishes. It must be pointed out that none of this is novel to the Republic but, as is the case with many features of "modern" Korea, was
originally decided by the Japanese. Then labor was controlled by the
Finance and Industry Departments, which provides an obvious clue
to the polity's notion of labor's expected contribution to the division of
labor. The Americans established a labor department, but Rhee diminished it to a bureau within the Ministry of Social Affairs. Park subsequently created a cabinet rank department, but this was a hollow
victory since by then it was perfectly clear that labor and its interests
were but an appendage to authority's organization and interests.

Third, subordination of labor's organization and interests to the
polity has been expedited by the union leaders themselves, since they
do not identify with their own rank and file but with the polity. Some
observers attribute this to the circumstance that the older leadership
received its training in the pre-World War II underground, primarily
in political struggle against the Japanese, and especially that much of
the younger leadership is well educated, and hence in this patrimonial division of labor politically ambitious. Whatever the source,
union leaders have little interest and even less experience in collective
bargaining or otherwise representing their nominal constituents, the
unionized workers.

Fourth, modern labor, in spite of its increasingly vital contribution
to the division of labor, has not been able to shake off the negative

(secondary) occupational image of its artisan predecessor; surveys indicate that even skilled workers have little or no occupational pride. This view has been reinforced by authority's decision not to upgrade the low (though rising) level of labor skills and discipline through formal, technical or on-the-job training, but rather to exploit an ever-available surplus of unskilled hands, so as to conserve the polity's investment capital for proliferating the often showy edifices that are internationally associated with a modern economy.

Fifth, private employers feel free to ignore existing laws and abuse labor, knowing full well that political contributions and the benign neglect of the government will allow them to do so. Among the worst abusers are foreigners who know that the authorities are less frightened of the wrath of workers than they are that the foreigners will withdraw from Korea if not placated. Industrial parks established for foreign enterprises thus are virtually extraterritorial enclaves, within which non-Koreans can set their own labor policies, typically unfavorable to the Korean workers.

Nevertheless, sixth, it is true that in spite of all these disabilities labor has always tried as best it could to pursue its occupational, especially wage, interests. Even in the Japanese period, though it was illegal and dangerous, workers did strike; in fact the Seoul Electric and Wonsan Dock strikes, solidarily supported by workers all over Korea, were among the few instances of effective protest of any sort by Koreans during the later occupation. Labor disputes are common enough these days, and ever increasing, in some measure because the labor force is growing, particularly among the more volatile young. However, most disputes are short-lived because the workers know and expect that a nervous government will soon prod employers to redress the economic grievances in the interest of general political peace and social harmony, and that if workers prolong the agitation or allow it to turn violent, then it will be the employers' turn to call on the polity to suppress the demonstrators as common criminals. In brief, labor is well aware that neither employers nor government will respond to labor demands unless political security is being threatened.

Seventh, although workers increasingly are being enrolled in unions which are universally affiliated occupational interest groups, and surveys attest that rank-and-file members would like their unions to defend vigorously their occupational interests, the members realize they have more to gain occupationally by exploiting their time-tested affiliations of kin and geography to *cliently* relate to union leaders and employers, and especially bureaucrats, as patrons than if those same union leaders, employers, and bureaucrats were confronted *impersonally* through the intermediation of unions![6]

## The Corporate Analysis of Korean Occupations

We can now draw some conclusions. Save for the learned-bureaucratic, no Korean occupational grouping is corporate; that is, no grouping can, as a legitimate *right*, define its own occupational interests and pursue them maximally through organizations of its own choosing and design. Rather, those initiatives are *privileges* which the learned-bureaucratic corporate occupational grouping alone can authorize and, equally pertinent, then only as a graceful prebend from particular *individuals* within the learned-bureaucratic occupational grouping to particular segments, or better yet to particular *individuals*, within the noncorporate occupational groupings. Even to grant the privilege to an occupational grouping in total might be viewed as a first step toward corporation recognition of that noncorporate occupational grouping which, a priori, is institutionally unacceptable. The notion of secondary occupational categories reinforces this principle, though of course agriculture is a primary occupation.

These axioms are valid regardless of whether an existing noncorporate occupational grouping's contribution to the division of labor is vitally augmented or a novel occupational grouping arises to respond to empirical changes in that division of labor. For the learned-bureaucratic corporate grouping has a perpetual mandate to determine the scope of occupational privilege of all the noncorporate, based on the learned-bureaucratic's assessment of the value of any noncorporate occupational grouping's contribution to the learned-bureaucratic design for the occupational order. We can see two implications: First, noncorporate occupations are forced to accept the premise that the only way they can hope to pursue and possibly achieve their occupational interests is through association with, nay subordination to, someone within the learned-bureaucratic grouping. And in doing so, second, the non-learned-bureaucrats, by definition, must subordinate their own occupational interests to interests which, if they are not prebendary, then are primarily political, and hence which fortuitously may or may not be compatible with non-learned-bureaucratic occupational interests.

This is why Korean interest organizations of noncorporate occupational groupings are mobilized "spontaneously" if not created by learned-bureaucrats to pursue their interests, while true voluntary organizations are rare in Korea. Only about a fifth of those which exist today concern themselves with "public" issues, and most of those have foreign ties, such as Rotary Clubs. And this is why, by default, Koreans have turned to other than occupational interest groups, such as associations based on kin, locality, and age grade, to protect and pursue their occupational interests. But such organizations often *cut across* occupations, and hence may be occupationally counterproductive and, if they are large, susceptible to factional divisiveness. And this is why, although I agree with Henderson's critics that intermediate affiliational (interest) groups of many kinds—youth, labor, teacher, farmer, women, commercial, industrial—do in fact exist in Korea, yet I agree with Henderson that what is crucial is that those groups are not (corporately) viable in Korea as they are in the West— which is what I prefer to think Henderson truly meant when he (mis-)stated that they have not existed in Korea. For he goes on to state that when groups act in concert—*mobilization*, in Henderson's argot—that concert comes from outside their organization, and in such a way that individuals must bargain separately and personally— in our argot, *patrimonially*—for occupational advantage.

Consequently, I can but conclude finally that the Korean patrimonial occupational order is not conducive to facilitating the emergence of novel organizations legitimately able to articulate and pursue potentially developmental occupational interests if those groups and interests run counter to the nondevelopmental patrimonial (political) interests of learned-bureaucrats.[7]

# 7

# Social Stratification

## The Estate System: The Privileged Strata

The Korean dynastic mode of social stratification was an estate (état, lande) order; that is, a system of legally (formally) defined and enforced differences in privileges and obligations among various social strata. Thus, in my view it is not valid that a key distinction between historic patrimonial and feudal orders is that the former are class orders while the latter are estate orders; rather, although all feudal orders are estate orders, historic patrimonial systems may be class (e.g., China) or estate.

Save for the royal family, with which the *yangban* (literally, the paired group of civil and military, though not unimportantly it was the civil element which came to predominate) interacted and could marry, the yangban constituted the nobility and thus the first of the four estates existent during the waning days of imperial Korea. Yangban were entitled to official rank according to their social prestige, a principle which was derived from an antique so-called bone-rank system of five sharply graded privileged strata and three additional tiers reserved for commoners but which survived the subsequent dissolution of "bone" classifications through creation of lineage genealogies, that is, documents which established the credentials, and hence the right to privilege, of contemporary descendants of some ancient prestiged ancestor. These documents demonstrate the tenacity of yangban lineages to survive the vicissitudes of power and prestige over the ages, though to be sure branches died out and migration and the forced extinction of lines by rulers took their toll.

The yangban were deferred to, rewarded with the economy's material benefits (especially its landed revenue), subject to distinctive and less-punitive laws and codes of conduct than their fellow Koreans, and relieved of onerous taxes and of degrading corvée drafts. But there were important distinctions within the estate. For one, any number of yangban were poor and otherwise lived much as commoners. There were great differences between those yangban who lived in the capital and decided Korea's fate and those, sometimes termed rustic yangban, whose prestige and prerogatives were limited to their local areas, and between those whose ancestors had served a great ruler of the past and those who were serving a contemporary ruler, and between those whose lineages were long and distinguished and those whose documents were recent or forged. And although in theory all yangban were eligible to take the civil service examinations, and those who passed were eligible for an official position according to their examination scores, a final screening assured that the low prestiged were kept out of key posts, especially the first three grades of the very elaborate grade-rank system. Finally, at least the immediate lineal descendants of honored officials were directly appointed to office by a patronal monarch without having to go through the examination system.

By the end of the imperial era, the yangban's luster was tarnishing, as was the image of the dynasty and the imperial order. Titles could be purchased outright or secured through bribery, while the examination route was opened to other than yangban. The Japanese destroyed the imperial estate system save for royalty, which in part was intertwined with the Japanese imperial lineage. But paradoxically, the Japanese also salvaged the estate by converting it into a rural elite which benefited from the new land tenure system. The Republic land reform, in turn, likewise did not destroy the yangban, a witness to the tenacity of consanguineal affiliation and solidarity (see the next chapter), especially in rural Korea. Only today, in a process set in motion by the Japanese, it takes more than ancestry to maintain yangban privilege and even status; the landownership and concubinage of the Japanese period having given way under the Republic to education and a prestigious role in Korea's modernizing.

The second privileged estate was the *chung'in*. The origin and even signification of the term, literally "the middle people," is obscure. The explanation that appeals to me has it that the chung'in were so named because the estate was socially positioned between the first, yangban, estate and the third, commoner, estate, serving as a porous buffer between them so as to diminish pressure from below on the first estate. In any case, in contrast to yangban who were destined for decision-making and administrative positions, chung'in were educated and examined for special skills, and then appointed only to lower civil service ranks as technicians, such as interpreters, accountants, astrologers, and lawyers. And though in theory all the privileged could take the distinctive military-official examination, it was usually the chung'in among them who availed themselves of this less-privileged opportunity. Chung'in also served on provincial staffs as clerks. Although a few of the more brilliant and manipulative of them did become magistrates, unlike the yangban they had no hope of moving beyond that entering level in the bureaucratic ladder.[1]

## The Deprivileged Strata

The remaining two classic estates consisted of commoners, termed *sangmin* in the last imperial dynasty to differentiate the estate from the yangban, or previously as *yangmin* to differentiate the estate from the lowest, fourth estate composed of mean people, termed *ch'ŏnmin*, a complex grouping of those bound in public and private service, certain artisans such as transport workers, and denigrated occupationalists such as entertainers and riverbed occupants, many of whom in all subcategories were forced to live in specially designated communities. The distinction between the commoner and the mean estates was not always either logical or clear-cut. For example, one had to prove that one's ancestors were not mean for eight generations to be eligible for public office, yet eunuchs, who were mean, were very influential at court. Commoners were liable for military corvée, while the mean were exempt. The mean in certain occupations were richer than most commoners. Lower-esteemed commoners were often treated as if they were mean, especially since such commoners could be reduced to mean status through debt, if their occupation was so specified by government patrimonial fiat (such as happened to salt-makers and smiths), or if, for some reason, e.g., treason or heinous crimes, they were forced to live in specially designated communities. Finally, certain commoners, such as butchers, were considered a people apart and treated as if mean. To be sure, all such anomalies are not atypical of the discrepancy between formal estate legal qualifications and the real world of prestige and privilege anywhere, although the Korean case does not conform to westerners' notion as to how that looseness of fit should apply! However, for all the sometimes deliberate blurring between commoner and mean, as a legally recognized estate, the mean were required to follow their distinctive estate sumptuary regulations, and their descendants were prohibited from taking civil service examinations. Their status was registered in the census rosters, which became the symbol of their discontent.

The bound segment of the mean is even more complex. It contained a number of often-overlapping categories, and I hesitate to use the western term "slave" to cover them all, though most observers do so. Interestingly, the indigenous Korean word for slave, *chong*, which consequently has no Chinese ideograph or equivalent, rarely turns up in discussions of the status of these individuals. I believe that true slaves, if in fact they existed, were limited to household aides living with and under the control of a master and his kin, a status and obligation peculiar to East Asia, termed in the literature *patriarchal slavery*. Consequently although I concede the Korean bondage system shows many similarities to classical slavery, yet certain not unimportant differences peculiar to East Asia in general and Korea in particular are evident and worth stating. First, although bound labor was considered vital for performing certain tasks—for example, in privately alienated estate agriculture during one period of Korean history—yet the bound never constituted even a majority of the total labor force. Second, although the causes of Korean bondage are typical—crime, debt, treason, captivity in war, and heredity—most bonding, as in China and unlike the West, was individual though it could be collective, as for treason. Third, although the bound were considered as property and hence could be bought and sold—though slave auctions did not exist, given as gifts, mortgaged, and inherited, they were not considered chattel, as were classical slaves. For example, since they were assumed to have personalities, the Korean bound had the same right to bring suit against their masters as did freemen (which was not so in either China or Japan), although, as was true of commoners, this could create serious status problems if the master was an official, which was likely to be the case. Yet the stakes were high enough to tempt the bound to try, since if they could prove illegal impressment they would be freed.

Some other characteristics of the Korean bound which may or may not have been shared by slaves elsewhere: the bound could be hired out, or even in some cases hire themselves out, to work for other than their masters. Most interesting, the bound had the same property rights as freemen; in fact the bound could own other bound, though if their ownership title was not clear their masters, or if they were subsequently freed the state, rather than heirs, inherited. The bound were prized because they were disciplined, cheaper, and above all constituted the means to insure that certain specialized revenue-producing and onerous tasks were performed. Those skilled in banking and commerce were highly desired by members of the political elite who themselves preferred not to engage in such patrimonially morally unworthy tasks. Some of the bound were highly prestiged, which sounds paradoxical to western ears. Among these were *kisaeng* and court eunuchs. Kisaeng were intelligent, skilled women who served not only as entertainers but as confidants and go-betweens for officials. The best of them, those assigned to the court, were treated deferentially and rewarded materially, as were their kin or the sponsors who used the women to mediate in factional court politics. As in China, eunuchs served court and officials, those in the upper grades being privy to the palace's inner circle. Eunuchs used their influence to get their relatives appointed to office or to secure lucrative prebendary grants for them, which is why most eunuchs were deliberately created by ambitious kinsmen.

A final example of the practical indistinction between commoner and bound may be seen in the polity's right to increase or decrease the numbers of commoners and bound by reckoning the offspring of mixed marriages as either bound—usually through the mother—or free—usually through the father. In this way, the polity could flexibly respond to the demands of insuring an adequate labor supply, especially on agricultural estates, through bondage, yet also increase the taxable and replenish ranks of low officials, both of whom had to be freemen.

A further confusion is public versus private bondage. When specific cases are examined, the distinction often blurs because, according to patrimonial reasoning, those assigned publicly to officials as aides could be in fact privately exploited according to officials' personal predilections, and on the officials' death the aides continued to serve their families for a subsequent three years. Moreover, although, unlike in private bondage, the period for which individuals were subject to private call—termed *body service* or *body tribute*—was prescribed and otherwise the individuals were subject only to a tax, yet the government could exercise a patrimonial right both to gracefully shorten individual service if others in the family were on call or if an individual was an orphan, as well as to accept a substitute or payment in exchange for service. Perhaps this then is the distinction: publicly bound body service was especially prevalent among artisans and those who served officials as unskilled manuals or bureaucratic clerks. Women, usually the relatives of traitors, were recruited as official entertainers, including for prostitution, the more accomplished of them being assigned to court. The private bound, on the other hand, were employed primarily as house servants and increasingly as cultivators.

In the final centuries of imperial rule, the conversion of household aides to indentured live-in hands, the privatization of land and the emergence of a free yeomanry, the commercialization of agriculture, the entrance of the bound into the military, which insured emancipation, and the erosion of the estate status system, all contributed to creating a universal deprivileged hand labor class of diverse elements in which distinctions of bound and free, and public versus private bondage, such as they previously existed, became increasingly irrelevant. The authorities formally recognized this fact when they abolished institutional bondage along with the estate system in 1894.

But that edict, and even the subsequent demise of imperial rule itself, did not terminate prejudice and discrimination against the descendants of the lowly. Once again the Japanese seem to have served to bridge the older and "modern" attitudes and social forms, in this case by drawing on their reactions to their own estate past. Japanese families hired deprivileged youngsters, male and female, as indentured servants. The status of the Korean public entertainer, the ki-saeng, was assimilated to that of the Japanese *geisha*, which became an acceptable career for the attractive daughters of the commoner poor. The Japanese also introduced a new occupation for poor girls, hostess and waitress, which often was a cover for prostitution. Most girls however became indentured factory workers in a system imitative of Japan's, in which, in return for a dowry payment to parents, employers were given *in loco parentis* rights, enabling them to underpay, to discipline harshly, and even incarcerate the girls in dormitories to isolate them from labor agitators. The Japanese police obligingly returned those girls who rashly fled. Although all such labor contracts were outlawed in 1946, the Japanese-period exploitive relationship between employers and employees, especially female employees in the industrial sector, lingers on with official blessing, since that relationship, to belabor the point, is a cornerstone of the export economic game plan. Also noticeable still is the exaggerated deference which, reminiscent of the imperial estate system, the privileged expect from the lowly, and the disdain felt for those who serve the public menially, especially if they happen to be women. For example, waitresses are universally assumed to be females of easy virtue and bus girls are intimidated when they try to collect fares. Butchers, A-frame laborers, and other descendants in truth or fiction from the historical mean are socially shunned—as are lepers, who are pathologically feared.

The virulence of discrimination persists in spite of the fact that all the lowly, now as in the past, are culturally, physically, and linguistically no different from other Koreans. It is rather the extreme kin consciousness and the psychological and material security that kin offers that is at the root of much Korean discrimination, kin distinctions taking priority over all the other potential sources of unity and fission in the Korean social order. To be sure, sometimes kin discrimination is ethnic, as in the case of children of mixed Korean and American parentage emerging from the Korean War, but lineage rather than race is the root. In sum, though it lacks many of the social cleavages plaguing other modernizing societies, Korea has its own peculiar obstacles to a more productive interaction among its historically rooted status groups.[2]

## Korean Social Stratification and Mobility: The Conventional Analysis

The barriers erected to separate and perpetuate the discrete categories (strata) of the classic Korean estate system were ever porous, especially in times of uncertainty and travail, which became increasingly routine as the twentieth century approached. Originally, commoners in general, though never formally excluded from taking the civil service examinations as were the mean, artisans, and merchants, nevertheless were for the most part discouraged from doing so by social and economic circumstance. However, by repeatedly expanding the examinations, the government made it feasible for commoners, including peasants and even seamen, to compete with the privileged in becoming yangban officials. Passing the initial examination did not entitle an individual to a position in the central administration, but rather gave him the right to enter the Confucian academy which prepared candidates for a further examination, passage of which did insure an official position. By manipulating such a complex system, the old elite, especially those in the top three grades or their relatives, were able to hold on to a sizable percentage of the key offices, and hence to their preeminent status. Lower-ranked center officials, however, were more widely recruited and local officeholders who constituted a local gentry even more so. It was these ranks that commoners increasingly were able to penetrate and through such offices they enhanced their prestige as dynastic Korea waned.

Moreover, increasing unrest required replenishing the pool of loyal government supporters by offering commoner status to the mean, even its bound segment, which not incidentally made them taxable subjects as well. The mean also took advantage of confusion to burn official registers which enshrined their low status, thus enabling a number of them to pass themselves off as commoners. Simultaneously, prosperous peasants and merchants (!) could buy yangban status from an ever fiscally embarrassed polity. At first the government tendered only temporary social advantages, and this fact was duly recorded next to individuals' names in the official census. But in time the offers became permanent and, consequently, degrading notations were deleted. In the north, where status differences were taken more lightly, perhaps because there yangban were few and commoners and mean moved about freely, the conversion of commoners into local yangban and the mean into commoners was much easier.

The distinction between yangban who held office and those who did not counted for little during the Japanese occupation, since few yangban held office and most of those that did filled only meaningless "advisory" positions. What did matter was whether a yangban was able to take advantage of the Japanese land survey and become a registered landlord, whereas most, though not all, cultivators became or remained tenant or day laborer commoners, thus reversing the late dynastic trend. This key dichotomy between landed and landless survived the American occupation and the early Republic, until the land reform divested the privileged of their holdings. Then they were forced to fall back on their prestige and political influence in the emerging conservative parties or to find new roots in the social order lest they disappear into the increasingly commoner society. A number of yangban used what wealth they were able to retain after land reform to acquire advanced education for their offspring and convert them into political leaders, higher civil servants, and lawyers, thus providing class continuity for the old elite in spite of the upheavals of colonialism, war, and economic deprivation. For although at least elementary education is both free and open in theory, fees and other expenses, especially on the more advanced levels, drain 5 to 30 percent of a family's income, and the need to be financially able to prepare adequately for the difficult entrance examinations restricts access to higher education, especially to those prestigious institutions which provide the society's preeminent employment. (The premier Seoul National University, for example, supplies approximately one-third of the higher civil-servants-to-be.) Even though at least some urban industrialists are pragmatically self-made men of limited education (as are some older professionals), many have yangban background themselves or have married into the ex-yangban elite to provide support for their careers, especially if they seek government favor. In contrast, the proprietors of small-medium industry, especially in the smaller towns, are recent rural migrants without connections and must rely on their own resources to improve their income and prestige.

The Park regime's policy of favoring export entrepreneurs exacerbated the cleavage between privileged and deprivileged which the government was not eager to remedy because of its economic game plan. Though, to reiterate, such contrasts are not as serious as they are in other undeveloped societies (see Chapter 5), the plight of the deprivileged, constantly buffeted by inflation while the favored entrepreneurs and professionals flaunt their advantages, prompted some concern in government circles, lest national morale suffer and the nation become vulnerable to pressure from the rival DPRK and the international community.

In sum, on balance the Korean system of social stratification has had neither sufficient vested interests nor vital structural obstacles inimical to the emergence of a productive modernizing elite. On the other hand, there are no obstacles to that society's contemporary elite exacerbating the modernizing problem because of that elite's choice of priorities and methods.[3]

## The Patrimonial View of Social Mobility and the Corporate Analysis of Class in Korea: An Alternative Analysis

The alternative analysis postulates that Korean social stratification is a two-class system, which is characteristic of all patrimonial systems of social stratification whether they be aristocratic, like dynastic Korea, or not, like China. This postulate is based on the conclusion that the Korean system of social stratification is better characterized by status groups rather than by classes in the conventional western sense, and that the vital cleavage in Korean society truly is between two categories, namely yangban officeholders and their descendants on the one hand, and all others in the society, regardless of their formal status-group affiliation, on the other hand. This conclusion in turn is based on the observation that for all the manifest Korean concern for hierarchy, status, and consanguineal purity, determining the distinctive characteristics of various social strata, including the formal estates of the last imperial dynasty, is most difficult. A few examples: Some of the nominally aristocratic yangban were in truth deprivileged farmers. Not only the free but also the bound could "own" bound-men. Because free and bound shared a common culture, when bound service was abolished they merged socially, save for one group, butchers, who, paradoxically to non-Koreans, were not technically among the bound at all! Korean obsession with purity of ancestry involved primarily only the small percentage of the populace seeking public office and at times even this was irrelevant because office was put on the auction block. Finally, the chung'in was not a true middle class but rather a way station for those moving up or down socially.

In the view of the present study, the Korean patrimonial two-class system contains a leadership class of officeholders who have beaten back all challenges to their perpetual domination of the social order in general and over the nonofficeholding class in particular. The officeholders have survived all the vicissitudes of Korean history—internal anarchy and foreign invasion, the threat of feudalization, disintegration of the classic order in the nineteenth and twentieth centuries, and finally occupation by modern nonpatrimonial Japan and the United States. Those who challenged the system, whether as individuals, as occupationalists, or as status groups, have been either neutralized or co-opted by converting their interests into officeholding interests (e.g., the military nobles of the twelfth and thirteenth centuries) or by transforming their privileges into prebends granted on grace by the officeholders (e.g., the ancient "bone" aristocracy) initially in land or labor service, then in commerce, and finally in industry. The only serious, persistent, and potentially effective threat to the officeholders' grip on the social order has come from consanguinity. But unlike the Japanese consanguinity which developed its own interests, interests which facilitated the emergence of feudalism, Korean consanguinity has been co-opted by the officeholders, as in China, by segmenting its lineages; that is, by bureaucratizing one segment in a lineage by offering its leader(s) the carrot of office and supporting that segment's—and hence indirectly that officeholder's—control over the other segments and thus over the lineage as a whole. Moreover, since Korean consanguinity commands loyalty across occupation, status group, and class lines, the officeholders have used consanguineal segmentation in particular but consanguinity in general to deflect potential challenge from any of those other sources. Thus has access to officeholding, no matter how it is obtained—whether by civil service, merit appointment, or even purchase, become the singular path to privileged social status and access to the society's prebendary benefices. Kinship does matter vitally, but primarily when it is exploited to obtain and legitimize access to prebendary advantage. Once this was done by claiming descent from an officially appointed merit subject, today by bureaucrats providing favorable treatment to their kinsmen.

In like patrimonial spirit, the formally specified privileges (or disabilities) and responsibilities of those within the various strata of the old estate system could be gracefully ignored and even countermanded at any time by the officeholders; for example, to recall, the officeholders decided whether the offspring of mixed marriages were free or bound simply by determining with which parent the young would be identified. The only way to insure that official decisions served an outsider's interest was through some connection—individual, kin, or whatever—to an appropriate officeholder, who considered his favorable decisions to be acts of patrimonial grace, not rights, and hence reversible at any time at the officeholder's option. Bribery often played a role in determining such decisions; for example, when commoners wanted to be classified in the registers as special communitarians to escape the onerous corvée (which indicates how slight many considered the formal status categories per se to be).

The members of the elite were required to place a kinsman in office, even by fakery, at least once every four generations, or have their affiliate—kin, faction, or whatever—lose its privileged status. That office vitally determined situs within the privileged status group, especially whether or not an individual ranked within the first three grades in the center adminstrative bureaucracy, whether he was a center or local bureaucrat, and finally whether he was an administrator or technician. Those who obtained public office were expected to then reward their status group by becoming both its protector-patron and a source of prebends, not only for contemporaries but for descendants as well. We can thus only conclude that it is the struggle to hold public office and to associate as intimately as possible with those who hold office that is the recurrent dynamic of the Korean social order, rather than the classic class struggle of the nonpatrimonial societies; though to be sure the struggle for office is one between the privileged and the disadvantaged—socially, occupationally, economically, and of course politically. Nevertheless, the course of the officeholding struggle determines how one fares otherwise, instead of vice versa, as in the feudal and its successor societies.

The ability of the officeholding privileged to dominate and exploit the nonofficeholders so persistently throughout Korean history also lies in the inability of nonofficeholders to create viable *corporate* organizations which not only can legitimately defend their own interests, but especially can prevent the officeholders from arrogating the right to define the interests of the nonofficeholders. For although Korea has abounded throughout its history with nonofficeholding organizations, those organizations at best rather have been cliental petitioners of, or organs co-opted by, officeholders or frustrated would-be officeholders.

Thus, I reiterate my support for Henderson's vortex theory, which postulates that a constant upper draft has sucked (co-opted) the crucial potential leadership talent of all nonofficeholding groupings into the privileged officeholding stratum. Because officeholding is the sole source of truly privileged status and security in the Korean patrimonial society, and because the possibility of securing such a position is always present, nonofficeholding leaders and potential leaders have been positively discouraged from creating and leading nonofficeholding corporate interest groups as the primary means by which those nonofficeholding leaders could improve their social prestige and obtain access to the material and nonmaterial rewards of the society. For this reason, mobility in the Korean patrimonial society must be characterized as *individual*, and not, as in a nonpatrimonial (especially feudal and its successor) society, as potentially *group*, in that the patrimonially mobile are individuals representing only themselves and do not, as in the nonpatrimonial social order, necessarily carry their former affiliates or their group interests (or values if you wish) with them when they ascend or descend the status ladder. For those who truly want to rise socially must not only enter the ranks of the officeholders, but in so doing also accept the interests of, and identify completely with, those of the prestiged officeholding group. Individual status then is all-important to Koreans; groups must be deliberately constructed flexibly enough to form and reform at will, since they exist primarily in order to facilitate the leaders as individuals perpetuating their membership in or entering the privileged officeholding group. Consequently, in spite of the existence of an estate system and the perseverance of "bone" and kin reckoning in spirit if not in form, the demands of patrimonial officeholding ever modified any estate or formal restriction on the requisite upper draft. Though precious few ever succeeded in rising, the potential always has been there; involuntarily in the old days by dynastic change, factionalism, and constantly rotating office, and voluntarily by a broadening or narrowing the eligibility requirement, and through purchase, special appointments, and purges.

Clearly, the Korean system of social stratification is being modernized; for example, privilege and prestige now are being offered to the movers and shakers of the industrial, especially export, economy. But the security of modern industrial interests, as interests in the past, depends on the prebendary grace of officeholders whose primarily political interests may not necessarily serve the nonpolitical interests of a truly modern industrial order, whether those interests exist within or without the officeholding group. Some Koreans who represent industrial interests do express their concerns to the officeholders. But without the legitimate right to organize corporate interest groups to articulate and express those concerns, those individuals represent only themselves or a few others without support in-depth, and hence can be ignored by the officeholders, if the individuals will not be prebendally bribed. At optimum, recalcitrant industrialists can support a counter officeholding group, which conceptually does not violate my basic thesis.

In conclusion, the Korean system of social stratification, now as in the past, dissipates pressure for *qualitative* change, that is, to develop the system, which in turn prevents the system from facilitating the development of the social order.[4]

# 8

# Kinship: Descent

## The Inheritance of Property

Two immediate caveats: First—determining the precise character of Korean inheritance is difficult because of a number of ambiguities in the sources. Among these are failures to distinguish between (1) formal prescriptions and reality, (2) the circumstances from dynasty to dynasty (and even changes within dynastic periods), (3) the rules for royalty and for others, and especially (4) strategic property—land in the classic period—and chattel, as well as (5) inheritance (of property) and status succession. Second—*uniogeniture*, that is, inheritance by a single heir, does not require that a single individual inherit all the strategic property of a predecessor, nor does it apply when one of all the heirs is given a modest extra share of the inheritance, typically to cover the cost of kin ritual. For, conversely, *homoyogeniture*, that is, inheritance (of strategic property) by all, does not require that all heirs must share the estate absolutely equally, only that no one heir inherit preponderantly what the predecessor controlled (that, in my reasoning, would be uniogeniture).

The hoary inheritance system for commoners is obscure, to say the least. Anthropological data on contemporary patriarchal kin villages (yet to be discussed) and on remote offshore islands, which may very well not truly represent early inheritance patterns, suggests homoyogeniture as the norm. One interesting example is that of a diminishing share system according to birth order with the first heir inheriting approximately half the estate. Aristocractic preference however is better known. It followed the Chinese model of primogeniture for royalty, enabling it to maintain its strategic property interests; that is, income from land, reasonably intact over the generations. In contrast, the landed income of the nobility during the last imperial dynasty was subject to homoyogenetic division—as at least the income from official cliental "merit" grants had been. Even the recording of land in one name may have been but a legal fiction to provide guarantors in case of default on taxes or other cliental obligations, and not indicative of uniogeniture. And although during the last dynasty only sons inherited and a preferential distinction was made between the heirs of first (legitimate) wives and those of other wives (concubines), such that the legitimate first son received an extra share—some 20 percent of the property—specifically for ancestor veneration and similar Confucian consanguineal observances, in my view these stipulations do not violate the homoyogenetic inheritance pattern since those other than the legitimate first son continued to share, equally or unequally; the first son's extra share was not personally alienable but had to be dissipated in the interest of the collective and, in any case, even with his extra share the eldest received nothing comparable to his predecessor's holding.

As the last imperial dynasty matured, landlord income increasingly became private, though not in the modern sense, forming the material base of the yangban class, especially for those retiring from office and returning to their rural native places. But under the iron law of homoyogenetic division, these landlord families were in constant need of replenishing their inheritance through purchase or some other form of acquisition, lest their incomes diminish, reducing them to tenancy or forcing them out of agriculture, and in the process depriving them of yangban status. Sometimes when the holding grew very small, homoyogeniture was ignored and only one son, or the consanguineous unit collectively, inherited. This does not truly violate the homoyogenetic rule since such inheritances were too minuscule to be strategic. Some large undivided private holdings did exist, but these were few and consanguineally collective whose income was dissipated ceremonially.

The Japanese made no attempt to convert the Koreans to their own primogeniture inheritance system, showing once again how selectively respectful the Japanese were of Korean customs which did not threaten, and might even serve, Japanese interests. However, in accord with their own patterns, the Japanese did make the Koreans give a greater share of the consanguineal inheritance to those in the main line in contrast to those in branch units; increased the eldest son's share to half the legacy and gave him the right to control the property of individual members of his family and to register the property in his name; and eliminated completely the right of females to share. The proof that none of this retarded the diminution process lies in the fact that the average size of a holding progressively declined during the Japanese occupation from 3.7 hectares in 1919 to 2.5 in 1945; incidentally, this trend continued into the Republic since inheritance was ignored in the land reform. It is worth observing that the Japanese were so thorough in their "modernizing" reforms that most contemporary Koreans believe that the Japanese code is their "traditional" inheritance system!

This is apparent in the currently valid 1960 inheritance code, which attempted simultaneously to eliminate grossly Japanese inheritance customs, preserve "cherished," supposedly eternal, Korean social practices such as first-son preference, and yet respond to the requisites of a modernizing society. A pertinent prescription is that the family head is entitled to a half-share of the inheritance in return for meeting certain family obligations, as under the Japanese. Though a female can inherit, as she could in the more remote past, she is entitled to only half a male's share. Antemortem testament and division can deviate from customary equal sharing, at least for males, but uniogeniture is ruled out. Nuclear inheritance is encouraged by setting a five-year maximum on undivided predecessor property and by eliminating the main-line preference of the Japanese period. In spite of stipulated formal legalities to the contrary, understandings exist among those who inherit minuscule estates to prevent further division by turning them over to a single heir (preferably an eldest son) to manage, but the income must be used to support surviving parents or be divided among the heirs. In sum, the 1960 code has not altered, and in fact in certain ways has further reinforced, the iron law of homoyogenetic inheritance.

We may conclude that the significance of Korean homoyogenetic inheritance is that, since unlike feudal lords who could transfer their strategic holding intact to succeeding generations through uniogeniture—a privilege only the Korean ruler himself enjoyed—the old Korean privileged had to parcel out an inheritance among many heirs, the only way they could insure that their land (-ed income), and hence their status, would not diminish over the generations was to constantly replenish their existing holdings. And this was feasible in patrimonial Korea not from conquest, as under feudalism, but from the graceful prebendary grants of a ruler who offered such gifts in return for personal service to him, most typically not from military duties but through public officeholding. Thus being included within the charmed circle of royalty or bureaucracy provided much more than political prerogatives; it provided the means to insure that one's descendants would not be reduced ultimately to commoner cultivators or worse—as symbolized by the truism that yangban status was lost in four generations if one's descendants could not obtain center public office. Those who out of political arrogance or great wealth refused to serve center authority, and hence were denied access to landed prebends, were simultaneously condemning their descendants to an adverse fate, not surprisingly considered a heinous case of criminal irresponsibility in Korean thinking. Consequently, literally without raising a hand in anger, the ruler and his officeholding aides were insured against persistence over time of any independent islands of political or economic opposition derived from nonprebendarily granted, and hence illegal, accumulations of strategic property. It is in this sense, as Weber and Marx pointed out, that no strategic property is truly "private," especially intergenerationally, in a patrimonial order such as Korea's.

Replacing land with commerce and then especially industry as the society's primary source of strategic wealth did not alter the fundamentals of patrimonial inheritance. True, as in feudal uniogeniture societies which have industralized, land, which is available in limited quantities, has been replaced by a source of virtually unlimited potential, and homoyogeniture also is positively encouraged. But in patrimonial Korea, since officeholding prebendary favor continues to determine access to significant industrially derived accumulation, replenishment against its diminution through inheritance also requires maintaining that prebendary grace, especially now that the polity is pressing for public ownership of all large enterprises and hence the demise of family-owned, potentially undivided corporations. Thus does "modernization" through acculturation of western patterns once again reinforce rather than qualitatively alter (that is, develop) existing institutions.[1]

## Consanguinity and the Inheritance of Status

Korean kin reckoning and organization are not easy to fathom since they are ill defined and ambiguous, perhaps deliberately so to exploit all possibilities to the maximum. Hence, specialists do not agree on the system's essentials, let alone their implications. With this caveat in mind, I fearlessly and perhaps foolishly attempt to describe briefly those aspects of the Korean kinship system which bear on the patrimonial concerns of the study, notably the relationship between consanguinity and the inheritance of status.

The fundamental Korean biologically related unit roughly translates into English as family, though technically it is a group of blood-related individuals living together under one roof and sharing one kitchen. Larger units are created from relatives reckoned more widely, living either in a single household or, more usually, in several households. These units are constructed on either or both of two principles. The first principle is patrilineality, which makes a distinction between a main stem and any number of secondary branches, each with a designated head, his spouse, children, and unmarried brothers and sisters. The heads of such subunits therefore are brothers and the stem head, normally the eldest brother, is simultaneously the head of the collectivity. The second principle is collaterality, the extended family or, more typically, the kindred. Although the degrees of kindred collaterality are formally (legally) defined—at present nine degrees on the male side and six on the female—custom also demands that a Korean be conscious of wider relationships, according to the three reckonings of one's own kin, one's father's kin, and, if a male, one's wife's father's kin. In fact, all are considered as kin who are expected to mourn the death of a collateral and his descendants.

Lineality and collaterality merge in an entity which can be visualized as either a kindred built up over time or a lineal construct claiming descent from a common great-grandfather. In the latter case the entity is a unit of the key consanguinity of Korean society, the patrilineage—those who claim descent from a specific ancestor, normally a great-great-grandfather, who is the symbol of the lineage's solidarity. There are some 15,000 lineages currently existent in Korea. Not all of those who live together—for example, maids—are considered members of the lineage and, conversely, lineage members need not live together. However, absentees can be called upon physically and morally to support the lineage, sharing the burden for its maintenance, such as the upkeep of its burial grounds.

Superior to the lineage is the clan, composed of those who claim to be the descendants of a common, often mythical, ancestor and who share a common surname. There are only some 250 clans, which accounts for the great number of Koreans with similar surnames. They vary considerably in size, but typically, especially when compared to the Chinese, all are extremely important, being nationwide in scope and commanding loyalties which transcend smaller parochial, geographic, and even provincial ties. The clan's major function has been to determine and enforce rules of exogamy on its members, since Koreans are enjoined not to marry anyone with either the same ancestral-geographic or the same clan names, even though most of the lineages within a clan may be only remotely, and more probably only theoretically, related. (A recent survey shows that 93 percent still conform to the clan-name exogamous taboo, while the remaining 7 percent accept only geographic exogamy.) Those related maternally, on the other hand, are freely eligible to intermarry unless they are close collaterally to each other.

Lineage authority has been fashioned out of two fundamentals— patriarchy and continuity. Patriarchy vests the male head with broad authority over lineage members, such as indenturing children, acting in the name of the lineage, and commanding all within to serve the lineage interests as the patriarch sees fit. Although the Korean patriarch never was as strong as his Japanese counterpart, perhaps because he never absolutely controlled his lineage's common property and was not chosen for his pragmatic ability, nevertheless he was stronger than his Chinese counterpart. Interestingly, in spite of differences among Korean, Chinese, and Japanese patriarchs, at least until recently the three societies have shared a common Confucian "ideology" stressing filial piety and authoritarian control by superiors within and without the consanguineal units.

Lineage viability over time (continuity) is reflected in consanguineal genealogies, which are records of the lineages' past privileges and prerogatives as well as lists of present members who could be called upon to defend their lineages' advantages and honor. In contrast, only the few most active and influential clans ever thought it worthwhile enough to provide fully comprehensive continuous records from ancient days. For it has been the individual lineages which have been primarily concerned with preserving the family fortunes, and hence chronicling the rise and fall of kin, reconstructing lost records whenever present fortunes required glorious roots. Such lineage continuity is maintained through status succession. Unlike the inheritance of property, status succession clearly devolves on one heir, whenever possible on the eldest son. If a proper, responsible first son is not available, a substitute must be found. The first choice is a younger son, hence the desire not to be content with only one son. The next choice is an adopted male relative of the proper generation from among those who bear the same (clan) surname. At first sons of brothers were preferred, taking precedence over the offspring of secondary wives, but in time distant cousins were preferred as a way of opening up the selection to talent. Adoption can occur at any time, even posthumously for those who hope against probability to produce their own heirs or who die unexpectedly without issue.

The interests of the lineage similarly determine the ground rules for divorce. Divorce could be instituted against a sonless wife. However, some observers argue that once adoption and the right to take concubines were accepted, albeit grudgingly in certain periods, factors considered inimical to the psychological health of the consanguineal unit, such as adultery and gossiping, have weighed more heavily in deciding whether or not to divorce. Widow remarriage has been frowned upon in the belief that such women, especially if they subsequently gave birth, would violate their commitment to serve the original consanguinity exclusively. Remarriage has been acceptable, however, if the woman was young, sonless, and without parents to defend her interests. If her former in-laws have not approved of her remarriage for any reason, the children born from her new union would be considered illegitimate; in the imperial period, the males were ineligible to hold public office, a dire consequence for the society's privileged.

Since a male heir is so essential to lineage continuity, Koreans have had a strong preference for male offspring. The belief is quite old, though it flagged during the period prior to the establishment of the last imperial dynasty. The eldest son, the heir-apparent, is treated specially in the household, commanding respect even when he is very young, particularly from his siblings, who one day will have to defer to his wishes.

Though it does not necessarily have to follow, Korean male preference has been matched by female discrimination. Because females have been ineligible to succeed to headships, save as a temporary expedient until suitable males could be found, or to establish independent households, women have been considered of secondary significance to consanguineal continuity. Symbolically, they once were without personal names save for the period from puberty to marriage. In rural areas husbands referred to their wives as their "inner house" while outsiders called them "male aprons"; after they gave birth they were referred to as their sons' mothers. Women have not been legally responsible for their own acts, yet have been liable for those of their male householders. Husbands could exploit, though not dispose of, their wives' assets. And since female relations were more broadly defined than those of males, males have had more freedom in mate selection. The overwhelming majority of females were illiterate in 1945, not surprising considering the close relationship between literacy and public officeholding, from which women were barred.

The very symbol of concern for consanguinity, especially its continuity, is ancestor veneration, which devolves upon the eldest son. Veneration ceremonies not only propitiate clan and lineage progenitors who protect and validate the status and privileges of present-day descendants, but also steel those descendants to stand solidarily against all outsiders who might threaten the consanguinity in any way. Consequently, the revenue from consanguineal property predominantly is devoted not only to veneration ceremonies, but also to maintaining consanguineal monuments and status symbols, such as ancestral halls, records, tombs, schools, and service centers.

Why such devotion to elaborating and perpetuating consanguinity? First and foremost, to return to the discussions of previous chapters, the consanguinity is *the* intermediary organization between the individual and the larger-scale, remote, and impersonal society in general, and formal authority in particular, in this patrimonial institutional order in which corporate occupational and class organizations are proscribed or co-opted by that authority. Second, the consanguinity is an individual's prime refuge in times of travail, such as during foreign invasion or occupation, frequent enough in Korean history, when the indigenous polity may not be able to protect the populace. Thus the consanguinity has been more important than in China, which has been less turbulent, and in nonpatrimonial Japan, in which alternative paths to concerted action and self-protection have been available. Third, the consanguinity has been the means for the privileged to validate their prerogatives through careful mate selection, hence the attention to genealogical records. In the Korean patrimonial estate system, the polity ever required evidence of long-term intergenerational purity from those seeking high-level official appointment, and it has been from office that vital prebends and status have flowed. It is for this reason perhaps that consanguinities are stronger and more rivalrous in the south, where the patrimonial court and central bureaucracy have located. Fourth, the consanguinity has provided a source of unity among those who might otherwise be split along class, political, or ideological lines. Fifth, by pooling the resources of its members, the consanguinity provides one of the few ways open to countervail the constant diminution of homoyogenetic inheritance, though this has brought on the confiscatory wrath of authority. Sixth, unlike the Japanese who developed strong loyalty to place, the Koreans have substituted consanguineal ties for geographical, perhaps because invasion often caused migration of whole communities. The consanguineal ancestral place therefore is often only a conventional symbol of an idealized past, though in the past whenever members of a privileged consanguinity were out of political favor at the capital they usually retreated to lick their collective wounds in their native rural place, though not necessarily their ancestral home, rebuilding their consanguineal strength and morale and marking time until the political wheel of fortune might turn in their favor. Seventh, in a society without many forms of social security, the consanguinity succors its members more readily and more persistently than do friends and work mates. Successful relatives expect kin to seek their favor, particularly to exploit personal contacts which are so vital in this patrimonial society. Eighth, one's consanguinity provides a psychological buffer against the difficulties of adjusting to a new environment; particularly today for ruralites migrating to the rapidly changing, impersonal prime urban centers.

Although lineal kin are vital, collaterals also are useful. Especially, a wife's kin may be able to provide the vital initial contact or economic wherewithal for an ambitious and talented male to launch a career when his own consanguineals are not in a position to help.

Perhaps the most fascinating persistent example of Korean kin organization is the consanguineous village, that is, a rural community in which (1) all the residents are members of a single lineage; or in which (2) the members of a single lineage predominate, while the other residents are descendants of the lineage's former (often bound) servants; or in which (3) the residents are members of a few, strongly competitive lineages; or finally, in which (4) the residents are distributed among a number of weak lineages, and hence lineality is of little or no consequence. Like lineages but unlike clans, all these consanguinities have an actual historical ancestor who may have been the leader of the original settlers of the village, the leader of later migrants, or an influential retired official returning to his native place. Village lineages expand by having younger sons move out of their parents' household to form new domiciles within the village or in the surrounding countryside. The heads of these individual households, however, meet annually to venerate their collective ancestors, and discuss a common budget and mutual problems. They act solidarily against nonmembers, especially in village politics and in protecting their collective privileges, such as the right to exploit forested uplands adjacent to the village. Land reform, which redistributed wealth and influence in the village, vitally affected the consanguinities. Some lineages reacted positively by investing their now more limited resources in advance, educating their youngsters so that they were able to compete effectively in today's struggle for advantage and expand their consanguinities' historic privileges. However, other consanguinities have not been able to stand against a rising tide of younger villagers' resentment or indifference toward lineage loyalty and responsibility.

In spite of all the advantages flowing from consanguineal solidarity, there have been serious drawbacks too, stemming primarily from the right of patrimonial authority to surveil and control intermediary organizations. Consanguineal elders conformed, if reluctantly, to authority's wishes because, first, under the principle of collective guilt lineages and even entire clans could be charged with treason. Treason could justify consanguineal annihilation; at the least it tainted the consanguinity so that all its descendants would be ineligible for public office, which in four generations under the rules of the last imperial dynasty implied the cessation of prebendary privileges and status, thus assuring the ultimate destruction of the consanguinity as effectively as immediate dissolution. Second, to recall the previous discussion on inheritance, the polity segmented the consanguinities, being assured that the elders of the prebendally favored segment would thus have both motive and means to keep the other segments in line with authority's wishes. Third, representatives of the larger and more ambitious consanguinities and their collateral allies became the nucleus of political factions. Consequently by playing the game of divide and conquer, that is, by gracefully offering and withdrawing prebendary favor from one and then another faction, the polity was able to rule not only the factions but also their supporting consanguinities and collateral allies. Fourth, when an individual has entered public service, he has been plucked from his consanguinity and relocated with peers from other consanguinities in the only corporately disciplined grouping in the society, a grouping which commands a loyalty that competes if not conflicts with consanguineal interests and solidarity (the "vortex" thesis once again; see the previous chapter). Fifth, the polity has levied and collected its taxes and corvée on households regardless of their internal consanguineal characteristics. The greater the number of households the greater the levy, and the more independent the households were of consanguineal ties the easier to collect that levy.

Although the nineteenth-century reformers preached, it was the Japanese, characteristically, who truly began the process of altering the existing kinship system, once again by preserving and even reinforcing prevailing patrimonial principles while adjusting the legal-formal ties to the demands of a modern, primarily commercial order. The Japanese were guided by their experience in reformulating their own family code only a few decades earlier. Thus, the new Korean code, like the older Korean and Japanese ones, was strongly patriarchal, eldest-son centered and female subservient. But the new code authorized personal names for women and provided them with property rights within and without the family circle. For the Japanese, as at home, wished to "alienate" Korean women from the confines of their kin-affiliated households to the extent that they could be exploited, especially as factory hands in the burgeoning Japanese-sponsored economy. But that strategy proved to be a mixed blessing since the men these women worked beside exposed them to Japanese-inspired leftist ideas and facilitated their coequal participation in the student-farmer-labor movements of the 1920s.

The 1960 family code, like its Japanese predecessor, is a compromise between the standards of international modernity and Korea's "beautiful customs," influenced at least subliminally by Japanese notions of both what is modern and what is worth preserving as fundamental from Korea's past. On the formal surface, the code sometimes drastically departs from the past, most notably in emphasizing a husband-wife rather than a father-son family axis and sex equality. The code gives women control over their personal property, authorizes them to establish branch families and become household heads, protects their vital interests in common-law marriages, permits them to marry without parental consent if they are of age, legalizes their adopting a child even if they are single, and accepts them as legally responsible individuals even when they are married. But these and other novel rights are counterbalanced either formally by code codicils or informally by older notions which have not been modified. For example, the historical ideal of the strong male ("patriarchal") household head "responsible" for his members, including especially his wife, permeates the entire code. Sons rather than daughters are responsible for the care of parents and succeed; if a female succeeds it is as a temporary expedient. Adoption still is limited to someone with the same surname. The children of divorced couples still go automatically with the father. The illegitimate children of a father may be registered as family members solely on the father's initiative, but those of the mother require her husband's consent. The age of marriage without parental consent for girls is deliberately set high enough to discourage them from waiting for it.

On the other hand and more to the point, many of the formal changes are more apparent than real. Regardless of statutes, the overwhelming number of Koreans do not approve the remarriage of divorced women, and many Koreans are reluctant to accept the remarriage of widows, especially if they have children. There is no equality of sex in the marketplace—the pay of women is half that of men; women are forced into earlier retirement than men; and women rarely enjoy such male perquisites as on-the-job training. Many women prefer not to marry an eldest son because public opinion demands that he be specially responsible toward his kin, particularly his parents. The patriarchal-conscious Park authority played on obsequience of the young to age by creating Parents Day to honor the worthy old and their pious children in the hopes that, according to the Confucian ideal, some of the filial piety would rub off on the polity. Prominent rural consanguinities still look with disfavor on intermarriage with less prestigious lineages. Though the number of members in urban households is diminishing, kin interhousehold contact is increasing. For example, urbanites expect to board their country-migrant kin temporarily when they come to town seeking either their fortune or advanced education. In fact the increasing interest in exploiting higher education to validate or improve existing status which facilitated post-1960 growth, though it cut the birthrate, simultaneously intensified the desire to have sons in the hopes that they subsequently would provide prebends or vital connections for kin.

In sum, too many interests in the society, political and popular, have too vital a stake in perpetuating the existing kinship system to support radical *qualitative* (that is, developmental) change, the desire of most Koreans to be simultaneously "modern" notwithstanding.[2]

# 9

# The Religious Heritage

## The Persistence of the Fundamental (Folk) Religion: *Sin'gyo*

The spirits of the folk religion are found everywhere in Nature and, as befits Nature's capricious blessing of water, soil, and weather, those spirits are either beneficial, like the Dragon Spirit which brings the vital water; or pranksters, such as the Spirit of the Dead who has not yet departed from the circle of the living; or are evil, like the Smallpox Spirit. In this way, the Korean spirit world mirrors this world and is as much a battleground between good and evil as our capricious world. Hence, to survive in this world, humans must somehow enlist the good spirits to at least stand off, but hopefully to defeat, the evil spirits. Thus, on the one hand, most individuals have favorite spirits which they rely on as their special patronal protectors against their spiritual and human enemies in this cosmic confrontation. Although some such spirit supporters are organized into sects, the majority, as in the patrimonial society in general, are content to pursue their (folk) interests singularly and in their own unique way. On the other hand, a number of folk practices are tricks to play on and outwit those spirits who perennially vex and do evil. For it is far wiser to beguile than to confront directly the (patrimonially) capricious authority of spirits—for example, open the house gates wide at New Year to tempt evil spirits to leave—and, by implication, the devilry of this world as well. Chinese Taoism gave depth to such folk beliefs, providing texts, techniques, and rituals, rather than becoming a distinctive religion.

216

Other vital Korean beliefs have been elaborated by, but predate, Chinese religious ways. One such has been geomancy, which originally was concerned with selecting an appropriate sacred place for making cliental offerings to spirits so that they would either grant favors or ward off disaster. By extension geomancy came to include finding a suitable spot on which to build a grave, and then a house site. Since all the phenomena in this world, whether natural or human, also exist in the spirit world, the two worlds being but aspects of one organic natural order, humans hope that by acting in accord with geomantic principles they will be in harmonic accord with the spirit world and receive its prebendal blessings now, here on earth. Consequently, even rulers have been attentive to geomancy in building their palaces and monuments, and especially the sites of their capitals, not only to legitimize dynasties in the eyes of both good, patrimonially moral spirits and this-world subjects, but also to neutralize both evil spirits and the regimes' equally patrimonially unworthy worldly predecessors and current and future political rivals.

A second Korean fundamental folk concern which has infused in it Chinese beliefs and practices is ancestor veneration. In sin'gyo, the dead are considered to be spirits whose peaceful passage to rest must be assured, lest they be forced against their will to hover about the living in an increasingly malevolent state. And when successfully dispatched, the spirits must be constantly appeased by periodic ceremonies and care for their graves by their descendants. If these dead ancestral spirits are properly cared for, they will serve as guardian patrons for any and all their descendants, not only those now living. Thus care and concern for the dead forges a vital link between the present living and the dead in a transcendental chain of unbroken continuity between past, present, and future. The rites of passage— in Korea, birth, coming of age, wedding, old age (the sixtieth birthday), and death—sanctify the linkage within the living generation and, at the extremes of birth and death rites, with respectively predecessor and successor generations and their spirits. The primary goal of ancestor veneration, then, is to insure prebendary benefices from one's ancestral spirits, not to obtain personal salvation, for prominent ancestors provide rationalization and protection of existing privileges, especially the authority of living patriarchs. Since maintaining generational continuity is so important to all this, ancestor veneration encourages and sanctifies consanguineal ties and the production of additional generations, especially male heirs, while the veneration ceremonies themselves provide the opportunity for consanguinities, the key collectivities of the Korean patrimonial society, to congregate and renew their solidarities and their vigor to pursue consanguineal interests.

Consanguineal spirit progenitors may be actual or mythological. The consanguineal ancestor of the Korean people is Tan'gun, the offspring of a male spirit and a woman who had been transformed from a totemic bear. Although he is not the sole Korean foundation spirit, even the last imperial house, in spite of its commitment to Confucianism, patronized Tan'gun to justify and legitimize *central* patrimonial authority, promoting Tan'gun to primacy as patriarchial spirit over other, especially consanguineal, spirits. After foreign imperialism increasingly penetrated Korea, the sophisticated seized upon Tan'gun as a national symbol. They revived the old royal services and created a religiously generated political sect dedicated to Tan'gun in order to keep faith in a Korean identity alive during the dark days of Japanese occupation.

In sin'gyo, as in most folk religions, formal doctrine is scarce and practice is all important. The cardinal practitioner is the shaman, who is prominent in all northeast Asian folk religions. Korean patrimonial rulers-as-shamans propitiated spirits, enlisting the good spirits to neutralize the evil ones, for example, to insure a good harvest. The rulers also reported to the spirits on state policies, entreating the good spirits to help to carry out patrimonially moral programs. And although shamanic specialists subsequently emerged, and other, sometimes antagonistic, court religious practices and thought (especially Confucianism) intruded, Korean rulers never relinquished their patrimonial folk shamanic role or interest. Blind shamans, serving as court astrologers, devised sham calendars to trick the evil spirits from interfering into vital agriculture and did all they could to insure a good harvest, lest the ruler be judged patrimonially unworthy. But certainly the most important government prebendal shamanic function, one required of all officials from the titular ruler on down to the village leaders in this land of uncertain moisture, was the appeal to the Dragon Spirits to provide Korea with an adequate rainfall for wet rice cultivation, especially in the spring.

The last imperial dynasty, for all its public involvement in shamanic practice—or, I suggest, because of it—grew increasingly intolerant of private shamans. It prohibited shamans from entering the capital under the excuse that their rituals were too noisy and disruptive of public order. But the shamans' activities were too much an essential of the popular religious sentiment to be summarily denied by rule-by-model fiat. Many individual shamans in disguise slipped into Seoul, while outside the city's walls shrines flourished as residents flocked to their services. In the waning days of the dynasty, a queen tried to lift the ban and founded new shaman sects. Local Confucian patrimonial bureaucrats were urged to participate in the new shaman rites and induce the populace to do likewise. Two charismatic shamans were given royal titles and royally patronized shrines were built in their honor to demonstrate court approval and facilitate their activities. Why such interest in these two shamans? A clue perhaps can be found in the fact that they patronized a deity who, according to legend, assisted Korea when it was invaded by Japan centuries earlier, and the queen hoped that that spirit would be persuaded to help once again against the new foreign intruders, since all other attempts to foil the imperialists had failed. With her assassination, the plan aborted.

There are many kinds of shamans. They need not be professional; for example, any healthy upright youngster may be selected to protect a village and its inhabitants for a coming year by propitiating the local spirits of earth and mountain. Some shamans, as we have seen, serve public, often political interests, while others serve family-individual interests. There are geomancers and (blind) fortune-tellers, either female or, more typically, male. But by far the most important shaman are the *mudang* who conduct *kut*, an act of mediation between spirits and humans which strives to establish rapport with good spirits and conquer, or at least neutralize, evil ones and provide humans with superhuman guidance to enable them to survive in this vale of tears. Mudang usually are female, though male mudang do exist; however, one expects to see males as helpers in a kut, such as musicians. Mudang are recruited variously; by heredity, normally passing to daughters-in-law; by enlistment of those who manifest unusual symptoms such as prolonged strange illness; or by volunteering or being selected by a mudang for training and disciplining. But regardless of how they get started, sooner or later all mudang are expected to be possessed by spirits if they are to validate their credentials.

Shamans in general and mudang in particular, although they are the professional practitioners of sin'gyo and thus propitiate sin'gyo spirits, are ever ready to call upon the spirits and exploit the folk aspects of Korea's other religions in their clients' behalf (consequently some observers refuse to call sin'gyo and the shaman role in it shamanism, and I concur). Sin'gyo has survived not only such inroads of alien, more sophisticated, and officially sanctioned beliefs, but also government indifference and occasional hostility. A primary source of sin'gyo's persistent strength lies in Koreans' conviction that in their patrimonial society this religion enables them both to know their future and, if necessary, to ameliorate or avoid an unfavorable destiny. Even scholars consult fortune-tellers to find out if they will pass their examinations; if the outlook is negative, a shaman is used to thwart the prediction or supply someone else's name to be used during the examination to trick a powerful but somehow not especially bright malevolent spirit.

Although Koreans appreciate the value of conciliation and subordination in ordering their essential social relations, often they also have to compete aggressively as individuals for their material survival, since corporate organization outside the limited consanguineal orbit is nonexistent. Sin'gyo has attempted to reconcile these contradictions by attributing the anxiety-generating, frustrating, and uncontrollable human conditions to forces beyond this world and by using the kut as surrogate dramatization of the spirit world in accord with cliental fantasies. Through the kut, a client controls his personal and social problems, such as poverty and illness, by reducing them to malfunctions (disharmonies) in the relationship between spirits and humans, brought on by sorcery, wandering spirits out for revenge, or dissatisfied ancestor spirits temporarily possessing some hapless descendant. Since such causes are beyond the rational control of human decision-making, the problem requires a metarational means to treat it, to wit, a kut which exorcises demons. Social and medical scientists have denounced the kut as confusing symptom with cause and, by treating only the former, contributing further to Koreans' rash behavior and paranoia, but alas to no avail. I suggest that the persistent underlying anxieties and frustrations in the patrimonial nature of Korean society are the true causes of the disease.

In spite of sin'gyo's concern with psychological and material anxiety and suffering and its spiritual remedy, the religion strongly affirms living in this social world. Sin'gyo is vague as to whether a future life exists and offers no transcendental mandate to fight against the social order, as oppressive and unreasonable as it may get, only rites to escape its pain. Individuals are thus encouraged to work out their problems in this world, rather than to reconstruct that world according to some religious ideal. Or to put it another way, as in all patrimonial religions, individuals are encouraged to accept their worldly fate and adjust as best they can to its demands, relying in this case on a shaman to ease their most frustrating, persistent burdens rather than to reconstruct the social environment in accord with clients' hopes. For ideals are the fantasy of the kut drama, not achievables in this society. The inability of critics and zealots of the other religions to stamp out sin'gyo attests to the persistence of Korean anxieties and frustrations, at least some of which I believe are attributable to the capricious patrimonial character of the Korean social order and the religion's persistence and effectiveness in addressing this character. In sum, sin'gyo indeed is primitive—not in the conventional meaning, but in the sense that it is vital and fundamental to Korea's persistent, patrimonially generated religious interests.[1]

## The Social Character of Buddhism

Buddhism has made three vital contributions to structuring Korean society. First, Buddhism rationalized loyalty to a centralized titular ruler by designating him the secular vicar of the Buddha, the ruler's laws as universally and morally valid, and the society which the ruler led as a universal brotherhood which transcended all parochial loyalties based, for example, upon consanguineous descent from common ancestors, real or imagined. In this reasoning, loyalty to Buddha and Buddhism implied loyalty to a centralized titular ruler, and vice versa, while spirituality implied centralized political loyalty and unity, and vice versa.

Second, Buddhism rationalized the (patrimonial) service role of the titular ruler and his staff. The ruler, as the Buddha's vicar, was expected to act on Buddhist scriptural principles, in Korea especially according to eight meritorious deeds (*pāramitā*), which are simultaneously spiritual and secular. When the ruler acts so, he governs under the Buddha's mandate, and is simultaneously a Bodhisattva, that is, a human whose essence (karma) is at the threshold of eternal bliss (nirvana) but who voluntarily stays in this mundane world expressly to *serve* others; a Maitreya, that is, a Buddha who has come personally to show humans how to achieve that bliss; and an intermediary for Amitaba, that is, a manifestation of that Buddha through whose patrimonially graceful mercy all are brought closer to secular and sacred happiness. If a ruler succeeds in meeting these religiously inspired but secular prebendal service responsibilities, the Buddha will compassionately watch over the Korean people and turn Korea into a Buddha land, that is, a land of both spiritual and material prosperity. Hence all Koreans, if they expect to survive and thrive, must join with their patronal ruler to help him carry out his Buddha-inspired patrimonial will, or so it is argued in the major Buddhist tract, the Sutra of the Golden Light.

Third, Buddhism interpenetrated sin'gyo. On the one hand, as it did elsewhere, Buddhism co-opted and reinterpreted the indigenous Korean religion and its beliefs, practices, and artistic forms to support

Buddhist morality. In fact, Buddhism succeeded so well that, although originally an alien faith, it overshadowed sin'gyo to become *the* medium of Korean religious expression. For example, sin'gyo natural forms were accepted as Buddhistically sacred; rocks, for instance, whether left as discovered or fashioned into more representative Buddha forms, were considered to be Maitreya. And as a universal faith, and because Buddhism appealed to all irrespective of class, occupation, or sex, the new religion provided Koreans with a sense of unity, mutuality, and identity which transcended sin'gyo's sacred and secular parochialism—hence Buddhism's special attraction to a centralizing patrimonial rulership. Yet, on the other hand, that very Buddhist association with sin'gyo and universal appeal directed Buddhism's religious interests to concerns beyond those of patrimonial rulership. Especially, sin'gyo directed Buddhism's attention to the Korean spirit world and the necessity to control it to serve the practical cause of protecting and nourishing the humble as well as the mighty mortals of the world here and now. For example, geomancy now could call upon a Buddhist pantheon of very potent spirits including Bodhisattvas to protect the inhabitants of humble dwellings as readily as those of the ruler's domicile, if they would but construct and comport themselves in accord with what was now a moral plan. Buddhist priests joined sin'gyo specialists in trying to control the weather, so as to protect the poor cultivators against poverty. Buddhist clerics, as intermediaries between the spirit and human worlds, were thought to have shamanistic magical capabilities, such as being able to travel quickly and widely to help travelers in distress, and their prized tracts, such as the tantric mandala, were those which were believed to have talismanic powers to divine or mobilize positive deities. Finally, of special pertinence, the goal of being reborn in a land of eternal bliss, which looms so prominently in northeast Asian Buddhism, gave way in Korea to a return to this imperfect world but under decidedly more pleasant secular circumstances.

Let us now examine the Buddhist element in two key patrimonial concerns which have been discussed extensively in earlier chapters. First, the use of the religion to foster (royal) *centralization*. The contribution of Wŏnhyo, the greatest Buddhist thinker of Korea and a towering figure in world Buddhism, was vital in creating such a truly centralizing doctrine. Wŏnhyo argued that making sectarian distinctions was an illusion, since all doctrines were only different aspects of the same Buddha truth. Since the doctrines of all schools were equally valid, why not boil them down to one, unique, essential doctrine which focused upon achieving religious perfection through demonstrating concern for humankind rather than striving to achieve individual, eternal, abstract bliss. Both principles, unity of doctrine and focus on this world, proved useful to a centralizing prebendally granting authority. However, Wŏnhyo only succeeded in reducing Buddhism to two constituents, namely, the doctrinal and meditative sects. I suggest that this was so because they represented two irreconcilable secular interests—the prebend-granting centralizers who were attracted to Amitaba's gracefully granted Pure Land bliss on the one hand; and those aristocrats opposing collective subordination to a central political will, nonaristocratic specialist-technicians who were being denied access to the higher echelons of the decision-making bureaucracy and hence to elite status, and local magnates trying to protect their landed revenue, all of whom saw value in a meditative doctrine which preached *individual* self-perfection as the correct path to bliss. The centralizers obtained primary support for their patrimonial nation-building not from exploiting any religious doctrine but rather from sponsoring visual expression of religious rectitude, that is, by building Buddhist temples and edifices. Since the royal centralizing constructors were able to mobilize corvée on a scale and in a manner which the competing aristocracy could not hope to match, the aristocracy could not match the royalists' religious, and by implication their patrimonial political, merit, which was the institutional point of it all. Kings also accumulated charismatic patrimonial merit by residing at temples, touring the land to spread the doctrines of the faith, presiding over great assemblages of priests who preached, and especially conducting a great court ceremony at which all in the audience swore allegiance to a ruler who patrimonially protected the Korean Buddha land.

A second patrimonially relevant Buddhist concern is the *failure* of the religion *to develop an independent corporate role* for itself and otherwise serve as a model and source of legitimacy for potentially corporate secular interests as occurred in the nonpatrimonial feudal societies, including neighboring Buddhist Japan, in spite of the fact that Buddhist interpenetration of sin'gyo seems to have led in that direction. Certainly by the tenth century Buddhism had become a power to be reckoned with. The current dynasty's founder had virtually established Buddhism as the state religion. Royal and noble second sons and any daughters became clerics, the upper reaches of the various orders being reserved for them. Additionally, since clerics were universally recruited and promoted through competitive examination, bright and energetic commoners could achieve middle-level clerical authority, positions in truth, if not legally, closed to them in lay administration (see Chapters 6 and 7). While in the cloth, all clerics, regardless of social origins, were members of a privileged class, exempt from corvée and taxes and sharing the government's prebendary benefices of land and conscript labor. In return for authority's favor, clerics served the ruler as aides and advisors, and when they did, they took precedence over their Confucian civil counterparts, which understandably was not appreciated.

Civil authority's occasional attempts to rein in the ever-growing power and wealth of the Buddhist order were not successful. The polity established an office to oversee the clerics, licensing them and requiring they carry identity and travel documents, in order to guarantee that the number of commoners evading taxes and military service would not get out of hand and to insure that the order would not grow so large as to become a political threat. However, individuals were not above bribing the appropriate official(s) to violate the quotas and, once in the order, to facilitate rising in the hierarchy. For both the prestige and the prerogatives of the higher clergy, especially the prebendary income from land and corvée, were at least comparable to those enjoyed by the secular privileged. As was true of civil property, Buddhist holdings were constantly being enlarged illegally by poaching on virgin territories and especially by commendations of land as acts of religious merit, either by small independent proprietors who were forced to surrender their land or by lay aristocrats who made voluntary gifts of land, hoping that offering the order nominal jurisdiction while retaining most of the land's income would circumvent confiscation by stronger rivals. However, no one was put off by the legal fiction of religious commendation, forcing the Buddhist order to turn to defending its holdings militarily, with conscript cultivators, lay recruits, and, when pressed, armed temple aides. Any number of these Buddhist domains were major integrated agricultural, artisan, and commercial establishments engaging in grain cultivation, stockraising, brewing, textile and paper manufacturing, military handicrafting, and the commercial handling of all these products and financed by their own capital, thus contributing significantly to the economic progress of Korea, including monetarization and artisan commercialization.

In sum, in many ways Korean "medieval" Buddhism had become very close to its contemporary Japanese Buddhism, which incidentally Wŏnhyo's thought helped spark! But there are significant *institutional* differences. First, unlike Japanese Buddhism, the Korean order, like its military ally-cum-rival, was never a serious countervailing political and economic institutional threat to central civil authority, and for the same reason—the order was dependent on central authority for prebends. Second, the Korean clerics did not, as the Japanese did, recruit from the populace to resist central or local civil oppression; in fact, the Korean order's patrimonial grinding of the peasantry through corvée and usury incited popular rebellion against it. Third, Korean Buddhism never consciously generated an ideology which served to rationalize popular rebellion against the existing patrimonial institutional order. Quite the contrary, the Maitreya-delivering-Buddha-to-come sect, so potent a legitimizer of popular dissent even in patrimonial China, was reinterpreted to drum up support for rather than confront centralized Korean authority. The meditative sect, even more than it did in either China or Japan, came closest to justifying local rights against centralization. And yet it too was never used to justify a movement to "break through" the existing social order and translate its ideals into notions of institutionally accepted legal rights and privileges, perhaps because the local civil or military lords, rather than being independent feudators like their Japanese counterparts, were themselves prebend-seeking patrimonialists.

The failure of Korean Buddhism to truly institutionalize a non-patrimonial independent corporate footing in the society is certainly attested by the ease with which the last imperial dynasty, favoring patrimonial Confucianism, was able to strip Buddhism of its seemingly redoubtable prerogatives. First, authority severed the religion and its hierarchs' intimate association with royal court and bureaucracy, clerical advisers and teachers being banished from court. Second, the order was isolated from the populace— ancestor veneration was purged of its Buddhist overtones, which ended the right of Buddhist clerics to participate in these ceremonies, and both temples and clerics were banned from the capital. Third, economically, Buddhist land prebends ceased, temples were taxed, and corvée prohibited. The smaller temples in particular were impoverished and literally crumbled, and so did the viability of the monastic orders within. Fourth, authority encouraged internal doctrinal disputation between and within the sects to divide and rule. Fifth and finally, clerics were degraded to the mean underclass, a condition which made commoners pause before taking the robe. Stripped of their prebends, clerics were forced to survive both by exploiting their talent as entertainers, which they had developed originally to attract audiences to their preaching, and by engaging in the occupations of the underclass, such as acting, magic, and geomancy. As was the intent, the order thus came to recruit primarily from the indigent and the ignorant who practiced a career characterized by routine ritual and prayer-reading learned by rote from a mentor for an unsophisticated audience. The sophisticated in contrast regarded the priests much as they regarded the underclass in general, as charlatans, parasites, and potential criminals. How low clerics had sunk in the public eye can be grasped by the fact that clerical actors in the popular theater found themselves increasingly satirizing their own beliefs and customs—the ultimate degradation whereby the ruled accept the master's deprecatory image!

All such harassment and machinations had two major effects on Buddhism. On the one hand, driven from their urban environment by government decree, the temples and the devout clergy relocated in the remote mountains where they were visited and supported by the dedicated minority of all classes and of both sexes. This assured the survival of the faith and the order, but it effectively cut them off from the realities of, and hence from an active role in, the contemporary society. On the other hand, in order to survive in the remote hinterland, Buddhist clerics even more than before accepted sin'gyo folk beliefs and practices as their very own, so that in many instances it became difficult to distinguish between a male mudang and a Buddhist cleric.

And yet, it cannot be overlooked that *particular* rulers, with typical patrimonial caprice, were quite lenient toward Buddhism, and even were its patrons. Of particular interest, usurper rulers considered what was by then a counterorthodox faith useful in legitimizing their rule in contradistinction to the entrenched authority sanctioned by Confucianism. But because they were capricious individual whims, such periods of favor never lasted, sometimes not even during the lifetimes of particular rulers or queens. Moreover, certain specialized Buddhist court roles, such as that of astronomer, thrived even during periods of overt hostility toward the faith. For as long as Buddhists were not numbered among the moral administrators or court pedagogical lecturers and ceremonial servants, the patrimonial court Confucians were not unduly agitated. Confucian court and local yangban were more than willing to have clerics, *as individuals*, chant to prebendally ward off or mitigate disasters. Further, because Buddhism had become so intimately intertwined with a particularly Korean identity and because at least some clerics stripped of their privileges and access to the privileged had established close ties to the populace, the authorities were never above using the clergy to mobilize the masses for those large-scale endeavors in the Confucian-devised and led local or national interest which the Confucians themselves would not or could not undertake. For example, clerics were used to organize corvée both to build and to repair the Seoul city walls. And in times of national peril, clerics helped raise Righteous Armies, served as spies, quartermasters, and chaplains, comforted the wounded and the bereaved, prayed for the dead, and otherwise kept up morale.

The reform movement of the late nineteenth century offered Buddhism the opportunity to recoup its earlier prestige. The faith profited by reformer negativism toward things Confucian; by the wave of anti-imperial nationalism which was suspicious of alien Christianity; by the fact that some of the reform leaders were Buddhist, even clerics; and by the fact that most Japanese, with whom many of the reformers identified, were Buddhist. The reformers, supported by an influential Buddhist priest, lifted the ban on priests and temples within Seoul and put an end to the special clerical dress. But most pertinent, Buddhist scholars strived to revitalize the faith by founding it on scientific rather than supernatural grounds and making it relevant to the social needs of the day. A 1902 convention reorganized the Seoul priesthood and temples and created a Buddhist-sponsored, secular educational system through middle schools. But these changes were too much for some; the Buddhist community, cleric and lay, as the society of the time in general, split along conservative and liberal reformist lines (see Chapter 11). The subsequent failure of the secular reform movement also dampened enthusiasm for religious change. However, even this modest Buddhist awakening did demonstrate the religion's viability in spite of the long night of dormancy and helped to pave the way for Buddhist modernization, for better or worse, under the Japanese.[2]

## Confucianism: Patrimonialism Triumphant

Although Buddhism predominated for a long period, Confucianism always took special hold among minor aristocrats who obviously preferred appointment and then promotion on merit—in patrimonial thinking, on intellectual competence and virtue—to prestiged birth alone. I say "alone" because these individuals were no more interested in opening the bureaucracy to commoners than were the higher ranked, since in Korean aristocratic Confucian thinking commoners were ordinary men devoid of the potential for cultivating virtue and intellect and hence unworthy to rule. The monarch too found Confucianism to his liking, because it provided him with advisers and aides who, in contrast to the aristocratic consanguinities of both capital and hinterland, were personally tied to him and supportive of his centralizing interests. Confucianism also enabled the provincial small landlords to justify expanding their holdings at the expense of the Buddhist temples.

All these Confucian partisans found their champion in the founder of the last imperial dynasty, whom the Confucians helped to turn Korea into a Confucian patrimonial society even more orthodox than its Chinese model. The founder's key adviser rationalized that properly cultivated humans were good, and hence did not need Buddha's redemption; that production, not Buddhist-inspired poverty, was the way to achieve bliss; and that the purpose of life and the foundation of morality was to serve, not escape from, this secular social order in general and the state in particular according to one's station—the ordinary man with his hands, the Confucian scholar with his mind. His philosophy found objective expression in the activities of the civil aristocrats, the yangban, who became the society's administrators, teachers, and cultural arbiters. In contrast to the Buddhists who channeled their religious interests into cosmology and ethics, the Confucians focused on creating and maintaining a patrimonial moral order which would serve their prebendary patron, the Korean monarch, and his patron in turn, the Chinese emperor, who, as the center of the Confucian world order, protected Confucian Korea from its physical and ideological-religious enemies.

Korean monarchs came to legitimize their patrimonial authority on a Confucian mandate of heaven; heaven in its Korean version being equated with the sin'gyo folk spirit world. However, such a mandate was a two-edged sword in that, although it could be used to demand the loyalty of the aristocracy in general and the bureaucratic representatives in particular, it also provided the bureaucracy with a weapon to criticize the ruler's performance in the light of Confucian ideal prescriptions which the censors especially could interpret rigidly and formalistically. Sooner or later a ruler was bound to violate some Confucian code.

As orthodox a Confucian order as Korea was, and as respectful—some were to say obsequious—of China as it was, nevertheless Korean Confucianism was never a pale imitation of the Chinese Confucian social order; rather one should say that Confucian general principles both modified and were modified by prevailing Korean beliefs and practices. For Confucianism sunk such deep roots into the Korean psyche that by the twentieth century few were able or cared to bother to make the distinction between patrimonial Confucian and sin'gyo shamanistic intervention into the spirit world through prayer during natural calamities, divination sacrifice at dangerous locations, and ritual plowing by a representative from the Confucian National Academy to open the spring agricultural season.

But perhaps the most significant example of the Confucian contribution to redefining social habits was in consanguineal relations. Confucian filial piety honors age, and through age superior authority. Although respect and deference to patriarchal elders predates Confucianism, while Korean Buddhism too extolled serving parents and their surrogates as a way of showing honor and thankfulness for patronal favors, Confucianism intensified and formalized such vertical submissiveness as a mandatory, moral ritual. The bureaucratic aristocracy, which had most to gain from such deference, were relentlessly indoctrinated in its moral vitality in school, questioned on it in their civil service examinations, rewarded for living according to it—given time off from official duties or put on special assignment to enable them to cater to their aging parents' needs, and, if they reached age eighty, given special rank. To one observer, such behavior was more than a virtue, it was a national cult. Why so? One reason is that the patrimonial ruler never seriously attempted to secure his subjects' loyalty by directly appealing to them *as individuals*. But if through filial piety he could insure their unquestioned loyalty and subordination to their superiors, especially the patriarchs of those local consanguinities which had been instrumental in bringing the dynasty to authority, and then the loyalty of the patriarchs to the ruler in turn, the ruler would solve his fundamentally Korean patrimonial control problem.

Filial piety projected generationally is ancestor veneration. Such veneration was a pre-Confucian (folk) practice which Buddhism embraced and went on to expand into a patriotic duty for aspiring Bodhisattvas to create a Buddha land in Korea. Confucianism's contribution was to clarify (validate) and glorify (vindicate) the lines of descent which guaranteed perpetual access to the privilege of public office for the descendants of those who came to authority with a dynasty's founder. These individuals dominated but did not monopolize elite status, which made them all but paranoid on maintaining the genealogical purity which Confucianism equated with patrimonial virtue. Confucian ancestor veneration was performed for the near (that is, for up to five generations above ego) at home involving only immediate kin, and for the remote (that is, for five to fifteen generations above ego) at grave sites where all the consanguineals who shared the same genealogical tie assembled, thus reinforcing vital consanguineal solidarity. And not to be overlooked was the special rite for those who reached their sixtieth birthday, since such individuals were considered living ancestors, that is, the symbolic link in the vital genealogical chain between the two worlds of the beyond and the here and now. Responsibility for venerating the ancestors was vested in the genealogical representative, the eldest male, whose activities were subsidized by a somewhat larger share of the common inheritance (see Chapter 8).

Confucian filial-ancestral practices are specialized and rationalized in the Chinese philosopher Chu-Hsi's "House Rules," a tract which, incidently, was rarely referred to in nonaristocratic imperial China. According to Chu-Hsi, all social practices and rules are the objective social expression of eternal universal principles of the natural order, which includes human society. Since, in Confucian thinking, that natural order is a moral order, conforming to the rules insures not only naturally correct but also morally worthy behavior, which is why it has been considered so important, especially to a patrimonial aristocracy determined to validate and perpetuate the legitimacy of its bureaucratic prerogatives. The aristocratic lineages drew up specific codes, rules, or customs to formalize the eternal principles of the House Rules. Typically these codes promised worldly success, especially prebendal public office, if house members conformed during their active years and taught the codes to and inspired the next generation in their retirement. These codes thus were meaningless to non-bureaucratic commoners, and precious few commoner codes exist.

Although the Confucians never monopolized, they and their ethos dominated formal education because both education and the religion were vitally concerned with socializing potential bureaucrats, a matter which Confucianism's chief rival, Buddhism, treated with tolerant indifference. The educational structure which blossomed by the last imperial dynasty had at the apex a national academy which admitted a limited number of carefully tested students destined to become authority's strategic decision-makers. In conformity with Korean aristocratic thinking, a clear distinction was made between this privileged group and those trained in halls and (ordinary) academies who became, respectively, civil specialists-technicians and military officials. Since both these latter categories of officials were considered to be morally inferior to the elite decision-makers, they were offered a (morally) inferior education, appointed to lesser ranks, and were recruited from the lesser nobility. Provincial academies, constituting the second level of the academic hierarchy, were established in every county. The most promising of their graduates were eligible to enter the national institutes of learning or to be appointed to local administrative posts. At the third, local level, schools catered to the very young. These schools were crucial because they socialized aristocrat and commoner alike in the fundamentals of Confucian patrimonialism, though aristocrats would in time move up the academic ladder, while commoners, in most cases, would cease their education upon graduation. The schools stressed rote memorization, and hence uncritical acceptance of alleged eternal moral truths; formalistic conformity to propriety; and obsequience to all superiors, from teachers and patrons in this and the spirit world beyond, to those in authority, especially the present ruler. The schools were popular in part because they used the vernacular alphabet which, along with publication of a Chinese-Korean dictionary, enabled ambitious commoners with even a limited education to master the sacred Confucian texts, and thus to challenge the aristocrats' virtual monopoly of public office and yangban status. Since they had sunk deep local roots and catered to local official and commoner needs so well, the schools managed to survive when the dynasty collapsed and with it the existing higher education system.

Retired or deposed officials founded a number of private academies in their local areas to instruct their kinsmen in the Confucian classics, literature, and history. The academies were especially attractive to those who were barred from attending the public institutions for political reasons, but all serious students sought them out because they set higher standards, their lecturers were more competent and inspired, and their curricula were more innovative than the government institutions. The government tried to prevent the academies from becoming potentially independent islands of resistance to the center by limiting the numbers of students they could accept, and especially by threatening to withdraw the prebendal subsidies. However, the academies countered by exploiting their consanguineal connections in high places. The academies' greatest challenge came in the mid-nineteenth century when a regent tried to eliminate their tax exemptions and set strict entrance quotas. Although this "reform" was countermanded when the regent fell from grace, the academies never truly recovered their old vitality. They were either abandoned or integrated into the emerging government education system.

One or more halls at all educational institutions were specifically set aside for religious homage to Confucius and his Chinese and Korean cohorts and disciples. All students were required to attend such rites. The monarch himself, or his personally designated representative, the crown prince or the head of the Board of Rites, presided over an elaborate twice-yearly pageant at the National Academy in honor of the Korean Confucian-defined moral-cum-social cosmic order. At lower levels, magistrates superintended ceremonies honoring the royal family. Thus were Korean authority, learning, religion, and the morally-religiously defined natural order all intertwined.

The primary goal of the Confucian-inspired educational system, whatever form it took, was to prepare candidates to take a civil service examination, the gate to national official appointment. Examinations had been introduced early in Korean history, but it was not until the Confucian-dominated last dynasty that high-ranking aristocrats fully accepted the validity of examinations to confirm social status. The system which came to prevail was the consequence of a long process of trial and error which determined that the system would be nationally competitive, would examine both in history and Confucian thought, and especially that it would separately examine those competing not only for different ranks but also for different careers of civil administrator, civil aide, and military officer, as symbolized by separate examinations in classics, literature, and the military arts. Introductory examinations were held three times a year at the lowest administrative levels. Successful candidates were allowed to sit for the regular provincial examinations, which were scheduled once every three years, although special provincial examinations were held more frequently as the dynasty matured. Those who passed the provincial examinations were eligible for immediate appointment to lesser posts in the central administration. But, if they preferred, they could compete in special national examinations held the following spring, at which occasion they were joined by sitting officials, the sons of merit officials, and the graduates of both the Seoul secondary institutes and the National Academy. This grand examination was given in three stages, the last stage being conducted before the ruler in his capacity as moral judge. All candidates were assured of passing, and hence obtaining some government post, but the examination determined at which of three possible grades candidates entered. The reformers of 1895 abolished all these examinations, and thus the primary incentive for most to study Confucianism, but by then the Confucian social order was crumbling.

Local and outside observers alike blame Confucianism for imperial Korea's ultimate travail, for a number of reasons: Confucian indifference and even hostility to a productive commercial and industrial economy, its espousal of unquestioned loyalty to incompetent superiors, its worship of the past, its penchant for social harmony whatever the effect on innovation, its preaching that frugality rather than production would liberate humankind from poverty, its refusal to accept other than ideal solutions to practical problems, its divisive petty bickering over abstractions, its elitist class consciousness, its anti-militarism even when survival was at stake, its investigation of moral and philosophical rather than scientific knowledge, and, above all, its insistence that nurturing individual perfection rather than worldly social effort would meet the challenges of the last two centuries. One can but point out that most if not all such charges have been made at one time or the other against most of the indigenous faiths of east and southeast Asia. Thus I prefer to rephrase the case, to postulate that Confucianism was dysfunctional in Korea because it was so intimately associated with rationalizing the then-existing and in many developmental ways inadequate Korean patrimonial order. When Confucianism functions in a nonpatrimonial order the verdict may not necessarily be negative, e.g., the case of nineteenth-century Japan, in which the very observers who deplore the Confucian role in Korea claim that the same religion played a positive, even vital, role in encouraging Japan's modernization *and* development![3]

## Christianity

Catholics were among the Japanese who invaded Korea in the late sixteenth century but, not surprisingly, we have no evidence that any Koreans were converted at that time. According to tradition, Korean Christianity formally began in the eighteenth century when a small group of yangban intellectuals met to discuss the religion and subsequently became disciples. Whether or not this is valid as the model for later yangban conversion, only an extreme minority ever followed their initiative. For although at least some yangban approved of Christian ethics, they found the concept of a personal creative deity wanting, if not inconceivable. And although most yangban were impressed with Jesuit science, they refused to accept the Jesuit claim that their scientific sophistication was derived from their faith, or that the Catholic social gospel was compatible with the Confucian rules of etiquette.

The new faith also had to contend with two more formidable obstacles. First, even the converts themselves were disturbed by the refusal of the church to accept ancestor veneration. To Korean yangban, ancestor veneration was much more than a moral code or ritual; it was the very symbol and essence of a way of life—an oath of loyalty not only to kin but also to ruler, to dynasty, to authority, and ultimately to the very social order. Hence, if Christianity frowned upon ancestor veneration, then the faith also questioned the vital patrimonial institutions with which that veneration was so intimately intertwined;

and thus Christianity was equated with political-moral treason. Second, the yangban Catholic partisans concentrated among the out-of-power "Southern" political factionalists who found in Christian thought a distinctive ideology around which to rally in the struggles against the dominant, established faction at court, and in Jesuit science a means to improve themselves economically. For all these reasons the authorities surveilled, harassed, and periodically persecuted all known Catholics. Whenever the polity uncovered the proscribed Catholic organizations it wiped them out, save during the early nineteenth century when their factional supporters were in power. Since they were considered traitors, yangban Catholics and their kin could be deprived of their aristocratic status. This perhaps more than any physical threat caused many a yangban to pause before converting and, once converted and discovered, to apostatize, lest social guilt fall collectively not only on contemporary kin but also on consanguineal descendants.

Those yangban Catholics who were exiled or who fled for their safety settled in remote areas, especially in the north where the government was the weakest and they could live unobtrusively among common peasants. Some of these yangban became humble potters to survive economically, to fool the authorities, and to justify traveling about to proselytize. In this way Catholicism spread geographically and from the elite to the masses who, deprived of close contact with Buddhism, found the Christian ideals of social equality and the promise of otherworldly relief from the sufferings of this world appealing. Commoner Christians, when discovered, were dealt with even more harshly than were yangban, perhaps because commoner converts were more likely to abandon their commitment to the established patrimonial order than were yangban. For example: if even one villager was discovered to be a Catholic, the whole village was razed, and all the former inhabitants reduced in status to the mean class. Females (of all classes actually) who became nuns, since they left their families and took an oath of chastity and hence threatened the very viability of their consanguineal units, were singled out for special reprisal.

International treaties with Japan and the European powers, particularly France, in effect legalized Catholicism and the right of French priests especially to proselytize for the faith. That clergy subsequently established an indigenous hierarchy and seminary program. By the end of the nineteenth century there were an estimated 42,000 Korean Catholics; even a royal princess was converted in 1896. But such prosperity was superficial. Foreign sponsorship intensified both official and popular suspicion that the religion was just another imperial tool to topple the existing social order, an attitude the unsubtle French, here and elsewhere in Asia, did nothing to disabuse. Thus persecution, though circumspect so as not to antagonize the well-armed foreigners, continued. Catholic lives were lost not only through organized movements inspired by both anti-foreign bureaucrats and nativists, but also through individual actions aided and abetted by colluding magistrates. In other words, in spite of expanding conversions, Catholic Christianity never shook off its negative image as a potential political and social subversive conspiracy. The consequent catacomb mentality and existence, as one church observer has termed it, induced the church to tread a very conservative path. For example, the prayer book adopted in 1886 was the very same one used in Europe to support absolute monarchy and familism by stressing that this world is an exile that must be bravely endured, and that the church through its agent the priest guaranteed survival in this and the next world. Translated into our terms, this implied God was the supreme patrimonialist, dispensing prebendary grace (salvation) through His yangban-like priesthood, in return for the faithful's cliental loyalty and obedience.

Although isolated Protestant missionaries had come to Korea as early as the eighteenth century, unlike the Catholics they did not arrive in strength until the country was officially opened to foreign intercourse in the 1880s. With the Catholic experience to guide them, the Protestants were determined not to be similarly categorized as subversive plotters and by and large they were successful for three major reasons. First, they entered the country openly and in the company of prestigious diplomats. Second, the early clerics were Presbyterians and Methodist-Episcopals who stressed biblical knowledge, personal piety, evangelical conversion, revivalism, and repentance, rather than the liberal social activitism certain to antagonize Korean officialdom. Third, intended or not, Protestantism was anything but asocial in the institution-building sense, which brought the religion prestige far beyond the small circle of converts. For the core of Protestantism, individual Bible-reading and study, requires literacy. Aghast at the prospect of transcribing the sacred book into classic Chinese or its Korean equivalent, *idu*, which few could read, the missionaries decided to use the popular alphabet, which they could teach to all, including the lowly classes and women, since they too had to read if they were to be saved. Learning to read religious tracts led to exposing Koreans, regardless of sex or class, to modern secular education, especially in the practical and scientific arts such as medicine. In Korean thinking, his combined scientific and spiritual skills made the

Protestant missionary a very wise and potent shaman at the very time that faith in the efficacy and moral superiority of the indigenous religions, including Confucianism, was waning.

But Protestant, like Catholic, proselytizing at first was restricted and personally dangerous. The faith's enemies spread rumors that missionary schools were literally and figuratively stealing children from parents, and that converts who cut their hair did so to fight alongside the foreign devils who were plotting to seize the country. Riots against Protestant clerics were as common as against Catholics. But by the 1890s all this had been overcome. The missionaries were free to move all over the land, especially in the north, where they set up their center in an old commercial metropolis where they were able to exploit the strong antibureaucratic, anti-Confucian sentiment and receptivity to a faith offering eternal bliss to all, including despised merchants. The missionaries penetrated the rural areas by relying on circuit Korean "helpers" to convert village leaders, who in turn converted kin and neighbors. Some of these helpers were peddlers who were used to traveling and were well known and trusted in the remotest sites in Korea. Spread thin, the competing Presbyterian and Methodist missionaries wisely decided to divide the country into areas open exclusively to either, but rarely to both. This not only husbanded valuable talent and resources in short supply, but also had the advantage of convincing the Koreans that they were being offered a consistent, truthful, universally valid corpus of thought and design for living, in sharp contrast to the factional contentiousness of Confucianism and the secular politicians. Finally, in the urban capital of Seoul, the churches established theological seminaries which created a self-sufficient indigenous clergy, a YMCA movement to attract the young, and a very popular dispensary service which demonstrated concern for all, regardless of sex and status.

Yet, in spite of such widespread appeal, apparent success, and ultimate government acquiescence, like Catholicism, Protestantism ever found itself up against formidable Korean religious and cultural barriers which were to restrict its numbers to a minor fraction of the population. Strong fundamentalist interdictions against using alcohol or smoking and disapproval of polygamy and ancestor veneration, though less strident than those of the Catholics, caused would-be converts to hesitate and to compromise after conversion. Those who flocked to the missionary schools and hospitals were eager to learn the ways of the foreigners, especially the English language, but very few were interested enough to discuss the new religion, let alone convert. The natural audience that the Protestants addressed in the United States and Canada, a true middle class, did not exist in Korea; the middle stratum chung'in and petty landlords, in contrast, were too strongly committed to patrimonial Confucian elitism to be receptive to Christianity. Those who were the most responsive to the new faith were the powerless, which made Protestantism as suspect as Catholicism in official circles.

And yet the Catholic-Protestant Christian notion of persevering in this vale of tears, secure within a fellowship of like believers equivalent to, and often more strongly tied together than, indigenous intermediary groups including consanguinities, stood the churches and Korean Christians well. This was especially true in the twentieth century, when the Japanese occupation of Korea created a situation in which sheer survival and personal faith rather than fruitless overt protest were the only feasible means for most Koreans to resist, albeit passively, their colonial masters. Thus it was that Korean Christianity had an influence far beyond the minuscule numbers of its adherents, and in spite of (perhaps because of) its historic reticence to redress grievances through social action.

In conclusion: If one discounts the Philippine case, in which the Spanish conquerors used the sword and their political power to convert, Korea has been the most receptive of all indigenous Asian societies to Christianity. Many explanations are offered for this; for example, the weakness of its potential key rival, Buddhism; its compatability with sin'gyo's central deity and the equation of Christian priests with shamans; anti-Confucian social attitudes which ultimately worked to Christianity's advantage as faith in the Confucian world order was shattered; its association with the West and its potent skills and modernity; and, for Protestantism in particular, the long dearth of any liberal or secular antireligious thought to challenge its fundamentalist claim to be *the* representative of modern, especially American, values. And yet in spite of all these advantages and the particular audience it addressed, Christianity ever compromised with existing Korean religious and institutional principles, ultimately even ancestor veneration, and, more important for our purposes, with the patrimonial character of the social order, which the religion refused to question in the light of its own nonpatrimonial convictions and its historical western European role in the development process.[4]

## The Transitional Modern Religion: Ch'ŏndogyo

It is axiomatic in the sociology of religion that in times of stress novel religious ideas and movements arise to enable individuals both

to understand and to persevere, if not to change their social environment, and the crises of mid-nineteenth-century Korea were no exception. Then, many religious sects appeared, offering both an opportunity to create a utopian social order in which all would enjoy bliss in
this world and beyond, and also a supranormal means to achieve that
goal against the will and formidable weaponry of institutional authority. Thus, on the one hand, the new sects preached a folk ideal of
equalitarian brotherhood to counter the popularized but nevertheless
hierarchical Confucianism which authority was then promoting to
tranquilize the masses; and, on the other hand, the leaders claimed to
be simultaneously Buddhist Maitreyas and Bodhisattvas, masters of
Tao magic able to appear and disappear at will and overcome enemies
effortlessly, and potent sin'gyo shamanic intermediaries who could
induce good spirits to support their causes.

The most significant of these sects was what was later called Ch'ŏndogyo—"the religion of heavenly way." At the time it appeared, yangban status and material security were declining rapidly while peasant
dreams for release from yangban incompetence and greed were rising. The sect's founder was highly intelligent, educated, and ambitious but, I think significantly, he found himself ineligible for public
office because, though his father's line was yangban, his mother's was
not, a situation which he bitterly resented. He had studied many religions, including Catholicism, but especially sin'gyo. Although he was
thus well aware of western religious learning, he was opposed to
western ideas and considered them and yangban culture to be the
twin causes of both his own and his nation's sorry plight.

The founder set about to provide a viable alternative. The heart of
the new religion was individual faith in the prime sin'gyo spirit,
Hananim. To the founder, however, Hananim was much more than a
sin'gyo spirit; he was an omnipotent, omnipresent, wise, and sincere
deity who provided salvation for all believers. The founder insisted
that Hananim was not an imitation of the God of the Christians; to
emphasize the point he wrote Hananim's name with Chinese ideographs, since the Christians wrote their deity's name in the vernacular
Korean. In contrast to Confucianism, whose medium, the yangban,
promised much while increasingly offering less and less, the founder
claimed that Hananim guaranteed his devotees prosperity and health.
If necessary, health could be restored by Hananim's spirit medicine,
most typically a formula written on paper which, when destroyed or
ingested, carried away not only the physical disability itself but also
the anxieties and economic distress which illness causes. The interpretation of omens replaced Taoist-Confucian geomancy. (Discussion

of Ch'ŏndogyo as a social movement—Tonghak—appears in the next chapter.)

The new religion involved much more than performing rituals for prizes. The cornerstone of the faith was the ethical-social principle that when an individual accepted Hananim as the supreme spirit of the universe, Hananim and the human spirit merged. Since all such humans now possessed Hananim's spirit, they were morally obligated to treat each other as equals, regardless of age, sex, and social status. The founder also preached that since spirit and matter, or mind and body, were one, the faithful had the responsibility of caring equally for their material and psychological health. Thus provided with a healthy body and mind, united with their neighbors in a moral, reasonable, and self-reliant community able to dispense with yangban services, the faithful could then go on to create the new social order that was free of both religious and secular evil, one in accord with Hananim's wishes and hence superior to what both the yangban and the West envisioned for Korea.

Keenly aware of the rashness and declining fortunes of his contemporaries, the Chinese T'aipings, the founder preached that only an individual, gradualist spiritual transformation was the proper way to change the existing social order for the better. However, since he also preached, at least by implication, that Hananim had abandoned (that is, removed heaven's mandate from) the morally wanting imperial dynasty and its prebend-granting yangban cohorts, the authorities could not but take a dim view of the new religion, and of the founder in particular. He was denounced as a traitor in patrimonial fashion, by equating heterodoxy with political error, taken into custody, and hanged. Suppression of the religion followed. Not surprisingly, the sophisticated elite overwhelmingly supported the government's actions. The yangban resented the suggestion that they should cut off their topknots as a symbol of social equality, since that directly attacked their patrimonially morally superior status and left them with the feeling that they were no better than the short-haired foreigners, while young intellectuals recoiled from such shamanic "superstitions" as the talismans which the faithful used to protect themselves against the government's superior weapons.

But all was not lost. The new head of the religion, a distant relative of the founder, created a local, sometimes secret organization which would insure the survival of the religion in the face of authority's determination to wipe it out and also clarified and expanded the founder's doctrines to discipline the faithful and weed out the opportunists. He denounced luxury, at least to the extent that it attracted

undue attention; proscribed concubinage, sexual inequality, and female exploitation of any sort; eliminated the worship of images; and
required abstinence from (1) smoking, drinking, or (2) meat-eating,
which went beyond the restrictions of either Protestants or Buddhists
respectively.

The new leader's refurbishing of Ch'ŏndogyo's spirit and organization certainly succeeded in the sense that he assured the survival of
the sect during the trying imperial days and the Japanese occupation
to follow. However, in contrast—and this is my conclusion—neither
founder or successor, on the one hand, nor yangban political reformers, on the other hand, were successful in the sense that none was
able to or saw fit to align Ch'ŏndogyo's potentially developmentally
relevant "ethic," religious interests, or social witness with developmentally productive *institutional* change in Korean society. Nor, for
that matter, was any even able to contribute positively to Korea's
modernization.[5]

## The Japanese Role in Korea's Religious Modernization

As was true for the other institutions of Korean society, the course
of Korea's religious modernization was initiated and defined by the
Japanese imperialists, in a form which would survive the influx of
American ideas and the Korean intellectuals' prejudice against things
Japanese.

### Sin'gyo

Japanese ethnologists, with official blessing, regarded sin'gyo as
equivalent to the Japanese folk religion, Shintō, that is, as the core of
the "real" Korean value system, and hence vital to understanding
Japan's new subjects. But unlike Shintō, which they honored, the
Japanese designated sin'gyo a "pseudo-religion," that is, a glorified
body of prescientific superstitions whose practitioners, especially the
mudang, were charlatans out to mislead and exploit the public and
otherwise stand in the way of the Japanese design for a modern
Korea. Why so? It would seem that besides striving to denigrate all
indigenous Korean culture to justify the occupation, the government
general needed an excuse to harass and suppress potential sin'gyo-
supported, if not inspired, movements whose philosophy might play
on popular resentment against Japan to spark agitation and even
open rebellion. The Japanese were especially worried by a prophesy
that a sectarian leader was one of a succession of Korean Maitreya-

like figures slated to rally the faithful and help them to obtain release from this world's—read Japanese—discontent.

The most significant pseudo-religion during the Japanese period was Ch'ŏndogyo. By so designating the sect, the Japanese continued the imperial practice of depriving its members of the right to worship freely and to organize. The Japanese acted so because they were ever suspicious of Ch'ŏndogyo after the unsuccessful revolt against the Korean-Japanese establishment by one of the sect's elements, the Tonghak, even though most of the sect's leaders subsequently tried, unsuccessfully it turned out, to mollify the Japanese by siding with them against the rival Russians and by otherwise supporting the Japanese effort to take over the peninsula, albeit in the mistaken belief that the Japanese would liberate and not colonize. Then the very disillusioned leader of Ch'ŏndogyo, ironically the same one who originated the pro-Japanese policy, responded to the Japanese challenge to the sect's viability by expelling the pro-Japanese faction (which created its own sect) and by reorganizing Ch'ŏndogyo. He promoted on merit, shored up the sect's finances, intensively trained and indoctrinated the faithful in general and the teachers in particular, and especially tried to strike a balance between central hierarchical control and district self-reliance to insure the sect's survival whether the authorities focused their attack on the center or on a particular geographical area. To help members stand firm spiritually, a 1906 doctrinal decree reaffirmed faith in the unity of thought and action, religion and social politics, and in living by—and if necessary dying for—principle. Refurbished Ch'ŏndogyo thought and organization were instrumental in generating and carrying out the March 1919 anti-Japanese demonstration (see Chapter 11), and hence became a special target of the government's vengeance, which included the incarceration of its leader, who died in 1922. Thereafter, the sect was forced to act very cautiously, eschewing violence for passive resistance against a Japanese drive to destroy the Korean cultural identity, national sentiment, and pride. Nevertheless, the sect's youth corps, reorganized into a party with a Marxist tinge, cooperated in a united front of laborers, farmers, students, and others to resist Japanese political-cultural aggression and economic exploitation more actively. Not surprisingly, the authorities intervened, and finally drove the party underground in 1934. The religion itself fared no better; for example, during World War II its cathedral was turned into a factory.

In conclusion, we can see that Ch'ŏndogyo profited from an excellent organization and widespread popular support for its programs, which enabled it to agitate under the very nose of authority. However, like all Korean intermediary groups, particularly in such troubled times, it suffered from doctrinal disputes, some of which had to do with differing views of the Korean modernizing process and whether or not to cooperate with authority or other groups in the society. These disputes, which the Japanese adroitly did not discourage, exacerbated factional tensions, which in turn vitiated Ch'ŏndogyo's potential influence.

## Confucianism

Confucianism was the Korean religion the Japanese favored, and hence they supported it physically and spiritually in every way they could. As early as 1911, with funds given directly by the Japanese emperor himself, the Japanese renovated the imperial center of Confucian learning in hopes of resuscitating what they considered a vital link to Korea's past. However, the Japanese authorities did change the center's name by requiring a Japanese rather than a Korean reading for the Chinese ideographs, thus simultaneously denying an exclusively Korean claim while affirming the Japanese right to determine the subsequent course of Korean Confucianism, especially its secular implications—specifically, patrimonial-moral support of Japanese rule per se and the Japanese patrimonial ruling style in particular. The center was considered so important to the Japanese that a Japanese crown prince and another emperor became its patrons, and its head was appointed by the Korean governor general. The attached temple continued the imperial semiannual ceremonies which Korean and now Japanese officials as well as prominent laymen attended. The scholars who lectured on Confucianism were sent out on circuit to instruct the populace on how to improve their morals and, not unimportantly, to drum up support for the Japanese design for a new Korea. Not content, the Japanese also rejuvenated provincial and local Confucian schools with generous land grants and subsidies from provincial and district officials, and prompted yangban local gentry to manage and participate in their activities. In 1930 an academy was founded to provide secondary-level instructors in the Confucian classics, followed two years later by the College of Confucian Classics, to train lecturers and religious ceremonialists. That the Japanese had more than old-style Confucianism on their minds may be inferred from the fact that the college's curriculum also included physical education, which was a frightening thought to genteel Confucian purists, and the Japanese language. From 1938 all Confucian ceremonies required an oath of allegiance to Japan and to its holy mission against anti-Confucian, western materialist Nationalist China.

Given the attention it received, the Japanese campaign to vivify and exploit Korean Confucianism does not seem to have been very fruitful. For all the talk about Confucian ethics, most of the government's Confucian budget went to support ritual and not academic study. The Japanese were never in doubt as to what they could expect from the religion, given their own experience with it in Japan, to justify authoritarian conservative rule, nor were they interested in playing the Korean Confucian intellectuals' game of trying to "adapt" the creed to facilitate Korean modernization. The Japanese soon learned that even the most religiously committed could not be relied upon to do what the Japanese wished. For example, the first head of the Confucian center was one of the heroes of 1919, and some of the institution's circuit leaders preached resistance to Japan's immoral rule to Korean exiles in Manchuria. And yet the Japanese did succeed in their goal of flattering and shoring up the status of those yangban compliant enough to support Japanese rule by paying homage to the patrimonial source of their strength and transferring their diffused religious sentiments of ancestor veneration, filial piety, and consanguineal loyalty from the dynastic rulers to the new patrimonial titular ruler of Korea, the Japanese emperor, notably after the bloody encounter of 1919. However, the Japanese were never fooled into believing that they could entice most of the populace to accept Confucian political moralizing, especially when every day the people could measure Japanese homilies against the stark reality of the occupation. Still, the Japanese were able to induce or force some quarter-million Koreans and Japanese residents to join a number of Confucian associations by 1945 and, of lasting significance, to educate the leaders of the Republic-to-be as to how historically rooted religious-ethical sentiments and organizations could be manipulated ("mobilized") to support patrimonial authority and its policies.

*Buddhism*

The Japanese interest in Buddhism in Korea predated their formal occupation by many years. Since most Japanese were at least nominally Buddhist, the religion was strongly represented among those Japanese who came to Korea after the country was formally opened to outsiders in 1876, much as Protestantism and a revived Catholicism similarly entered Korea through incoming Americans and Europeans. Japanese influence and pressure forced the Korean government (1) to rescind the requirement that Buddhist clerics wear a distinctive, degrading dress, not inherit property, be nameless, and especially be barred from living and preaching in the capital; (2) to establish direct civil jurisdiction over the order through creation of an administrative Buddhist Affairs Office (1902); (3) to separate the monasteries from palace jurisdiction (1904); and (4) to unite the rival sects under the abbot of a prestigious monastery (1908). In 1910 this abbot returned the courtesy by proposing to affiliate the new united order with a Japanese sect, but his attempt aborted as three abbots withdrew, splitting Korean Buddhism into what came to be termed north (pro-Japanese) and south (dissenting) factions.

During the Japanese occupation, which dates from that year, not surprisingly the leaders of the north faction rose to prominence in the ecclesiastic hierarchy and were appointed as abbots of the Japanese-sponsored monasteries. But it would be simplistic to interpret the split as but another Korean factional squabble at worst, or a political conflict between pro- and anti-Japanese partisans at best, and Japanese involvement as a devious political maneuver to divide and rule the faithful, although undoubtedly all these considerations were involved. For, as was true of all thinkers and doers during the occupation (see Chapter 11), being pro- or anti-Japanese also implied whether, respectively, one supported the Japanese lead in modernizing, in this case Buddhism, or believed it was feasible to somehow resuscitate the old faith. For example, should clerics participate in secular society? The pro-Japanese group, like their Japanese counterparts, married, ate flesh, and actively worked on secular problems, aided by laymen, termed lay cerics, who not only helped provide social services but also preached. The nationalist clerics, however, as in the last imperial dynasty, wanted to be secluded from secular temptation as much as possible, preferably in isolated monastic communities. Unfortunately, such controversy goaded the anti-Japanese partisans into resisting any and all attempts to face up to a number of thorny theological and organizational problems and thus paralyzed creative innovation in the order as long as the Japanese were to rule Korea.

One notable exception was Han Yong'un. Han was one of those who had scuttled the attempt to affiliate the order with a Japanese sect, was a signer of the 1919 independence manifesto and a supporter of the 1929 student strike, and was active in Buddhist resistance circles throughout the occupation, believing that Korean Buddhism must preserve its long-standing role of rallying the people to resist a foreign invader, physically and spiritually. And yet, for all his unquestioned nationalist credentials, Han eloquently argued that Buddhism must revitalize and adapt to contemporary life. He preached accepting western science and purging those outmoded, unnecessary "superstitions" left over from another age. Like his eminent predecessor Wŏnhyo, who inspired him, Han called for Buddhism to drop its obsession with meaningless ritual and refocus upon the timeless fundamentals of equality, other-interestedness, and practicality. He attacked those meditative clerics who preached mind rather than body quiescence and that meditation's purpose was other than to prepare one to participate actively in the affairs of this world. Clerics must be productive contributors to Korean society, rather than, as many of them had become, beggars dependent on the handouts of the faithful. He rejected the Japanese Buddhist concept of "other power," not on theological grounds but because it could be used to rationalize and thus perpetuate a mental and physical dependence of Koreans on their Japanese masters and could vitiate the Koreans' will to overcome the sufferings of this life. In brief, Han believed that a revitalized Buddhism generating productive cooperation and working in tandem with modern science would enable the Koreans to persevere, overcome their occupation mentality, and eventually regain their independence and create a true Buddha land as was their destiny.

Although the most prominent, Han was not the only Buddhist reformer, but, alas, their influence did not go beyond a small circle of concerned intellectuals. What changes did occur were such limited achievements as creating a Young Buddhist Association and a cooperative intersect publishing and educational program. And, although it was now respectable to be a Buddhist, according to a 1938 census only some 5000 priests and 1000 nuns were serving only 20,000 congregants, the majority of whom were Japanese residents! Most Korean Buddhists were content to restrict their religious participation to temple pilgrimages, and without the Japanese program of preserving and rebuilding "national treasures" it would have been unlikely that the faithful would have been able to carry on even such modest reverence. Very few temples had resident scholars; in fact, most clerics were barely literate. Instead, they relied on gratuities which they received for chanting prayers which they had learned by rote, from patrons who likewise did not comprehend the chants, or competed with sin'gyo occultists. An attempt to maintain a three-year training seminary had to be soon abandoned and the building sold to the Ch'ŏndogyo sect. To the Japanese, including Buddhists, in the prevailing colonial atmosphere, all this was but further vindication of the stereotype of Koreans as hopelessly backward.

The major Japanese contribution to Korean Buddhism bequeathed to the Republic was to reorganize the order along modern administrative lines, albeit to facilitate control. The 1911 Temple Act confiscated most of the land then held, forcing the temples into dependency upon government prebendary economic grace, and hence into subservience to government policy. The same act and subsequent legislation created a hierarchy of thirty-one head temples in Seoul overseeing some 1300 branch units with a still greater number of minor establishments affiliated with each of the branches. Supervising all this was a general headquarters in the office of the government general which was responsible for insuring discipline and especially political neutrality. Periodic seminars, particularly in the Seoul head temple, kept personnel up-to-date on government innovations. A 1935 religious act formally unified the order but, because of Korean resistance, this did not end the millennial split between meditationists and tractists, nor did it heal the conflict between pro- and anti-Japanese wings of the order. However, government-Buddhist relations, even during World War II, were reasonably amicable. This was undoubtedly due to the great number of Japanese residents who were Buddhist, but also to the fact that, save for a few intellectuals and some individual activists among the younger clergy, hierarchy and members alike were tolerant as ever of any regime that did not actively persecute them and were appreciative of Buddhism's Japanese-inspired respectability; an insight and precedent, as we soon shall see, which a subsequent patrimonial republican president was to appreciate and exploit.

*Christianity*

The Japanese always considered Christian indigenous and foreign clergy and organizations as obstructions to firm control and mobilization of the Korean populace, but especially during the early days of the occupation, before overt resistance to Japanese rule had been crushed. It is worth pointing out that this confrontation was not welcomed by the Christians, especially by those foreign missionaries who regarded the Japanese as agents of progress in backward Asia. The Japanese, using the same tactics they were then (1911) employing in the home islands against political radicals, accused various church leaders of conspiring to assassinate an unpopular governor general. Although the secret and obviously farcical trial subsequently was repudiated, the move was successful in frightening the clergy into being more circumspect in their secular activities. After the 1919 protests, many clergymen, whether they were implicated or not, were arrested and churches were charged with allowing their property to be misused for political purposes, even though the conspirators had deliberately kept virtually all clerics in the dark so as not to compromise them or the church. Political pressure finally eased with the arrival of a new governor general in August 1919, and the inauguration of the conciliatory "culture program." Some attribute the governor general's religious tolerance to his having a Christian wife. However, it was obvious by then that the Christians, like the populace in general, had been so bullied by Japanese ruthlessness that the older ham-handed aggressive policy was no longer necessary to insure that the Japanese would have their way. Some churchmen continued exposing Japanese physical and psychological brutality, but since they did so to a largely indifferent outside world, the authorities could gracefully look aside and point to their tolerance as proof of religious freedom in Japanese Korea, especially since most clergy, Protestants in particular, were turning their attention rather to buttressing their congregants' personal courage in the vale of Japanese occupational tears. Even the Salvation Army's militant slogan of fighting a war against sin, an issue which figures prominently in the 1911 conspiracy case, was muted.

The next source of tension between Japanese authority and Christians, which as usual was decided in the government's favor, was over the teaching of religion and ethics in the Christian mission schools. According to a 1917 decree, all religious teaching (the very rationale for the mission schools) was to be prohibited in "recognized" schools, a designation which was vital to the mission schools if their graduates were not to be discriminated against in advanced education or employment. Simultaneously, the mission schools were required to teach State Shintō's version of loyalty, duty, and veneration toward the Japanese emperor, which the government insisted was not propagating religion but civic ethics. The fundamentalist Protestant sects in particular considered this "secularistically" compromising, and thus were reluctant but were forced to comply.

As Japanese militarism intensified, the Japanese went a step further, insisting that all religious leaders participate in Shintō, nonreligious "civic" ceremonies. Some clergymen accepted Japanese rationalizations to save their churches, congregants, and schools from discrimination and even persecution; those who did not were incarcerated and their churches closed. When World War II broke out, foreign missionaries were either interned or expelled from Korea; indigenous Christians were interrogated and some were punished; church buildings were converted to war use, such as factories; and, as in Japan, the sects were consolidated into a united church organization, which took instructions from the government. Those who refused to go along were driven out of the church. By 1945 the number of Christian congregants dwindled to half what it was before the war.

In addition to Japan's relentless antagonism and intimidation, Christianity perhaps was also prevented from playing a positive developmental role in Korea because the corpus of liberal Christianity—especially the sects then prevalent in the United States—which questioned dogmatic authority, viewed religion primarily as a spiritual experience in a modern utilitarian world, accepted science and treated scripture as symbol rather than veritable truth, and above all stressed the social gospel, was unknown to Koreans save a few intellectuals. Moreover, Christian education reinforced the existing institutional order by churning out low-level bureaucrats and teachers to serve the Japanese patrimonial state. And yet the church did provide a conduit for non-Japanese modernizing ideas and practices. For example, the "Y" program enabled young Koreans of both sexes to express themselves artistically and intellectually in their own culture and to explore their individual and social aspirations free of both conservative parental and political surveillance. And because it shored up the spirit to resist internally and occasionally overtly arbitrarily established authority on grounds of individual conscience, Christianity did provide an important precedent for Korea's republican future.

### The Japanese Religion: Shintō

The government general propagandized both Sectarian (religious) and State Shintō. The sects that attracted the Koreans were those that practiced faith healing and preached a spiritual rejuvenation not unlike sin'gyo. State Shintō, supposedly a civic creed rather than a religion (though its rituals and priesthood were identical to Sectarian Shintō), was introduced soon after the occupation began to encourage loyalty to the new government. A state shrine dedicated to the Japanese patron goddess and to the Japanese emperor was constructed on the site of an older sin'gyo temple on South Mount overlooking Seoul. Lesser shrines devoted to Japanese imperial ancestors sprung up all over the peninsula. Students, as in Japan proper, were required to attend one or another of these shrines periodically, to bow to imperial portraits, and to attend lectures extolling loyalty and sacrifices to a Japanese emperor. But since State Shintō was clearly a political enterprise, the Koreans treated it indifferently, and even hostilely, especially when the authorities tried to force Koreans to include State Shintō rites in their indigenous religious observances. Many Koreans certainly visited the shrine on South Mount, but then it had always been a favorite picnic spot because it afforded an excellent view of the capital. Thus when the Japanese left Korea in 1945, all Shintō shrines were dismantled and the sin'gyo spirits allowed to reclaim South Mount, but not before another lesson in how to exploit politically relevant, religiously diffuse sentiments, while simultaneously claiming religious freedom, had been learned by the future leaders of the republican patrimonial authority.

*Secular Education*

We need to consider secular education in this discussion of religion in Korea because of its contribution to the diffusion and secularization of Korean patrimonial religious values in that society and the exploitation of formal secular education by the patrimonial authority in proselytizing those diffused-secularized values. Diffused-secularized religious values are those guides to social behavior which are either (1) historically derived from religious values or (2) are logically derived from or compatible with historical or contemporary religious values.

The 1895 reformers, inspired by the Japanese modernizing model, established a Ministry of Education and a modern educational bureaucracy to replace the sporadic, primarily European-infused private or aristocratic system. A Japanese was appointed education advisor in 1905; full Japanese control over education followed the next year, four years before the occupation actually began. In 1911 the Japanese Imperial Rescript on Education was extended to Korea, establishing the primacy of state interests in education. Step by step, the Japanese introduced their own elementary track, technical institutes, and finally an Imperial University in 1926. By 1945, 1.7 million students were enrolled in the Japanese-sponsored education system.

But as is true for all Japanese enterprise in Korea, one must look beyond structure and statistics. Certainly it is unrealistic to expect the Japanese overlords to create in Korea what they were unwilling to do at home, but, even with that caveat, there still were wide discrepancies between what was being offered in Korea and in Japan proper, and certainly between what Japan was telling the world it was doing and reality. Especially, the system discriminated in the Japanese residents' favor. No attempt was made to create a truly universal elementary educational system for Koreans. Save in elementary school, the language of instruction was Japanese, which automatically put Koreans at a disadvantage. Japanese were specially tracked and provided a superior education, except at the university level, for which few Koreans qualified and where they were kept out of fields which trained leaders and would enable Koreans to criticize Japanese rule. And, although Koreans were channeled into nonintellectual, economically productive tasks which served Japanese interests, all the better technical schools discriminated in favor of the Japanese.

However, increasing economic pressures, on urban Koreans especially, encouraged more and more of them to seek the kind of education which the Japanese public system would not accommodate. Private schools mushroomed. Most of those who could afford a higher education went abroad, paradoxically primarily to Japan, where they constituted a sizable proportion of the student body of many second-ranked private institutions. Such students majored in fields closed to them in Korea, particularly law, economics, and politics, fields for which there were few employment opportunities when they returned to Korea. In the long run their efforts were not in vain, for most of the first-generation leaders of the Republic, for better or worse, were to come from these graduates, as well as from the few fortunate enough to be admitted to the liberal arts programs at the Imperial University in the Korean capital. Then, as Japan militarized and industralized Korea, labor shortages developed, and the Japanese were compelled to expand Korean access to advanced, especially technical, education. But the authorities simultaneously tightened political control over all schools, forcing exclusive use of the Japanese language, expanding indoctrination, and punishing nonconformers.

In sum, the Japanese provided the infrastructure and organizational foundations of the modern Korean educational system. But they did nothing to alter, and even reinforced by modernizing, prevailing patrimonial didactic, authoritarian, pedagogical techniques; political control of education; and especially the notion that an advanced education was the primary path to elite status. This was especially true of those branches of modern learning compatible with yangban pursuits and prerogatives, namely, law and politics, whose content reflected, perhaps even was distorted to facilitate, the quest for patrimonial prestige. What was novel and in time significant was that through modern education commoners could compete with yangban for the glittering patrimonial prizes. Modern education thus served to diffuse patrimonial aspirations and values more widely among Koreans. Such were the educational system and sentiments the Japanese passed on to the Republic.[6]

# 10

# Contemporary Religion

## Christianity in Contemporary Korea

Liberation from Japanese rule in 1945 provided a great impetus for Christianity's expansion. Leaders were released from confinement or the shadows, and their activities, including proselytizing, were freed from government harassment. Religious schools, hospitals, orphanages, and youth hostels were either reactivated or newly created. The New Testament was retranslated into contemporary Korean and serious consideration given to creating an ecumenical text. Korea's first Catholic cardinal was appointed in 1969. Refugees from the north, some 60,000 of the 164,000 POWs captured in the Korean War, and returnees from abroad all swelled the ranks of the faithful. Denominations novel to Korea, like Friends and Mennonites, expanded the Protestant vision. In sum, the 1950s was a period of explosive expansion; the number of Protestants doubled to 3.5 million, while Catholics increased fivefold to 800,000.

A key stimulus was a close relationship between Christianity and authority. As in Japan, American occupation officials facilitated the early return not only of those American missionaries and Korean Christians who had been expelled, but also of American religious leaders who were able to advise their Korean counterparts how to take advantage of recent propagation techniques, such as the media and campus crusades. Catholic Cardinal Spellman stood beside General Hodge as he received the formal Japanese surrender for the United States, and joint Easter sunrise ceremonies were held by American and Korean servicemen. The American authorities awarded a share of Japanese vested property to the churches and provided them with U.S. Public Law 480 food aid, while various American religious relief agencies gave succor throughout the liberation and Korean War periods. A number of the new Korean leaders were Christian, especially the first president, Syngman Rhee, as were half the assembly members and many professionals and civil servants. Also the new military, since it organizationally imitated the American services, contained a chaplain corps which for a long time was thus exclusively Christian and predominantly Protestant. Even in 1970, of the 372 chaplains only 41 were Catholic, and even more pertinently only 21 were not Christian, although only 15 percent of the troops were professed Christians. The significance of the virtual Protestant monopoly of the chaplaincy is that the corps is an excellent medium by which to recruit and hold potential congregants. Military service is a time when individuals are religiously vulnerable; church-related benefit centers provide continuing religious exposure to the servicemen's families even after the men are demobilized or die; and many Koreans in and out of service consider the military and what it likes as both modern and prestigious, and that includes the religion which those individuals believe the military sponsors or at least favors. Finally, delinquent youth were turned over to church shelters and clerics were allowed to minister in prisons, which had been expressly forbidden by the Japanese.

And yet, in spite of all these advantages and opportunities, Christianity has not lived up to its potential. For one, both the church in general and specific congregations were torn apart by factional bickering. As in the political world, disputes arose over who had been truly anti-Japanese during the occupation. Although most Protestants decided to continue the Japanese-initiated ecumenical organization, a number of individual denominations decided to reestablish their own identity to take advantage of an emerging competitive recruiting atmosphere. The Americans added to the din by introducing sects hitherto unknown in Korea and the liberal wings of denominations long dominated by conservative thinking. The sects also split on how to respond to the ever-changing social scene, such as the problems of urbanization, labor relations, and poverty. Finally, one must mention the competitive scramble for Japanese vested property. All such dissension could not but tarnish Christianity's image in the eyes of Koreans, who looked askance at such feuding among those who claimed to be dedicated to goodwill.

Second, Christianity suffered from a progressively deteriorating relationship with authority once the military came to power. As Park increasingly tightened his grip on the society (see Chapter 3), the church either chose or by default found itself to be one of the few means to express political dissent. Bearing witness in this way certainly was a radical departure from its stance—in contrast to acts of individual clerics—under the Japanese, and may have been prompted by guilt over the church's previous compromising, if not collaborating. Or perhaps the new attitude was due to the winds of religious change from abroad. Whatever the reason, the church decided it should no longer be indifferent to the question of the Kingdom of God on earth and hence must morally judge the social-cum-political order, which it found wanting. Catholic and most Protestant denominations created human rights committees and demanded an end to press censorship, release of political prisoners, and university freedom. The authorities responded as they did to all political protest, with bile and charges of treason. But in this instance the polity was forced to tread more cautiously than it might otherwise have because foreign, especially allied American, religious interests were involved, and because the issue of religious freedom is one the government likes to use against the DPRK. However, tread the authorities have, often using ingenious tactics. For one, the polity has claimed that the church opposition is playing the game unfairly; the church involves itself in politics but uses an irrelevant, suprapolitical argument to justify antistate activities. Second, if foreign clerics support causes and individuals who are breaking the law, then the polity is justified in expelling them, or at least not renewing their visas. Third, the church is treated as any potentially corporate intermediary group; that is, it is surveilled and, when necessary, harassed. Prior consent is required for meetings and church activities, sermons and statements are screened. Financial aid to the families of incarcerated clerics constitutes fraud in the government's eyes. Fourth, the polity argues, how can it stand strong in its struggle with the DPRK when the churches are forever finding political fault, pitting Korean against Korean? Rather, Christianity by its very nature should be in the vanguard of the government's ideological anti-Communist crusade. Fifth and finally, the government has split the church by convincing some of the older, more conservative senior hierarchs to moderate their political views and by organizing more militant nationalists into a Christian Salvation Mission to denounce less-pliant colleagues and agitate for clerical military training to help prepare for an inevitable invasion of the ROK by godless hordes from the north. To be sure, such church-state tension is not novel either to Christianity or to the ROK. All Korean authority has shared the view that the state has the moral right and obligation to supervise the political activities of religious bodies and that religion is politically free only as long as it supports or at least does not work at cross-purposes to the decisions of patrimonial authority; in modern jargon, as long as the church is willing to support the attempts of the government to build social consensus. However, when in contradiction the religion turns the tables and demands, as a corporate right, to judge the polity, this is unacceptable; in patrimonial terms, it is heretical, and hence the religion must be chastized by the polity in its capacity as the moral watchdog of the patrimonial order.

A third indication that the church has not lived up to its potential is that even if the political controversy should somehow be settled amicably, the church still would be confronted with the more fundamental, vexing problem of defining a religious role in a contemporary society. The ROK clearly lacks both a coherent national ideology (save perhaps for anti-Communism) and an ethic for a rapidly modernizing (and politically developing) community, yet the church has been reluctant to fill the vacuum. In spite of American Protestant and French Catholic traditions of strong parish involvement, Korean Christians prefer to insure their personal salvation in a future life. They cling tenaciously to a morally simplistic, individualistic view of the causes and cures of suffering and to an ideal code of conduct—and the Protestants in particular to a very puritanical one—which is increasingly unrealistic, if not irrelevant to the psychological and material requirements of coping with a competitive, amoral society. For example, ancestor veneration, grave services, and all the other symbolic expressions of consanguineal solidarity, which were so vital in the past in forging links to the spirit world to guarantee this-worldly happiness, now seem more vital in today's uncertainty, yet certain church denominations are as reluctant as ever to accept any of this as suitable for Christian concern. Conversely, non-Catholic Koreans, like patrimonial religionists in general, find sacerdotal celibacy irrational and Catholic priests are discovering their congregants, as happens elsewhere, are ignoring their advice on birth control and abortion. Some clerics consider psychological counseling no better than modern shamanism. And finally, contrary to the past and to the church's claim, Christians in office or business nowadays are not discernably more upright than non-Christians. In brief and in consequence, the image most Koreans have of Christians is one of affluent, self-satisfied hypocrites, too often indifferent to the mundane interests and problems of their non-Christian fellows.

To be sure, any number of individual clerics are ahead of their parishioners, and non-Christians too, on many pressing social issues. But most such clerics bear their witness through political protest, which is the very expression which most Koreans, Christian and non-Christian alike, are reluctant to support. For those Koreans who are not members of the elite or sophisticated politically—which means most Koreans—regard authority as worthy of support, even when they disagree with official policy, because in patrimonial reasoning loyalty and respect for superiors are morally binding on ordinary men, even when laws are unjust. Similarly, most of the congregants who support their church leaders who struggle for human rights do so out of the same attitude of loyalty to superiors, irrespective of whether or not the congregants agree with what the leaders preach. To be sure, some congregants do so out of conviction, while still others cynically use the churches as fronts for prohibited political agitation, though definitely not in the numbers the government charges. But clearly, supportive or not of religiously led or motivated agitation, precious few Koreans, Christian or not, understand, let alone support, the nonpatrimonial Christian, especially Protestant-inspired, idea of individual and radical salvation which calls on the faithful to transcend and ultimately actively transform (i.e., develop?) the society so that it will be in accord with Christian ideals. To conclude, given the patrimonial character of the society, those religiously concerned Christian Koreans willing to bear witness to their conscience and face whatever the consequences may be, though certainly present, are as unusual as they are brave.[1]

## Contemporary Buddhism

Most of the property that the Buddhist order had managed to hold on to during the Japanese occupation was lost during the republican land reform, although some fields were restored and new virgin forest areas were acquired and successfully exploited. The order received government bonds for the surrendered land, which, as was the government's intent, the order reinvested in commerce and industry. In doing so, not only was organized Buddhism's economic foundation transformed from agriculture to business, but the faith's attention was now drawn to an urban constituency and its religious concerns. One significant consequence was an upsurge in membership of educated, young urban males and their appointment to boards of directorship of the order, radically altering the prevailing image of Buddhism as the religion of women and the aged.

As was true of all religious bodies, Buddhism was freed of government control in 1945, a decision which also terminated the forced unity of the sects. However, one sect continues to dominate as it had before unification, comprising about half the estimated eight million Buddhists, which makes it the largest organized religious body in Korea. By implication, this has facilitated the ability of the government to surveil the religion. The sect's hierarchy, which follows the Japanese-period-inspired bureaucratic principles with only minor modifications, consists of a central executive board with an attached legislature and judiciary—that is, inspecting and financial functionaries—overseeing twenty-five head temples, which in turn are the administrative district nerve centers for controlling 1200 individual temples and 7000 male and 600 female clerics. And, in spite of their independence, the various sects continue to use the Japanese-created Korea Buddhist Association to coordinate activities. Monasteries now enjoy a measure of autonomy, but nothing like the splendid isolation or the private power of a past age. On the other hand, indicative of a new wave of modernizing interest, the Buddhist Institute, founded in 1914 under the Japanese and primarily devoted to politically innocent theoretical esoterica, has been converted into a highly respected university with full liberal arts and law curricula. Its divinity school trains new clerics but also upgrades the credentials of existing clerics, especially the long-neglected monastery residents. The university is complemented by, and acquires a number of its students from, a Buddhist college, and twelve middle and many elementary Buddhist schools. The income derived from factories acquired after the land reform has enabled the order to expand both its social welfare programs and its publications, consisting of learned tomes, translations of religious classics into modern Korean, and popular magazines. And although this has been strongly resisted by the Christian establishment, Buddhist chaplains are being appointed and Buddhist service centers are being built on military bases throughout Korea.

Another significant evolvement has been a compromise on the issue of celibacy. During the Japanese period, Korean Buddhist clerics were allowed to marry. Immediately after independence, however, the heads of certain sects agitated for the purging of all noncelibates, and incidentally all those who wore Japanese clerical dress. The reformers thus wanted to eliminate Japanese cultural influences; to return clerics to pre-Japanese monastic isolation so that those in the cloth would better resist the secular temptations of this ethically dubious world; to preserve resources which were being squandered to support clerical families; to wed the clerics socially and psychologically to the order, considered to be even more pertinent in consanguineally conscious

Korean society than in western-Catholic medieval Europe; and, for the meditative leaders in particular, to refocus attention away from social witness. The head of the meditative sect was able to persuade President Rhee to relocate married and Japanese-garbed priests in separate though adjacent dwelling units, if not as outcasts then certainly as second-rate clerics. But this only exacerbated existing tension. In 1962 a compromise was worked out; no more noncelibates would be admitted to the order, but those already married would be tolerated, provided they practiced celibacy while on duty at the monasteries and were not appointed to an ecclesiastic office at or above the rank of archbishop.

The significance of the compromise is that although it did not sever clerical contact with the society, it did require that someone other than clerics henceforth care primarily for the parishioners' personal religious needs. That role was taken up enthusiastically by lay believers; that is, as in Japan, those nonordained who fervently strive to live secularly in full accord with the principles of Buddhism and who bring the fruits of their insight and experience to the attention of the larger circle of Buddhists, congregant or not. These believers have stimulated the formation of many kinds of Buddhist groups. Some are highly organized and bureaucratized, while others are informal get-togethers in private homes. Some groups cater to particular age, sex, class, occupation, or education categories, while others cut across such boundaries. One of the most interesting is the Young Buddhist Association which, though it recruits through college and university Buddhist associations, has been able to hold on to its followers after they are graduated and go on to professional careers. The YBA holds frequent social meetings and study sessions at which all are encouraged to explore how to apply Buddhist principles practically to daily life. Clerics often are invited to these sessions, performing a brief introductory religious service and delivering a sermon which may serve as point of departure for the discussion to follow. In this way at least some of Korea's emerging elite come to appreciate that to be modern does not mean either to be secularly western or to become Christian, as some unscrupulous foreign Christian missionaries have claimed. The Buddhist lay movement also has made respectable headway in the business community, which, like the educational establishment, until recently has been virtually a preserve of Christianity.

This Buddhist resurgence has been one of the reasons for the sluggish growth of Christianity since the 1960s. Another, and potentially more consequential, reason was a shift in government patronal support from Christianity to Buddhism under Park. True, Park was at least a nominal Buddhist while Rhee was a militant Christian, but I believe that this was not at the heart of the matter. Rather it was that Park saw much in Buddhism which he believed Christianity lacked. For one, in an era when third-world leaders are reaching for a source of nonwestern pride and identity, Buddhism's association with and contributions to Korea's ethical and artistic culture are visually evident in the temples and monuments which dot the landscape. Buddhism offers an Asian ethic which even westerners are coming to recognize increasingly as valid. In this age characterized by mass media hoopla, Park was aware of the advantages of exploiting the order's organization to drum up support for his interests. And finally, and most pertinently, as the relationship between Park and the Christians deteriorated, he turned increasingly to the Buddhists for moral-religious support for his patrimonial regime and his policies. The Buddhists undoubtedly were flattered by this newfound attention, especially after the dark days from the last imperial dynasty through the Rhee regime, and responded enthusiastically to Park's overtures. It must be pointed out, however, that the order always has been willing to be the moral sanctifier of patrimonial authority if its titular head was not unduly tempted by the materialism of this world and thus would inspire the masses to act similarly, if he rules wisely so as to prevent moral degradation and social chaos, and especially if he was willing to be the protector and patron of the faith. Park played these prescribed roles well, including that of patron by renovating and building new monasteries and monuments, by subsidizing a reprint of the sacred Buddhist texts in imitation of his imperial predecessors, by introducing the Buddhist chaplaincy and a circuit sermon program in the armed forces and in prisons, and by proclaiming Buddha's birthday a national holiday in 1975. In return, Buddhists actively supported the government by, for example, dutifully turning out for anti-DPRK rallies, by bringing Buddhist children to the presidential palace to honor Park on his birthday, and by swearing an oath of allegiance to the government during the celebration ceremonies of the Buddha's birthday. This cozy relationship between the polity and especially the dominant sect of Buddhism has been a mixed blessing. It certainly has brought prestige and material (prebendary) advantage to the religion which it has not enjoyed for centuries. But it also tied the faith visibly to the regime in power. Hence there always could be a negative reaction toward Buddhism if there were a search for scapegoats among those held responsible for the acts of the Park administration, as happened at the time the last imperial dynasty came to authority. Moreover, as in the past, patrimonial authority clearly is the dominant party in any such church-state relationship, and hence is the one who calls the tune. Consequently, like all intermediary organizations, the order is surveilled and, if found wanting in any way, prodded, sometimes not subtly, by a Ministry of Culture and Information. When university student groups were disbanded in 1975, for example, the Buddhist ones were not exempted.

For Buddhism as for the other faiths, the problem of working out a mutually satisfactory relationship with a patrimonial polity, as troublesome as it is, is not as difficult as redefining a religious role in the Korean society of today. Should clerics return to their monastic isolation now that lay believers are carrying the day-to-day religious burden, or should the clerics assist the laymen in disseminating the faith, at least through moral support? Should the folk elements and the old rituals which had been incorporated into the religion over the ages be eliminated as Wŏnhyo preached long ago, since today's youth reject miracles and without their rejuvenating sustenance the religion will die? Are the monasteries primarily centers of devotional retreat, or essentially national treasures and tourist attractions as the government is determined to make them? All these issues are as divisive today as was the marriage-celibacy controversy of the past and cannot be ignored, contributing, along with the relationship to patrimonial authority, to the order's failure to create a potentially developmental productive force in Korean society.

Another expression of the Buddhist renascence is the Wŏn sect, a "new religious" movement (see the next section) of some three-quarters of a million followers, organized into over a hundred branches, and active in education, welfare, and, not unimportantly, in industry, particularly in pharmaceuticals, hospital supplies, and ginseng. Wŏn, which in Korean denotes a circle, in the sect's thinking connotes the essential unity or oneness of existence. Achieving that oneness is the core of Wŏn. It requires overcoming this world's false (illusionary), contentious, secular or sacred dissonance, which is needlessly and foolishly driving human beings apart. For this reason, the founder was one of the few prelates at the time who refused to take sides in the married-celibate clerical controversy. Similarly he refused to accept the long-standing mediation-practice dichotomy as valid, and, since he equated religious practice with daily life, he considered the distinction between cleric and layman too as irrational.

Oneness achieved is the "perfect circle," which lifts the veil of darkness, suffering, and insecurity that prevents all from fully expressing the Buddha nature existent within all living things. To come to this worthy state, individuals must respect, be loyal to, and be responsible toward the deserving, initially and especially parents, but ultimately toward all humankind. Those who do so are capable of attaining the mutual cooperation and productive fellowship with all which is the foundation of an ideal Buddhist society. Social renovation, as important as it is, alone cannot end humanity's travail. For there still will be those who have not achieved peace of mind and hence soundness of body—in Wŏn thinking the two interrelate. Thus individuals must reexamine themselves and not blame others or the society for their failures, searching out personal faults, such as following false leaders, being tempted by greed, superficial materialism, and impatience, and bearing false witness against neighbors. Nothing is impossible to those who trust their faith and diligently persevere, because they have pure Buddha nature within them at this point, and thus their goals are noble. They are truly their own creators, for their destiny (karma) is in their minds, in their actions, and not in mollifying ancestral spirits.

My conclusion: On the one hand, although clerics, older Buddhist precepts, and practices are respected, they are not considered as essential as Wŏn fundamentals to be carried out by laymen in their daily life, which is where Wŏn preaches the Buddhists of today will work out their religious destiny. Wŏn and the lay movement in general are emerging as the vital element of a modernizing Buddhism. On the other hand, however, Wŏn theology is based on such time-tested Korean secularly diffused, patrimonially relevant religious values as consanguineal loyalty, consensus, mutual aid, and physical-cum-psychological health. Wŏn also provides a sense of personal worth no matter how civil overlords abuse and degrade, and a pragmatic, this-worldly ethic similar to what Wŏnhyo preached long ago. This enables the faithful to come to terms with but not overcome the increasing tensions and contentious partisan controversies of the ephemeral contemporary patrimonial society. On balance then, Wŏn, like Buddhism in general and Korean religion in turn, is modernizing but not simultaneously becoming a potential agent of Korean development.[2]

### Sin'gyo and the New Religions

In spite of Japanese and republican authorities' negative attitude toward and even use of force against sin'gyo, the folk religion continues to maintain its hold on the Korean people, as I have argued previously, because the (in my focus, patrimonial) social and cultural conditions which incubate the tensions and frustrations which this always has addressed so well have not changed, the modernizing process notwithstanding. For example: I attended a kut ceremony at which a wealthy man was receiving assurance that if he did in fact participate in a risky business venture he would not become bankrupt, which is only too possible in the present volatile Korean economy. That this individual was educated and a member of Korea's emerging elite should not startle. A Seoul survey shows that 71 percent of males and 66 percent of females in all walks of life use the services of some thousand full-time and twice that number of part-time mudang, although this is contrary to the conventional wisdom that folk religions are the special preserve of uneducated women.

The vitality of the folk religion is even more evident in the organized "new religions" which have enrolled more than 10 percent of the populace. "New" is a misnomer, since at least some of them predate independence, although they have mushroomed since 1945. In many theological and organizational ways they resemble their Japanese counterparts, which is not strange since a number of them were founded during the Japanese occupation or are presently led by Koreans who could not be unaware of what is going on in Japan since many of them lived there at one time or another. One must not, however, overrate Japanese influence. Much more pertinent are the indigenous roots of the new religions, especially the kinship between the new and folk religions. For the new religions, like sin'gyo, first, are syncretic. They culled even Christianity, adopting its rituals; its organizational insights, such as the use of women and youth affiliates; its aggressive recruiting; and its concept of Jesus as a potent healer. Second, the new religions engage in sin'gyo fortune-telling and medium activities, though they do not use mudang. Third, the new religions and sin'gyo are nationalistic, for their ideal new order of plenty and happiness will be constructed in Korea and hence it is a Korean privilege and duty to serve mankind by taking the lead in creating such an order. Fourth, the primary goals of both the new religions and sin'gyo are this-worldly material success, physical health, and psychological peace of mind. Fifth, both religions eschew theology and dogmatics, relying rather on simple, direct messages or, even better, physical expression and evidence of their leaders' powers, such as talismans of their handwriting. Sixth, both religions are led by charismatic figures who claim easy access to the spirits and the spirit world. In the case of the new religions access is direct if the leader is the sect's founder, but if he is not then access is through the leader's possession of the founder's spirit. Seventh, rituals are commonly designed to cheer and reassure, for joy is an expression of religious bliss. Eighth, both sin'gyo and the new religions offer quick and easy answers to often vexing, eternally recurrent problems. Ninth, both preach that personal adjustment to this worldly order rather than social reform will achieve religious perfection, for the millennium comes only gradually and from redirecting personal lives. Thus both sin'gyo and the new religions are fundamentally conservative. However, tenth, for this very reason, the individual and his concerns matter very much in both systems.

Nevertheless there are pertinent differences between sin'gyo and the new religions, because the latter are responding more directly to the requisites of contemporary life than sin'gyo can. In doing so, the new religions may be said to be modernizing sin'gyo, making it more respectable to those people who are not totally receptive to it, yet at the same time are not prepared to reject sin'gyo outright. For example, in contrast to sin'gyo the new religions are organized into definite communities of the like-minded who expect mutual comfort and security that they cannot find in a society in which old loyalties of consanguinity and geography are breaking down, while new intermediary organizational affiliations have yet to form. The new religions thus have special appeal in areas of intense social disintegration, such as rural Chŏlla Province, and where life is particularly dangerous, such as contemporary Seoul; that is, where the consequences of a modernizing but fundamentally unaltered (patrimonial) institutional order are most acute.

Some three hundred new religious sects exist. The most historically significant, though by no means the largest, of these is Ch'ŏndogyo, the oldest new religion, which now has about 600,000 followers. Most of the faithful lived in the north in 1945, but in 1948, when the government there demanded that the sect's leaders actively support the regime, those who refused but escaped purging fled south with their followers. Rather than honoring them as non- if not anti-Communists, Rhee persecuted them; I suggest for much the same reason as in the north—namely, Rhee, ever the patrimonialist, was just as determined to mobilize all intermediary organizations to serve his rather than their own corporate interests as were Rhee's Communist antagonists, and Ch'ŏndogyo was no exception. He was also especially suspicious of any organization that professed to be indifferent to pensinsula politics, which were soon to erupt in the Korean War. Moreover, the sect's penchant for supporting reformist causes, which turned out to be far leftist in the political climate of Rhee, and its formation of a Young Friends party in spite of the sect's profession that government was no substitute for self-improvement, also energized Rhee's ire and suspicion and ultimately his wrath. The relationship between Ch'ŏndogyo and Park was more amicable, for the sect came around to conforming patrimonially by supporting Park's confrontation politics with the DPRK and by restricting its social program to succoring the neglected and advocating the upgrading of the society's quality of life without being too specific in its suggestions. Park was also appreciative of Ch'ŏndogyo's balancing its interests in human rights with a call for social responsibility and the sect's reiteration of its long-standing insistence that Koreans must develop a distinctive national ethic, which in the present context implies freeing Korea of ideological dependence on either superpower—all of which suited Park's notion of a distinctively Korean "guided democracy." It is not easy to assess the sect's viability since it has a history of learning to prevail by keeping a low political profile when necessary. Clearly, however, Ch'ŏndogyo's historic role as a rallying point for dissident political behavior is over, but then with independence other channels to express that concern have appeared.

Unfortunately, space precludes discussing more than two further new religions. No claim is made that these two typify the many, often colorful sects or their leaders. Nevertheless I trust a brief review will provide insight into the character and patrimonial pertinence of the new religious movement. First, there is the New Capital Movement, which derives its name from the fact that its adherents crave compensation for the dislocations of the present age not through foreign-influenced "modern," secular, pragmatic means, but through the creation of a sanctuary where disease, poverty, and discrimination will be banished, the Armageddon of coming World War III bypassed, and the coming of a messiah, who now is hiding, awaited. Until that day, however, the community residents are obliged to perform certain religious rituals related to sin'gyo practice, and more pertinently to lay the foundation for the promised land of virtue to come by helping others, building personal pride, engaging in diligent labor, and educating the young both to cope better with the here and now as well as to live productively in the blissful society of tomorrow. Since the leaders are treated as if they are consanguineal patriarchs, their commands are obeyed. As in all millennial communities, the failure of the impending judgment day to arrive and recent improvements in the national economy have prompted the young and the less religiously committed to abandon the New Capital. But it must be said that in its heyday during the early Republic, the movement, like all the new religions, filled a definite need by buoying the spirits of the psychologically and materially depressed, encouraging them to lead useful and rewarding lives as best they can within the existing parameters of a capricious patrimonial social order.

A number of new religions claim to be Christian at least in inspiration. Certainly the most newsworthy of these is the Unification Church of the Rev. Moon (Sun Myung). Moon lived and was educated in Japan. Subsequently he became a Presbyterian minister, but later (1945) received a revelation to lead a reconstituted Christian Church, which he accomplished in Seoul in 1954 in the form of the Church of the Holy Spirit Association for the Unification of World Christianity— Unification Church for short—with himself as the chief minister.

Theologically, the church claims to be a Christianity which can both explain and offer the means to ameliorate humankind's suffering, neither of which, Moon insists, historic Christianity can do. This is because Jesus only could address Himself to redeeming the human mind and not the body, since He did not marry and hence could not personally establish God's kingdom on earth, which requires divinely inspired mating. By default then it was Satan who became the progenitor of human union by illicitly congressing with an Eve who could not be redeemed by Jesus. And until the divinity intervenes, all humankind must suffer for this transgression. That intervention is Moon's precise function, since by mating with his second wife, "the Mother of the Universe," Moon has given birth to sinless children, as have all couples selected and married by Moon under his divine direction. The exact relationship between Jesus as the Christ and Moon is obscure. Moon has talked, especially abroad, of only preparing for the Christ, referring to himself as a mere prophet of God. But in Korea especially Moon has claimed that the messianic return of Christ is not certain, and hence that Moon's role as redeemer is crucial. In any case, Moon is Jesus' successor for this age, authorized by Him to fulfill His divine plan for creating His kingdom of God on earth. Since Moon is Korean—and this is the pertinence of this theological digression—that divine plan will be realized not as hitherto in the West, but in Korea, the new Israel, and through a Korean path to salvation. This is Korea's divinely designed mission, a mission which will save all humankind but Koreans in particular from their present psychological and material suffering.

There are two major secular sources of church strength of significance to the present study; the first is its skillful organization. Authority is hierarchical, flowing down from the center in Seoul through intermediary levels to fundamental units which are rooted in villages and urban neighborhoods. Simultaneously, functional cells proliferate among students, businessmen, women, and youth, which also are organized hierarchically under Seoul's direct control. Centralization assures immediate response to directives from above, especially from Moon himself, who commands obedience by virtue of his special mission and his designation as parent of all the church members. Individuals are encouraged to rise in the organization by converting others who will become their clients or through the competitive examinations which are held periodically at all levels. In brief, the church's organization is the model of a time-tested but very "modern" patrimonial administration. And Moon, as its charismatic patrimonial leader, has wide jurisdiction over his flock, not only spiritually but physically. Members "volunteer" labor service, and church entrepreneurial activities have made him rich. But like other new religious leaders, and as all patrimonial rulers must, Moon claims that his wealth is the organization's, but that he and his aides must live well as a sign of God's approval of physical redemption and God's promise that one day all believers will enjoy a similar material life.

The second source of the church's strength is its controversial, often denied, but not unexpected connection to patrimonial authority, especially under Park. It was no secret that Moon's Christianity was the kind of Christianity that Park liked; that is, one that flatters Korean nationalism, is a spokesman for the old virtues of family and responsibility, and above all not only does not criticize, but on the contrary actually supports the existing polity, since both Park and Moon considered Communism their prime moral enemy. Moon still preaches that Korea will be the new paradise because it is the very place where a successful confrontation with the anti-Christ Satan, in the form of the DPRK, can and should take place. Hence Moon was at least urging his followers to rally for Park's mass politics, preaching at government anti-Communist indoctrination centers, and going abroad to the hellish West to propagate the idea that the ROK was the last bastion of anti-Communism and hence worthy of American support. But Moon's obviously well-financed American tour did not generate much public attention, in part because he had to speak through an interpreter, save from American Protestant clergymen who denounced Moon as a heretic and from a number of young seekers moving cafeteria-style among the many religious offerings of the contemporary scene. But the church's aggressive tactics, the Asian-centricity of Moon's message, and the close-knit but isolated life of the members, however, caused the converts' parents to panic, denouncing Moon as an occult brainwasher, hiring professionals to deprogram their sometimes kidnapped offspring, and noisily pressing the courts and legislatures to proscribe the Church. The parents' campaign coincided with growing American interest in Korean influence-peddling in high American government circles. Moon, though he consistently denied his church had any official, especially Korean, intelligence connections, still was implicated in scandal, at the least through various front organizations such as the Korean Cultural Association in Washington, D.C., and through his followers' busy lobbying of American congressmen. Within the Asian patrimonial context, nothing Moon has thought or done (or has been accused of doing), inside or outside Korea, is in any way either unusual or illegal, although his opinions and conduct often horrify nonpatrimonial Americans. Moon sees the campaign against himself and his church as the work of Satan, especially in the devious Communist form which he believes is so prevalent in a corrupt United States. His followers also point out, with justification, that at least some of the spleen vented against Moon comes from those who cannot accept that the East has anything to offer, especially from a Christian Messiah, while westerners see nothing amiss in expecting Asians to accept a western God as universal. Back in Korea, therefore, defensive nationalism assures that Moon's prestige has not diminished, perhaps even has been enhanced by the church's problems abroad.[3]

## Contemporary Confucianism

Confucianism is enjoying a modest revival, profiting from two trends, one national and one institutional. *Nationally* the ROK sees itself, rather than what it claims is an iconoclastic, alien-imitating DPRK, as the true successor to the Korean national heritage, which includes inter alia Confucianism. Thus, properly purged of Chinese superficialities, the semiannual official rites at the old imperial National Confucian Shrine have been revitalized, with the minister of public information and culture among other government officials conspicuously in attendance and the last dynastic heir presiding as high priest. The pedagogical arm of the shrine has been turned into a modern, full-fledged university. The first postwar head was a nationalist of unquestioned credentials who had resisted collaborating with the Japanese. Both he and his successor have taken a strong anti-Communist and non- if not anti-American ideological stand, claiming that only through a revivified Confucian-inspired Korean ethic can the nation both sustain its independence and be true to its heritage— the kind of message ROK governments like to hear. *Institutionally,* this Confucian role in rationalizing political patrimonialism, especially loyalty to authority, is too valuable for the polity to abandon now that most of the older sources of patrimonial support have dried up and modern secular, often blatantly high-handed, techniques of control are being both resorted to and resented.

Yet, although most of its vocal partisans are government officials and aged aristocrats, it would be folly to assume that Confucianism is a propped-up relic of an nonviable past that will ultimately expire. Four and a half million Koreans claim to be Confucians, more than those on Chinese Taiwan where the government too has sponsored a Confucian revival. The old Confucian rural social centers and schools are holding their own as are village temples, which numbered 231 at recent count. But above all Confucianism lives in the network of con-sanguineal ties and obligations, which now more than ever are considered vital in an increasingly insecure, though "modern," Korean patrimonial social and economic environment.

A word on TAOISM. It thrives, not only in its popular geomantic form, but also as the mode of thought of organized Moral Associations which claim to be repaying a Korean debt to China by revitalizing the religion at the very time it is being harassed in the Peoples' Republic of China.[4]

## The Ethos and Organization of Contemporary Secular Education

The American educational record in Korea is the quintessence of the Americans' success and failure in reshaping Korean society to an American image of a modern society. On the positive side, a number of American proposals were eagerly accepted because they did away with blatant expressions of Japanese cultural imperialism—such as using the Korean language once again to instruct, purging texts of pro-Japanese sentiments, and replacing Japanese educational bureaucrats with Koreans—or because the Americans were doing what the Koreans wanted to do on their own but had been prevented from doing by the Japanese—such as providing both a universal, compulsory elementary and a readily available secondary-higher education for Koreans. However, on the negative side, first, reforms which the Americans highly prized and assumed the Koreans would too, committed as the Koreans said they were to democratizing education, somehow did not work out as the Americans thought they should. For example, freeing education from the control of the Ministry of Home Affairs did not simultaneously free education from the control of the local bureaucracy; hence the educational boards set up with American blessing did not become the autonomous popular organs the Americans had envisioned. Second, the Americans soon came to realize that certain of their innovations were accepted because they could be redefined in a way that reinforced rather than undermined, as the Americans assumed they would, certain educational values inherited from the Japanese period. For example, the American goal of turning out individuals capable of pursuing their personal aspirations yet who simultaneously would be useful citizens was reinterpreted to a goal of creating individuals who would be useful to society and themselves because they were useful to the state. Third, in certain instances nothing changed substantively from the Japanese days save that new American titles and jargon were substituted for existing ones. For example, educational inspectors were now called superintendents. Fourth, the Koreans claimed to be *formally* conforming to American desires, when in fact they were not. For example, all Korean regimes have claimed that education is democratic and popular, when clearly it is neither, as we shall see. Finally, as was true of the Korean institutional order in general, the Americans, in spite of all they thought they had accomplished by the time the occupation ended, did not alter one whit most of the existing education patterns, either out of ignorance of what truly was going on in this alien patrimonial society or because the Americans thought it expedient to work with what they had and who was on hand.

Consequently, when the Republic was proclaimed and the Americans relinquished control of education, Koreans trained under the Japanese, using *their* assumptions, structures, and operating procedures, became the new decision-makers and managers. Thus, Seoul continues to control local education directly by financing all higher education, and indirectly through the Ministry of Home Affairs administrative control of provincial government. The center minister of education reviews all texts, faculty credentials, and the character of public as well as private institutions of learning. Retained are: independent divisions on the college level; separate tracking of regular, normal, and special-technical students; cleavage between compulsory-elementary and secondary education, signified by a stiff entrance examination; six-year professional training directly after completing secondary education; administrative staffs which are not professionally specialized; and the very symbol of the Japanese system, black-uniformed elementary and secondary students. Finally, still viable is the prewar Japanese view that education is the primary means to create pliant, egoless, obedient, prebendary-seeking, politically passive, and dependent subjects. None of this should startle, I suggest, because the

ROK is as interested in having the educational system turn out patrimonialists as were the Japanese (and the dynasts before them).

The desire of the government to indoctrinate, and of parents to obtain the validating credentials which would enable their offspring to exploit opportunities denied most Koreans under the Japanese, generated strong pressures to expand the educational system. Though not to be faulted, such enthusiasm has been a mixed blessing since the great numbers pressing against limited resources, for example, enabled the government for too long to put off extending compulsory education beyond the first six grades. Moreover, education may be free, but books and services are not, eliminating most of the poor in rural areas. Entering numbers are high, but attrition is high also. Hence, although education is legally open to all, increasingly as one goes up the educational ladder the system serves the select few. Yet, simultaneously, even at the highest level, the numbers of students are many in relation to the available faculty. The consequence is didactic lecturing rather than discussion, and authoritarian methods to control great numbers of potentially disruptive students. All this smacks of the Japanese colonial past.

Another consequence is that since the economic and social stakes—ultimately the modern equivalent of elite yangban status and privileges—are so high, yet places in the public institutions are limited and elimination along the way is as ruthless as under the Japanese, private organs at all levels and of all kinds have proliferated. A significant minority of these institutes, primarily those going back to the imperial era but properly updated in 1945, are highly reputable. But too many are diploma mills, which have mushroomed to exploit especially wealthy parents with not-too-promising children but high-status aspirations. By paying generous fees, these parents can count on sympathetic faculty and administrators, but the schools themselves are perpetually at the brink of insolvency because of the dearth of organizational talent and buccaneering attitude. The government, recognizing such institutions as the money-making schemes they truly are, has denied them subsidies, has taxed them as business enterprises, has reviewed their financing, and has forced them to accept students which the public middle and higher institutions cannot accommodate under threat of withdrawing accreditation.

Vocational-technical schools, public or private, are ranked lower in prestige than are general education institutions, in spite of the fact that the chronic shortage of competent technicians in the expanding Korean economy is axiomatic. The Japanese left a rudimentary vocational education program, most of which was respectable. But the Americans, although they often talked about expanding the program, did little, and Rhee abandoned it. The situation changed dramatically under Park, who not only was committed to industrialization, but was irked by the great number of liberal arts institutions turning out candidates for nonexistent government positions who then became chronic political discontents. Although Park was his usual forceful self and was undoubtedly helped by an expanding economy offering opportunities for the vocationally trained, he was not truly successful. The primary reason is that career choice continues to reflect a patri-monial division of labor (see Chapter 6); to wit, the yangban work ethic persists, especially in dismay over being associated with hand work and in the wish that eldest sons in particular find a secure, sta-tused, and potentially prebendally rewarding government career, re-gardless of the increasingly unfavorable odds of doing so by climbing the liberal arts ladder. Consequently, the ambitious and capable con-sider the vocational track as their last choice. Even a commercial edu-cation is preferred because it will assure a white-collar career. And for those who do enter the vocational track, textile is preferred to ma-chine industry because, although remuneration is more rewarding in the latter, it is historically associated with unskilled labor. By like rea-soning the last choice is agriculture; for although, or because, so many Koreans are farmers, even being a technically trained and com-petent one is considered lowly since it still is believed that farming requires neither ability nor ambition. Thus rural families see little point in using scarce funds to send their youngsters to agricultural institutes.

The negative attitude toward vocational education, which seems so strange to Americans and certainly is economically counterproduc-tive, is not necessarily irrational, given the fact that the system is ill adapted to teach skills. First, the curriculum has too many unrelated courses because students clamor for such courses, hoping against hope that somehow such a program will qualify them to enter a non-vocational college or, failing that, provide a watered-down version of the liberal arts curriculum for which they originally did not qualify. Second, students have scant interest in practical, especially labora-tory, training. They demand rather the lectures characteristic of the prestigious liberal arts, which even in that program are unimaginative, unrealistic, and out-of-date because they use obsolete foreign texts in unreliable translation, shortcomings critical in vocational training. Third, save in the case of Taegu City, there is little coordination be-tween potential employers' and the schools' spokesmen, the Vocational Education Association, a situation not unknown in technologically advanced economies but extremely wasteful in resource-short Korea. Perhaps this is not an unwise decision, given the nature of vocational education. Whatever the reason, Korean managers, taking their cue from their Japanese predecessors, prefer to train on the job and they make a creditable performance of it. But this only intensifies the already low morale of the vocational institutes.

Colleges and universities are not the most modern segment of Korean education, perhaps because they were the least affected by the changeover from Japanese colonial to independent control. Hence, although the Republic charter mandating higher education sets lofty goals, the government claims it wants skills for its modernizing programs, and students claim they seek knowledge and character-building, yet in fact all expect education to reinforce the status quo. Though public higher education is subsidized, the student body primarily is drawn from the conservative well-to-do with roots in the dynastic and especially Japanese past. And although most students say they want to be useful once they are graduated, they show little interest in social issues, especially in the question of reform of the existing order. Rather, like their parents, they strongly desire a society which offers them material opportunity and psychological security. And there is little in their higher educational experience, much of it a carbon copy of the Japanese past, which will alter their thinking for a number of reasons.

First, the higher education process is not conducive to creative (productive) learning. Lecturing predominates, rote memory is rewarded, regurgitating the instructor's opinions is required if one expects to get a good grade, precious little attention is given to contemporary problems, and citizenship skills are rarely taught. Once enrolled in a particular program it is most difficult to change faculties, no matter how indifferent or incompetent the students find themselves to be in their present curricula. There are too many courses and other requirements to graduate, discouraging students from trying to master anything. And it is so difficult to qualify that, once accepted, most students will be graduated unless they personally antagonize the administration, and hence what and how well one learns also is left to whim.

Second, the faculty, a potential major source of productive change, is unable to fulfill that role for two major reasons. One source is the morale problem. Base salaries are low, a not unusual situation the world over. However, in Korea the problem is acute because a good portion, and sometimes all, of personal research and most books must be financed out of faculty resources. Moreover, educating children to advanced levels, so socially and economically vital these days, is a burden for all but the wealthy, which few faculty are. Hence they are constantly aware that their own hard-earned status may not be transferrable, a transgression against consanguinity, especially ancestors. The second obstacle against the faculty changing the system is tenure. Once tenured, professors are most difficult to dislodge, which would be a useful protection for agents of change, but tenured openings are not always filled. Consequently, tenured faculty are overburdened and staff deficiencies must be made up by moonlighters who have only a superficial interest in the affairs of their institutions. Tenure is acquired primarily through nepotism, often by being selected while still a student as a potential client of some faculty patron. Returnees from overseas, even though (but perhaps because) they have novel skills, find it difficult to surmount such patron-client paths to appointment, especially in the fiercely contested tenured positions. Some such individuals contribute to the "brain drain," but most make their way in the academic establishment by putting aside their alien notions how academe might be rationally reorganized and accepting the discipline of their group's patronal leader.

Third, higher education is vexed by the same bureaucratic organizational constraints on innovation which exist in the larger society. There is too much required paperwork, which cuts seriously into faculty time better devoted to creative research. Educational regulations are conflicting and unclear, which exacerbates tension and generates unproductive factional strife between government bureaucrats and educational administrators, between administrators and faculty, and finally between faculty and students. The consequent confusion and bickering enables authoritarian decision-makers to bully the less resourceful into accepting their desires, irrespective of what the majority may want or the formal rules may require. This is especially evident in relations between government and faculty. According to the Korean constitution, all faculty at either public or private institutions of higher learning are guaranteed academic freedom and tenure is inviolable, unless a criminal act has been committed; all charges of criminality must be aired by specially appointed committees and reviewed by the presidents of the respective institutions; and if the accused faculty member is of high rank, the charge must be further reviewed by the education minister and then the president of the Republic. However, the emergency and martial law decrees which all Koreans, including of course academics, must obey take precedence over such assurances. Thus, for example, faculty can be dismissed for "neglect of duty" if they participate in unauthorized political activity.

Such faculty are incarcerated, banished from academe, or exiled to less prestiged campuses without seniority, depending on the seriousness of the offense in authority's eyes. Faculty know very well that they dare not teach, publish, or even research controversial matters, as almost anything can be denounced as irresponsibly aiding Korea's enemies, whether that foe is the DPRK or carping American congressmen. The law enabling authority to enter the campus whenever the government considers its laws violated has been on the books since 1964, and has been used to send in occupying troops or to completely close down especially noisy and troublesome institutions.

Fourth, the Education Ministry itself is not exempt from those problems besetting all government agencies, which dissipate energy and reduce performance. Among these are (1) petty bickering, self-serving, lack of coordination within the ministry and with outsiders, and arrogant indifference to input from the public, all of which have discouraged the emergence of an education constituency within either government or society interested in, and able to articulate and represent, the higher educational aspirations of Koreans; (2) rapid turnover in ministry personnel accompanied by constant curriculum "reform" to enable new appointees to put their distinctive mark on programs, both of which have made it difficult to draw up and implement long-range plans; (3) as under the Japanese, appointment of those without professional education qualifications to decision-making and even staff positions, which facilitates political interference into and control of purely educational concerns of all levels, for example, clerks in minor (myŏn level) government offices being authorized to supervise and "guide" school principals in their duties; (4) educational projects chosen more for their tangible quantity than their intangible quality, often selected ad hoc without supportive feasibility research and without regard to priorities in spite of limited educational resources; and yet (5) the expansion of Education Ministry responsibility—e.g., for hospitals on grounds that they are affiliated with medical schools—which spreads the ministry's resources too thin, so that what it does is often of marginal quality and what it supervises is rarely monitored and evaluated.

The polity has at its disposal a number of subtle and effective means to get its way with academics without recourse to overt force. Foremost is the character of higher education budgeting. Only little more than half of faculty salaries are "base." The remainder is made up of special and "merit" allowances which can be politically manipulated to reward or punish particular individuals or a whole university's faculty and staff. Likewise, the Ministry of Education is authorized to set standards for both public and private institutions. Its mandate is patrimonially vague, enabling it to subsidize those which it (politically) likes and to find fault with, and hence refuse to help, those which it (politically) dislikes. Perpetually indigent students can also be pressured into conforming by government threats to withdraw their prebendally granted scholarships and allowances. Foreign students are prescreened abroad, put on scholarships, and assigned on arrival in Korea. They are made aware that their support and even their stay in Korea is a patrimonial privilege which can be revoked at government option and that students can be deported just like any troublesome foreign national.

Second, everyone on campus fears ubiquitous secret observers, the modern equivalent of the dynastic censors and Japanese academic spies. Whether they are actually present or not, the fact that they might be is intimidating enough to discourage students and even the most hardy faculty and administrators from joining together to resist government campus policies or to press for change in the academic or social status quo.

A third instrument the polity exploits to control academia and ultimately the role of the educated in the society is the power to determine the structure of the curricula. A prime example is legal education. To recall (Chapters 5 and 6), law faculties are chartered primarily to turn out legal bureaucrats and not legal specialists to serve the populace's public or private interests. Hence, precious little education time is spent on the function of law in society, the responsibilities of lawyers in society, rural or business law, and civil liberties, since the polity will define all those issues in terms of its own political interests. Many legal texts are Japanese—in Korean translations to be sure—because, in spite of formal political freedom from Japan and in spite of certain formal changes carried out in response to American inspiration and prodding, the pre-World War II, patrimonially inspired, "modern" Japanese legal apparatus and reasoning, which took root in the occupation, continues to be viable.

A fourth prerogative, also a Japanese legacy, which the government exercises most vigorously, is to control education texts, negatively by extirpating what it considers to be subversive thoughts and positively by pressing for support of authority and its policies. The Ministry of Education is authorized to review all texts used in private as well as public institutions and to set guidelines for which kinds of texts are acceptable and which are not. Firms printing texts are required to obtain ministry clearance before they can legally execute orders. The ministry, though most diligent about protecting textual moral purity, is unfortunately not equally diligent about how thorough, accurate, clear, stimulating, and realistic texts are. An early UNESCO review, for example, found most high school texts ill organized, formalistic in application to the real world, slogan-studded, and overloaded with rarely explained technical jargon and formulae without examples.

Fifth, the government controls and simultaneously exploits education by mobilizing the young to serve the state, either through organizing campus youth corps (the favorite of Rhee) or through inspiring, and even participating in, drafting lecture material (the favorite of Park), both techniques being learned from the Japanese colonialists. Moreover, according to a government scenario, Korean Confucianism, as noble as it is, is defunct. Consequently, Koreans, thrashing about in moral confusion and tempted to fill the vacuum with the dubious, shallow values of the materialist West (especially its notions of extreme democracy and individualism inappropriate for Korea), require ethical revitalization to create that consensus necessary both to modernize and to confront their enemies; and that implies ethical indoctrination at all levels. Thus, as the Japanese did in the case of State versus Sect Shintō, Park claimed that ethics was not synonymous with religion and hence did not need to be separated from politics or education as the constitution required in the case of religion. After an alleged subversive plot was discovered among the Federation of Democratic Youth in 1974, Park ordered that anti-Communist material also be incorporated into texts and that special courses and examinations on the Communist threat be mandatory.

In sum and in conclusion, much of Korean education has been found wanting by internal and external critics. Westerners' judgments not surprisingly reflect their societies' notions of what an efficient productive education has to be in order to generate a useful, satisfied citizenry capable of assuming responsibility in a modern social order—a goal which the Korean polity professes to desire and with which one cannot logically quarrel. However, if we are willing to consider Korean education as the means by which the existing institutional order expects to socialize the next generation into its patrimonial ways, albeit in a *modern* version, much of what seems obscure and faulty by nonpatrimonial standards becomes both rational and functional, though it is questionable indeed whether such a system is conducive to Korea's *development*.[5]

# 11

# The Social Order and Social Change: How Korea Has Reacted to the Challenge of Modernization

## Patrimonial Persistence, Morality, Corruption, and Cathartic Moral Renovation

In patrimonial reasoning, an institutional order, to accord with the natural scheme of things, above all must be a moral, nonexpedient order. Hence, problems when they arise are ascribed to immoralities committed by immoral individuals, quintessentially symbolized by corruption. Corruption is much more than a loss of individual innocence and uprightness, as important as they are. Rather, corruption implies a decline in performance, since those who are corrupt turn their attention away from primarily serving the interests of society to primarily serving their own advantage, which in turn encourages others to do likewise through rule by model. Thus both morality and (material) practicality are inevitably intertwined, such that if the social order is morally weak (that is, corrupt) it simultaneously must be practically weak, and conversely, if it is materially weak, it must be morally weak as well. Yet, since a social order must be patrimonial if it is to be both morally and practically viable, corruption and practical weakness call into question the moral worth of specific individuals or, at most, the moral worth of the specific social order, but never the *patrimonial* character of any social order. Hence, patrimonial social change is thought of as a process by which all specific social orders are subject to cycles of modest and thus tolerable corruptibility accompanied by high material performance, giving way sooner or later to high corruptibility and poor performance, either in shorter, repetitive cycles within a particular social order's time span or as major cycles which separate one social order from another.

The course of Korean history until this century seemed to vindicate this philosophy. In fact the patrimonial character of the Korean social order was never challenged even to the modest extent that it was in its patrimonial neighbor, China. First, there were fewer dynastic changes and the average dynastic span was longer in Korea than in China. In part this was because there was less internal interference in Korea by foreign intruders, and in part because, second, the Korean monarchy was not as crucial to the elite's maintaining its privileges as the Chinese ruler was. Third, the Korean elite, though it had its ups and downs, never had its monopolistic access to power and privilege seriously challenged. The major challenge to the institutional order came rather from possible feudalization, but that threat soon evaporated when the military elite decided to collaborate with, rather than overturn, and even supply fresh blood for the patrimonial elite. Finally, neither persistent, popular oppositional secret societies nor a mandate of heaven signaling a propitious time to replace an existing social order, both renowned in China, were ever present in Korea.

For all these reasons the Korean elite never perceived that it had to compromise patrimonially to prevail, since no qualitatively distinct nonpatrimonial counter interest ever arose to challenge the patrimonial idea. Only some among the patrimonially committed periodically were dissatisfied with their share of the prebendary political, economic, or social spoils and they could be mollified as individuals. Thus, the Korean moral guardians of the institutional order, rather than being forced to question or change prevailing patrimonial norms, could devote their attention to trying to minimize intra-elite conflict, especially disruptive factional antagonisms over prebends, and to perfecting a social policy which validated their claim that it was indeed serving the best interests of the populace through equal doses of didactic moral lecturing and benevolence. Consequently, although its record of exploitation and inefficiency was no better than its neighbors', the Korean elite was the most successful in holding on to what sociologists term integrative, inner-cultivating goals, smug in the belief that no matter how serious the difficulties of the moment the patrimonial institutional order would prevail. In sum, innovation, though certainly not unheard of, was carefully measured so that it never worked against fundamental patrimonial assumptions and structures.

Lest we believe that this reasoning and this overview of history are quaint, obsolete notions of the causes and consequences of Korean social change, I point out that contemporary Korean observers have interpreted the internal restructuring and the transition from predecessor to successor of the republican Rhee, Chang, and Park social orders in such terms, especially of cyclic corruption. According to the scenario, in all three cases the need to create and distribute prebends to build loyal cliental followers in order to consolidate power, which at least one observer has argued is not necessarily self-serving since such consolidation may facilitate productive nation-building, has turned decision-makers' attention away from performance to major preoccupation with fund-raising and hence tolerance, if not encouragement, of personal spoliation of the society's resources. In spite of a temporary (cyclic) reversal of priorities from prebendary exploitation to performance, corruption so dominated the Rhee regime that it inevitably gave way to the Chang regime which, unable to act decisively on the problem, was replaced by the Park regime, which in turn trod the same path to inevitable destruction. The only way any of these regimes could have survived, the argument goes, was through periodic tightening up of discipline and at least a noticeable diminution, if not elimination, of corruption.

Such a response, as useful as it may be, clearly is not institutional change but *cathartic renovation*—in Korean *yusin*—which in a patrimonial context implies moral crusading against individual venality through disciplinary action and didactic preaching (rule by model). Well aware of the unpopularity of his regime, especially at the end, Park periodically launched cathartic campaigns against those whom he termed corrupt bureaucrats. But the campaigns were short-lived, more show than substance, and disruptive of office routine, since when they were on officials procrastinated and absented themselves lest they inevitably violate some formal regulation. Above all, they begged what to me seems the key issue—namely, the need to ascertain what it was in the very patrimonial nature of the social order that encouraged bureaucrats and nonbureaucrats alike to bribe and scramble so for material security in spite of the professed moral focus and the multitudinous regulations and legal sanctions. Certainly the campaigns did not save Park from his fall from patrimonial grace.[1]

I now shall discuss briefly the various kinds of cathartic renovations during the nineteenth and twentieth centuries, a period of Korean history which I will attempt to demonstrate may be characterized as one of ever-escalating challenges to the existing patrimonial character of the institutional order, challenges which sparked *modern* responses that not only did not contribute to but often positively thwarted Korean *development*.

With this goal in mind and because I am not a historian, I restrict myself to examining patrimonially relevant character and consequence, and hence, as has been true of my treatment of the historical evidence throughout the study, I do not claim that I am doing full justice to the often controversial complexities of the material. (Please review the methodological discussions of Chapter 1.)

### Cathartic Positive Renovation: The Taewŏn'gun's Yusin

Salvational catharsis is by no means limited to periodic soul-searching and the weeding of the bureaucratic garden, as characteristic as these are. Catharsis also can involve large-scale administrative and even structural reform. We must never fall into the western theoretical trap of viewing patrimonial dynastic societies as static and their decision-makers as passionately antagonistic to innovation. Nevertheless, I do suggest that most of those decision-makers did everything possible to insure that innovation was cathartic, and hence renovative, and not institutionally qualitative in the development sense.

Korean cathartic renovation prior to this century predominantly strived to increase the ruler's share of the economy's surplus without unduly arousing the populace's ire; for example, by increasing the effectiveness of existing tax collection to prevent leakage; by introducing new sources of revenue and eliminating existing, nonproductive sources, such as altering the cropping pattern; by augmenting the productivity of existing sources of revenue through technical or material aid, such as irrigation; by surveying the cadastre to uncover hidden sources of productive taxable wealth; and by removing overzealous and overbearing officials to induce the populace to be more cooperative in paying its taxes. One of the most ambitious of these renovative campaigns was the one carried out by the taewŏn'gun, or regent for the king, in the 1860s. Though this was not strictly an orthodox cathartic response to an internal crisis, in that foreign pressures intruded in all the regent's decisions, many observers consider the program as the last imperial attempt to renovate in response to the popular resentment against official ineptness and hanky-panky which had crystalized in a major peasant rebellion the year before the regent came to power.

The regent's program comprehensively touched upon political, cultural, and especially economic matters. Many of its specifics are familiar, for example, extortive local officials were punished with dismissal, banishment, and confiscation of illegally seized wealth. However, the regent went further: Of political patrimonial interest, first he reorganized the civil and military machinery; second, he recruited and promoted additional "merit" officials particularly from regions previously discriminated against and from those elements in the society largely then excluded from public office, in order to reduce if not eliminate corruption, raise the efficiency and morale of the bureaucracy, build a personal loyal following to carry out the reforms, and create a patrimonial clientele far more broadly based than the old-time factions; third, he puffed up the royal prestige in hopes of reviving the monarch's declining fortunes and centralized authority; and fourth, all but a mere handful of the local private academies, the very political nerve centers of out-of-power yangban, were closed, both to weaken aristocratic opposition to the regent and to tie yangban fortunes more closely to the patrimonial royal house. In the academies' place he substituted a central, refurbished Confucian academy and Confucian schools to siphon off the ambitious and talented into center (read, regent) service.

On the economic front, first, the regent moved against those corrupt officials who either unlawfully appropriated or refused to collect the land tax; second, he replaced a commoner-evaded and yangban-exempt (military support) tax with a universally levied and collected (household cloth) tax; third, he reformed grain loaning, by writing off most of the principal and most of the loan debt, not only as an act of prebendary grace, but also to insure repayment of the interest which, as in all usurious loaning, was considerable. The loans, rather than being controlled by corrupt magistrates and their aides, henceforth were dispersed by village yangban, who along with village notables were made responsible for insuring the quotas now set on all loans; and fourth, to cover the heavy expenses he incurred by palace-building and military renovation, for which cathartic economic reform alone could not hope to suffice, the regent debased the coinage, generating great inflation, which he unsuccessfully tried to ameliorate by administratively controlling prices and which ultimately led to his downfall.

Looking beyond the specific historical events, the regent's failure perhaps was inevitable because, first, he could not hope to accomplish his goal of increasing the state revenue on the scale he envisioned by tightening rather than qualitatively altering the collection process. Especially critical was depending on a cooperative relationship between magistrates-cum-local-notables and producers, without providing any novel (nonpatrimonial) workable scheme to insure that magistrates and notables suddenly would become universally competent and honest. Moreover, the land tax, still the primary source of revenue, was left untouched; the grain loan reform did not regulate existing interest rates and thus, intentionally or not, legitimized unproductive private usury; and the yangban elite continued to be exempt from grain or corvée levies. Second, the regent's programs were not integrated into any comprehensive, realistic, qualitatively novel economic plan but were ad hoc ameliorative expediencies, some of which helped, some of which did not, while others were counterproductive. Third, for all the heat the reform generated among the privileged, the regent never truly struck at the institutional status quo. He had no interest whatever in destroying the patrimonial yangban society; quite the contrary, he was doing all he could to preserve it. He thus found himself in the worst of all possible situations; that is, he made no serious attempt to solve any of the root institutional causes of the society's malaise, yet he still managed to alienate the governing yangban elite, more out of fear than out of reality. Fourth, he failed to build a viable constituency of his own to resist yangban pressure. Most of the regent's newly created clients, the men of merit, did not stand with him at the critical moment of truth and, in fact, always were more interested in refurbishing their local power bases than in creating a novel, truly national interest group. Then as now, viable corporate, intermediary interest groups, occupational or otherwise rooted, did exist for the regent to exploit in his contest with the entrenched patrimonial civil-military bureaucracy. On the other hand, the yangban purists stood virtually as one against any tinkering with their way of doing things, piously asserting that frugality and didacticism which would morally cleanse men rather than changes in the rules of the game were the proper path to national, renovative salvation. Finally, the regent's centralizing effort to insure yangban loyalty to the sovereign failed, and with it the ability to transcend the very limited political maneuverability he possessed by virtue of being regent.

Some of the regent's specific cathartic renovations survived his downfall, but his failure served to assure the yangban that once again the moral foundation of the institutional order had been successfully defended against heresy. In winning the day, the yangban eventually facilitated the triumph of the Japanese, not because what the yangban specifically opposed in the regent's program would have made all that much difference had the program succeeded but because failure reinforced the notion that the existing institutional order was eternally viable. Though written with the same Chinese ideographs, the regent's yusin was not the equivalent of the Japanese *Ishin* of 1868 and thereafter, which was a true social revolution. Rather, the regent's reform was the equivalent of the age-old Chinese patrimonial cathartic restoration, which in this case did not succeed even to the very limited extent that its contemporary Chinese *T'ung-chih* period renovation did in postponing the ultimate day of reckoning for both the dynasty and the old social order. To bring the discussion up to date, the reader should have no difficulty in deciding which interpretation of yusin applies to Park's use of the term.[2]

### The Philosophy of Catharsis: Silhak

The failure of Korean productive reform was certainly not due to any dearth of relevant criticism of the existing malaise or of imaginative remedial suggestions. The most persistent and creative scrutiny was that offered by *Silhak* which, as the name implies, extolled the *sil;* that is, relevant, practical solutions to the real problems of an age, as contrasted to idle speculation and inadequate, outdated ideas retained primarily through inertia ("tradition"). The concept of sil was not original with Silhak, nor even with Korea. What was unique to Silhak was that it used the notion of sil first to question the hitherto sacrosanct premise that Koreans were obligated to support the existing social order, even if it was unworkable, if it supposedly conformed to an eternal Confucian ideal (because to do otherwise would tempt the wrath of Heaven and its secular Chinese arm of repression), and then to review the Korean social order and offer sometimes radical practical solutions to that order's ills.

Perhaps because they involved only formal changes in administrative procedure and brought in additional state revenue, some of Silhak's proposals were put into practice, in spite of carping criticism by old-line bureaucrats—such as substituting a rice tax for tribute. But those suggestions which involved much more than formal reform— for example, willingness to come to terms with emerging commercial agriculture, commercial enterprise, and incipient industry and the need to rationalize social and economic relationships between managers and producers—were denounced and opposed successfully by orthodox thinkers and interests as threats to the very moral foundations of the social order.

Notwithstanding the fact that Silhak can thus be judged a failure, its ideas about the causes of social malaise and even many of the solutions have a pertinent and contemporary ring. Examples include: the warning that an overly complex agricultural administration encourages corruption; the recommendation that villagers develop cooperatives to eliminate exploitive middlemen; the suggestion that technological inputs such as irrigation and novel cropping and a reward system for productive cultivators are ways to rehabilitate agriculture; the plea to build government-certified and monitored markets and shops and situate them in locations accessible to all; the proposal to improve public transport both to facilitate commerce and to stabilize prices; the approbation of manual labor and denunciation of unproductive idleness by the society's privileged; the requirement that individuals be assigned to the division of labor on merit rather than on influence; the argument that the polity must refrain from demanding bribes to allow the people to do economically what they should be entitled to do as a legitimate right. All these sound very modern and familiar. Similarly, would not recent fiscal reformers be at home with the assurance that directly collected, equitably levied taxes rather than moral preachment (rule by model), as well as taxes which are easy to assess and collect and are readily accepted as just by the people, will both end corruption and increase the revenue? And like the present modernizing leadership, Silhak thinkers too were firm in the conviction that improved technology would increase both production and revenue, and hence national prosperity and social stability, though, like the debate within the Economic Planning Board these days, they disagreed among themselves about which economic activities to apply that technology to. Also, like the reformers of today (see Chapters 2 and 3), Silhak philosophers acted as one in demanding administrative revitalization (yusin!), given the pervasive government influence which both they and their contemporaries considered inevitable. To one observer, the key administrative problem was finding and holding on to trustworthy low-level officials, especially those interacting with the public, who would serve the people and not themselves—an appeal sure to be found almost any day in the contemporary press. However, another observer believed the only way to obtain an efficient, honest corps of officials was to select them on realistic, rather than formal, grounds and then continuously rotate, supervise, and if necessary discipline them. Still another believed that a corruption-free administration required a constitutionally limited executive, a political order which not only passed but enforced laws, a bureaucracy whose size was determined by need and not by the desire to validate social status, and precise administrative decrees and job descriptions.

Even though I agree that Silhak struck at the very heart of Korea's persistent problems, however, I cannot support those who believe that it did or could provide a catalyst for productive change. Beyond certain obvious historical circumstances (Silhak's alliance with the wrong political faction and the wrong [chung'in] class) and the fact that, although Silhak may have posed the right questions, many of its solutions managed to be both behind the needs of particular times and beyond the capacity of the society to implement, I believe lies an intrinsic institutional flaw. For, even if Silhak had succeeded in having all its programs adopted, at best this would have helped to set in motion only a modernizing process, which would have reinforced and not altered prevailing patrimonial presuppositions and goals by helping to make existing operational procedures, especially exploitation of the economy, more effective. For example, the proposal for an annual audit of government finance and the separation of public and private expenditures by officials, the counsel to spend according to a budget, now facts of Korean economic life, have not had any appreciable impact on bureaucratic diligence or uprightness, to judge from contemporary commentary. What I am driving at is that Silhak was seeking a cathartic renovation, not an institutional revolution. For Silhak was as committed to patrimonialism as were both its rivals in the establishment and the reformers to follow, those whom Silhak inspired and for whom it set the ground rules on the nature and limits of reform—which I see as Silhak's contribution to modern Korea. All this is to be contrasted with what went on simultaneously in Japan, ironically influenced in part by Silhak thought. There, Silhak's equivalent, *jitsugaku*, played a significant role not only in altering the prevailing, similarly entrenched Confucian view of an eternal natural-cum-social universe but, more pertinently, in legitimizing a pragmatically creative "amoral" response to society's ills, thus helping to pave the way for Japan's modernization *and* development. If similar ideas are present, why didn't development happen in Korea? I suggest once again that the difference is that, in spite of recurrent influences from both China and Korea, Japan is not *institutionally* patrimonial.[3]

## Korea Reacts to the Outside World with Cathartic Reform

It is patently false to argue that Korea had little contact with foreigners and their ideas until the middle of the nineteenth century. Yet it is true that Korea was more successful than were its neighbors in isolating itself from other than East Asians, and hence was less experienced in responding effectively to western and modern Japanese intrusion after the Treaty of 1876 forcefully opened the "Hermit Kingdom" to the outside world. Moreover, Korea's previous experience in successfully accommodating itself to East Asians, especially its ritually obsequious cliental relationship to China, gave Koreans a false sense that, first, selective temporizing would always be sufficient to mollify any intruder and survive; second, legal interchange could be limited to official missions which could be carefully screened for subversive potential; and finally, isolation of foreign residents would suffice to prevent popular contact with outsiders and their ideas and to protect the society's basic institutions from foreign contamination.

At first, very few Korean decision-makers, even those sympathetic to western or Japanese technology, were willing even to believe that their cherished beliefs and customs might not be perpetually viable; in fact, on the contrary, the Korean innovators argued that absorbing the foreigners' superior technology was the only way to resuscitate and preserve the existing institutional order and hence assure Korea's survival. Yet some conservatives resisted even the simplest changes, often with a logic we now find quaint and amusing—for example, that the telephone would cause drought by depriving heaven of moisture. But such conservatives soon found themselves defending a lost cause. Whether they liked it or not, relentlessly, item by item, foreign technology was coming to Korea, and so were foreign technicians to install and then train Koreans in maintaining the new devices. Subsequently, students were sent abroad to learn the new technological secrets firsthand. Finally, to better exploit the technological potential, new administrative agencies such as a Mining Bureau were established, initially directed and sometimes staffed by foreigners. In other words, step by step, reluctantly, and sometimes without realizing it, the Koreans were being forced to retreat from total rejection, to limited rejection, to selective acceptance—first of technology, but then of certain associated alien social practices and even ideas which the Korean elite considered at the least as of dubious value, if not actually detrimental to Korea's welfare. For example, a modern mint not only required accepting foreigners, and having them in decision-making positions, but it also required accepting the belief that facilitating rather than merely tolerating commerce was worthy of elitist attention. When it finally became absolutely clear to all in the elite that technological innovation required more than the introduction of potent gadgets—and in this the conservative warning was only too prescient—the vital struggle between conservatives and reformers over the society's destiny was joined.

The decisive moment in that struggle occurred in 1894, when the Japanese victors in their war with China helped the Korean reformers (once again) to come to power and initiate major changes, changes which the Japanese, with an eye to turning Korea into a colony, were vitally interested in instituting. Some of these measures had been discussed for some time but never implemented, but others were considered daring even by the reformers themselves. Some examples pertinent to the patrimonial concerns of the study are: *Administrative innovation.* A cabinet and state council free of control of the titular leader now directed functional government bureaus. Surviving old-line agencies were given novel responsibilities, e.g., the Agriculture Ministry now built and maintained irrigational and other rural works, rather than focusing on prebendally exploiting the countryside. Finances were centralized in a discrete ministry, rendering the collection and disbursement of funds by prebend-granting individual bureaucrats or organs obsolete. Taxes were levied by statute rather than official whim. Novel local organs reined in the magistrate's diffused and arbitrary authority. Universal conscription and a system of primary and normal education were introduced to stimulate *nationalism* and actively involve the populace in creating the new reformist society. The Japanese were especially interested in *commercialization;* hence their prodding the Koreans to standardize weights, measures, and the currency and to create joint stock companies. And above all, the *yangban* and his way of life were singled out for *obsolescence.* On the one hand, the old civil service examinations were abolished and public office opened to new blood, while conversely yangban, whether officials or not, could now legally engage in private trade. The most controversial innovation was abolition of the male topknot which, as intended, struck at the very heart of the existing social system. A yangban male could not be married until the topknot ceremony was performed, and without marriage male descendants, who would venerate ancestors and hence preserve consanguineal integrity, would be impossible. Shorn of the knot, the Confucian yangban resembled not only the despised Buddhist clerics but, even worse, foreigners, especially the hated reformist Japanese. The aroused yangban were able to capitalize on widespread fear of so many changes being enacted so abruptly, on pressures by the international community for Japanese retreat from Korea, and on Japan's overplaying its political hand. Thus armed, they prevailed on the Korean king and his conservative backers to oust the reformers from power and sabotage their program.

Yet many of the reforms survived and new ones, such as a modern postal system, military renovation, and modern functional education, were introduced, because even the most conservative now conceded that changes were essential if Korea was to ward off foreign domination. Moreover, the ever-optimistic reformers created novel organizations, e.g., the Independence Club, to continue to press for meaningful reform. In spite of all this ferment and some cases of individual success, it cannot be said that late imperial productive reformism was other than a failure as a social movement.

From our patrimonial point of view, at least some of the roots of that failure may be attributed to a number of factors. First, the often sweeping proposals which, though undoubtedly required and not unrealistic given the desperate situation, were beyond the society's institutional ability to handle. Especially pertinent, even the most worthy proposals could not be implemented effectively with so inefficient and inadequate a bureaucracy used to patrimonially exploiting rather than leading. Consequently, superficial sloganeering became a convenient alternative to productive action.

Second, too often the wisest decisions, especially by nonpatrimonial western and Japanese standards, turned out to be disasters in the prevailing Korean patrimonial context. For example, the creation of a modern military can intensify nationalism. But in Korea that military was immediately embroiled in factional strife, including rivalry with the police (which persists to the present day); its officer corps, as before, was more interested in prestige and prebends than in command; and that corps continued to regard the enlisted ranks as members of the patrimonially nonmoral, despised classes, thus perpetuating the long-standing denigration of military service in the popular mind, making it a corvée obligation rather than a chance to serve the nation with dignity.

Third, the gap between the elite innovators and the masses whose support was required to implement the reforms was never bridged. All initiatives, revisions, reservations, and even questions from below were brushed aside as antipatrimonial impertinence by the impatient innovators. Intermediary organizations enjoying mass support were considered patrimonially dangerous troublemakers and ignored or, like the Tonghak, suppressed (see the next section).

Fourth, given the uncertainty inherent in Korean patrimonial society, and consequently the penchant of Koreans to prefer to profit here and now and avoid long-term, especially painful, sacrifices for potentially unrealizable future bliss, most Koreans found it difficult to accept that the benefits of true reform often must be other than immediate and refused to support many admirable projects.

Fifth, the reforms were never integrated into a coherent reform plan with definite objectives. The Koreans rationalized that they were only being realistic when, as usual, they rejected this or that program (especially if it originated abroad), if it appeared alien to the cherished Korean (read, patrimonial) way of life.

Sixth, by successfully associating the reform movement with the patrimonially nonmoral foreigners and their ways, especially with the unsubtle, abusive, and deeply resented Japanese, the conservative establishment was able to deny that any reform it objected to or did not patronally initiate had indigenous roots. Hence such a reform first had to be justified as morally worthy to be seriously considered, a ploy republican authority was to inherit and use.

Seventh, the Koreans underestimated the sagacity and persistence of the Japanese. While other foreigners, especially the Russians, concentrated on politics, the Japanese went about methodically creating a modern social and economic infrastructure that took root in spite of the vicissitudes of their political fortunes. Hence, by the time of the occupation, Japanese reformist ideas and practices were in situ, which the Japanese then elaborated upon to direct Korea's progress thereafter, although some Koreans in time would claim that a viable indigenous reformism did exist in pre-Japanese Korea and would have succeeded had not Korea been deprived of its political independence at a critical moment.

Consequently, and in sum, the reform movement, whether primarily local or Japanese-inspired and initiated, or both, was conceived and implemented in a way which did not impede and even reinforced the fundamental, existing patrimonial character of the Korean institutional order. That a patrimonial order could be reformed and even *modernized* was to be demonstrated conclusively by the Japanese and their successors. However, whether that Korean institutional order simultaneously could (or can) be *developed* is an issue which neither the Korean or Japanese reformers ever seriously confronted. In other words, Korean reformism was, and is today, *cathartic*.[4]

## Cathartic Rebellion and Resistance, and the Failure of Revolution

Rebellion is well known to Koreans. In the dynastic age, most typically it took the form of peasants forcefully resisting their official and private exploiters, whether because those predators were excessively greedy or because adverse natural conditions made it impossible for the cultivators to meet their assigned quotas of commodities, labor, or military service. On such occasions, peasants might abandon their fields, placing an increased burden on those who remained, which further aggravated dissatisfaction. Those who fled became rural or urban vagrants, surviving on official charity or drifting into banditry on land or sea; or they joined other socially aggrieved, such as the despised underclass, to petition and pressure the government for redress by burning and looting aristocratic property, destroying tax and class registers, or forcefully demanding a diminution or cancellation of debt. The polity tried to mollify them by replacing offending officials, by remitting overdue obligations, and by offering graceful prebends such as land to commoners and commoner status to the bound. But these palliatives did not always succeed. Especially when Korea was invaded and the government was forced to organize popular "Righteous Armies" to resist, recruits might not be willing to continue to support authority and its policies once the invader was turned out or if the authorities came to terms with an oppressive invader.

Most dangerous to authority were those instances in which local officials joined rebels, since bureaucrats, who commanded the only truly viable corporate organization in the society, could provide the coherent planning, organization, communication, tactics, and access to resources necessary to sustain a successful rising. Moreover, unlike commoner rebels who contented themselves with personal ameliorative goals, officials could not always be bought off with comparable prebends of rank, office, or landed revenue. Rather, disaffected officials might interpret the distress of the deprivileged as a signal that existing authority had run its course and that the opportunity was at hand for themselves to mobilize commoner manpower and pent-up violence to become the nucleus of an alternative authority. According to the accepted scenario, once in authority these officials lessened the burden, or even creatively modified the obligations, of both commoners and lowly in order to correct the flagrant inequities and irregularities which originally had sparked rebellion. In this way the new rulers won popular support to refurbish the economy in general and replenish the prebends of officials in particular. In time, however, those officials would move from a commitment to equality and harmony and benign supervision, and reasonable extraction, of the producers' surplus to unreasonable seizure of that surplus by force and even violence. Then followed a political style characterized by increasing repression, inequality, and resentment against the exploiters, until inevitably rebellion would break out anew, with a new group of dissatisfied, non-officeholding or local aristocrats. We may call this pattern of change *cyclic cathartic renovation.*

Although, as suggested, some rebellions were long and fierce and even contributed to the demise of dynasties, for a number of reasons none of these insurrections ever succeeded in breaking through the accepted pattern of cyclic cathartic renovation to challenge the very patrimonial foundations of the social order. First, those who had the least stake in that order, namely, the commoners, were unable to mount a rebellion on their own, free of bureaucratic control and hence bureaucratic co-optation. Each geographic area had its distinctive interests and grievances, which made it difficult to forge a common front, especially to mount sufficient numbers to threaten the united authorities. Yet, ironically, in contrast to Japan, local loyalties were never so intense, even in those areas particularly discriminated against, such as Chŏlla Province, that geography alone could forge a bond strong enough to unite individuals against oppressive authority. Second, the upward draft of center prebendal status and privilege continually tempted noncenter bureaucratic rebel leaders to desert their comrades-in-arms and otherwise work against the formation of occupational or class corporate groups interested in and potentially able to institutionalize a qualitatively different kind (that is, non-patrimonial) social order. Finally, officeholders were always willing to side with foreign invaders if the invaders were willing to accept and defend the officeholders and their patrimonial interests against fellow (commoner) Koreans, which the invaders certainly were willing to do since they required the indigenous bureaucrats to control and exploit the Korean populace. In patrimonial reasoning, such loyalty was proper (that is, moral) because it assured the survival of the patrimonial character of the social order and reduced the need for moral bureaucrats to depend upon, and hence to bargain with, morally deficient nonbureaucrats, which might sustain a polity but might also open the entire institutional order to nonpatrimonial changes.

The most determined cathartic rebellion of the late nineteenth century was the Tonghak movement. The Tonghak were incited to act out of such perennial complaints as cultivators' anger at the central government's rotating rather than dismissing disgraced officials and at investigators who took bribes to treat easily those whom the movement had denounced as leeches. But this time the introduction of foreign, most notably Japanese, booty-commercial capital into an unprepared, largely subsistence, patrimonial agricultural Korean economy created greater than usual resentment. In particular, the Japanese policy of encouraging the export of vital Korean local consumer commodities not only made them scarce but drove up their price. Simultaneously, the Japanese flooded Korea with imported western-style textiles, which destroyed local handicrafts and hence the side income of many farmers while providing them with such newly vital foreign articles as kerosene at prices not commensurate with the value of the raw materials the Korean producers were delivering to Japanese exporters. Consequently, peasants became indebted and were increasingly losing their land because of forces beyond their control, yet the current regent (whom we discussed earlier in the chapter), although he resented the foreigners as much as the peasants did, nonetheless was determined to exchange Korean commodities for Japanese technology and capital, with which he hoped to renovate the dynasty, while he was just as determined not to consider the internal institutional (development) changes which were necessary to solve Korea's economic difficulties.

When three Tonghak petitions for redress were rejected by the government, the movement openly rebelled (February 1894). At first the king tried to mollify the rebels in the accepted fashion by offering to set up a corrections office and to grant amnesty to the insurrectionists if they would surrender. But then, intimidated by the magnitude of the revolt and thus fearful for his throne and the social order, the king called on Chinese and Japanese help to suppress the rebellion—a move morally justified by patrimonial reasoning, especially in the case of patronal China, but one which prompted hitherto uninvolved Tonghak members and even outsiders to join the cause. Thus it was, as in the case of the Chinese T'aiping, that foreign armies had to be used to put down an indigenous, largely peasant rebellion. Even so the Tonghak were not easy to defeat. For one, they were skillfully riding a wave of popular political and economic discontent. Second, their antiforeign and moral-cleansing battle cries struck responsive chords well beyond their partisan ranks. Third, although they were modestly armed, unlike earlier insurrectionists they were militarily competent. Fourth, their claim that those who stood fast in battle were invincible buoyed the spirits of warriors armed with primitive weapons against mighty Japan's modern military technology. Finally, the Tonghak exploited an excellent organization, especially a well-trained and disciplined local leadership, which had been contrived when their religiously related arm, Ch'ŏndogyo, was forced to go underground.

Nonetheless, the Tonghak failed. Beyond the obvious circumstances of having superior, often brutally applied force arrayed against them by the Japanese in particular, the fact is that the rebels were not a concerted socially (in Marxist terms, class-) conscious group of revolutionaries committed to a bitter-end struggle, but rather congeries of individuals seeking patrimonial amelioration of their everyday grievances, and hence were ready to desert the cause, especially at the next agricultural season when the survival of their families required their services away from the battlefield. Most of the leaders remained faithful to the throne, blaming their plight not on the patrimonial institutional order, but on the way specific individual bureaucrats miscarried the king's rule-by-model moral will. The decentralized sectarian organization and leadership, so effective at first, became a two-edged sword once the leaders began to bicker over authority and followers. The Tonghak's erstwhile allies dropped out when the going became rough, the most opportunistic of them burning and looting the ever-suffering peasantry, though not to the extent the government and foreigners claimed. Finally, and most relevant to our concerns, the rebels, representing a social movement initiated from below, never gained widespread sympathy beyond the peasantry, especially not from the aristocratic reformers, who viewed the Tonghak as a substantive threat to themselves and their patrimonial interests and prerogatives. Thus, when they had to make the choice, the reformers sided with the foreigners against the Korean rebels, a precedent for republican authority.

But anti-Japanese militancy flared anew in other quarters. Local officials who were being replaced by pro-Japanese reformers organized disaffected peasants and the mean class into Righteous Armies and led them in open rebellion or, for example, inspired railway workers to sabotage Japanese lines of communication. The Righteous Armies continued to resist after the Japanese formally occupied Korea in 1910, until they were ruthlessly suppressed at home or driven over the northern border. Some of these exiles slipped back into Korea to destroy Japanese installations throughout the period of foreign rule. The most significant act of defiance toward the Japanese, however, was that of March 1919, termed *Samil*. Samil was a peaceful demonstration—a strike—and not an act of forceful resistance, but it was crucially important because it was the first nationwide overt expression of social discontent. The immediate energizer was the conviction of Koreans in all walks of life that their Japanese overlords were determined to make all Koreans regardless of status or occupation, even those who served the Japanese such as the Korean police, into second-class human beings in their own land. Caught off guard, in shock and fearful, the Japanese determined to extirpate any threat to their rule and to make examples of the demonstrators. They goaded some Koreans into self-defensive actions to justify Japanese retaliation, but, even without provocation, they killed some 7000, and beat up, incarcerated, and tortured many more. This campaign of deliberate terror, however, did not end Korean resistance. For example, in 1929, the abuse of a Korean girl by a Japanese who went free while her Korean male defender was jailed touched off a four-month countrywide student protest. Violence also was not unknown; Japanese government officials, especially those who had served or were serving in Korea, were assassinated within and without Korea, and in 1933 an attempt even was made against the Japanese emperor, certainly not an inviolate person to Koreans. What was the contribution of such resistance and suppression to the successor Republic? That patrimonial authority can resort to ever more "modern" methods of legalized violence to break the back of, if not completely eliminate, resistance to its policies, no matter how widespread and intense the opposition might be.

With the consolidation of Japanese rule, however, a more liberal "Culture Policy" allowed indigenous self-expression, albeit within carefully monitored bounds. One consequence, not unanticipated by the Japanese, was to set Korean against Korean. Rejectionist intellectuals considered all non-Korean, and hence all Japanese, ways as unacceptable and Korea's past as the sole determinant of her future. The gradualist intellectuals, in contrast, preached facing up to existing Korean social and technical shortcomings, adapting whatever was useful in the Japanese experience to overcome such deficiencies, and using Korean history as an object lesson in escaping from the failures of the past. The business community was similarly divided. An Economic Independence Group stimulated indigenous enterprise, organized boycotts of Japanese goods, and refused to sell more land to the voracious Oriental Development Company, but most Korean businessmen were forced to accept the reality that they could survive economically only on terms dictated by the Japanese. The consequence of all this? Koreans were unable to create a singular, energizing national ideology or indigenous system of cultural, social, and economic values to replace the discredited and defunct ideas and practices of the old dynastic order. Hence, by default, the rising generation of political and economic leaders of the Republic trained in Japanese schools did not escape being profoundly influenced by the colonialist's image of what Korea and Koreans should be, an image which I have suggested many times is patrimonially modern but undeveloped.

The Communist movement was the most successful, yet simultaneously the most faulted, of the national struggles under Japanese rule. The Communists initially recruited within Korean communities which had sprung up on the Manchurian border and in Siberia from the early 1800s. They were also successful in forming cells among other exiles. Especially was this true in Japan, where they took advantage of widespread discrimination against Koreans, support from the Japanese left and later the Japanese Communist party, and hometown or consanguineal ties both to recruit and to maintain solidary discipline. By 1925, Communists within Korea were availing themselves of the opportunities afforded by the post-Samil modest thaw to found a party. They organized cooperative fronts, a sound strategy given the conservatism of Korean society and the ever-present Japanese police. As elsewhere the Communists were most successful in recruiting some professionals and white-collar workers, the young, journalists, and (often unemployed) intellectuals, all of whom were organized into a Proletarian Culture Movement front. The Communists also gained influence in the labor and agricultural tenant movements. In this instance, contrary to Communist conventional wisdom, the workers proved to be the poorer prospect. Besides being few in number until the war economy of the 1930s, they were predominantly temporarily employed females who were indifferent to institutional reform and political agitation, and after the 1930s factory working conditions and wages were good by prevailing Korean standards. A key exception was the Wonsan dock workers' strike of 1929. The peasants, on the other hand, were well organized, used to resisting, and not at all conservative given the vicious exploitation by Japanese and Korean alike. However, although in specific instances a significant element, the Communist party was never able to dominate any of these movements, not to speak of the national movement in general. The party's influence was further limited by the Kremlin's confusing tactics of continually driving non-Soviet parties to change their course. Especially this was true of the so-called Otto Kusinen thesis, which denounced a cooperative mass line and demanded that the parties turn themselves into hard-line, militant revolutionaries, which in Korea invited unrestrained police repression. Moreover, like all Korean intermediary groups, the party had to rely on geography and kin to recruit and maintain itself. Hence if a cell was penetrated, the authorities could round up all the members without too much difficulty. The few Korean Communists who survived went underground or fled to China or Japan, where they joined those Communist movements.

In spite of all the party's historical difficulties and inherent structural weaknesses, for a number of reasons the end of Japanese rule in 1945 seemed to afford an excellent opportunity for a Communist upsurge. For one, the party had managed to survive both within and without Korea. Especially those who had remained in Korea at great risk to their lives could justifiably claim that they had a more legitimate right to the cloak of authority than did many of the politicians who had not been in the country for some thirty-five years. Second, the party's leaders, never in authority, were untainted by collaboration with the Japanese. Third, the intellectuals, those in the media, students, and youth—the opinion makers of the society—were soon once again under the spell of Communist dogma. Fourth, another traditional potential Communist constituency, the aggrieved peasantry, was anxious for amelioration of its plight, aggravated by Japanese rule. Fifth, the party, reconstituted quickly from among underground survivors and returned exiles, was one of the few interests in the society with an organization immediately in place. Sixth, the Kremlin sponsors, unlike during the Japanese period Kusinen-inspired disaster, were determined not to alienate their current ally, the United States, through strident militancy, so they prevailed upon the Korean Communists to propagandize for a two-stage revolution in which the first stage would be carried out through a popular united front. Especially in the south the Communists seemed to have an excellent chance to come to power. But there the American occupiers prevailed and were induced by their Korean supporters (clients?) to play the historic role of repressing an internal threat to patrimonial rule, especially when, out of both Kremlin policy and Korean goading, the Communists turned revolutionary. With the cold war and the Korean War, even sympathy for a Communist-sponsored cause was considered unpatriotic and subversive.

Of more institutional moment, since it is a singular example of much of what we have been examining discretely in this section, was the Autumn Uprising of 1946. In essence, the rising was a mass protest against the first year of American occupation in the south, in my interpretation, especially against America patronal support of deeply resented, patrimonially inspired policies inherited from the imperial and Japanese periods. The uprising, like many similar movements in Korea's past—the Tonghak coming immediately to mind, began innocently enough as a strike of railway workers in the port city of Pusan, but spread rapidly both geographically in a band west of that city and occupationally to the peasantry, through the medium of dissident leftist political activists, labor unions, peasant associations, and, most notably, locally generated, nondenominational "People's Committees." Additionally, any number of the unaffiliated joined in what was a protest of the desperate, who felt it was then or never if they were to have any say in, if not dramatically alter, the course of Korean social history which had worked persistently against their interests. Their specific grievances revolved about the three major issues of the first year of American rule; namely, (1) the fate of politically and economically active collaborators of the Japanese and their ruling style, especially the use of the police; (2) for the peasants in particular, parasitic (that is, nonentrepreneurial, rent-extracting) landlords and the system of tenure which sustained them; and (3) the once Japanese-conscripted and now demobilized Korean laborers who had been left adrift in a modern, yet undeveloped, especially rural society—all issues which had polarized Korean society.

In one camp were those who had profited in one way or another by association with the Japanese themselves or with their policies, and hence were vitally supportive of the patrimonial status quo. These "rightists" had become convinced that American patronal support was essential if they were to protect their interests, even if necessary by accepting an American stewardship. The Americans in turn felt that their political interests in the peninsula required supporting the cause of the right against those they had come to believe would turn the south over to their Russian adversary. Arrayed against the first camp were moderates to radicals who wanted redress for their various constituents—out-of-power politicians, professionals, laborers, women, and especially peasants. Each side had its own organized supporters. The right was rooted in the patrimonial bureaucracy, the police, and the Korean Democratic party, which the Americans relied upon to nominate and provide personnel for the various political organs and intermediary groups being created or purged of repatriated Japanese and "unreliables," that is, those suspected of leftist sympathy, who conceivably might threaten the status quo. The opposition was popularly based and certainly, when compared to the first camp, disunited, but had managed to create a virtual government in place, the Korean People's Republic, and, more important in my view, autonomous, ubiquitous people's committees at all hierarchical levels, composed of all shades of political thinking. It was these committees, in the rural provincial periphery especially, that were to be the backbone of the Autumn Uprising.

To the Americans and their Korean clients the uprising was a Communist North Korean-directed plot to take over the south; in fact at first the Americans believed the rising was an invasion from that quarter. But the uprising was not universal, being concentrated in those areas where suffering was greatest from the unresolved, even ignored, economic and social problems; where American local military government rule was late in coming, thus giving locals a chance to organize people's committees; where, contrary to American belief, *all* shades of political thought were represented on the committees; and where communication was either good, thus facilitating local organizing and action, or bad, thus denying access to the opposition concentrated in the urban centers (in this one sense the rising can be seen as a rural-popular versus urban-patrimonial contest).

The successful suppression of the uprising was a crucial watershed in determining American-Korean relations, the destiny of South Korea, and, for our purposes, the patrimonial institutional character of the Republic-to-be. Specifically, the right and its fists, the bureaucracy, the rightist youth organs, and especially the police, had triumphed over leftism and its organs, but particularly over the peasantry, who once again had been cowed into survivable passivity. Anti-Communism had proved to be both a viable way of legitimizing regimes and the means to justify an increasingly authoritarian rule on the one hand, and the assurance of American patronal support for Korea and its version of patrimonial "democracy" on the other hand. But most pertinent for the discussions of this chapter was the lesson that the pursuit of independent, unsolicited corporate organizational action within this patrimonial society would never be tolerated. Certainly, as noted elsewhere in the study, all manner of popular dissent, some of it confrontational, would continue—from university students, underground labor (e.g., the Industrial Mission Group), and peasant marketers—but by associating *all* potentially viable opposition with Communism, not even leftism, the ROK decision-makers have justified stifling resistance not only to themselves and their particular polity, but to the patrimonial institutional order in general, assuring that change, if and when it occurs, at best will be cathartic.[5]

# Conspectus:
# Why Didn't Korea
# Enter the State
# of Developmental
# Modernization?

Many Korean observers are convinced that the preconditions for successfully modernizing Korean society were present in the closing years of the imperial era. They cite, for example, the emergence of new productive agricultural techniques such as rice transplantation which made double-cropping feasible, improved weeding and furrowing which opened the upland to cultivation, and larger, more reliable irrigation systems which expanded production. These improvements both encouraged and were encouraged by commercialization of agriculture, such as novel cash-cropping in ginseng, hemp, and tobacco and a continually expanding national market to facilitate their sale. Rural entrepreneurs, contriving new managerial techniques, emerged. The more successful increased their holdings by acquiring or renting some of the land of the less successful—some 60 percent in an 1846 survey—who became tenants of or day laborers for the successful, or were forced out of agriculture into craftsmanship and mine labor. The tenants were not at all like the bound, subordinated cultivators who continued to work the royal land, but rather were renters in kind or specie under civil contract to those who were legally registered as landowners, proprietors whose claim was revocable only for a crime, a disputed claim, or unauthorized seizure of reclaimed tracts. In other words, socially as well as economically, agriculturalists were differentiating. The economically successful commoners among them were claiming to be yangban and taking over control of village affairs. Concurrently, the urban commercial economy was expanding rapidly.

A rural and urban *manufaktur* stage of artisan-incipient industrial enterprise, free of government constraints, was burgeoning. And Korea, like other east Asian societies and unlike the western societies at a similar point in their modernizing, had already achieved national political unity, bureaucratic organizational maturity, and popular acceptance of nonreligious, rational modes of thinking. In brief, according to the observers, in the light of the experience of the developed western and Japanese societies, the prospect for modernizing, even developing, nineteenth-century Korea logically was most promising.

And yet, with the wisdom of hindsight, we know that though those changes were necessary, they still were not sufficient to fulfill that promise. Though in my estimation the observers have rightly blamed Japanese occupation policies, I believe, as I have stated throughout the study, that this cannot be the whole account. I therefore concur with those critics who suggest that these observers are overemphasizing the similarities and slighting the differences between the agriculture, commerce, and artisan-industry of nineteenth-century Korea and the developed West and Japan at the appropriate period. The critics cite, for example, Korean failure to create a truly local, autonomous political consciousness  Consequently, those at the center and those whom the center appointed never developed any local identification with or loyalty toward the local people, primarily land cultivators, for whom they were responsible. The officials regarded the locals rather as servants of center interests and felt no hesitation in stifling all local efforts to restrain center control, for example, over local, rural-generated capital, which the centrists frivolously dissipated or at best used to purchase land which was not productively improved but held for usurious rent or social prestige. Thus, economically and socially satiated, the centrists could be but marginally interested in developing commerce and industry, and since they were in a position to do so, they succeeded only too well in neutralizing all those developmentally potential circumstances described in the previous paragraph. In the process, the centrists prevented the emergence of an economy able to protect Korea from political and economic imperial aggradisement, especially by the Japanese, who then proceeded to modernize Korea selectively to serve Japanese interests, which was not all that different institutionally from the existing pattern of exploitation. By thus leaving certain vital considerations unattended, the Japanese provided the Republic with precedent to perpetuate the original gap between late imperial developmental modernization potential and nondevelopmental modernization reality.

It is also worth pointing out that the gap did not generate the kind of social and individual tension and subsequent productive (developmental) action which western scholars, misapplying their own experience to Korea, anticipate, in spite of the fact that with independence such ideals as popular control of decision-making (termed in Korea "liberal democracy") and economic affluence ("the consumer society") for all have been widely diffused from the developed societies. Rather, save for a few intellectuals who agonize over the disparity between potential and reality, as long as the social milieu appears to offer minimal personal security, the pursuit of self-interest seems possible, and the economy gives the appearance of being dynamic, Koreans are not particularly concerned about where their society is heading. Why, Koreans argue, should they care whether their personal goals or the means they have to achieve those goals are logical and foresighted when, after all, seizing upon "lucky opportunities" truly spells the difference between success or disaster. True enough, a sense of nationalism emerged from the Korean War and the cold war, but this is viewed more as a government ploy to justify authoritarian rule than as a viable means to organize and motivate people to break through the legacy of their nondeveloped past. Nor, contrary to conventional wisdom, is there any major tension-filled, potentially creative intergenerational ideological gap between pre- and post-Korean War Koreans. Both generations, for example, are spiritually idealistic and share an awesome reverence for authority and patronal obligation. Intergenerational conflict, such as it is, is limited to the younger generation's feeling that its elders are preventing youth from achieving commonly held goals through the elders' ineptness and corruption, which I cannot but observe is the classic Korean cathartic explanation for unproductive action. Psychological profiles of Koreans confirm this social profile. Loss of respect for the old is not significant in schizophrenic cases. Neurotics project their problems on neighbors and not on either the cosmos or the social order, and hold on to their dependency with great tenacity. Psychologists regard those who are personally maladjusted in these ways as least likely to be the misfits who initiate creative, constructive social change as a means to relieve their discomfort. What I am driving at is that the shakers and doers of postindependence Korea, whether they are the generation socialized under the Japanese or the present generation, are not members of a class of alienated individuals apt to be developmentally interested as were those "middle" or bureaucratic class members who catalyzed productive institutional change in the developed societies.

In sum, Korea's development potential, at least from the western standpoint, is confusing, even contradictory. Koreans are personally nimble in responding quickly to opportunity, are nationally unified, technologically and commercially sophisticated, and tolerant toward novelty including alien ideas, but they have not generated the kind of personal drive or social institutional building associated with twentieth-century development. This observation brings the discussion full circle to the opening query of the preface, and I wish it to serve as introduction to the study's primary conclusions. I postulate that the Korean road to modernization is one which accepts change, sometimes hesitantly, sometimes eagerly, but always deliberately only within certain specified limits, which I designate as the Korean (model) version of a patrimonial institutional order. Thus if, in the course of the development process, in spite of all precautions, certain values, goals, or procedures which contradict patrimonial characteristics do find their way into Korean society and in consequence dislocations arise, the dialectic tension is not necessarily resolved in development's favor, as western theory would have us believe. This is because something more than the familiar cultural-social conflict over accepting or rejecting innovation (from without) is involved; namely, preservation of the patrimonial institutional order. I further suggest that the consequent tensions, confusions—and contradictions, if you wish—will persist as long as the Korean decision-makers use the modernizing techniques of the developed societies to perfect, that is, to *modernize*, the existing *patrimonial* ways of doing things, rather than using those techniques to *develop* the society, no matter what the consequences may be for the society's patrimonial character. To be sure, Korean decision-makers have every moral right to continue to do as they please. But this in no way precludes our using the patrimonial model to make sense of what, from the conventional western approach, is a confusing and sometimes ineffective Korean road to modernization and, to date, (non-) development.[1]

# Abbreviations for Notes and Bibliography

CG     Chōsen Gakuhō (Tenri City, Japan)

CH     Chintan Hakpo (or Hakbo)

ILCORK     International Liaison Committee for Research on Korea of the Social Science Research Institute, University of Hawaii; working papers

JAS     Journal of Asian Studies (U.S.A.)

JKCRI     Journal of the Korean Cultural Research Institute, Ehwa Woman's University

JSSH     Journal of Social Sciences and Humanities (Seoul)

KA     Korean Affairs

KASS     Korean Agricultural Sector Study, of the Agricultural Economics Research Institute, Ministry of Agriculture and Forestry, Seoul and the Department of Agricultural Economics, Michigan State University, East Lansing, Michigan

KH     Korea Herald (Seoul daily newspaper)

KJ     Korea Journal (UNESCO, Seoul)

KO     Korea Observer

KPT     Korean Press Translations (Seoul)

KQ     Koreana Quarterly

KT     Korea Times (Seoul daily newspaper)

RAS     Transactions of the Royal Asiatic Society, Korea Branch

USCT     Universitas Seoulensis Collectio Theseon, Humanitas-Scientia Sociales

YH     Yŏksa Hakbo (alternately Ryoksa, Hakho), also known as the Korean Historical Review

# Notes

Titles are abbreviated after the initial citation. Works in Korean and Japanese which have English titles are cited using those titles, followed by a * for those in the Korean language and ** for those in Japanese. If an English résumé accompanies the text it is noted. Japanese and Korean authors writing in their own languages are cited family name first, in English according to usage in the citation.

## Preface

1. Norman Jacobs, *The Origin of Modern Capitalism and Eastern Asia*, 2d ed. (New York, 1981) (contrasting China and Japan). The author now is preparing a major revision of the contrasting Japanese case, tentatively entitled *Feudalism, Patrimonialism and Japanese Development*. See also *The Sociology of Development: Iran as an Asian Case Study* (New York, 1966), and *Modernization without Development: Thailand as an Asian Case Study* (New York, 1971).

## Chapter 1

1. Max Weber, *Economy and Society* (New York, 1968), vol. 3, chs. 12 and 13; Schlomo Avineri, *Karl Marx on Colonialism and Modernization* (Garden City, N.Y., 1969); Karl Marx, *Pre-Capitalist Economic Formations*, trans. Jack Cohen with intro. by Eric Hobsbawn (London, 1964); Karl A. Wittfogel, *Wirtschaft und Gesellschaft Chinas* (Leipzig, 1931) and *Oriental Despotism* (New Haven, 1957); Ferenc Tökei, *Essays on the Asiatic Mode of Production* (Budapest, 1979), esp. pp. 87–91; Lawrence Krader, *The Asiatic Mode of Production* (Assen, The Netherlands, 1975); George Lichtheim, *The Concept of Ideology and Other Essays*

(New York, 1967), pp. 62–93; Institute of Asian Economic Affairs, *The Developing Economies*, 4.3 (1966); Paek Namun, *Chōsen Shakai Keizaishi* (Tokyo, 1933); Moritani Katsumi, *Tōyōteki Shakai no Rekishi to Shisō* (Tokyo, 1948), has a section specifically on Korea as well as a general discussion.

2. Jacobs, *Modernization*, chs. 1 and 12; *Korean Studies Today* (Seoul, 1970), pp. 247–48, 302; Bryan Turner, *Marx and the End of Orientalism* (London, 1978).

3. Jacobs, *Modernization*, pp. 13–21, and *Sociology*, ch. 10, have fuller systematic treatments of this model, including discussion of the theoretical problem of integrating the various discrete institutions into a coherent viable societal analysis. For a critical discussion of the limitations of value and motivational analyses of development problems in Korea see Kim Kyong-dong, *Industrialization and Industrialism: A Comparative Perspective on Values of Korean Workers and Managers*, ILCORK, no. 1 (Seoul, 1971).

## Chapter 2

1. The discussion owes much to Pow-key Sohn, "Social History of the Early Yi Dynasty, 1392–1592" (Ph.D. diss., University of California, Berkeley, n.d.); Edward W. Wagner, *The Literati Purges: Political Conflict in Early Yi Korea* (Cambridge, Mass., 1974), esp. the early chapters; James B. Palais, *Politics and Policy in Traditional Korea* (Cambridge, Mass., 1975), esp. the introduction. On the conciliar theory, see Gregory Henderson, *Korea, the Politics of the Vortex* (Cambridge, Mass., 1968); Hi-woong Kang, "The Development of the Korean Ruling Class from Late Silla to Early Koryŏ" (Ph.D. diss., University of Washington, 1964), the first essay and from p. 326; Chong-sun Kim, "The Emergence of Multi-Centered Despotism in the Silla Kingdom: A Study of the Origin of Factional Struggle in Korea" (Ph.D. diss., University of Washington, 1965), pp. 445–63; Pyong-choon Hahm, *The Korean Political Tradition and Law* (Seoul, 1967), ch. 2.

The formal structure of contemporary government is well surveyed by Edward R. Wright, Jr., ed., *Korean Politics in Transition* (Seattle, 1975), ch. 2, and Se-jin Kim and Chang-hyun Cho, eds., *Government and Politics of Korea* (Silver Spring, Md., 1972), pp. 70–90. The dynamics of that structure are insightfully discussed in C. I. Eugene Kim, ed., *A Pattern of Political Development: Korea* (Kalamazoo, Mich., 1964), pp. 158–69 (on various constitutions); Dong-suh Bark, "Policy Making in the Korean Executive Branch," in Byung-chuil Koh, ed., *Aspects of Administrative Development in South Korea* (Kalamazoo, Mich., 1967), pp. 30–114. The contention between the president (and his spokesmen) and the National Assembly is best approached through the press, but see also W. D. Reeve, *The Republic of Korea: A Political and Economic Study* (Oxford, 1963), esp. pp. 39–51; Henderson, *Vortex*, ch. 9; Byung-kyu Woo and Chong-lim Kim, *Legislative Recruitment and Political Representation in South Korea* (Iowa City, 1970).

2. The literature on public administration is prolific and rightly so; see especially Suk-choon Cho, "The Bureaucracy," in Edward R. Wright, Jr., *Politics*,

ch. 3; Dong-suh Bark, *A Historical Development of the Bureaucracy in Korea*\* (Seoul, 1961) (Eng. résumé, pp. 1–14); E. Grant Meade, *American Military Government in Korea* (New York, 1951), pp. 109–18; U.S. Operations Mission to Korea, *Rural Development Program Evaluation Report* (Seoul, 1967), sections on the "innovating bureaucracy." Prof. Hahn-been Lee's study is *Korea, Time Change and Administration* (Honolulu, 1968); his basic argument is summarized by him as "The Role of the Higher Civil Service under Rapid Social and Political Change," in Edward W. Weidner, ed., *Development Administration in Asia* (Durham, N.C., 1970), pp. 107–31.

3. Wagner, *Literati*, esp. the introduction; and Choi Suk, "The Factional Struggle in the Yi Dynasty of Korea, 1575–1725," *KQ*, 7.1 (1965), 60–91 and 7.2, 70–96, are very useful. See also Chong-sun Kim, "Despotism," pp. 184, 360–431, 485–97; Key P. Yang and Gregory Henderson, "An Outline History of Korean Confucianism, Part I," *JAS*, 18.1 (1958), 81–101; Murayama Chijun, *Chōsen no Gunshu* (Keijō, 1926), sec. 5.

For modern Korea—Henderson, *Vortex*, pp. 254–91; Meade, *American*, sec. "Political"; Man-gap Lee, "Social Organization," in Man-gap Lee and Herbert R. Barringer, eds., *A City in Transition: Urbanization in Taegu, Korea* (Seoul, 1971); the government's attitude toward party dissent can be gleaned from *KPT*, e.g., 15 (Oct. 5, 1974), 11.

4. The literature on local government is extensive and multifaceted. For a general interpretation, Henderson's thesis of the vortex and its critics perhaps is central among the English language sources—thus see Henderson, *Vortex*, and his "Centralization," pp. 309–22 in International Conference on the Problems of Modernization in Asia, *Report* (Seoul, n.d.). See also Pyung-kun Kang, "Sub-Bureaucracy and Community Structure of the Yi Dynasty," *KO*, 2.1 (1969), 68–83; Wagner, *Literati*; Hatada Takashi, *Chōsen Chusei Shakaishi no Kenkyū* (Tokyo, 1972), the first five essays; Paek Namun, *Chōsen Hōken Shakai Keizaishi-Jōkan* (Tokyo, 1937), pp. 116–32; Lee Ki-baik, *Studies on the Koryō Military System*\* (Seoul, 1968) (Eng. summary, pp. 299–312), and its review by Chin-chol Kang in *JSSH*, no. 29 (1968), 118–20. Chang-hyun Cho, "Bureaucracy and Local Government in South Korea," in Se-jin Kim and Chang-hyun Cho, *Government*, pp. 91–126; Suk-choon Cho, "Administrative Decentralization: A Case Study of the South Korea Military Government," in Byung-chul Koh, *Administrative*, ch. 4; Meade, *American*, ch. 11; Sang-gee Kim and Lawrence W. Libby, *Rural Infrastructure* (Seoul, 1972), sec. on local government; Hyo-jae Lee, "Life in Urban Korea," *RAS*, no. 46 (1971), 21–33; Dong-suh Bark, "Comparison of Provincial Development Administration in Korea," *JSSH*, no. 34 (1971), 1-23; Wan-sang Han, "A Conceptual Clarification of Mass Society," *KO*, 3.4 (1971), 3–22; Henderson, *Vortex*, pp. 195–99.

5. For the "Asiatic" nature of the Korean village see Byong-jip Moon, *A Study on Village in Korea*\* (Seoul, 1973) (Eng. summary, pp. 191–203); Hatada, *Chusei*, chs. 4 and 17, criticized by Sil-song Ch'oe in his "Shiragi ni okeru Jizen Sonrakusei-teki Kindensei," *Rekishigaku Kenkyū*, no. 237 (1960), 40–47; Ouchi Takeji, "Lichō Makki no Nōson," in Keijō Teikoku Daigaku Hōbun-

gakubu, *Chōsen Shakai Keizaishi Kenkyū* (Tokyo, 1933). On consanguinity see Too-hun Kim, *Study on the Family System in Korea*\* (Seoul, 1949), ch. 2 (Eng. table of contents only); Byong-ho Park, "Traditional Korean Society and Law," reprinted from *Seoul Law Journal*, 15.1, 125. On village articulation with the formal apparatus see U-song Lee, "A Study on Paik-song of the Koryŏ Dynasty,\* *YH*, no. 14 (1961), 25–44. On intravillage communal organization and labor see Suzuki Eitarō, *Chōsen Nōson Shakai no Kenkyū* (Tokyo, 1973); In Chŏngsik, *Chosŏn Nong'ŏp Munje Sajŏn* (Seoul, 1948), esp. pp. 1–12. On comparisons of Chinese and Japanese communalism see Man-gap Lee's perceptive "National Characteristics of Korea and Japan and Their Social Background," *KQ*, 7.4–8.1 (1965–66), 86–87.

The most up-to-date and useful general guide to village Korea is Vincent S. R. Brandt, *A Korean Village, between Farm and Sea* (Cambridge, Mass., 1971). Also useful are Taik-kyoo Kim, *The Cultural Structure of a Consanguineous Village*\* (Seoul, 1964) (Eng. résumé pp. 1–52); Hoe-su Yang, *A Study on the Structure of the Korean Farming Village*\* (Seoul, 1967), (Eng. résumé, pp. 609–16); Jaiseuk Choi, *Studies on Korean Rural Society*\* (Seoul, 1975) (Eng. résumé, pp. 605–18); Man-gap Lee, *The Social Structure of Korean Village and Its Changes*\* (Seoul, 1973) (Eng. summary, pp. 357–93—ch. 15 of an earlier edition has been translated as "Korean Village Politics and Leadership" by Lee Man-gab in *KA*, 1.4 (1962), 398–412; Ki-hyuk Park and Seung-yun Lee, *Three Clan Villages in Korea* (Seoul, 1973); Cornelius Osgood, *The Koreans and Their Culture* (New York, 1951); Syn-duk Choi and Chae-yoon Kim, "Hyo-ri: A Traditional Clan Village," *Cultural Anthropology* (Seoul), 5 (1972), 269–313.

## Chapter 3

1. There are many excellent reviews of Korean legal principles by Koreans; see esp. Pyong-choon Hahm, *Tradition*, the initial article; his *Religion and Law in Korea* (Berkeley, 1969) and "Korea's Initial Encounter with Western Law: 1866–1910 A.D.," *KO*, 1.2 (1969), 80–93, and with Seung-doo Yang, *A Study of Five Decisional Outcomes Involving the Judicial Process of Korea*, 2 vols. (Seoul, 1972, 1973); Woong-shik Shin, *Comparative Analysis of Korean and American Judicial Systems* (Chicago, 1974); Il-kyo Suh, *A Study on the Criminal Law and Procedure of the Chosun (Yi) Dynasty (1392–1910)*\* (Seoul, 1968) (Eng. summary, pp. 1–21) (reviewed by William Shaw in *JAS*, 31.2 (1972), 417–19; Yun Paengnam, *Chosŏn Hyŏngjŏngsa* (Seoul, 1948); Byeong-ho Park, *A Study on the Legal History of Korea*\* (Seoul, 1960) (Eng. summary, pp. 133–47). Also useful are William Shaw, "Traditional Korean Law: A New Look," *KJ*, 13.9 (1973), 40–53 (a provocative article); Chin Kim, "Legal Privileges under the Early Yi Dynasty Criminal Codes," *KJ*, 15.4 (1975), 34–44 and 15.5, 19–28; Hi-dok Lee, "Koryo's Criminal Law and the Ideals of Filial Piety,"\* *YH*, no. 58 (1973), 77–103 (Eng. summary, p. 104); David I. Steinberg, "Law, Development and Korean Society," *KQ*, 13.3 (1971), 43–80; Yasu Morioka, "A Study on the Law Prohibiting the Accusation of One's Superiors in the Reign of King Injo in the Yi Dy-

nasty,"** *CG*, nos. 21–22 (1961), 817–43 (Eng. summary, p. 32); Ch'ang-gyu Ch'oe, "Traditional Legal Systems," in *Korean Studies Today*, pp. 264–87.

2. A number of the works cited in n. 1 apply for this period, esp. the writings of Hahm and Shin. See also Edward R. Wright, Jr., *Politics*, pp. 57–62; Jay Murphy et al., *The Legal Profession in Korea: The Judicial Scrivener and Others* (Seoul, 1967); Jay Murphy, *Legal Education in a Developing Nation: The Korea Experience* (Seoul, 1967).

3. Sung-joo Han, *The Failure of Democracy in South Korea* (Berkeley, 1974), is basic. See also John Kil-chiang Oh, *Korea: Democracy on Trial* (Ithaca, 1968), esp. the conclusion. Compare these views with the official version, e.g., Chung-hee Park, *Our Nation's Path, Ideology of Social Reconstruction* (Seoul, 1962), ch. 4.

4. James Wade, ed., "Mass Communication in a Developing Korea," *RAS*, 45 (1969); John L. Mitchell and John Hyun Kim, *Survey of Mass Communication in Korea, 1968* (Seoul, 1968); Ministry of Public Information, ROK, *Mass Communication* (Seoul, n.d.). For the *Tong'a-Ilbo* and similar controversies, see *KPT*, esp. Feb. 15, 1975.

5. Kwang-rin Lee, "Census Taking under the Yi Dynasty," *RAS*, no. 35 (1959), 33–50; Yi Kwang-nin, "Hop'aego," in *Yongjae Paek Nakchun Paksa Hwan'gap Kinyŏm* (Seoul, 1955), pp. 549–612; Henderson, *Vortex*, ch. 6; Young-ho Lee, "The Politics of Democratic Experiment," in Edward R. Wright, Jr., *Politics*, ch. 1; Meade, *American*, pp. 151–89; *KPT*, Mar. 21, 1975, on the "flunky law"; U.S. House of Representatives, Committee on Foreign Affairs, Subcommittee on Asian and Pacific Affairs and International Organizations and Movements, *Human Rights in South Korea: Implications for U.S. Policy, Hearings*, 93d Cong., 2d sess., 1974; U.S. House of Representatives, Committee and Subcommittee on International Relations, *Investigation of Korean-American Relations, Hearings (seven parts) and Report*, 95th Cong., 2d sess., 1977–78.

6. Sung-joo Han, "Political Dissent in South Korea, 1948–1961," (ch. 3) and Y. C. Han, "Political Parties and Elections in South Korea" (ch. 6) in Se-jin Kim and Chang-hyun Cho, *Government;* Y. H. Lee, "The Politics of Democratic Experiment" (ch. 2) and Ki-shik Hahn, "Underlying Factors in Political Party Organization and Elections" (ch. 4) in Edward R. Wright, Jr., *Politics*; Kyong-il Yim, "Interest Aggregations," in C. I. Eugene Kim, *Pattern*, ch. 6; Henderson, *Vortex*, chs. 6, 9, and 10; Chung-hee Park, *Path*, ch. 1 (wherein he criticizes Rhee and Chang for patrimonial political actions he himself would use in time); Hyoung-sup Yoon, "Party Systems in the Stage of Nation Building: U.S. vs. Korea," *KO*, 5.1 (1973), 3–41. On the left see Henderson, *Vortex*, ch. 11, and esp. Robert Scalapino and Chŏng-sik Lee, *Communism in Korea*, part 1, *The Movement* (Berkeley, 1972), ch. 4.

7. Byung-hun Oh, "Students and Politics," in Edward R. Wright, Jr., *Politics*, ch. 5; C. I. Eugene Kim, *Pattern*, ch. 4; *KPT*, Apr.–May, 1975.

8. Henderson, *Vortex*, esp. the introduction and pp. 225–35, is basic. Among his critics see Wan-sang Han, "Clarification," and Bruce Cumings, "Is Korea a Mass Society?" in James B. Palais, *Occasional Papers*, no. 1, pp. 65–81;

see also the excellent Man-gap Lee, "Social Organizations," in Man-gap Lee and Herbert R. Barringer, *City;* Sang-ch'e Sin, "Interest Articulation, Pressure Groups," in C. I. Eugene Kim, *Pattern,* pp. 41–47. Recent attitudes can be found in *KPT,* esp. May 1975 issues.

9. Most national character studies by foreigners suffer from bias, but then Korean studies have their own blind spots. In any case, I have used, inter alia, Sung-jik Hong, *A Survey of Korean Values\** (Seoul, 1962) (Eng. summary, pp. 341–55); Yun T'aerim, *Han'gugin ŭi Songgyŏk* (Seoul, 1964); Ham Sŏkhŏn, *Ttŭsŭro Bon Han'guk Yŏksa* (Seoul, 1975); Yi Pyŏngdo, *Tugye Chapp'il* (Seoul, 1956); Yi Haenam, *Han'guk Hyŏndae Chŏngch'i Munhwasa* (Seoul, 1963), esp. from p. 169; Hwa-soo Lee, "A Study of Political Socialization Process: Family, Political Efficacy and Legitimacy: The Case of Secondary School Students in Korea," *KQ,* 10.2 (1968), 156–97; Eui-young Ham, "A Study of the Political Socialization Process in Korea," *KO,* 4.4 (1972), 131–91; Kyu-hwan Lee, "A Study of Democracy as Manifested in Every Day Behavior of Korean Students" (in English), *JKCRI,* 19 (1972), 309–24; Yi-sup Hong, *Korea's Self Identity* (Seoul, 1971), pp. 1–25; Chin-man Kim, "Korean Thought Patterns: How Koreans Think and Solve Problems," *KQ,* 11.4 (1969–70), 67–82.

10. Andrew J. Grajdanzev, *Modern Korea* (New York, 1944), chs. 13 and 14; Henderson, *Vortex,* ch. 4; Jong-hae Yoo, "A Study of Korean Local Government under Japanese Rule; Pu and Myon Systems," *KO,* 4.3 (1972), 205–15; Ch'ol-hun Kim, "History," in *Korean Studies Today,* pp. 221–61; Scalapino and Lee, *Communism,* ch. 3; Dae-sook Suh, *The Korean Communist Movement,* 1918–1948 (Princeton, 1967). Japanese government secret reports of the radical and related "social movements" during the occupation are now public property and many have been reprinted commercially in Tokyo by, for example, Gannando Bookstore.

11. Bruce Cumings, *The Origin of the Korean War, Liberation and the Emergence of Separate Regimes, 1945–1947* (Princeton, 1981); Meade, *American;* Philip H. Taylor and Donald McDonald, "Military Government Experience in Korea," in Carl Friedrich et al., *American Experiences in Military Government in World War II* (New York, 1948), ch. 16; Scalapino and Lee, *Communism,* ch. 4; Joung-won A. Kim, *Divided Korea, the Politics of Development, 1945–1972* (Cambridge, Mass., 1975), ch. 7 and conclusion; Won-sul Lee, "The Embryo of Korean Bureaucracy in 1945," *KQ,* 7.3 (1965), 32–49; Yong-sik Ahn, "Efforts of U.S. Military Government in Personnel Administration of Korea," *KO,* 4.4 (1972), 306–22; Henderson, *Vortex,* ch. 5 and passim thereafter.

## Chapter 4

1. The source material for this section is excellent but elephantine. Of particular interest has been: Chinch'ol Kang, "Traditional Land Tenure Relations in Korean Society," in Hugh H. W. Kang, ed., *The Traditional Culture of Korea: Thought and Institutions* (Honolulu, 1975), pp. 43–104 (with editor's comments)—an excellent introductory essay; also do not overlook the discussions

on land in the standard historical texts in the English language (see the Bibliography); Chong-sun Kim, "Despotism," ch. 3 and from p. 202; Palais, *Traditional*, ch. 4; Ho-chin Choi, *The Economic History of Korea* (Seoul, 1971); Yong-ha Shin, "Land Tenure System in Korea, 1910–45," *Social Science Journal*, 1 (1973), 65–84; Ki-hyuk Pak, *A Study of Land Tenure System in Korea* (Seoul, 1966), esp. the historical introduction; Hoon K. Lee, *Land Utilization and Rural Economy in Korea* (Chicago, 1936), section on "Ownership and Tenure"; Ching-young Choe, *The Rule of the Taewŏn'gun 1864–1873* (Cambridge, Mass., 1972), ch. 1; Susan S. Shen, "Some Aspects of Landlord-Tenant Relations in Yi Dynasty Korea," in Palais and Lang, *Occasional Papers*, no. 3, pp. 49–88; Yong-sŏp Kim, "Absentee Landlord System during the 19th-20th Century in Korea," *JSSH*, no. 37 (1972), 27–63; Paek Namun, *Shakai* (1933), esp. pp. 207–13, 259–71, 339–40; the works of In Chŏngsik, esp. *Chosŏn Nong'ŏp Kyŏngjaenon* (Seoul, 1949) and *Chōsen no Nōgyō Kiko* (Tokyo, 1940); Yi Sangbaek, *Yijo Kŏn'guk ŭi Yŏn'gu* (Seoul, 1949); Kim Chunbo, *Han'guk Chabonchu ŭi Sa Yŏn'gu*, vol. 2 (Seoul, 1974) (a very important work); Hatada, *Chusei*, part 2, a controversial but significant series of essays; Paek Namun, *Hōken*, much criticized both by Marxists and non-Marxists but still a classic; Nongchi Kaehyŏksa, *Nongchi Kaehyŏksa Pyŏnch'an Wiwŏnhoe* (Seoul, 1970); Pak Sihyŏng, *Chosŏn T'oji Chedosa*, vol. 1 (P'yŏngyang, 1960)—I regret I had access only to the first volume. Such scholarly publications, in contrast to propaganda dribble from the DPRK, are virtually impossible to obtain in the United States; Kim Sŏkhyŏng, *Chōsen Hōken Jidai Nōmin no Kaikyū Kōsei* (Tokyo, 1960), from p. 261 (this is a Japanese translation of a work originally published in Korean in P'yŏngyang in 1957, similarly impossible to obtain in the original); Chŏn Sŏktam, *Chosŏn Kyŏngjaesa* (Seoul, 1949), from p. 107; Chŏn Sŏktam et al., Chosŏn Sahoe Kyŏngjaesa (Seoul, 1946, mimeo). On the controversy whether or not the land economy of the Japanese period was modern, see e.g., the essays in Keijō Teikoku Daigaku Hōbungakubu, *Shakai*.

2. Clyde Mitchell, *Final Report and History of the New Korea Co.* (Hdq. U.S. Army Military Government in Korea, 1948), and his Land Reform in South Korea (1949, mimeo); Ki-hyuk Pak, *Tenure*; Ki-hyuk Pak, "Economic Analysis of Land Reform in the Republic of Korea, with Special Reference to an Agricultural Economic Survey, 1954–55" (Ph.D. diss., University of Illinois, 1956); Robert B. Morrow and Kenneth H. Sherper, *Land Reform in South Korea* (Washington, D.C., 1970); Kenneth H. Parsons, Issues in Land Tenure Policy for Korea, (Seoul, 1965, mimeo); Ki-hyuk Pak and Seung-yun Lee, *Villages*, pp. 52–82, 238–46; for more recent details, see *KPT*, e.g., July-Aug., 1974 issues.

3. The classic on the tribute system is Kōzō Tagawa's *Study on the Tribute System of the Ri Dynasty*** (Tokyo, 1964) (Eng. summary, pp. 1–9); Toichi Miyahara, "A Study on Formation of the Military Labor System of the Yi Dynasty,"** *CG*, no. 28 (1963), 112–31 (Eng. summary, p. 2), Tomonori Arii, "Statutory Labor in the Early Period of I Dynasty,"** *CG*, no. 30 (1964), 64–106 and no. 31, 58–101 (Eng. summary in no. 30, p. 2) and his "On the Census Registration Law in the Early Period of Yi Dynasty,"** *CG*, nos. 39–40 (1966),

42–93 (Eng. summary, p. 3 (542)). For the recent period see R. A. Musgrave, *Revenue Policy for Korea's Economic Development* (Seoul, 1965); Korean Development Association, *A Study of Property Tax in Korea* (Seoul, 1967).

4. The key work is Yong-sop Kim, *Studies in the Agrarian History of the Late Yi Dynasty*,* 2 vols. (Seoul, 1971) (alas, Eng. table of contents only!, but see a critical review in English by Yong-ho Kim, *JSSH*, no. 34 (1971), 149–53); see also Kwang-rin Lee, *History of Irrigation in the Yi Dynasty** (Seoul, 1961) (Eng. summary, pp. 169–83); Keijō Teikoku Daigaku Hōbungakubu, *Shakai*, the second essay by Ouchi and the third by Moritani; Hojin Ch'oe, "A Study of Laborer Forces in the Lee Dynasty,"* in *Commemorative Theses, Thirtieth Anniversary, Chungang University* (Seoul, 1955), pp. 1–22.

5. Seoul Municipal College of Agriculture, *An Economic Analysis of Upland Cropping Patterns* (Seoul, 1969); Seoul National University, College of Agriculture, *Economic Analysis of Double Cropping in Paddy Fields* (Seoul, 1967); Yong-sam Cho, *"Disguised Unemployment" in Underdeveloped Areas with Special Reference to South Korean Agriculture* (Berkeley, 1963); Felix Moos, *Social Science Factors and Considerations in Korean Rural Development* (USOM, [Seoul?], 1965).

6. Sung-chick Hong and Bok-soo Lee, "The Expressway and the Process of Changes in Rural Villages," *Social Science Journal*, vol. 1 (1973), 85–113; Mangap Lee, "Rural People and Their Modernization," in International Conference on the Problems of Modernization in Asia, *Report*, pp. 665–78; George L. Mehren, *Preliminary Analysis of the Third Five Year Plan for the Agricultural Sector, Republic of Korea* (New York, 1969); William R. Gasser et al., *Planning Korea's Agricultural Development* (Seoul, 1970); EXOTECH Systems, Inc., *Farm Mechanization Program for Korea* (Washington, D.C., 1972).

7. Pal-young Moon, *A Brief Review of the Evolution of Rice Policy in Korea* (Seoul, 1974), is a basic introduction. See also Gilbert T. Brown, *Korean Pricing Policies and Economic Development in the 1960's* (Baltimore, 1973); USAID/Korea, *Korean Agriculture Food Grain Subsector: Supply and Demand, Farm Mechanization, Storage and Fertilizer* (Seoul, 1971); Young-kim Shim, *Marketing of Rice and Other Grains in Suwon, Report of a Field Survey, 1965–67* (Suwon, 1968); Agency for International Development, *Korean Irrigation*, (Washington, D.C., 1980), pp. F 1–15.

8. For rural taxation see Kim Sang-gee and Lawrence W. Libby, *Rural Infrastructure*; Ki-hyuk Pak, "Reform," pp. 124–56. On kye see Kang C. Kyu, *The Influence of "Ke" Societies upon Ri-Dong Agricultural Cooperative Association* (Washington, D.C., 1973). For general credit, John Brake et al., *The National Agricultural Cooperative Federation, an Appraisal* (Seoul, 1972), pp. 13–30; U.S. Operations Mission to Korea, *Evaluation*, section on "agricultural finance"; Robert B. Morrow and Paul E. White, *Farm Credit in Korea* (Washington, D.C., 1973); National Agricultural Cooperative Federation, *Rural Credit Survey in Korea, 1965* (Seoul, 1966).

9. National Agricultural Cooperative Federation, *Agricultural Cooperatives in Korea* (Seoul, 1975); National Agricultural Cooperative Federation, Research Dept., *The Evaluation of Success of the Primary Cooperatives in Korea* (Seoul, 1971); Adlowe L. Larson and Helim H. Hulbert, *Study of Agricultural Cooperatives in*

*Korea* (Seoul, 1966); Brake, *Federation;* National Agricultural Cooperative Federation, Research Dept., *Cooperatives;* Morrow and White, *Credit;* Jun-bo Kim, "Conversion of Farming into Enterprise and Cooperative Forms for Agricultural Modernization," *KQ*, 9.3 (1967), 58–81.

10. Moo-nam Chung et al., *Agricultural Research and Guidance* (Seoul, 1972); Ministry of Reconstruction, ROK, *Community Development in Korea* (Seoul, 1961); Korean Overseas Information Service, *Saemaül Undong* [New Community Movement] (Seoul, 1973); Seh-kyun Seok and Yun-sook Lee, *Kwangju Gun Survey* (UN Command, 1958) and Combined Economic Board, UN Command, *Kwangju-gun, a Supplementary Report*, Survey no. 5 (Seoul, 1958); Brandt, *Village*, esp. on solidarity beyond kin; Man-gap Yi, "Socio-Cultural Aspects of the Community Development Movement in Korea," *KJ*, 13.1 (1973), 25–33 (penetrating!); Kwang-kyu Lee, "Rural Development and Role of Leadership,"* *Cultural Anthropology*, 5 (1972), 151–93 (Eng. summary, p. 194); Hoon Yu, "Perception of Villagers on Community Development Activities in Korea,"* *Korean Journal of Public Administration*, 9.2 (1971), 83–99; David I. Steinberg, The Economic Development of Korea, Sui Generis or Generic? (Washington, D.C., 1982, mimeo), pp. 8–9, 14–19; Ronald Aqua, *Local Institutions and Rural Development in South Korea* (Ithaca, 1974); David I. Steinberg et al., Korean Agricultural Research, the Integration of Research and Extension (Washington, D.C., 1981, mimeo); Sung-hwan Ban et al., *Rural Development* (Cambridge, Mass., 1980), esp. pp. 260–80 by Brandt; Sung-hwan Ban, "The New Community Movement," in Chuk-kyo Kim, ed., *Essays on the Korean Economy*, vol. 2, *Industrial and Social Development Issues* (Honolulu, 1977), pp. 206–35; Byung-nak Song, "Economic Development and Rural Urban Transformation" in Chuk-kyo Kim, *Essays*, vol. 3, *Macroeconomic and Industrial Development in Korea* (Honolulu, 1980), pp. 352–70; Hyŏng-hiu Kim, "Revolution of Consciousness among Farmers," *KJ*, 18.10 (1978), 24–26; Dong-il Kim, *Social Impact Assessment, Korean Irrigation Funded by USAID* (Seoul, 1980); Agency for International Development, *Irrigation*, pp. 1–15, secs. D and G; Hae-joang Cho, "A Study of Changing Rural Communities in Korea," *KJ*, 21.6 (1981), 18–25, 34.

## Chapter 5

1. Jung-sae Kim, "Recent Trends in the Government's Management of the Economy," in Edward R. Wright, Jr., *Politics*, ch. 9; L. L. Wade and B. S. Kim, *Economic Development of South Korea, the Political Economy of Success* (New York, 1978), esp. pp. 195–96 and 240–41; Leroy P. Jones and Sa-kong Il, *Government, Business and Entrepreneurship in Economic Development: The Korean Case* (Cambridge, Mass., 1980), esp. pp. 67–78 and the final chapter; Edward Mason et al., *The Economic and Social Modernization of the Republic of Korea* (Cambridge, Mass., 1980), pp. 16–17, 54–57, 244–55.

2. Korea Industrial Development Research Institute, *Survey of Government Enterprise in Korea* (Seoul, 1972); U.S. Operations Mission to Korea, *Third Interim Report* (Seoul, 1967), section on "innovating bureaucracy"; Sa-kong Il,

"Macroeconomic Aspects of the Public Enterprise Section," in Chuk-kyo Kim, *Essays*, vol. 3, pp. 99–128; Leroy P. Jones and Sa-kong Il, *Government*, ch. 5; Mason, *Modernization*, pp. 273–75, 476.

3. John J. McCloy et al., *The Great Oil Spill* (New York, 1976); WNET (New York), The MacNeil-Lehrer Report, "Korea and Congress: The Scandal So Far," script for June 20, 1977 telecast; *KPT*, 1975–76.

4. The literature on planning is prolific. The texts of the Five-Year Economic Plans are available in English, published by the government of ROK. I have found the following interpretive material useful: Soo-kon Kim, "Role and contribution of Social Scientists in Planning National Development," *KJ*, 18.5 (1978), 33–40; David C. Cole and Princeton N. Lyman, *Korean Development, the Interplay of Politics and Economics* (Cambridge, Mass., 1971); Duk-woo Nam, "Korea's Experience with Economic Planning," in International Conference on the Problems of Modernization in Asia, *Report*, pp. 517–31; Robert R. Nathan Associates, *Preliminary Report on Economic Reconstruction of Korea* (New York, 1952); Andrew C. Nahm, *Studies in the Developmental Aspects of Korea* (Kalamazoo, Mich., 1969); John G. Gurley, *Financial and Real Aspects of South Korea's Industrial Development* (Seoul, 1971); Irma Adelman, ed., *Practical Approaches to Development Planning, Korea's Second Five Year Plan* (Baltimore, 1969); Sung-hwang Jo and Seong-yawng Park, eds., *Basic Documents and Selected Papers of Korea's Third Five Year Economic Development Plan (1972–1976)* (Seoul, 1972); Princeton Lyman, "Economic Development in South Korea" (ch. 8) and Junsae Kim, "Recent Trends in the Government's Management of the Economy" (ch. 9), in Edward R. Wright, Jr., *Politics*.

5. A thorough but uncritical summary may be found in Taek-il Kim et al., *The Korean National Family Program* (New York, 1972). See also pertinent articles in the two-volume *Population and Family Planning in the Republic of Korea*, vol. 1 by Ministry of Health and Social Affairs, ROK (reissued Seoul, 1976) and vol. 2 by Korean Institute for Family Planning (Seoul, 1974).

6. The vernacular press is the best guide, see *KPT*; also F. L. Larkin, *Report on Public Relations for Korea Electric Company* (Seoul, 1966); Shin-pyo Kang, "Fatalism in Korea," *KJ*, 15.11 (1975), 14–16; Paul S. Crane, *Korean Patterns*, 2d ed. (Seoul, 1969), pp. 100–104.

7. Ho-chin Choi, *History*, sections on commerce; Won-sun Park, *Kaekju (Factors)** (Seoul, 1968) (Eng. résumé, pp. 317–57), his *Pubosang, a Study on Native Korean Merchant** (Seoul, 1965) (Eng. résumé, pp. 1–22), and in English his briefer "Merchant System Peculiar to Korea," *JSSH*, no. 26 (1967), 100–113 and his "Korean Factor," *JSSH*, no. 35 (1971), 64–84; Eisuke Zenshō, "Merchants of Gaiseng and Their Business Customs,"** *CG*, no. 46 (1968), 105–24 (Eng. summary, p. 4) and his "Traditional Commercial Customs of Korea,"** *CG*, no. 9 (1956), 185–216; Kang Man'gil, *Chosŏn Hugi Sang'ŏp Chabon ŭi Paltal* (Seoul, 1973)—a challenging work; Kyo-song Yu, "Organization and Function of the Peddler Merchants in the Late Yi Dynasty, as Seen in Chung-chong U-do,"* *YH*, no. 10 (1958), 167–96 and his (Romanized as Kyo-sung Ryu) "A Study on Ryukichun in Seoul: The Character of City Commerce in Yi Dy-

nasty,"* *YH*, no. 8 (1955), 377–434; Ch'oe Hojin, *Kindai Chōsen Keizaishi* (Tokyo, 1943); Kim Chunbo, *Han'guk*, vol. 2; Hoon K. Lee, *Economy*, pp. 252–80 (for market conditions under the Japanese); Won-dong Yoo, *History of Commerce and Industry in the Latter Part of the Yi Dynasty*\* (Seoul, 1968) (Eng. résumé, pp. 247–57); Hyoun-young Lee, "A Geographic Study of the Korean Periodic Markets," *KJ*, 15.8 (1975), 12–24; Dae-heui I, "On the System of Water Transportation in the Period of Yi Dynasty,"\*\* *CG*, no. 23 (1962), 83–102 (Eng. summary, pp. 3–4); Toichi Miyahara, "Local Markets in 15th and 16th Century Korea,"\*\* *CG*, no. 9 (1956), 165–84; Mun Chŏngch'ang, *Han'guk Nonch'on Tanch'esa* (Seoul, 1961); Palais, *Traditional*, ch. 7; Ho-chin Choi, "On Usury Capital in the Late Yi Dynasty," *JSSH*, no. 16 (1962), 12–22. A useful brief introduction to Korean monetary history is in Edgar J. Mandel, *Cast Coinage of Korea* (Racine, Wis., 1972), pp 6–15, but see also the many articles of Yu-han Wŏn in English, e.g., "A Study on the Circulation of Coin in the Latter Period of the Chosun Dynasty," *KO*, 6.2 (1975), 166–85 and in Korean *A Study of the Monetary History of the Latter Period of the Chosun Dynasty*\* (Seoul, 1975) (Eng. résumé, pp. 1–4).

8. John N. Ferris et al., *Investment Priorities in the Korean Agricultural Sector* (Seoul, 1972), pp. 96–120; Sang-kuk Han et al., *Organization and Performance of the Agricultural Marketing System in Korea* (Seoul, 1972); Gasser et al., *Planning*, section on marketing; Business Management Research Center, Korea University, *Report on the Management and Accounting Survey of the Office of Monopoly of the Republic of Korea Government* (Seoul, 1965); *KPT* on price inflation and government commodity pricing and market control. Such works as Hishimoto Nagatsugu, *Chōsen Mai no Kenkyū* (Tokyo, 1938); Zenshō Eisuke, *Chōsenjin no Shōgyō* (Keijō, 1925) and his *Chōsen no Shijō* (rpt. Seoul, 1969) all are useful in understanding what the Japanese did (modernize) and did not do (develop) for the Korean marketing system.

9. Korea Development Finance Corporation, *Money and Capital Markets in Korea and the Potential for their Improvement* (Seoul, 1970); Edward S. Shaw, *Financial Patterns and Policies in Korea* (Seoul, 1967); Homer Jones, *Korean Financial Problems* (Seoul, 1968); Business Management Research Center, Korea University, *Report on Research of Commercial Banking in Korea* (Seoul, 1971); Yung-moh Chung, ed., *Financial System in Korea* (Seoul, 1974); Research Institute for Economics and Business, Sogang University, *A Study of Money Market and Industrial Investment Finance in Korea* (Seoul, 1970); John Gurley, Hugh T. Patrick, and E. S. Shaw, *The Financial Structure of Korea*, preliminary draft (Seoul, 1965); Byong-kuk Kim, *Central Banking Experiment in a Developing Economy* (Seoul, 1965); Arthur I. Bloomfield and John P. Jensen, *Reports and Recommendations on Monetary Policy and Banking in Korea* (Seoul, 1965); Medium Industry Bank, *Financing Small Industry in Korea* (Seoul, 1968); Chang-nyol Lee, *Mobilization of Domestic Capital* (Seoul, 1965); Hyong-chun Kim, *Financial Policies and Industrialization in Korea*, ILCORK, no. 5 (Seoul, 1971); Kim-jung Sae, *The Evolution of the Financial Structure for Industrialization*, ILCORK, no. 13 (Seoul, 1971); R. H. Johnson, "The Role of Fiscal Policies in the Third Five Year

Plan," in Sung-hwan Jo and Seong-yawng Park, *Documents*, pp. 95–129; Sang-soo Kwak, *A Study of Taxation in Korea\** (Seoul, 1961) (Eng. résumé, pp. 231–33); Moon-ok Park, "Urban Land Value and Taxation—the Case of Korea," *KO*, 3.1 (1970), 62–78; Wan-soon Kim, *The Equalizing Effect of Financial Transfers: A Study of Inter-governmental Fiscal Relations in Korea* (Seoul, 1974), pp. 199–249; Steinberg, *Development*, pp. 20-26; Mason et al., *Modernization*, pp. 16–28, ch. 8, pp. 339–41, 475; Mahn-je Kim and Yung-chul Park, "A Study on the Savings Behavior 1953-1972" (pp. 155–91) and Kwang-suk Kim, "Household Savings Behavior" (pp. 192–218), in Chuk-kyo Kim, *Essays*, vol. 1 (Honolulu, 1977); Leroy P. Jones and Sa-kong Il, *Government*, chs. 8, 9, and Appendix B.

10. The key study is Ko Sŭngje's controversial 1959 study, *Kunse Han'guk Sanŏpsa Yŏn'gu* (Seoul, 1959); this work is critically reviewed in English by Kizun Zo in *JSSH*, no. 15 (1961), 84–96. See also Sang-woon Jeon, *Science and Technology in Korea, Traditional Instruments and Techniques* (Cambridge, Mass., 1974); Ho-chin Choi, *History*, the sections on handicrafts under each dynasty, esp. pp. 162–71; Chun-yung Lee, *A History of Agricultural Technology in the Yi Dynasty\** (Seoul, 1964) (Eng. résumé, pp. 1–5) and his (Romanized as Ch'unyŏng Yi) "History of Agricultural Techniques in Korea," *KJ*, 14.1 (1974), 21–27; Won-dong Yoo, "A Study of Privileged Manufacturers in the Latter Period of the Yi Dynasty," *JSSH*, no. 38 (1973), 1–18; Yong-ho Kim, "The Manual Industries Prior to Korea's Opening," *JSSH*, no. 39 (1974), 1–36; Chŏn Sŏktam et al., *Sahoe*, pp. 1–61, 161–208.

11. P. W. Kuznets, *Korea's Emerging Industrial Structure*, ILCORK, no. 6 (Seoul, 1971); Bertrand Renaud, *Regional Policy and Industrial Location in Korea*, ILCORK, no. 7 (Seoul, 1971); Moon-taik Shim, *Research and Development and Industrialization in Korea*, ILCORK, no. 19 (Seoul, 1971); Ki-pyok Cha, *The Political Implications of Industrialization in Korea*, ILCORK, no. 16 (Seoul, 1971); Man-gap Lee and Herbert R. Barringer, *City*, many chapters by individual authors are very pertinent; R. H. Johnson, "Comments on Regional Aspects of the Third Five Year Plan," in Sung-hwan Jo and Seong-yawng Park, *Documents*, pp. 194–206; Yun-hwan Kim, *A Study of Labor Problems in Korea\** (Seoul, 1971) (Eng. résumé, pp. 353–66); International Cooperation Administration, Office of Labor Affairs, *The Labor Situation in South Korea* (Washington, D.C., 1956); George Ogle, "Development of the Korean Labor Movement" (Master's thesis, University of Wisconsin, 1966), pp. 92–101; Business Management Research Center, Korea University, *Report on Survey of Selected Manpower Problems in Korea* (Seoul, 1966); Kie-wook Lee, *A Study of the Determinants of Farm Income in Korea* (Seoul, 1972); Korean Social Science Research Institute, *Report on Field Study in Employment and Income Pattern of Farm Household in Rural Community in Korea* (Seoul, 1969); Vincent S. R. Brandt, "Mass Migration and Urbanization in Contemporary Korea," *Asia*, no. 20 (n.d.), 31–47; Byung-nak Song, *The Distribution and Movement of Jobs and Industry-the Case of the Seoul Metropolitan Region* (Seoul, 1974); Urban Population Studies Center, School of Public Health, Seoul National University, *The Progress and Findings of the Urban Slum*

*Population Study, an Interim Report* (Seoul, 1966); Chang-shub Roh, *A Study of a Residential Community in Seoul** (Seoul, 1964) (Eng. résumé, pp. 173–189); J. Allen Beegle et al., *Population, Migration, and Agricultural Labor Supply* (Seoul, 1972); George Nez, *Evaluation of Metropolitan Planning Practice in Korea* (Seoul, 1968); Russell J. Sveda, Regional Planning Efforts in the Republic of Korea (Seoul, 1972, mimeo); Steinberg, Development, pp. 1–2, 32–37; Kwang-suk Kim and Michael Roemer, *Growth and Structural Transformation* (Cambridge, Mass., 1979); L. L. Wade and B. S. Kim, *Development*, ch. 2; Hae-joang Cho, "Study"; Song-ung Kim and Peter Donaldson, "Seoul's Population Growth: Plans and Implementation," in Chuk-kyo Kim, *Essays*, vol. 4 (Honolulu, 1980), pp. 3–18; Chuk-kyo Kim and Chul-hee Lee, "The Growth of the Automobile Industry" (pp. 277–311) and Byung-nak Song, "Economic Development and Rural Urban Transformation" (pp. 339–51), in Chuk-kyo Kim, *Essays*, vol. 3; Edwin S. Mills and Byung-nak Song, *Urbanization and Urban Problems* (Cambridge, Mass., 1979); Sung-hwan Ban et al., *Rural*, ch. 12; Hak-chŏng Choo, "Economic Growth and Income Distribution" (pp. 277–335) and Sang-mok Suh, "The Patterns of Poverty" (pp. 336–71), in Chuk-kyo Kim, *Essays*, vol. 4; Irma Adelman and Sherman Robinson, *Income Distribution Policy in Developing Countries: A Case Study of Korea* (Stanford, 1978); Mason et al., *Modernization*, pp. 442–44, 482–83; Larry E. Westphal and Kwang-suk Kim, *Industrial Policy and Development in Korea*, IBRD Staff Working Paper, no. 263 (Washington, D.C., 1977); Roger Norton and Seung-yoon Rhee, "A Macroeconomic Model of Inflation and Growth" (pp. 3–54) and Sang-woo Nam, "The Dynamics of Inflation" (pp. 55–97) in vol. 3, and Suk-kim Kwang, "The Causes and Effects of Inflation" (pp. 219–27) in vol. 4 of Chuk-kyo Kim, *Essays*; Ki-jun Jeong, "Achievement and Failures of the Korean Economy in the 1970's," *KJ*, 20.1 (1980), 12–17; *KPT* references to labor policy in 1974–75 recession, e.g., the series on worker conditions from Jan. 30 through Feb. 6, 1975.

12. Ronald Toby, *State and Diplomacy in Early Modern Japan* (Princeton, 1984); Byung-ha Kim, *A Study of the Trade between Korea and Japan during the Early Yi Dynasty** (Seoul, 1969) (Eng. résumé, pp. 193–203); Hae-jong Chun, "A Historical Survey of the Sino-Korean Tributary Relationship," *JSSH*, no. 25 (1966), 1–31; Ki-jun Cho, "The Impact of the Opening of Korea on Its Commerce and Industry," *KJ*, 16.2 (1976), 27–44; Ui-hwan Kim, "Japanese in Pusan after Opening of Port," *JSSH*, no. 40 (1974), 87–102; Sung-chai Koh, "The Decline of the Cotton Industry at the Close of the Yi Dynasty"* *Journal of Social Sciences* (Seoul), no. 2 (1958), 99–129 (Eng. summary, pp. 203–5).

13. Ann Krueger, *The Developmental Role of the Foreign Sector and Aid* (Cambridge, Mass., 1979); Sung-hwan Jo, "Direct Foreign Private Investment" (pp. 129–81), Yung-bong Kim, "The Growth and Structural Change of Textile Industry" (pp. 185–276), and Lin-su Kim, "Stages of Development of Industrial Technology" (pp. 312–38), all in Chuk-kyo Kim, *Essays*, vol. 3. Mason et al., *Modernization*, pp. 5–6, 123–24, 163–64; Reeve, *Republic*, ch. 7; Gene M. Lyons, *Military Policy and Economic Aid, the Korean Case, 1950–1953* (Columbus, Ohio, 1963); Byung-kwon Cha, *Import Substitution and Industrialization*,

*the Korean Case* (Seoul, 1971); Nak-kwan Kim, *Is Korea's Export Promotion Scheme Consistent with Her Industrialization?* ILCORK, no. 9 (Seoul, 1971); Roger Norton, "Planning with Facts" and Bela Balassa, "Trade Policy and Planning in Korea," in Sung-hwan Jo and Seong-yawng Park, *Documents;* Jong-chul Lim, "Economic Development in Korea and United States Economic Missions' Reports and Advice," *KQ*, 9.4 (1967), 41–54; Mahn-je Kim, *Alternative Strategies for Korea's Industrialization* (Seoul, 1974); Kee-chun Han, "An Analysis on the Relationship between U.S. Aid and Korea's Balance of Payments," *KO*, 1.2 (1969), 3–25; Norman Jacobs, "Economic Rationality and Social Development: An Iranian Case Study," *Studies in Comparative International Development*, 2 (1966), 137–42, and his "Donor-Recipient Relationship and Development: Some Lessons from the Iranian Experience," in *Accelerated Development in Southern Africa*, ed. John Barratt et al. (London, 1974), pp. 595–614.

14. Takashi Hatada, *A History of Korea* (Santa Barbara, Calif., 1969), section on Japanese rule; Henderson, *Vortex*, ch. 4; Ho-chin Choi, *History*, "Japanese Colonialism" with excellent tables; Bank of Chōsen, *Economic History of Chōsen* (Seoul, 1920); Edward de Schwinitz Brunner, "Rural Korea: A Preliminary Survey of Economic, Social, and Religious Conditions," in Jerusalem Meeting of the International Missionary Council, *The Christian Mission in Relation to Rural Problems* (London, 1928), vol. 6, pp. 84–112; Hoon K. Lee, *Economy;* Sang-chul Suh, *Growth and Structural Changes in the Korean Economy, 1910–1940* (Cambridge, Mass., 1978); Grajdanzev, *Korea*, an excellent, very critical study; Sun-keun Lee, "The Extent to Which the Japanese Colonial Policy toward Korea Contributed to Her Modernization" (pp. 323–38) and Yong-kwang Bae, "The Role of Entrepreneurs in the Modernization Process of Korea" (pp. 754–67), in International Conference on the Problems of Modernization in Asia, *Report;* Karl Moskowitz, "The Creation of the Oriental Development Co.," in Palais, *Occasional Papers*, no. 2, pp. 73–121; Chǒn Sǒktam, *Ilcheha ǔi Chosǒn Sahoe Kyǒngjaesa* (Seoul, 1947); Murayama Chijun, *Gunshu*, pts. 1 & 2; essays by Shikata and Park in Keijō Teikoku Daigaku Hōbungakubu, *Shakai;* Fujii Tadajiro, *Chōsen Musan-Kaikyū no Kenkyū* (Tokyo, 1926); In Chǒngsik, *Kiko* (in Japanese), esp. pp. 48–67; Takahashi Kamekichi, *Gendai Chōsen Keizairon* (Tokyo, 1935), pp. 161–218, 402–3; Ik-whan Kwon, "Japanese Industralization on Korea, 1930–1945: Idealism or Realism?" *KQ*, 8.2 (1966), 80–95; Sung-jae Koh, "The Role of the Bank of Chōsen (Korea) and the Japanese Expansion in Manchuria and China," *JSSH*, no. 32 (1970), 25–36.

15. Sang-bok Han, "The Effects of Local Enterprise on Social Change in a Korean Fishing Village," *Cultural Anthropology* (Seoul), 5 (1972), 255–66; Norman Strand, *Revue and Recommendation on Collection and Handling of Farm Statistics in the Ministry of Agriculture and Forestry* (Seoul, 1969); Yi-sup Hong, "Science," in *Korean Studies Today;* Daniel Sun-gil Juhn, "The Development of Korean Entrepreneurship," in *Korea under Japanese Colonial Rule*, ed. Andrew C. Nahm (Kalamazoo, Mich., 1973), pp. 113–34; and Juhn "Korean Industrial Entrepreneurship, 1924–1940," in *Korea's Response to the West*, ed. Yung-hwan Jo (Kalamazoo, Mich., 1970), pp. 219–54; Ki-zun Zo, "Types of the Entrepreneur in Modernization Process of the Korean Economy," in Interna-

tional Conference on the Problems of Modernization in Asia, *Report*, pp. 616–26; Sung-jae Koh, "Contrasting Characteristics of Industrial Entrepreneurship in Japan, India and Korea," *JSSH*, no. 29 (1968), 16–51; Man-gap Lee, "Social Organization," in Man-gap Lee and Herbert R. Barringer, *City;* Doh-chull Shin, "Socio-economic Development and Democratization in South Korea: A Time Series Analysis" (Ph.D. diss., University of Illinois, 1972), conclusion; Kah-kyung Cho, "Philosophical Aspect of Modernization or the Modern Consciousness and the Problem of Subjectivity" (pp. 61–86), Tae-kil Kim, "How to Harmonize the Traditional Moral Values and Present Day Needs in Korea" (pp. 114–26), and Chiu-yuan Hu, "On the Conception of Modernity" (pp. 181–96), all in International Conference on the Problems of Modernization in Asia, *Report*; Hong Sung-jik, *Values.**

## Chapter 6

1. Chang-hyun Cho, "Bureaucracy and Local Government in Korea," in Se-jin Kim and Chang-hyun Cho, *Government*, pp. 91–126; Byung-chul Koh, *Administrative*, pp. 9–29; Pung-ku Kim, "The Image of Korean Intellectuals," *KJ*, 8.6 (1968), 17–25; Sun-chik Hong, *The Intellectual and Modernization* (Seoul, 1967) and (Romanized as Sung) his "Consciousness Structure of the Korean Intellectuals," *KO*, 3.3 (1971), 26–40; Byung-hun Oh, "Students and Politics," ch. 5 in Edward R. Wright, Jr., *Politics;* Chong-keun Bae, "Impact of the Brain Drain on Korea," *JSSH*, no. 41 (1975), 79–91; *KPT*, May 29, 1974, pp. 9–20; Doo-jong Kim, "The Study of Women-Doctor's Institution during the Yi Dynasty,"* *Journal of Asian Women*, 1 (1962), 1–15 (Eng. summary, pp. 15–16); George Won and Jang-hyun Lee, "The Korean Lawyer: A General Profile," *JSSH*, no. 30 (1969), 107–16; George Won et al., "Korean Private Law Practitioner," *JSSH*, no. 35 (1971), 1–10; Murphy, *Education*, passim.

2. Yi Ch'ŏngwon, *Chōsen Shakaishi Tokuhon* (Toyko, 1936), pp. 129–54; Chŏn Sŏktam et al., Sahoe, pp. 92–170.

3. Henderson, *Vortex*, ch. 12; Ki-baek Lee, "Korea—the Military Tradition" (pp. 1–42) and Hugh Kang, "Epilogue" (pp. 141–50), in Hugh Kang, *Traditional;* Wanne J. Joe, *Traditional Korea, a Cultural History* (Seoul, 1972), pp. 217–43; Ki-baik Lee, *Studies in Silla Politico-Social History** (Seoul, 1974) (Eng. summary, pp. 310–21) and his *Military;* Masaaki Ebara, "A Study on the Provincial Army of Gorie Period,"** *CG*, no. 28 (1963), 35–74 (Eng. summary, pp. 1–2); Byong-ha Min, "On the Military Officials of Government during the Koryeo Dynasty,"* *Sahak Yuenku*, no. 6 (1959), 27–68 (Eng. summary, pp. 110–12); Tae-sup Pyon, *Studies in the Political System of Koryo Dynasty** (Seoul, 1974) (Eng. table of contents only, p. 10), see esp. from p. 276; Paek Namun, *Hōken*, esp. part 6 and pp. 661–75; Jong-gug Gim, "Inquiry into the Characteristics of the Military Government of Goryeo,"** *CG*, no. 17 (1960), 51–80 (Eng. summary, pp. 1–2).

4. Most important is Jong-ha Ree, *Labour Legislation in Josun Dynasty** (Seoul, 1969) (Eng. summary, pp. 1–4—most inadequate); Won-dong Yoo, *Commerce;* Man-gil Kang, "A Study of Artisans in the First Half of the Lee Dynasty,"*

*Sahak Yuenku*, no. 12 (1961), 1–72 (Eng. summary, pp. 129–30); Paek Namun, *Shakai*, pp. 184–205, 216–55; U. (should be Toichi) Miyahara, "Employees and Labourers in Korea in 15th-16th Centuries,"** *CG*, no. 11 (1957), 93–116; Hochin Choi, *History*, references to "handicrafts," e.g., pp. 162–69, 290–92; Song-mo Huang, "The Role of Industrial Laborers in the Modernization of Korea," in International Conference on the Problems of Modernization in Asia, *Report*, pp. 768–78; Choon-ryang Chung and Hy-chai Lee, "Study of Women's Occupations and Labor Problems during the Japanese Government,"* *JKCRI*, 22 (1973), 307–43 (Eng. table of contents only, p. 344).

5. Hi-woong Kang, "Class," pp. 158–67; Won-sun Park, "Factor," pp. 64–84; Johannes Hirschmeier, *The Origins of Entrepreneurship in Meiji Japan* (Cambridge, Mass., 1964), esp. ch. 5.

6. Paek Namun, *Hōken*, ch. 79; Ch'oe Hojin, *Kindai*, up to p. 158; Yun-hwan Kim, *The Korean Labor Movement in the 1960's*, ILCORK, no. 17 (Seoul, 1971); Kyong-dong Kim, *Industrialization*; Chae-jin Lee, *Labor Movement and Political Development in Korea*, ILCORK, no. 2 (Seoul, 1971); Sang-joon Hahn, *Manpower Development for Industrial in Korea*, ILCORK, no. 18 (Seoul, 1971); Edward D. Hollander, *The Role of Manpower in Korean Economic Development* (Seoul, n.d.); Federation of Korean Trade Unions, Activity Report, 1973, ([Seoul?], n.d., mimeo); International Cooperation Administration, *Labor*, pp. 34–58, 76; Sumiya Mikio, "Hankoku no Rōdōchiba: Sono Kōzō to Kinō," *Ajia Keizai*, no. 16 (1975), 2–12, 47–62; Young-ki Park, "Unionism and Labor Legislation in Korea," *KO*, 1.2 (1969), 94–102; Se-jin Kim, "Attitudinal Orientations of Korean Workers," *KJ*, 12.9 (1972), 18–30.

7. Henderson, *Vortex*, pp. 256–72, 286 and his critics, e.g., Cumings in Palais and Lang, *Occasional Papers*, no. 1. On mass mobilization see Dae-sook Suh, *Movement*, pp. 132–41; and Scalapino and Lee, *Communism, Part 1*, pp. 112–19 and ch. 3.

## Chapter 7

1. On bone rank see Lee Ki-baek, *Silla*,* esp. the section on *yukdup'um* (see Eng. summary, pp. 312–13, for help); Chŏng-sun Kim, "Despotism," pp. 232–55 and his "Kol'pum System: Basis for Sillan Social Stratification," *Journal of Korean Studies* (Seattle), 1.2 (1971), 43–70; Ehara Masaaki, "Kopponsei-Shiragi no Jibunsei ni kansuru Oboegaki," *Shicho*, no. 92 (1965), 50–55. For the military see Pyon Tae-sup, *Political*.* For yangban see Hi-woong Kang, "Class," from p. 104; He-sung Chun Koh, "Religion, Social Structure and Economic Development in Yi Dynasty Korea" (Ph.D. diss., Boston University, 1959), pp. 70–82; Pow-key Sohn, "The Concept of History and Korean Yangban," *International Journal of Korean Studies* (Yonsei University), 1 (1973), 91–113; Kim Taik-kyoo, *Village*; Lee Man-gap, *Village* (but see pp. 367–68 of Eng. summary for help). For chung'in see Henderson, *Vortex*, pp. 46–49; He-sung Koh, "Religion," pp. 83–100; Tai-chin Yi, "Discriminating System for the Descendants of Concubines in the Early Yi Dynasty,"* *YH*, no. 27 (1965),

65–104 (Eng. summary, p. 180); Makoto Hiraki, "On the Standing of Slaves (Mean Class), Wives of Common People and Their Children in 17th and 18th Centuries,"** CG, no. 61 (1971), 45–76 (Eng. summary, pp. 2–3).

2. Chong-sun Kim, "Despotism," pp. 158–75, 200; He-sung Koh, "Religion," pp. 103–11; Kyu-tae Yi, *Modern Transformation of Korea* (Seoul, 1970), pp. 39–53, 97–102; Susan Shin, "Some Aspects of Landlord-Tenant Relations in Yi Dynasty Korea," in Palais and Lang, *Occasional Papers*, no. 3, pp. 50–54; Sang-beck Lee, "On the Ch'onja Sumo,"* CH, 25–27 (1964), 155–83 (Eng. summary, pp. 482–85); Byong-ho Park, "Social Castes and Legal Rights under the Modern Korean Law," KQ, 4.2 (1962), 35–44; Hatada, *Chusei*,** essays 3, 4, 15, 16; Paek Namun, *Hōken*, Introduction, pp. 1–11, 298–384; Ree Jong-ha, *Labour*,* pp. 19–21, 118–23, 150–53, 203–11, 233, 397–414; Woo-chul Lee, "Consideration on the Eunuch in the Koryeo Dynasty,"* *Sahak Yuenku*, no. 1 (1958), 18–44 (Eng. summary, pp. 140–41); Byung-sak Koo, "A Study on the History of Law in Korea,"* *Woo Sok University Journal*, 1 (1967), 295–421 (Eng. table of contents, pp. 422–23, but alas an inadequate summary on pp. 424–25 of a very important work); Paek Namun, *Shakai*, pt. 3; Ellen Unruh, "The Landowning Slave: A Korean Phenomenon," KJ, 16.4 (1976), 27–34— this is a prelude to an important forthcoming work on the medieval bound.

3. Henderson, *Vortex*, pp. 40–44, 390–91; Edward Wagner, "The Ladder of Success in Yi Dynasty Korea" (pp. 1–8) and his "Social Stratification in 17th Century Korea" (pp. 36–54), and Susan Shin, "The Social Structure of Kumhwa County in the Late 17th Century" (pp. 9–35), all in Palais and Lang, *Occasional Papers*, no. 1; Yong-mo Kim, "The Social Background and Mobility of State Ministers of the Yi Dynasty," KA, 3.2 (1964), 238–60 and (as Kim Yongmo) his *Han'guk Sahoehak* (Seoul, 1972), pp. 189–216; Yŏng-ho Ch'oe, "Commoners in Early Yi Dynasty Civil Examinations," JAS, 33.4 (1974), 611–31; Bae-ho Hahn and Kyu-taik Kim, "Korean Political Leaders, 1952–1962; Their Social Origins and Skills," *Asian Survey*, 3.7 (1963), 305–23; Jang-hyun Lee, George Won, and In-hwan Oh, "The Korean Lawyer," JKCRI, 20 (1972), 405–29; Dong-suh Bark, "Korean Higher Civil Servants," in Byung-chul Koh, *Administrative*, pp. 9–29; Hoon Yoo, "Social Background of Higher Civil Servants in Korea," KQ, 10.1 (1968), 34–55; Yong-mo Kim, "A Study on the Educational Opportunity and Social Class in Korea,"* CH, 35 (1973), 121–65 (Eng. summary, pp. 174-75); Herbert R. Barringer, *Social Stratification and Industrialization in Korea*, ILCORK, no. 11 (Seoul, 1971), and his "Social Change and Social Differentiation in Korea," in C. I. Eugene Kim and Ch'ang-boh Chee, *Aspects of Social Change in Korea* (Kalamazoo, Mich., n.d.), pp. 203–27; Wolfram Eberhard, "Social Mobility of Businessmen in a Small Korean Town," JSSH, no. 16 (1962), 23–32; R. H. Johnson, "Social Development Aspects of the Third Five Year Plan," in Sung-hwan Jo and Seong-yawng Park, *Documents*, pp 184–93; Steinberg, Development, pp. 12, 28–32. For contemporary income maldistribution see *KPT*.

4. Bae-ho Hahn, "The Authority Structure of Korean Politics," in Edward R. Wright, Jr., *Politics*, ch. 10; William E. Henthorn, "Traditional Korea and

Modernization," in International Conference on the Problems of Modernization in Asia, *Report*, pp. 229–40; Murayama Chijun, *Gunshu*, pp. 168–204; He-sung Koh, "Religion," pp. 112–16.

## Chapter 8

1. Ch'in-ch'ol Kang, "Traditional Land Tenure Relations in Korean Society," in Hugh Kang, *Traditional*, ch. 2; Ki-hyuk Pak, *Tenure*, pp. 242–97; Kyung-sook Bae, *Women and the Law in Korea* (Seoul, 1973), pp. 147–54; Brandt, *Village*, pp. 68–70, 86, 100–102, 112–14; Jai-seuk Choi, "Changes in Korean Family Values,"* *CH*, 28 (1965), 135–90 (Eng. summary, pp. 191–92); Young-kyun Oh, "Agrarian Reform and Economic Development," *KQ*, 9.2 (1967), 91–137; Byong-ho Park, "Traditional Korean Society" and his "Legal Nature of Land Ownership in the Yi Dynasty," *KJ*, 15.10 (1975), 4–10; Susan Shin, "Some Aspects of Landlord-Tenant Relations in Yi Dynasty Korea," in Palais and Lang, *Occasional Papers*, no. 3, pp. 49–84; Noboru Niida, "The Law of Succession to a Property of Gorye and I Dynasty and the Chinese Law,"** *CG*, no. 30 (1964), 1–10 (Eng. summary, p. 1); Hatada, *Chusei*, part 4, essay 14; Paek Namun, *Hōken*, ch. 92; Nakane Chie, *Hankoku Nōson no Kazoku to Saigi* (Tokyo, 1973), essays 2 and 3; Kim Too-hun, *Family*,* ch. 4.1.

2. The two standard sources on kinship are Jai-seuk Choi, *A Study of the Korean Family*\* (Seoul, 1966) (Eng. résumé, pp. 1–50) and Kim Too-hon, *Family*.\* See also Kwang-kyu Lee, *Kinship System in Korea*, 2 vols. (New Haven, 1975); Zenshō Eizuke, *Chōsen no Shuraku*, 3 vols. (Keijō, 1935; rpt. Seoul, 1974) and reply by Shikata Hiroshi, "Chōsen ni Okeru Dai-Kazokushi to Dōzoku Buraku," *Chōsen*, 11 (1937), 26–42; He-sung Koh, "Religion," pp. 47–69; Nakane, *Hankoku*, essays 2 and 3; Hwang-yŏng Ko et al., *A Study of Korean Rural Family*\* (Seoul, 1963) (Eng. résumé, pp. 257–79); Takashi Akiba, "A Study of Korean Folkways," *Folklore Studies*, 16 (1957), 1–106; Ki-hyuk Pak and Seung-yun Lee, *Villages*, pp. 188–96, 262; Mark Peterson, "Adoption in Korean Genealogies," *KJ*, 14.1 (1974), 28–35, 45; Edward Wagner, "The Korean Chokpo as a Historical Source," in Spencer J. Palmer, *Studies in Asian Genealogy* (Provo, Utah, 1972), pp. 141–50; Chu-gun Chang, Korean Culture, trans. Charles Goldberg (Seoul, 1975, mimeo), pp. 9–11, 25–48, 108–40; Sang-yŏl Park, "The Social Structure of a Korean Village under the Control of Consangunity," *JSSH*, no. 17 (1967), 70–98; Hyo-chai Lee, "Patterns of Change Observed in the Korean Marriage Institution," *JSSH*, no. 26 (1967), 34–55, and his *Industrialization and the Family in Korea*, ILCORK, no. 8 (Seoul, 1971); Jai-seuk Choi, "Composition of Korean Family Members,"* *CH*, 24 (1963), 101–27 (Eng. summary, pp. 128–30) and his "Institution of Inheritance during the Yi Dynasty,"* *YH*, nos. 53–54 (1972), pp. 98–148 (Eng. summary, pp. 149–50); Hyoung Cho, "The Kin Network of the Urban Middle Class Family in Korea," *KJ*, 15.6 (1975), 22–33; Roger L. Janelli, "Anthropology, Folklore and Korean Ancestor Worship," *KJ*, 15.6 (1975), 34–43; Young-koo Yun, "Factors Affecting Mate Selection in Korea," *JSSH*, no. 17 (1962), 24–45; C. S. Kim, *A Study of Marriage and Divorce in the New Civil Code of Korea*\*

(Seoul, 1958) (Eng. summary, pp. 1–22); Bom-mo Chung, Jae-ho Cha, and Sung-jin Lee, *Boy Preference and Family Planning in Korea* (Seoul, 1974); Jae-un Kim, "Psychological Structure of the Korean Family," *JSSH*, no. 40 (1974), 1–27; Eun-woo Kim, *A Study of Korean Woman's Inner Conflict\** (Seoul, 1963) (Eng. résumé, pp. 1–9); *KH*, May 9, 1975, on Parent's Day.

## Chapter 9

The references I have used for this chapter are very many. I cite only a representative sample and rarely repeat the same work in different notes.

1. Charles Allen Clark, *Religions of Old Korea* (Seoul, 1961), pp. 127–216; He-sung Koh, "Religion," pp. 148–60; Minjok Munhwa Yŏn'gusa, *Han'guk Munhwasa Taegye*, vol. 6, parts 1 and 2 (Seoul, 1970); Byung-kil Chang, *Korean Background Series: Religion* (Seoul, 1974), ch. 2; George Jones, "The Spirit Worship of the Koreans," *RAS*, 2 (1902), 37–58; Akiba, "Folkways"; Yong-joon Hyun, "Family and Religion in South Korea," in Chie Nakane and Akira Goto, eds., *The Symposium on Family and Religion in East Asian Countries*, East Asian Cultural Studies, vol. 11, nos. 3–4 (Tokyo, 1972), pp. 113–24; Douglas Romoli, "Female Shamans of Seoul," *Asian Pacific Quarterly of Cultural and Social Affairs*, 3 (1971–72), 64–69; Kwang-iel Kim, "Folk Psychiatry in Korea, II,"\* *Cultural Anthropology*, 5 (1972), 79–105 (Eng. résumé, pp. 105–6) and (Romanized as Kwang-il Kim) "Traditional Concept of Disease in Korea," *KJ*, 13.1 (1973), 12–18; Tong-shik Ryu, "The World of 'Kut' and Korean Optimism," *KJ*, 13.8 (1973), 13–20; Tae-gon Kim, "Korean Shamanism and Its Outlook on Future Life," *JSSH*, no. 39 (1974), 83–104; Crane, *Patterns*, pp. 121–36; J. Robert Moose, *Village Life in Korea* (Nashville, Tenn., 1911), pp. 189–203; Pyong-choon Hahm, *Religion*; Sang-il Rhie, "Dramatic Aspect of Shamanistic Rituals," *KJ*, 15.7 (1975), 23–28; Nam-young Lee, "Tan'gun Myth and the Korean Thought," *KJ*, 16.4 (1976), 35–44; Hong-jik Lee, "The Tan'gun Myth and the National Consciousness," *KQ*, 1.2 (1960), 103–14; Ki-hyuk Pak and Seung-yun Lee, *Villages*, pp. 173–83; Chu-gun Chang, "Culture," pp. 13–30; Noritada Kubo, "Belief of Samsi Doctrine during Yi Dynasty,"\*\* *CG*, nos. 37–38 (1966), 270–95 (Eng. summary, p. 8); Osamu Kumagai, "On Dong-je, the Festival Commemorating Community Gods,"\*\* *CG*, no. 74 (1975), 97–110 (Eng. summary, pp. 1–2); *Korean Studies Today*, sections on religion, philosophy, classical literature, and customs and folklore; Kim Tuhŏn, *Kungmin Yulli* (Seoul, 1972), pp. 224–26; Ham Sŏkhŏn, *Bon*, pp. 83–143; Yi Pyŏngdo, *Tugye*, from p. 94; Nakane, *Hankoku*,\*\* the fourth essay; Akamatsu Chijo and Akiba Takahashi, *Chōsen Fuzoku no Kenkyū*, 2 vols. (Tokyo, 1938; rpt. Seoul, 1970); Murayama Chijun, various investigations for the Chōsen Sotokufu, e.g., *Chōsen no Fusai* (1931), *Chōsen no Semboku to Yogen* (1933), *Chōsen no Ruiji Shūkyō* (1935), *Chōsen no Kishin* (1929), *Burakusai* (1937), and *Shakuson, Kiu, Antaku* (1938)—all these were reprinted in Seoul in 1971.

2. Charles Clark, *Religions*, part 1; Peter H. Lee, *Lives of Eminent Korean Monks* (Cambridge, Mass., 1969); Frederick Starr, *Korean Buddhism* (Boston, 1918); Shin-yong Chun, ed., *Buddhist Culture in Korea* (Seoul, 1974) and Dong-

guk University, *Buddhism and Its Culture in Korea* (Seoul, 1964) (both have significant interpretations); James Bissett Pratt, *The Pilgrimage of Buddhism* (New York, 1928), ch. 21; Byung-kil Chang, *Religion*, pp. 26–30. *KJ*, 4.5 (May 1964) is a special issue devoted to Buddhism in Korea; Ky-yong Rhi, "Wŏnhyo and His Thought," *KJ*, 11.1 (1971), 4–9, 14; his (Romanized as Ki-young) "Won Hyo's Moral Concepts," *KO*, 1.2 (1969), 103–15; his (Romanized as Ki-young Lee) "Buddhism and Modern Man," *KJ*, 7.10 (1967), 10–16; and his essay "Religion" in *Korean Studies Today*, pp. 10–47—all but snippets in English of this great scholar's work on Korean Buddhism in general and Wŏnhyo in particular in the Korean language. Roger Leverrier, "Buddhism and Ancestral Religious Beliefs in Korea," *KJ*, 12.5 (1972), 37–42; Jong-gug Gim, "A Study on the Contentions between the Warrior's Regime and the Buddhist Monks in the Goryeo Period,"** *CG*, nos. 21–22 (1961), 567–89 (Eng. summary, p. 20); Masataka Nakai, "On the Organs for Controlling Buddhism in Silla,"** *CG*, no. 59 (1971), 1–22 (Eng. summary, pp. 1–2); Ke-hyun An, "On the Buddhist Priesthood in the Koryeo Dynasty,"* *Toong Gook Sa Hak*, no. 5 (1957), 95–105; Yukio Takeda, "Management of the Temple Estate in the Koryeo Period,"* *Tōyōshi Kenkyū*, 251.1 (1966), 70–91 (Eng. summary, pp. 2–3); Yi Ch'ŏngwon, *Tokuhon*,** pp. 76–114; Kim Ch'ŏlchun, *Han'guk Kodae Kukka Paltalsa* (Seoul, 1975), pp. 282–302; Minjok Munhwa Yŏn'gusa, esp. pp. 269–364; Han Yong'un, *Chosŏn Bulgyo Yusin Non* (Seoul, 1973) (a significant original source); Paek Sŏn'guk Paksa Sŏngsu Kinyŏm Saŏp Wiwŏnhoe, *Paek Sŏn'guk Paksa Sŏngsu Kinyŏm Bulgyo Nonmunjip* (Seoul, 1959), many articles are pertinent, see esp. pp. 567–604, 605–26, and 1135–74; Woo-keun Han, "A Study on the Government vis-a-vis Policy Buddhist Influence and Belief in Korea, from the Late Koryŏ Dynasty to the Early Yi Dynasty,"* *USCT*, 6 (1957), 1–80.

3. Pow-key Sohn, "Social," from p. 213; Palais, *Traditional*, ch. 6; He-sung Koh, "Religion," pp. 117–30, 170–99; Ministry of Education, ROK, *Education in Korea* (Seoul, 1972); Charles Dallet, *Traditional Korea* (New Haven, 1954), pp. 137–42; Charles Clark, *Religions*, ch. 3; Richard Rutt, "The Chinese Learning and Pleasures of a Country Scholar," *RAS*, 36 (1960), 1–100; Chong-guk Kim and Chin-man Kim, "Notes on the Sŏnggung'wan," *RAS*, 38 (1961), 69–91; Key P. Yang and Gregory Henderson, "Confucianism, Part II," *JAS*, 18.2 (1959), 259–76. *KJ*, 3.9 (1973) is a special issue devoted to Confucianism. Hyŏn Sang'yun, *Chosŏn Yugyosa* (Seoul, 1960); Martina Deuchler, "Neo-Confucianism in Early Yi Korea," *KJ*, 15.5 (1975), 12–18; Doo-hun Kim, "The Rise of Neo-Confucianism against Buddhism in Late Koryo," *JSSH*, no. 12 (1960), 11–29; Sang-ok Lee, "Society in the Middle Age of Koryo and Neo-Confucianism,"* *Woo Sok University Journal*, 1 (1967), 1–45 (Eng. summary, p. 46); Hi-dok Yi, "A Study on the Development of the Thought of Filial Piety in the Koryo Dynasty,"* *YH*, no. 55 (1972), 37–70 (Eng. summary, pp. 71–72); Ki-baek Lee, "Confucian Political Ideology in the Silla Unification and Early Koryo Periods," *JSSH*, no. 42 (1975), 1–23; Hyung-jin Yoo, "Private Educational Institution in Korea, a Study of the Sŏwon System," *KQ*, 3.1 (1961), 126–59; Manabu Watanabe, *Kinsei Chōsen Kyoiku Kenkyū* (Tokyo, 1972); Nakamura Hidetaka, "Richō Jidai no Kirosho ni Tsuite," in *Ichimura Hakase*

*Koki Kinen Tōyōshi Ronsō* (Tokyo, 1933), pp. 813–42; *Korean Studies Today*, the various discussions on Confucianism; Yun T'aerim, *Han'gugin*, pp. 131–46; Tameo Tabana, "Official Instructions and Mutual Control, Two Moralistic Elements in the Village-Contract of Li Dynasty,"** *CG*, no. 5 (1963), 127–54.

4. Charles Clark, *Religions*, ch. 7; Lak-geoon George Paik, *The History of Protestant Missions in Korea, 1832–1910* (Seoul, 1970); Allen D. Clark, *A History of the Church in Korea* (Seoul, 1971), to p. 175; Joseph Chang-mun Kim and John Jae-sun Chung, *Catholic Korea, Yesterday and Today* (Seoul, 1964), to p. 320; William E. Biernatzki et al., *Korean Catholicism in the 1970's* (Maryknoll, N.Y., 1975), chs. 1 and 2; Spencer J. Palmer, *Korea and Christianity* (Seoul, 1967); Kyu-tae Yi, *Transformation*, pp. 185–201; Chai-sik Chung, "Christianity as a Heterodoxy," in Yung-hwan Jo, *Response*, pp. 57–86; Sung-bum Yun, "Korean Christianity and Ancestor Worship," *KJ*, 13.2 (1973), 17–21; Ki-shik Han, "The Christian Impact and the Indigenous Responses in the 18th and 19th Century Korea," *KQ*, 10.1 (1968), 1–25.

5. Benjamin Weems, *Reform, Rebellion and the Heavenly Way* (Tucson, 1964), intro. through p. 18; Charles Clark, *Religions*, ch. 5 and Appendix 1; William Junkin, "The Tong Hak," *Korean Repository*, 2 (1895), 56–60; "Seven Months among the Tonghak," *Korean Repository*, 2 (1895), 201–8; Yong-choon Kim, "The Essentials of Ch'ondogyo Ethics," *JSSH*, no. 38 (1973), 85–100; Dong-hee Choi, "Tonghak and Korean Thought," *KO*, 3.2 (1971), 26–50.

6. Wi-jo Kang, "Japanese Rule and Korean Confucianism" (pp. 67–74) and Frank Baldwin, "Missionaries and the March First Movement" (pp. 193–219), in Nahm, *Colonial*; Government-General of Tyosen, *Annual Report on Administration of Tyosen, 1937–1938* (Keizyo, 1938), pp. 100–103; Brunner, "Rural"; Allen Clark, *History*, pp. 186–231, 366–71, 409–59; Yi-sup Hong, *Korea's Self Identity* (Seoul, 1971), pp. 40–63; T'ae-gon Kim, "Korean Folklore Data Collected Prior to Liberation," *KJ*, 12.4 (1972), 33–39; *Korean Studies Today*, pp. 20–21, 223–35; Mu-wong Yom, "The Life and Thought of Han Yong-woon," in Shin-yong Chun, *Buddhist*, pp. 97–117; Warren W. Smith, Jr., *Confucianism in Modern Japan* (Tokyo, 1959), pp. 166–84 (on Korea); Spencer J. Palmer, ed., "The New Religions of Korea," *RAS*, 43 (1967), see esp. 28–103; Weems, *Reform*, intro. and pp. 50–86; James E. Fisher, *Democracy and Mission Education in Korea* (Seoul, 1970); Wŏn-mo Dong, "Assimilation and Social Mobilization in Korea," in Nahm, *Colonial*, pp. 146–82.

## Chapter 10

1. Allen Clark, *History*, from p. 234; Joseph Kim and John Chung, *Catholic*, from p. 326; Biernatzki et al., *Korean*. KPT for Park regime protests.

2. Kyung-soo Shu, "The Present Situation of Korean Buddhism," in Nakane and Goto, *Family*, pp. 97-105; *KJ*, 4.5, special issue devoted to Buddhism; Kyŏng-su Sŏ, "The Present Situation of Korean Buddhism," *KJ*, 11.5 (1971), 15–20; Kyung-bo Seo, "Characteristics of Korean Zen," *KJ*, 12.5 (1972), 29–36; Ki-du Han, "Practical Tendency in Modern Korean Buddhism," *KJ*, 13.7 (1973), 24-28; Do-ryun Sok, "Modern Son Buddhism in Korea," *KJ*, 5.1 (1965),

26–30; Won Buddhism, Hdq., *Manual of Won Buddhism* (Iri City, Korea, n.d.); Pal-khn Chon, trans., *The Canonical Textbook of Won Buddhism* (Seoul, 1971).

3. Palmer, "New," is basic in English; see also Byung-kil Chang, *Religion*; Gernot Prunner, "The Birthday of God: A Sacrifice Service of Chŭnsan'gyo," *KJ*, 16.3 (1976), 12–26; Minjok Munhwa Yŏn'gusa, vol. 6, pp. 781–866 (article by Chŏng Pyŏnkil on new religions); advertisements by the Unification Church in *New York Times*, Jan. 4, 1976.

4. Warren Smith, *Confucianism*, pp. 182–84; Yoon-joon Hyun, "Family and Religion in South Korea," in Nakane and Goto, *Family*, pp. 113–24; Brian Wilson, "Values and Religion," in Man-gap Lee and Herbert R. Barringer, *City*, pp. 383–422.

5. Noel McGinn et al., *Education and Development in Korea* (Cambridge, Mass., 1980); Steinberg, Development, pp. 28–32; Yung-bong Kim, "Education and Economic Growth," in Chuk-kyo Kim, *Essays*, vol. 4, pp. 234–73; Mason et al., *Modernization*, pp. 222–23 and ch. 10; reports of the Central Education Research Institute, e.g.: *A Study of Compulsory Education in Korea* (Seoul, 1968), *A Comprehensive Study of the Contents of Higher Education—Faculty Development* and *Curriculum* (Seoul, 1967), and *Korean Education and Foreign Assistance Programs* (Seoul, 1965); Bom-mo Chung, *An Image of Education in Korea—a Critique* (Seoul, 1966); Meade, *American*, pp. 213–18; Murphy, *Education*; Sung-chik Hong, "A Pilot Study of the Korean Students' Values," *KA*, 2.1 (1963), 1–11; Bartz, "Higher Learning in the Third Republic," in Nahm, *Developmental*, pp. 98–127; UNESCO-UNKRA Educational Planning Mission to Korea, *Rebuilding Education in the Republic of Korea* (Paris, 1964); Hyung-jin Yoo, "On the Charter of National Education," *KQ*, 11.1 (1969), 60–66; Si-joon Yu, "Educational Institutions," in Man-gap Lee and Herbert R. Barringer, *City*, pp. 423–53; Joon-hee Park, "A Brief Review of Educational Attitudes of Korean Parents in Rural Areas,"* *JKCRI*, 19 (1972), 101–16 (Eng. summary, p. 117); Jae-un Kim, "A Study on Educational Socialization Programs by Content Analysis of Primary School Curriculum,"* *JKCRI*, 20 (1972), 119–43 (Eng. summary, pp. 144–45); Sung-il Kim, "A Study of Historical Roots of Educational Administration in the Republic of Korea," *JSSH*, no. 22 (1965), 1–25; Woong Huh and Sung-nyong Lee, "Han-gŭl and Hanmum," *KJ*, 12.4 (1972), 45–52; *KPT*, May 1, 1975.

## Chapter 11

1. Hae-jong Chun, "Dynastic Changes in China and Korea," *KJ*, 11.4 (1971), 32–36; He-sung Koh, "Religion," the summary; Jong-won Kim, *Divided*, from p. 115.

2. Palais, *Traditional*, and Ching-young Choe, *Rule*, are the key sources (see also Palais's review of Choe in *JAS*, 33.1 [1973], 130–33); Henderson, *Vortex*, pp. 60–62, has his usual stimulating views; and Yu-han Won, "An Observation on Monetary Policy of Taewongun in Power," *JSSH*, no. 39 (1974), 43–62, is useful. For comparisons see Mary C. Wright, *The Last Stand of Chinese Con-*

*servatism, the T'ung-chih Restoration, 1862–1874* (Stanford, 1957) and William Beasley, *The Meiji Restoration* (Stanford, 1972).

3. Woosung Lee, "Korean Intellectual Tradition and the Silhak School of Thought," in Hi-woong Kang, *Traditional*, pp. 105–38; Yi-sup Hong, *Identity*, ch. on Confucianism; and his "Silhak School's Criticism on Feudal System," *JSSH*, no. 20 (1964), 1–10; and his *Politico-Economic Thought of Yak-yong Chŏng, 1762–1836\** (Seoul, 1959) (Eng. summary, pp. 1–23); Hugh Walker, "The Weight of Tradition," in Yung-hwan Jo, *Response*, pp. 1–14; Ching-young Choe, *Rule*, ch. 2; Kyung-tak Kim, *A Study on Yul-gok Lee, 1536–1584\** (Seoul, 1960) (Eng. summary, pp. 1–18); Woo-keun Han, "Sung-ho Yi Ik and His Socio-Economic Views in 18th Century Korea,"\* *CH*, 20 (1959), 5–78 (Eng. summary, pp. 181–83); Chu-yŏng Song, "Yu Hyŏng-wŏn," *KJ*, 12.7 (1972), 33–39; Wŏn-gu Hwang, "An Chŏng-bok: New Discovery of Korean History," *KJ*, 13.1 (1973), 43–49; Yong-sŏp Kim, "Two Sirhak Scholars' Agricultural Reform Theories," *KJ*, 14.10 (1974), 13–26; Yu-han Wŏn, "Socio-Economic Thought of Kim Yuk," *KJ*, 15.1 (1975), 44–54; Michael C. Kalton, "An Introduction to Silhak," *KJ*, 15.5 (1975), 29–46; Chong-hong Park, "Empiricism of Ch'oe Han-gi," *KJ*, 15.6 (1975), 54–69; Jong-gyn Bag, "An Analysis of Jeng Jagiong's Reformation on Land System,"\*\* *CG*, 28 (1963), 75–111 (Eng. summary, p. 2); Kang Man'gil, *Chosŏn*, ch. 1; Yong-sŏp Kim, *Studies,\** vol. 1, ch. 1 and his "Modern Agrarian Reforms Claimed by the Reformists in 1884–1894,"\* *Dong Bang Hak Chi*, 15 (1974), 125–95. For Japanese jitsugaku see, e.g., the index to H. D. Harootunian, *Toward Restoration* (Berkeley, 1970), which provides many additional references.

4. Henderson, *Vortex*, pp. 65–71; Chong-sik Lee, *The Politics of Korean Nationalism* (Berkeley, 1963), pp. 46–98; Young-ick Lew, "An Analysis of the Reform Documents of the Kabo Reform Movement, 1894," *JSSH*, no. 40 (1974), 29–85; Yi-sup Hong, *Identity*, pp. 145–62, 234–42; Chung-hyun Ro, "A Study on Administrative Reorganization in Yi Dynasty (Korea), 1894–1910," *JSSH*, no. 28 (1968), 51–103; Byong-ik Koh, "The Role of Westerners Employed by the Korean Government in the Late Yi Dynasty," in International Conference on the Problems of Modernization in Asia, *Report*, pp. 249–60; X, Y, Z, "The Attack on the Top Knot," *Korean Repository*, 3 (1896), 263–72; Felix Moos, "Acculturation in Korea," in Nahm, *Developmental*, pp. 71–83; his *Social*; and his *Some Observations on Korean Cultural Change, 1966–1967* (USOM, Korea, 1967); Brandt, *Village*, pp. 78–85; Young-bok Koh, "A Review of Postwar Social Change in Korea," *Asian and Pacific Quarterly of Cultural and Social Affairs*, 3 (1971–72), 9–33; Hy-sop Lim, "Continuity and Change of Development Values in Korea," *KJ*, 15.10 (1975), 38–43; Thomas Ho-suck Kang, "Confucian Behavior toward the Modernization of Korea, 1864–1910," *KJ*, 13 (1973), 4–15; Jacobs, *Origin*; and his *Sociology*; Hong-ryol Ryu, "The Acceptance of Western Culture in Korea," *KO*, 1.1 (1968), 57–72; Young-ho Kim, "Yu Kil Chun's Idea of Enlightenment," *JSSH*, no. 33 (1970), 37–60.

5. Ching-young Choe, *Rule*, ch. 3; Yi Ch'ŏngwon, *Tokuhon*,\*\* pp. 179–216; Chŏn Sŏktam, *Kyŏngjaesa*; Charles Clark, *Religions*, ch. 5; Weems, *Reform*;

Young-hee Ch'oe, *A Study of Social Movements in the "Imjin Wainan"—with Righteous Army as Center*\* (Seoul, 1975) (Eng. résumé, pp. 1–6); Bok-ryong Shin, "A Study of Characteristics of the Dong-Hak Revolution (1860–1894)," *JSSH*, no. 39 (1974), 63–81; Murayama Chijun, *Gunshu*, secs. 3 and 4; Chong-sik Lee, *Politics*, from p. 119; Ki-baek Lee, "Historical View of Nationalism in Korea under Japanese Occupation," *JSSH*, no. 27 (1967), 1–18; Kim Chunbo, *Han'guk*, vol. 1; Scalapino and Lee, *Communism*, Part 1; Dae-sook Suh, *Movement*; Cumings, *Origin*, esp. ch. 10; Meade, *American*; Seok-choong Song, "Grammarians or Patriots: Struggle for the Linguistic Heritage," *KJ*, 15.7 (1975), 129–44.

### Conspectus

1. Kim Yong-sŏp, *Studies*; Kim Chunbo, *Han'guk*, vol. 2; Yŏng-mo Kim, "Social Background to Mobility of the Landlords under Japanese Imperialism in Korea," *JSSH*, no. 34 (1971), 87–109; for comparison to Japan see, e.g., Thomas C. Smith, *The Agrarian Origins of Modern Japan* (Stanford, 1959). Wansang Han, "Perception of Limited Opportunity and Self-Ability and Deviation among Urban Adolescents, a Test of the Anomie Hypothesis in Korea," *Social Science Journal*, 1 (1973), 114–23; Kwang-eil Kim, "Culture and Mental Illness in Korea," *KJ*, 14.2 (1974), 4–8; Dong-shick Rhee, "Philosophical Ground-laying for Psychotherapy and Counseling in Korea," *KJ*, 14.12 (1974), 32–37; Tae-kil Kim, "On the Difference of Values between the Old and New Generations in Korea," *KO*, 1.1 (1968), 76–90; Young-ho Lee, "The Korean People's Distributive Consciousness: An Analysis of Attitudes," *KJ*, 12.9 (1972), 17, 31–39; Man-gap Lee, "Conditions and Factors of Modernization of Korea," *KQ*, 7.4–8.1 (1965–66), 74–81; C. I. Eugene Kim and Ch'ang-boh Chee, *Aspects*, esp. the article by David Lewis Daeh Chang, "Rural and Urban Backgrounds of the Students and Their Orientations to Change," pp. 187–202; Ch'ang-gyu Ch'oe, "Concept of Loyalty and Filial Piety vs. Democracy," *KJ*, 12.6 (1972), 13–20; International Conference on the Problems of Modernization in Asia, *Report*, see esp. 61–86, 114–26, 181–96, and 241–48; Crane, *Patterns*, pp. 175–76, 183–89; Sŭng-jik Hong, "The Impact of American Culture on Korea," *KJ*, 11.7 (1971), 9–14.

# Bibliography

This bibliography is not exhaustive. It is limited to works cited in the foot-notes save for a few additional pertinent survey histories or bibliographies which are indicated thus (+). Because of space limitations, chapters from an-thologies individually cited in the footnotes are not separately listed in the bibliography, only the books themselves are. Some of the citations exist in a number of editions; reference is to the edition actually used, although in some cases this is not necessarily the one most readily available. Works in En-glish, Korean, and Japanese are distinctively listed, in that order. If English summaries or résumés—the choice of terms is the authors'—exist for works in Korean or Japanese, these are noted, though the reader is forewarned that many are hopelessly brief or inadequate. For works cited in English or by En-glish title, titles and authors' names are cited as they appear, including gram-matical errors and preferred spelling. I have decided not to reconcile the vari-ous transcriptions of authors' names especially, but to cite as they are in the material, since I assume that specialists knowledgeable in the languages can make the adjustment, while my choice will most facilitate the (solely) English reader locating the material. One caveat: Korean names are standardized ac-cording to Korean usage; that is, the family name is cited first, followed by the two given names, regardless of how they are cited. Additionally, in order to clearly differentiate family and given names for the sake of readers unfamiliar with Korean (or Japanese), the given names are joined by hyphen with the first of the two capitalized, regardless of how they appear in the case of either English works or works in Korean and Japanese cited with English titles, but the hyphen is omitted for Korean authors of material in Korean or Japanese so as to conform to current practice among Korean specialists.

## I—Books and Articles in English

Adelman, Irma, ed. *Practical Approaches to Development Planning, Korea's Second Five Year Plan*. Baltimore, 1969.

Adelman, Irma, and Sherman Robinson. *Income Distribution Policy in Developing Countries: A Case Study of Korea*. Stanford, 1978.

Agency for International Development. *Korean Irrigation*. AID Project Impact Evaluation Report, no. 12. Washington, D.C., 1980.

Ahn, Yong-sik. "Efforts of U.S. Military Government in Personnel Administration of Korea." *KO*, 4.4 (1972), 306–22.

Akiba, Takashi. "A Study of Korean Folkways." *Folklore Studies*, 16 (1957), 1–106.

Aqua, Ronald. *Local Institutions and Rural Development in South Korea*. Ithaca, 1974.

+ Asiatic Research Center, Korea University. *Bibliography of Korean Studies*. Vol. 1 (1945–58). Seoul, 1961. Vol. 2 (1959–62). Seoul, 1965.

Avineri, Shlomo. *Karl Marx on Colonialism and Modernization*. Garden City, N.Y., 1969.

Bae, Chong-keun. "Impact of the Brain Drain on Korea." *JSSH*, no. 41 (1975), 79–91.

Bae, Kyung-sook. *Women and the Law in Korea*. Seoul, 1973.

Ban, Sung-hwan, Pal-yong Moon, and Dwight Perkins. *Rural Development*. Cambridge, Mass., 1980.

Bank of Chōsen. *Economic History of Chōsen*. Seoul, 1920.

Bark, Dong-suh. "Comparison of Provincial Development Administration in Korea." *JSSH*, no. 34 (1971), 1–23.

Barringer, Herbert R. *Social Stratification and Industrialization in Korea*. ILCORK, no. 11. Seoul, 1971.

Beasley, William. *The Meiji Restoration*. Stanford, 1972.

Beegle, J. Allen, Tom W. Carroll, Dale E. Hathaway, and Byeong Do Kim. *Population, Migration, and Agricultural Labor Supply*. KASS, no. 6. Seoul, 1972.

Biernatzki, William E. et al. *Korean Catholicism in the 1970's*. Maryknoll, N.Y., 1975.

Bloomfield, Arthur I., and John P. Jensen. *Reports and Recommendations on Monetary Policy and Banking in Korea*. Seoul, 1965.

Brake, John R., Carl F. Frost, Henry E. Larzelere, George E. Rossmiller, James D. Shaffer, and Vernon L. Sorenson. *The National Agricultural Cooperative Federation, an Appraisal*. KASS, no. 1. Seoul, 1972.

Brandt, Vincent S. R. *A Korean Village, between Farm and Sea*. Cambridge, Mass., 1971.

———. "Mass Migration and Urbanization in Contemporary Korea." *Asia*, no. 20 (n.d.) 31–47.

Brown, Gilbert T. *Korean Pricing Policies and Economic Development in the 1960's*. Baltimore, 1973.

Brunner, Edward de Schwinitz. "Rural Korea: A Preliminary Survey of Economic, Social and Religious Conditions." In Jerusalem Meeting of the International Missionary Council, *The Christian Mission in Relation to Rural Problems*. Vol. 6, pp. 84–172. London, 1928.

Business Management Research Center, Korea University. *Report on Research of Commercial Banking in Korea*. Seoul, 1971.

———. *Report on Survey of Selected Manpower Problems in Korea*. Seoul, 1966.

———. *Report on the Management and Accounting Survey of the Office of Monopoly of the Republic of Korea Government*. Seoul, 1965.

Central Education Research Institute. *A Comprehensive Study of the Contents of Higher Education—Curriculum*. Seoul, 1967.

———. *Faculty Development*. Seoul, 1967.

———. *Korean Education and Foreign Assistance Programs*. Seoul, 1965.

———. *A Study of Compulsory Education in Korea*. Seoul, 1968.

Cha, Byung-kwon. *Import Substitution and Industrialization, the Korean Case*. ILCORK, no. 15. Seoul, 1971.

Cha, Ki-pyok. *The Political Implications of Industrialization in Korea*. ILCORK, no. 16. Seoul, 1971.

Chang, Byung-kil. *Korean Background Series: Religion*. Korean Overseas Information Series. Seoul, 1974.

Chang, Chu-gun. *Korean Culture, a Brief Historical Survey*. Trans. by Charles Goldberg. Korea Tourist Service. Seoul, 1975. Mimeo.

Cho, Hae-joang. "A 'Study' of Changing Rural Communities in Korea." *KJ*, 21.6 (1981), 18–25, 34.

Cho, Hyoung. "The Kin Network of the Urban Middle Class Family in Korea." *KJ*, 15.6 (1975), 22–33.

Cho, Ki-jun. "The Impact of the Opening of Korea on Its Commerce and Industry." *KJ*, 16.2 (1976), 27–44.

Cho, Yong-sam. *"Disguised Unemployment" in Underdeveloped Areas, with Special Reference to South Korean Agriculture*. Berkeley, 1963.

Ch'oe, Ch'ang-gyu. "Concept of Loyalty and Filial Piety vs. Democracy." *KJ*, 12.6 (1972), 13–20.

Choe, Ching-young. *The Rule of the Taewŏn'gun, 1864–1973*. Cambridge, Mass., 1972.

Ch'oe, Yŏng-ho. "Commoners in Early Yi Dynasty Civil Examinations: An Aspect of Korean Social Structure, 1392–1600." *JAS*, 33.4 (1974), 611–31.

Choi, Dong-hee. "Tonghak and Korean Thought." *KO*, 3.2 (1971), 26–50.

Choi, Ho-chin. *The Economic History of Korea*. Seoul, 1971.

———. "On Usury Capital in the Late Yi Dynasty." *JSSH*, no. 16 (1962), 12–22.

Choi, Suk. "The Factional Struggle in the Yi Dynasty of Korea, 1575–1725." *KQ*, 7.1 (1965), 60–91 and 7.2, 70–96.

Choi, Syn-duk, and Chae-yoon Kim. "Hyo-ri: A Traditional Clan Village." *Cultural Anthropology* (Seoul), 5 (1972), 269–312.

Chon, Pal-khn, trans. *The Canonical Textbook of Won Buddhism*. Seoul, 1971.

Choy, Bong-youn. *Korea, a History*. Tokyo, 1971.

Chun, Hae-jong. "Dynastic Changes in China and Korea." *KJ*, 11.4 (1971), 32–36.

————. "A Historical Survey of the Sino-Korean Tributary Relationship." *JSSH*, no. 25 (1966), 1–31.

Chun, Shin-yong, ed. *Buddhist Culture in Korea*. Seoul, 1974.

Chung, Bom-mo. *An Image of Education in Korea—a Critique*. Seoul, 1966.

Chung, Bom-mo, Jae-ho Cha, and Sung-jin Lee. *Boy Preference and Family Planning in Korea*. Korean Institute for Research in the Behavioral Sciences. Seoul, 1974.

Chung, Moo-nam, Mason E. Miller, and Sylvan H. Wittwer. *Agricultural Research and Guidance*. KASS, no. 5. Seoul, 1972.

Chung, Yung-moh, ed. *Financial System in Korea*. Seoul, 1974.

Clark, Allen D. *A History of the Church in Korea*. Seoul, 1971.

Clark, Charles Allen. *Religions of Old Korea*. Seoul, 1961.

Cole, David C., and Princeton N. Lyman. *Korean Development, the Interplay of Politics and Economics*. Cambridge, Mass., 1971.

Combined Economic Board, UN Command. *Kwangju-gun, a Supplementary Report*. Survey no. 5. Seoul, 1958.

————. *Vocational Survey of Seoul City Women*. Survey no. 4. Seoul, 1958.

Crane, Paul S. *Korean Patterns*. 2d ed. Seoul, 1969.

Cumings, Bruce. *The Origin of the Korean War, Liberation and the Emergence of Separate Regimes, 1945–1947*. Princeton, 1981.

Dallet, Charles. *Traditional Korea*. New Haven, 1954.

Deuchler, Martina. "Neo-Confucianism in Early Yi Korea." *KJ*, 15.5 (1975), 12–18.

Dongguk University. *Buddhism and Its Culture in Korea*. Seoul, 1964.

Eberhard, Wolfram. "Social Mobility of Businessmen in a Small Korean Town." *JSSH*, no. 16 (1962), 23–32.

EXOTECH Systems Inc. *Farm Mechanization Program in Korea*. Washington, D.C., 1972.

Federation of Korean Trade Unions. Activity Report, 1973. [Seoul?], n.d. Mimeo.

Ferris, John N., William J. Haley, Glenn L. Johnson, Young-sik Kim, Lawrence W. Libby, George E. Rossmiller, In-joon Seol, Han-hyeck Suh, and Sylvan H. Wittwer. *Investment Priorities in the Korean Agricultural Sector*. KASS. Seoul, 1972.

Fisher, James E. *Democracy and Mission Education in Korea*. Seoul, 1970.

Gasser, William R., James B. Cavin, Richard S. Magleby, Edward S. Micka, Troy Mullins, and Charles A. Breitenbach. *Planning Korea's Agricultural Development*. Foreign Economic Development Service, U.S. Dept. of Agriculture. Seoul, 1970.

Government of the Republic of Korea. *Summary of the First Five Year Economic Plan, 1962–1966*. Seoul, 1962.

————. *The Second Five Year Economic Development Plan, 1967–1971*. Seoul, 1966.

————. *The Third Five Year Economic Development Plan, 1972–1976*. Seoul, 1971.

Government-General of Tyosen. *Annual Report on Administration of Tyosen, 1937–1938*. Keizyo, 1938.

Grajdanzev, Andrew J. *Modern Korea*. New York, 1944.

Gurley, John G. *Financial and Real Aspects of South Korea's Industrial Development*. ILCORK, no. 12. Seoul, 1971.

Gurley, John G., Hugh T. Patrick, and E. S. Shaw. *The Financial Structure of Korea*. Preliminary draft. Seoul, 1965.

Hahm, Pyong-choon. *The Korean Political Tradition and Law*. Seoul, 1967.

———. "Korea's Initial Encounter with Western Law: 1866–1910 A.D." *KO*, 1.2 (1969), 80–93.

———. *Religion and Law in Korea*. Kroeber Anthropological Society Papers, no. 41. Berkeley, 1969.

Hahm, Pyong-choon, and Seung-doo Yang. *A Study of Five Decisional Outcomes Involving the Judicial Process of Korea*. Preliminary Report, 1972 (pp. 1–121), Final Report, 1973 (pp. 122–353). Seoul.

Hahn, Bae-ho, and Kyu-taik Kim. "Korean Political Leaders, 1952–1962: Their Social Origins and Skills." *Asian Survey*, 3.7 (1963), 305–23.

Hahn, Sang-joon. *Manpower Development for Industrialization in Korea*. ILCORK, no. 18. Seoul, 1971.

Ham, Eui-young. "A Study of the Political Socialization Process in Korea." *KO*, 4.4 (1972), 131–91.

Han, Ki-du. "Practical Tendency in Modern Korean Buddhism." *KJ*, 13.7 (1973), 24–28.

Han, Kee-chun. "An Analysis on the Relationship between U.S. Aid and Korea's Balance of Payments." *KO*, 1.2 (1969), 3–25.

Han, Ki-shik. "The Christian Impact and the Indigenous Responses in the 18th and 19th Century Korea." *KQ*, 10.1 (1968), 1–25.

Han, Sang-bok. "The Effects of Local Enterprise on Social Change in a Korean Fishing Village." *Cultural Anthropology* (Seoul), 5 (1972), 255–66.

Han, Sang-kuk, Yong-sun Hong, Chang-seo Park, James D. Shaffer, Won-jun Song, Kee-won Suh, and Won-ho Suh. *Organization and Performance of the Agricultural Marketing System in Korea*. KASS, no. 7. Seoul, 1972.

Han, Sung-joo. *The Failure of Democracy in South Korea*. Berkeley, 1974.

Han, Wan-sang. "A Conceptual Clarification of Mass Society: For a Better Understanding of Mass Tendencies in Korean Society." *KO*, 3.4 (1971), 3–22.

———. "Perception of Limited Opportunity and Self-Ability and Deviation among Urban Adolescents: A Test of the Anomie Hypothesis in Korea." *Social Science Journal* (Seoul), 1 (1973), 114–23.

+ Han, Woo-keun. *The History of Korea*. Honolulu, 1970.

Harootunian, H. D. *Toward Restoration: The Growth of Political Consciousness in Tokugawa Japan*. Berkeley, 1970.

Hatada, Takashi. *A History of Korea*. Santa Barbara, Calif., 1969.

Henderson, Gregory. *Korea, the Politics of the Vortex*. Cambridge, Mass., 1968.

+ Henthorn, William E. *A History of Korea*. New York, 1971.

Hirschmeier, Johannes. *The Origin of Entrepreneurship in Meiji Japan*. Cambridge, Mass., 1964.

Hollander, Edward D. *The Role of Manpower in Korean Economic Development*. Seoul, n.d.

Hong, Sun(g)-chick. "Consciousness Structure of the Korean Intellectuals." *KO*, 3.3 (1971), 26–40.

———. *The Intellectual and Modernization*. Seoul, 1967.

———. "A Pilot Study of the Korean Students' Values." *KA*, 2.1 (1963), 1.11.

Hong, Sun(g)-chick, and Bok-soo Lee. "The Expressway and the Process of Changes in Rural Villages." *Social Science Journal* (Seoul), 1 (1973), 85–113.

(as) Hong Sŭng-jik. "The Impact of America Culture on Korea." *KJ*, 11.7 (1971), 9–14.

Hong, Yi-sup. *Korea's Self Identity*. Seoul, 1971.

———. "Silhak School's Criticism on Feudal System." *JSSH*, no. 20 (1964), 1–10.

Huh, Woong, and Sung-nyong Lee. "Han-gŭl and Hanmun." *KJ*, 12.4 (1972), 45–52.

Hwang, Wŏn-gu. "An Chŏng-bok: New Discovery of Korean History." *KJ*, 13.1 (1973), 43–49.

Institute of Asian Economic Affairs. *The Developing Economies*, 4.3 (1966).

International Conference on the Problems of Modernization in Asia, June 28-July 7, 1965. *Report*. Seoul, n.d.

International Cooperation Administration, Office of Labor Affairs. *The Labor Situation in South Korea*. Washington, D.C., 1956.

Jacobs, Norman. "Economic Rationality and Social Development: An Iranian Case Study." *Studies in Comparative International Development*, 2 (1966), 137–42.

———. "The Donor-Recipient Relationship and Development: Some Lessons from the Iranian Experience." In *Accelerated Development in Southern Africa*, edited by John Barratt, Simon Brand, David S. Collier, and Kurt Glaser, pp. 595–614. London, 1974.

———. *The Origin of Modern Capitalism and Eastern Asia*. 2d ed. New York, 1981.

———. *Modernization without Development: Thailand as an Asian Case Study*. New York, 1971.

———. *The Sociology of Development: Iran as an Asian Case Study*. New York, 1966.

Janelli, Roger L. "Anthropology, Folklore and Korean Ancestor Worship." *KJ*, 15.6 (1975), 34–43.

Jeon, Sang-woon. *Science and Technology in Korea, Traditional Instruments and Techniques*. Cambridge, Mass., 1974.

Jeong, Ki-jun. "Achievement and Failures of the Korean Economy in the 1970's." *KJ*, 20.1 (1980), 12–17.

Jo, Sung-hwan, and Seong-yawng Park, eds. *Basic Documents and Selected Papers of Korea's Third Five Year Economic Development Plan (1972–1976)*. Seoul, 1972.

Jo, Yung-hwan, ed. *Korea's Response to the West*. Kalamazoo, Mich., 1970.

+ Joe, Wanne J. *Traditional Korea, a Cultural History*. Seoul, 1972.

Jones, Homer. *Korean Financial Problems*. Seoul, 1968.

Jones, Leroy P., and Sa-kong Il. *Government, Business and Entrepreneurship in Economic Development: The Korean Case*. Cambridge, Mass., 1980.

Junkin, William. "The Tong Hak." *Korean Repository*, 2 (1895), 56–60.

Kalton, Michael C. "An Introduction to Silhak." *KJ*, 15.5 (1975), 29–46.

Kang, [Hugh] Hi-woong. "The Development of the Korean Ruling Class from Late Silla to Early Koryǒ." Ph.D. diss., University of Washington, 1964.

——, ed. *The Traditional Culture and Society of Korea: Thought and Institutions*. Occasional Papers of the Center for Korean Studies, no. 5. Honolulu, 1975.

Kang, Pyung-kun. "Sub-Bureaucracy and Community Structure of the Yi Dynasty." *KO*, 2.1 (1969), 68–83.

Kang, Shin-pyo. "Fatalism in Korea." *KJ*, 15.11 (1975), 14–16.

Kang, Thomas Ho-suck. "Confucian Behavior toward the Modernization of Korea, 1864–1910." *KJ*, 13.7 (1973), 4–15.

Kim, Byong-kuk. *Central Banking Experiment in a Developing Economy*. Seoul, 1965.

Kim, C. I. Eugene, ed. *A Pattern of Political Development: Korea*. Kalamazoo, Mich., 1964.

Kim, C. I. Eugene, and Ch'ang-boh Chee, eds. *Aspects of Social Change in Korea*. Kalamazoo, Mich., n.d.

Kim, Chin. "Legal Privileges under the Early Yi Dynasty Criminal Codes." *KJ*, 15.4 (1975), 34–44 and 15.5, 19–28.

Kim, Chin-man. "Korean Thought Patterns: How Koreans Think and Solve Problems." *KQ*, 11.4 (1969–70), 67–82.

Kim, Chong-guk, and Chin-man Kim. "Some Notes on the Sǒnggung'wan." *RAS*, 38 (1961), 69–91.

Kim, Chong-sun. "The Emergence of Multi-Centered Despotism in the Silla Kingdom: A Study of the Origin of Factional Struggle in Korea." Ph.D. diss., University of Washington, 1965.

——. "The Kol'pum System: Basis for Sillan Social Stratification." *Journal of Korean Studies* (Seattle), 1.2 (1971), 43–70.

Kim, Chuk-kyo, ed. *Essays on the Korean Economy*
   Vol. 1. *Planning Model and Macroeconomic Issues*. Honolulu, 1977.
   Vol. 2. *Industrial and Social Development Issues*. Honolulu, 1977.
   Vol. 3. *Macroeconomic and Industrial Development in Korea*. Honolulu, 1980.
   Vol. 4. *Human Resources and Social Development in Korea*. Honolulu, 1980.

Kim, Dong-il. *Social Impact Assessment, Korean Irrigation Funded by USAID*. Korean Rural Economics Institute. Seoul, 1980.

Kim, Doo-hun. "The Rise of Neo-Confucianism against Buddhism in Late Koryo." *JSSH*, no. 12 (1960), 11–29.

Kim, Hyong-chun. *Financial Policies and Industrialization in Korea*. ILCORK, no. 5. Seoul, 1971.

Kim, Hyǒng-hiu. "Revolution of Consciousness among Farmers." *KJ*, 18.10 (1978), 24–26.

Kim, Jae-un. "Psychological Structure of the Korean Family." *JSSH*, no. 40 (1974), 1–27.

Kim, Father Joseph Chang-mun, and John Jae-sun Chung. *Catholic Korea, Yesterday and Today*. Seoul, 1964.

Kim, Joung-won A. *Divided Korea, the Politics of Development, 1945–1972*. Cambridge, Mass., 1975.

Kim, Jun-bo. "Conversion of Farming into Enterprise and Cooperative Forms for Agricultural Modernization." *KQ*, 9.3 (1967), 58–81.

Kim, Kwang-iel. "Culture and Mental Illness in Korea." *KJ*, 14.2 (1974), 4–8.

(as) Kim, Kwang-il. "Traditional Concept of Disease in Korea." *KJ*, 13.1 (1973), 12–18.

Kim, Kwang-suk, and Michael Roemer. *Growth and Structural Transformation*. Cambridge, Mass., 1979.

Kim, Kyong-dong. *Industrialization and Industrialism: A Comparative Perspective on Values of Korean Workers and Managers*. ILCORK, no. 1. Seoul, 1971.

Kim, Mahn-je. *Alternative Strategies for Korea's Industrialization*. Seoul, 1974.

Kim, Nak-kwan. *Is Korea's Export Promotion Scheme Consistent with Her Industrialization?* ILCORK, no. 9. Seoul, 1971.

Kim, Pung-ku. "The Image of Korean Intellectuals." *KJ*, 8.6 (1968), 17–25.

Kim, Sang-gee, and Lawrence W. Libby. *Rural Infrastructure*. KASS, no. 2. Seoul, 1972.

Kim, Se-jin. "Attitudinal Orientations of Korean Workers." *KJ*, 12.9 (1972), 18–30.

Kim, Se-jin, and Chang-hyun Cho, eds. *Government and Politics of Korea*. Silver Spring, Md., 1972.

Kim, Soo-kon. "Role and Contribution of Social Scientists in Planning National Development." *KJ*, 18.5 (1978), 33–40.

Kim, Sung-il. "A Study of Historical Roots of Educational Administration in the Republic of Korea." *JSSH*, no. 22 (1965), 1–25.

Kim, Tae-gon. "Korean Shamanism and Its Outlook on Future Life." *JSSH*, no. 39 (1974), 83–104.

(as) Kim, T'ae-gon. "Korean Folklore Data Collected Prior to the Liberation." *KJ*, 12.4 (1972), 33–39.

Kim, Tae-kil. "On the Difference of Values between the Old and New Generations in Korea." *KO*, 1.1 (1968), 76–90.

Kim, Taek-il, John A. Ross, and George C. Worth. *The Korean National Family Planning Program*. New York, 1972.

Kim, Ui-hwan. "Japanese in Pusan after Opening of Port." *JSSH*, no. 40 (1974), 87–102.

Kim, Wan-soon. *The Equalizing Effect of Financial Transfers: A Study of Intergovernmental Fiscal Relations in Korea*. Seoul, 1974.

Kim, Yong-choon. "The Essentials of Ch'ondogyo Ethics." *JSSH*, no. 38 (1973), 85–100.

Kim, Yong-ho. "The Manual Industries Prior to Korea's Opening." *JSSH*, no. 39 (1974), 1–36.

Kim, Yong-mo. "The Social Background and Mobility of State Ministers of the Yi Dynasty." *KA*, 3.2 (1964), 238–60.

————. "Social Background to Mobility of the Landlords under Japanese Imperialism in Korea." *JSSH*, no. 34 (1971), 87–109.

Kim, Yong-sŏp. "Absentee Landlord System during the 19th-20th Century in Korea." *JSSH*, no. 37 (1972), 27–63.

————. "Two Sirhak Scholars' Agricultural Reform Theories." *KJ*, 14.10 (1974), 13–26.

Kim, Young-ho. "Yu Kil Chun's Idea of Enlightenment." *JSSH*, no. 33 (1970), 37–60.

Kim, Yun-hwan. *The Korean Labor Movement in the 1960's.* ILCORK, no. 17. Seoul, 1971.

+ Knez, Eugene I., and Chang-su Swanson. *A Selected and Annotated Bibliography of Korean Anthropolgy.* Seoul, 1968. (Korean and Japanese sources.)

Koh, Byung-chul, ed. *Aspects of Administrative Development in South Korea.* Kalamazoo, Mich., 1967.

Koh, He-sung Chun. "Religion, Social Structure and Economic Development in Yi Dynasty Korea." Ph.D. diss., Boston University, 1959.

Koh, Sung-jae. "Contrasting Characteristics of Industrial Entrepreneurship in Japan, India and Korea." *JSSH*, no. 29 (1968), 16–51.

————. "The Role of the Bank of Chōsen (Korea) and the Japanese Expansion in Manchuria and China." *JSSH*, no. 32 (1970), 25–36.

————. "Studies of Korean Economic History: Review Article." *JSSH*, no. 40 (1974), 119–38.

Koh, Young-bok. "A Review of Postwar Social Change in Korea." *Asian and Pacific Quarterly of Cultural and Social Affairs*, 3 (1971–72), 9–33.

Korea Development Finance Corporation. *Money and Capital Markets in Korea and the Potential for their Improvement.* Seoul, 1970.

Korea Industrial Development Research Institute. *Survey of Government Enterprises in Korea.* Seoul, 1972.

*Korea Journal* (UNESCO, Seoul). "Buddhism in Korea." 4.5 (special number) (1964).

Korean Development Association. *A Study of Property Tax in Korea.* Seoul, 1967.

Korean Institute for Family Planning. *Population and Family Planning in the Republic of Korea.* Vol. 2. Seoul, 1974.

Korean Overseas Information Service. *Saemaŭl Undong* [New Community Movement]. Seoul, 1973.

Korean Social Science Research Institute. *Report on Field Study in Employment and Income Pattern of Farm Household in Rural Community in Korea.* Seoul, 1969.

*Korean Studies Today.* Seoul, 1970.

*Koreana Quarterly.* Special Issue on the Fourth Republic. 14.4 (1972–74).

Krader, Lawrence. *The Asiatic Mode of Production.* Assen, The Netherlands, 1975.

Krueger, Ann. *The Developmental Role of the Foreign Sector and Aid.* Cambridge, Mass., 1979.

Kuznets, P. W. *Korea's Emerging Industrial Structure*. ILCORK, no. 6. Seoul, 1971.

Kwon, Ik-whan. "Japanese Industrialization on Korea, 1930-1945: Idealism or Realism?" *KQ*, 8.2 (1966), 80–95.

Kyu, Kang C. "The Influence of 'Ke' Societies upon Ri-Dong Agricultural Co-operative Association." In *Small Farmer Credit, Informal Credit, A.I.D. Spring Review of Small Farmer Credit*. Vol. 15 (June 1973). Washington, D.C., 1973.

Larkin, F. L. *Report on Public Relations for Korea Electric Company*. Seoul, 1966.

Larson, Adlowe L., and Helim H. Hulbert. *Study of Agricultural Cooperatives in Korea*. Seoul, 1966.

Lee, Chae-jin. *Labor Movement and Political Development in Korea*. ILCORK, no. 2. Seoul, 1971.

Lee, Chang-nyol. *Mobilization of Domestic Capital*. Seoul, 1965.

Lee, Chong-sik. *The Politics of Korean Nationalism*. Berkeley, 1963.

Lee, Hahn-been. *Korea: Time Change and Administration*. Honolulu, 1968.

———. "The Role of the Higher Civil Service under Rapid Social and Political Change." In Edward W. Weidner, ed., *Development Administration in Asia*, pp. 107–31. Durham, N.C., 1970.

Lee, Hong-jik. "The Tan'gun Myth and the National Consciousness." *KQ*, 1.2 (1960), 103–14.

Lee, Hoon K. *Land Utilization and Rural Economy in Korea*. Chicago, 1936.

Lee, Hwa-soo. "A Study of Political Socialization Process: Family Political Efficacy and Legitimacy: The Case of Secondary School Students in Korea." *KQ*, 10.2 (1968), 156–97.

Lee, Hyo-chai. *Industrialization and the Family in Korea*. ILCORK, no. 8. Seoul, 1971.

———. "Patterns of Change Observed in the Korean Marriage Institution." *JSSH*, no. 26 (1967), 34–55.

(as) Lee, Hyo-jae. "Life in Urban Korea." *RAS*, 46 (1971), 21–33.

Lee, Hyoun-young. "A Geographic Study of the Korean Periodic Markets." *KJ*, 15.8 (1975), 12–24.

Lee, Jang-hyun, George Won, and In-hwan Oh. "The Korean Lawyer." *JKCRI*, 20 (1972), 405–29.

Lee, Ki-baek. "Confucian Political Ideology in the Silla Unification and Early Koryo Periods." *JSSH*, no. 42 (1975), 1–23.

———. "Historical View of Nationalism in Korea under Japanese Occupation." *JSSH*, no. 27 (1967), 1–18.

Lee, Ki-young [see also Rhi, Ki-young]. "Buddhism and Modern Man." *KJ*, 7.10 (1967), 10–16.

Lee, Kie-wook. *A Study of the Determinants of Farm Income in Korea*. Seoul, 1972.

Lee, Kwang-kyu. *Kinship System in Korea*. 2 vols. New Haven, 1975.

Lee, Kwang-rin. "Census Taking under the Yi Dynasty." *RAS*, 35 (1959), 33–50.

Lee, Kyu-hwan. "A Study of Democracy as Manifested in Every Day Behavior of Korean Students." *JKCRI*, 19 (1972), 309–24.

Lee, Man-gab. "Korean Village Politics and Leadership." *KA*, 1.4 (1962), 328–412.

(as) Lee, Man-gap [see also Yi, Man-gap]. "Conditions and Factors of Modernization of Korea." *KQ*, 7.4-8.1 (1965–66), 74–81.

———. "National Characteristics of Korea and Japan and Their Social Background." *KQ*, 7.4–8.1 (1965–66), 86–87.

Lee, Man-gap, and Herbert R. Barringer, eds. *A City in Transition: Urbanization in Taegu, Korea.* Seoul, 1971.

Lee, Nam-young. "Tan'gun Myth and the Korean Thought." *KJ*, 16.4 (1976), 35–44.

Lee, Peter H. *Lives of Eminent Korean Monks.* Cambridge, Mass., 1969.

Lee, Sung-nyong, ed. See *Korean Studies Today.*

Lee, Won-sul. "The Embryo of Korean Bureaucracy in 1945." *KQ*, 7.3 (1976), 32–49.

Lee, Young-ho. "The Korean People's Distributive Consciousness: An Analysis of Attitudes." *KJ*, 12.9 (1972), 17, 31–39.

Leverrier, Roger. "Buddhism and Ancestral Religious Beliefs in Korea." *KJ*, 12.5 (1972), 37–42.

Lew, Young-ick. "An Analysis of the Reform Documents of the Kabo Reform Movement, 1894." *JSSH*, no. 40 (1974), 29–85.

Lichtheim, George. *The Concept of Ideology and Other Essays.* New York, 1967.

Lim, Hy-sop. "Continuity and Change of Development Values in Korea." *KJ*, 15.10 (1975), 38–43.

Lim, Jong-chul. "Economic Development in Korea and U.S. Economic Missions' Reports and Advice." *KQ*, 9.4 (1967), 41–54.

Lyons, Gene M. *Military Policy and Economic Aid, the Korean Case, 1950–1953.* Columbus, Ohio, 1963.

McCloy, John J., Nathan W. Pearson, and Beverley Matthews. *The Great Oil Spill.* New York, 1976.

McGinn, Noel, Donald R. Snodgrass, Yung-bong Kim, Shin-bok Kim, and Quee-young Kim. *Education and Development in Korea.* Cambridge, Mass., 1980.

Mandel, Edgar J. *Cast Coinage of Korea.* Racine, Wis., 1972.

Marx, Karl. *Pre-Capitalist Economic Formations.* Translated by Jack Cohen with introduction by Eric Hobsbawn. London, 1964.

Mason, Edward, Mahn-je Kim, Dwight Perkins, Kwang-suk Kim, and David Cole. *The Economic and Social Modernization of the Republic of Korea.* Cambridge, Mass., 1980.

Meade, E. Grant. *American Military Government in Korea.* New York, 1951.

Medium Industry Bank. *Financing Small Industry in Korea.* Seoul, 1968.

Mehren, George L. *Preliminary Analysis of the Third Five Year Plan for the Agricultural Sector, Republic of Korea.* Agribusiness Council. New York, 1969.

Mills, Edwin S., and Byung-nak Song. *Urbanization and Urban Problems.* Cambridge, Mass., 1979.

Ministry of Education, ROK. *Education in Korea.* Seoul, 1972.

Ministry of Health and Social Affairs, ROK. *Population and Family Planning in the Republic of Korea*. Vol. 1. Seoul, 1976.

Ministry of Public Information, ROK. *Mass Communication*. Seoul, n.d.

Ministry of Reconstruction, ROK. *Community Development in Korea*. Seoul, 1961.

Mitchell, Clyde. *Final Report and History of the New Korea Co*. Hdq. U.S. Army Military Government in Korea, 1948.

————. Land Reform in South Korea. n.p. 1949. Mimeo.

Mitchell, John L., and John Hyun Kim. *Survey of Mass Communication in Korea, 1968*. Seoul, 1968.

Moon, Pal-young. *A Brief Review of the Evolution of Rice Policy in Korea*. Seoul, 1974.

Moos, Felix. *Some Observations on Korean Cultural Change, 1966–1967*. USOM, Korea, 1967.

————. *Social Science Factors and Considerations in Korean Rural Development*. USOM, [Seoul?], Korea, 1965.

Moose, J. Robert. *Village Life in Korea*. Nashville, Tenn., 1911.

Morrow, Robert B., and Kenneth H. Sherper. *Land Reform in South Korea*. In *A.I.D. Spring Review of Land Reform*. Vol. 3 (June 1970). Washington, D.C., 1970.

Morrow, Robert B., Kenneth H. Sherper, and Paul E. White. *Farm Credit in Korea*. In *Small Farm Credit in Asia, A.I.D. Spring Review of Small Farm Credit*. Vol. 11 (1973). Washington, D.C., 1973.

Murphy, Jay. *Legal Education in a Developing Nation: The Korea Experience*. Seoul, 1967.

Murphy, Jay, Shi-yun Lee, Alberta B. Murphy, Tai-ro Lee, Tai-joon Kwon, and Choong-hyun Paik. *Legal Profession in Korea: The Judicial Scrivener and Others*. Seoul, 1967.

Musgrave, R. A. *Revenue Policy for Korea's Economic Development*. Seoul, 1965.

Nahm, Andrew C., ed. *Korea under Japanese Colonial Rule*. Kalamazoo, Mich., 1973.

————. *Studies in the Developmental Aspects of Korea*. Kalamazoo, Mich., 1969.

Nakane, Chie, and Goto Akira, eds. *The Symposium on Family and Religion in East Asian Countries, Tokyo, June 18–20, 1971*. East Asian Cultural Studies, 11, nos. 1–4. Tokyo, 1972.

Nathan, Robert J., Associates. *Preliminary Report on Economic Reconstruction of Korea*. New York, 1952.

National Agricultural Cooperative Federation. *Agricultural Cooperatives in Korea*. Seoul, 1975.

————. *Rural Credit Survey in Korea, 1965*. Seoul, 1966.

————. Research Dept. *The Evaluation of Success of the Primary Cooperatives in Korea*. Seoul, 1971.

Nez, George. *Evaluation of Metropolitan Planning Practice in Korea*. Seoul, 1968.

Ogle, George. "Development of the Korean Labor Movement." Master's thesis, University of Wisconsin, 1966.

Oh, John Kil-chiang. *Korea: Democracy on Trial*. Ithaca, 1968.

Oh, Young-kyun. "Agrarian Reform and Economic Development: A Case Study of Korean Agriculture." *KQ*, 9.2 (1967), 91–137.

Osgood, Cornelius. *The Koreans and Their Culture*. New York, 1951.

Paik, Lak-geoon George. *The History of Protestant Missions in Korea, 1832–1910*. Seoul, 1970.

Pak, Ki-hyuk. "Economic Analysis of Land Reform in the Republic of Korea, with Special Reference to an Agricultural Economic Survey, 1954–55." Ph.D. diss., University of Illinois, 1956.

———. *A Study of Land Tenure System in Korea*. Seoul, 1966.

Pak, Ki-hyuk, and Seung-yun Lee. *Three Clan Villages in Korea: Socio-economic Study, 1961–1962*. Seoul, 1963.

Palais, James B. *Politics and Policy in Traditional Korea*. Cambridge, Mass., 1975.

———. Review of "The Rule of the Taewŏn'gun, 1864–1873" by Ching-young Choe. *JAS*, 33.1 (1973), 130–33.

———. *Occasional Papers on Korea*. Joint Committee on Korean Studies of the American Council of Learned Societies and the Social Science Research Council, nos. 1–2 (1974).

Palais, James B., and Margery D. Lang. *Occasional Papers on Korea*. Joint Committee on Korean Studies of the American Council of Learned Societies and the Social Science Research Council, nos. 3–5 (1975–77).

Palmer, Spencer J. *Korea and Christianity*. Seoul, 1967.

———, ed. "The New Religions of Korea." *RAS*, 43 (1967).

———, ed. *Studies in Asian Genealogy*. Provo, Utah, 1972.

Park, Byong-ho. "The Legal Nature of Land Ownership in the Yi Dynasty." *KJ*, 15.10 (1975), 4–10.

———. "Social Castes and Legal Rights under the Modern Korean Law." *KQ*, 4.2 (1962), 35–44.

———. "Traditional Korean Society and Law." Reprinted from *Seoul Law Journal*, 15.1 (n.d.), 107–34.

Park, Chong-hong. "Empiricism of Ch'oe Han-gi." *KJ*, 15.6 (1975), 54–69.

Park, Chung-hee. *Our Nation's Path, Ideology of Social Reconstruction*. Seoul, 1962.

Park, Moon-ok. "Urban Land Value and Taxation—the Case of Korea." *KO*, 3.1 (1970), 62–78.

Park, Sang-yŏl. "The Social Structure of a Korean Village under the Control of Consanguinity." *JSSH*, no. 27 (1967), 70–98.

Park, Won-sun. "Korean Factor." *JSSH*, no. 35 (1971), 64–84.

———. "The Merchant System Peculiar to Korea." *JSSH*, no. 26 (1967), 100–113.

Park, Young-ki. "Unionism and Labor Legislation in Korea." *KO*, 1.2 (1969), 94–102.

Parsons, Kenneth H. Issues in Land Tenure Policy for Korea. Seoul, 1965. Mimeo.

Peterson, Mark. "Adoption in Korean Genealogies: Continuation of Lineage." *KJ*, 14.1 (1974), 28–35, 45.

Pratt, James Bissett. *The Pilgrimage of Buddhism*. New York, 1928.

Prunner, Gernot. "The Birthday of God: A Sacrifice Service of Chŭnsan'gyo." *KJ*, 16.3 (1976), 12–26.

Reeve, W. D. *The Republic of Korea: A Political and Economic Study*. Oxford, 1963.

Renaud, Bertrand. *Regional Policy and Industrial Location in Korea*. ILCORK, no. 7. Seoul, 1971.

Rhee, Dong-shick. "Philosophical Ground-laying for Psychotherapy and Counseling in Korea." *KJ*, 14.12 (1974), 32–37.

Rhi, Ki-yong. "Wŏnhyo and His Thought." *KJ*, 11.1 (1971), 4–9, 14.

(as) Rhi, Ki-young. "Won Hyo's Moral Concepts." *KO*, 1.2 (1969), 103–15.

Rhie, Sang-il. "Dramatic Aspect of Shamanistic Rituals." *KJ*, 15.7 (1975), 23–28.

Ro, Chung-hyun. "A Study on Administrative Reorganization in Yi Dynasty (Korea), 1894–1910." *JSSH*, no. 28 (1968), 51–103.

Romoli, Douglas. "Female Shamans of Seoul." *Asian Pacific Quarterly of Cultural and Social Affairs*, 3 (1971–72), 64–69.

Rutt, Richard. "The Chinese Learning and Pleasures of a Country Scholar." *RAS*, 36 (1960), 1–100.

Ryu, Hong-ryol. "The Acceptance of Western Culture in Korea." *KO*, 1.1 (1968), 57–72.

Ryu, Tong-shik. "The World of 'Kut' and Korean Optimism." *KJ*, 13.8 (1973), 13–20.

Sae, Kim-jung. *The Evolution of the Financial Structure for Industrialization*. IL-CORK, no. 13. Seoul, 1971.

Scalapino, Robert A., and Chŏng-sik Lee. *Communism in Korea*. Part 1, *The Movement*. Berkeley, 1972.

Seo, Kyung-bo. "Characteristics of Korean Zen." *KJ*, 12.5 (1972), 29–36.

Seok, Seh-kyun, and Yun-sook Lee. *Kwangju Gun Survey*. UN Command, 1958.

Seoul Municipal College of Agriculture. *An Economic Analysis of Upland Cropping Patterns*. Seoul, 1969.

Seoul National University, College of Agriculture. *Economic Analysis of Double Cropping in Paddy Fields*. Seoul, 1967.

"Seven Months among the Tonghaks." *Korean Repository*, 2 (1895), 201–8.

Shaw, Edward S. *Financial Patterns and Policies in Korea*. Seoul, 1967.

Shaw, William. "Traditional Korean Law: A New Look." *KJ*, 13.9 (1973), 40–53.

Shim, Moon-taik. *Research and Development and Industrialization in Korea*. IL-CORK, no. 19. Seoul, 1971.

Shim, Young-kim. *Marketing of Rice and Other Grains in Suwon, Report of a Field Survey, 1965–67*. Suwon, 1968.

Shin, Bok-ryong. "A Study of Characteristics of the Dong-Hak Revolution (1860–1894)." *JSSH*, no. 39 (1974), 63–81.

Shin, Doh-chull. "Socio-economic Development and Democratization in South Korea: A Time-Series Analysis." Ph.D. diss., University of Illinois, 1972.

Shin, Woong-shik. *Comparative Analysis of Korean and American Judicial Systems.* Chicago, 1974.

Shin, Yong-ha. "Land Tenure System in Korea, 1910–45." *Social Science Journal* (Seoul), 1 (1973), 65–84.

Smith, Thomas C. *The Agrarian Origins of Modern Japan.* Stanford, 1959.

Smith, Warren W., Jr. *Confucianism in Modern Japan.* Tokyo, 1959.

Sŏ, Kyŏng-su. "The Present Situation of Korean Buddhism." *KJ*, 11.5 (1971), 15–20.

Sogang University, Research Institute for Economics and Business. *A Study of Money Market and Industrial Investment Finance in Korea.* Seoul, 1970.

Sohn, Pow-key. "The Concept of History and Korean Yangban." *International Journal of Korean Studies* (Yonsei University), 1 (1973), 91–113.

———. "Social History of the Early Yi Dynasty, 1392–1592; with Emphasis on the Functional Aspects of Government Structure." Ph.D. diss., University of California, Berkeley, n.d.

+ Sohn, Pow-key, Chol-choon Kim, and Yi-sup Hong. *The History of Korea.* Seoul, 1970.

Sok, Do-ryun. "Modern Son Buddhism in Korea." *KJ*, 5.1 (1965), 26–30.

Song, Byung-nak. *The Distribution and Movement of Jobs and Industry—the Case of the Seoul Metropolitan Region.* Seoul, 1974.

Song, Chu-yŏng. "Yu Hyŏng-wŏn." *KJ*, 12.7 (1972), 33–39.

Song, Seok-choong. "Grammarians or Patriots: Struggle for the Linguistic Heritage." *KJ*, 15.7 (1975), 29–44.

Starr, Frederick. *Korean Buddhism.* Boston, 1918.

Steinberg, David I. The Economic Development of Korea, Sui Generis or Generic? AID Evaluation Special Study no. 6. Washington, D.C., 1982. Mimeo.

———. "Law, Development and Korean Society." *KQ*, 13.3 (1971), 43–80.

Steinberg, David I., Robert I. Jackson, Kwan S. Kim, and Hae-kyun Song. Korean Agricultural Research, the Integration of Research and Extension. Washington, D.C., 1981. Mimeo.

Strand, Norman. *Revue and Recommendation on Collection and Handling of Farm Statistics in the Ministry of Agriculture and Forestry.* Seoul, 1969.

Suh, Dae-Sook. *The Korean Communist Movement, 1918-1948.* Princeton, 1967.

Suh, Sang-chul. *Growth and Structural Changes in the Korean Economy, 1910–1940.* Cambridge, Mass., 1978.

Sveda, Russell J. Regional Planning Efforts in the Republic of Korea. Seoul, 1972. Mimeo.

Taylor, Philip H., and Donald McDonald. "Military Government Experience in Korea." In Carl J. Friedrich et al. *American Experiences in Military Government in World War II.* New York, 1948.

Toby, Ronald. *State and Diplomacy in Early Modern Japan.* Princeton, 1984.

Tökei, Ferenc. *Essays on the Asiatic Mode of Production.* Budapest, 1979.

Turner, Bryan S. *Marx and the End of Orientalism.* London, 1978.

UNESCO-UNKRA, Educational Planning Mission to Korea. *Rebuilding Education in the Republic of Korea*. Paris, 1954.

USAID/Korea. *Korean Agriculture Food Grain Subsector: Supply and Demand, Farm Mechanization, Storage and Fertilizer*. Seoul, 1971.

U.S. House of Representatives, Committee on Foreign Affairs, Subcommittee on Asian and Pacific Affairs and International Organizations and Movements. *Human Rights in South Korea: Implications for U.S. Policy, Hearings*. 93d Cong., 2d sess., 1974.

U.S. House of Representatives, Committee and Subcommittee on International Relations. *Investigation of Korean-American Relations, Hearings (seven parts) and Report*. 95th Cong., 2d sess., 1977–78.

U.S. Operations Mission to Korea. *Rural Development Program Evaluation Report*. Seoul, 1967.

————. *Third Interim Program*. Seoul, 1967.

Unruh, Ellen. "The Landowning Slave: A Korean Phenomenon." *KJ*, 16.4 (1976), 27–34.

Urban Population Studies Center, School of Public Health, Seoul National University. *The Progress and Findings of the Urban Slum Population Study, an Interim Report*. Seoul, 1966.

Wade, James, ed. "Mass Communication in a Developing Korea." *RAS*, 45 (1969).

Wade, L. L., and B. S. Kim. *Economic Development of South Korea, the Political Economy of Success*. New York, 1978.

Wagner, Edward W. *The Literati Purges: Political Conflict in Early Yi Korea*. Cambridge, Mass., 1974.

Weber, Max. *Economy and Society*. Vol. 3. New York, 1968.

Weems, Benjamin. *Reform, Rebellion and the Heavenly Way*. Tucson, 1964.

Westphal, Larry E., and Kwang-suk Kim. *Industrial Policy and Development in Korea*. IBRD Staff Working Paper, no. 263. Washington, D.C., 1977.

Wittfogel, Karl A. *Oriental Despotism*. New Haven, 1957.

————. *Wirtschaft und Gesellschaft Chinas*. Leipzig, 1931.

WNET (New York), The MacNeil-Lehrer Report. "Korea and Congress: The Scandal So Far." Script for June 20, 1977 telecast.

Won, George, In-hwan Oh, and Jang-hyun Lee. "Korean Private Law Practitioner." *JSSH*, no. 35 (1971), 1–10.

Won, George, and Jang-hyun Lee. "The Korean Lawyer: A General Profile." *JSSH*, no. 30 (1969), 107–16.

Won, Yu-han. "An Observation on Monetary Policy of Taewongun in Power." *JSSH*, no. 39 (1974), 43–62.

————. "Socio-Economic Thought of Kim Yuk." *KJ*, 15.1 (1975), 44–54.

————. "A Study on the Circulation of Coin in the Latter Period of the Chosun Dynasty." *KO*, 6.2 (1975), 166–85.

Won Buddhism, Hdq. *Manual of Won Buddhism*. Iri City, Korea, n.d.

Woo, Byung-kyu, and Chong-lim Kim. *Legislative Recruitment and Political Representation in South Korea*. Iowa City, 1970.

Wright, Edward R., Jr., ed. *Korean Politics in Transition*. Seattle, 1975.

Wright, Mary C. *The Last Stand of Chinese Conservatism, the T'ung-chih Restoration, 1862–1874*. Stanford, 1957.

X.Y.Z. "The Attack on the Top Knot." *Korean Repository*, 3 (1896), 263–72.

Yang, Key P., and Gregory Henderson. "An Outline History of Korean Confucianism." *JAS*, 18.1 (1958), 81–101 and 18.2 (1959), 259–76.

Yi, Ch'un-yŏng. "A History of Agricultural Techniques in Korea." *KJ*, 14.1 (1974), 21–27.

Yi, Kyu-tae. *Modern Transformation of Korea*. Seoul, 1970.

Yi, Man-gap. "Socio-Cultural Aspects of the Community Development Movement in Korea." *KJ*, 13.1 (1973), 25–33.

Yoo, Hoon. "Social Background of Higher Civil Servants in Korea." *KQ*, 10.1 (1968), 34–55.

Yoo, Hyung-jin. "On the Charter of National Education." *KQ*, 11.1 (1969), 60–66.

———. "Private Educational Institution in Korea, a Study of the Sŏwon System." *KQ*, 3.1 (1961), 126–59.

Yoo, Jong-hae. "A Study of Korean Local Government under Japanese Rule; Pu and Myon Systems." *KO*, 4.3 (1972), 205–15.

Yoo, Won-dong. "A Study of Privileged Manufactures in the Latter Period of the Yi Dynasty." *JSSH*, no. 38 (1973), 1–18.

Yoon, Hyoung-sup. "Party Systems in the Stage of Nation Building: U.S. vs. Korea." *KO*, 5.1 (1973), 3–41.

Yun, Sung-bum. "Korean Christianity and Ancestor Worship." *KJ*, 13.2 (1973), 17–21.

Yun, Young-koo. "Factors Affecting Mate Selection in Korea." *JSSH*, no. 17 (1962), 24–45.

## II—Books and Articles in Korean

*A—Works with English Titles*

An, Ke-hyun. "On the Buddhist Priesthood in the Koryo Dynasty." *Tong Gook Sa Hak*, no. 5 (1957), 95–105.

Bark, Dong-suh. *A Historical Development of the Bureaucracy in Korea* (Eng. résumé, pp. 1–14). Seoul, 1961.

Ch'oe, Hojin. "A Study of Labor-Forces in the Lee Dynasty." *Commemorative Theses, Thirtieth Anniversary, Chungang University*. Seoul, 1955, pp. 1–22.

Ch'oe, Young-hee. *A Study of Social Movements in the "Imjin Wainan"—with Righteous Army as Center* (Eng. résumé, pp. 1-6). Seoul, 1975.

Choi, Jai-seuk. "Changes in Korean Family Values." *CH*, 28 (1965), 135–90 (Eng. summary, pp. 191–92).

———. "Composition of Korean Family Members." *CH*, 24 (1963), 101–27 (Eng. summary, pp. 128–30).

———. "The Institution of Inheritance during the Yi Dynasty: An Analysis of Inheritance Records." *YH*, nos. 53–54 (1972), 98–148 (Eng. summary, pp. 149–50).

————. *Studies on Korean Rural Community* (Eng. résumé, pp. 605–18). Seoul, 1975.

————. *A Study of the Korean Family* (Eng. résumé, pp. 1–50). Seoul, 1966.

Chung, Choong-ryang, and Hyo-chai Lee. "Study of Women's Occupations and Labor Problems during the Japanese Government." *JKCRI*, 22 (1973), 307–43 (Eng. table of contents only, p. 344).

Han, Woo-keun. "A Study on the Government vis-a-vis Policy Buddhist Influence and Belief in Korea, from the Late Koryŏ Dynasty to the Early Yi Dynasty." *USCT*, 6 (1957), 1–80.

————. "Sung-ho Yi Ik and His Socio-Economic Views in 18th Century Korea." *CH*, 20 (1959), 5–78 (Eng. summary, pp. 181–83).

Hong, Sung-jik. *A Survey of Korean Values* (Eng. summary, pp. 341–55). Seoul, 1962.

Hong, Yi-sup. *The Politico-Economic Thought of Yak-yong Chŏng, 1762–1836* (Eng. summary, pp. 1–23). Seoul, 1959.

Kang, Man-gil. "A Study of Artisans in the First Half of the Lee Dynasty." *Sahak Yuenku*, no. 12 (1961), 1–72 (Eng. summary, pp. 129–30).

Kim, Byung-ha. *A Study of the Trade between Korea and Japan during the Early Yi Dynasty* (Eng. résumé, pp. 193–203). Seoul, 1969.

Kim, C. S. *A Study of Marriage and Divorce in the New Civil Code of Korea* (Eng. summary, pp. 1–22). Seoul, 1958.

Kim, Doo-jong. "The Study of the Women-Doctor's Institution during the Yi Dynasty." *Journal of Asian Women*, 1 (1962), 1–15 (Eng. summary, pp. 15–16).

Kim, Eun-woo. *A Study of Korean Woman's Inner Conflict* (Eng. résumé, pp. 1–9). Seoul, 1963.

Kim, Jae-un. "A Study on Educational Socialization Programs by Content Analysis of Primary School Curriculum." *JKCRI*, 20 (1972), 119–43 (Eng. summary, pp. 144–45).

Kim, Kwang-iel. "Folk Psychiatry in Korea, II." *Cultural Anthropology*, (1972), 79–105 (Eng. résumé, pp. 105–6).

Kim, Kyung-tak. *A Study on Yul-gok Lee, 1536–1584* (Eng. summary, pp. 1–18). Seoul, 1960.

Kim, Taik-kyoo. *The Cultural Structure of a Consanguineous Village* (Eng. résumé, pp. 1–52). Seoul, 1964.

Kim, Too-hun. *Study on the Family System in Korea* (Eng. table of contents only). Seoul, 1949.

Kim, Yong-mo. "A Study on the Educational Opportunity and Social Class in Korea." *CH*, 35 (1973), 121–65 (Eng. summary, pp. 174–75).

Kim, Yong-sŏp. "Modern Agrarian Reforms Claimed by the Reformists in 1884–1894." *Dong Bang Hak Chi*, 15 (1974), 125–95.

————. *Studies in the Agrarian History of the Late Yi Dynasty* (Eng. table of contents only). 2 vols. Seoul, 1971. Reviewed in English by Yong-ho Kim, *JSSH*, 34 (1971), 149–53.

Kim, Yun-hwan. *A Study of Labor Problems in Korea* (Eng. résumé, pp. 353–66). Seoul, 1971.

Ko, Hwang-yŏng, Hyo-jae Yi, Man-gap Yi, and Haeyŏng Yi. *A Study of Korean Rural Family* (Eng. résumé, pp. 257–79). Seoul, 1963.

Koh, Sung-chai. "The Decline of the Cotton Industry at the Close of the Yi Dynasty" (Eng. summary, pp. 203–5). *Journal of Social Sciences* (Seoul), no. 2 (1958), 99–129.

Koo, Byung-sak. "A Study on the History of Law in Korea." *Woo Sok University Journal*, 1 (1967), 295–421 (Eng. summary, pp. 422–25).

Kwak, Sang-soo. *A Study of Taxation in Korea* (Eng. résumé, pp. 231–33). Seoul, 1961.

Lee, Chun-yung. *A History of Agricultural Technology in the Yi Dynasty* (Eng. résumé, pp. 1–5). Seoul, 1964.

Lee, Hi-dok. "Koryo's Criminal Law and the Ideals of Filial Piety." *YH*, no. 58 (1973), 77–103 (Eng. summary, p. 104).

Lee, Ki-baik. *Studies in Silla Politico-Social History* (Eng. summary, pp. 310–21). Seoul, 1974.

———. *Studies on the Koryŏ Military System* (Eng. summary, pp. 299–312). Seoul, 1968. (Reviewed by Chin-chol Kang in *JSSH*, no. 29 [1968], 118–120 —in English.)

Lee, Kwang-kyu. "Rural Development and Role of Leadership." *Cultural Anthropology*, 5 (1972), 151–93 (Eng. summary, p. 194).

Lee, Kwang-rin. *History of Irrigation in the Yi Dynasty* (Eng. summary, pp. 169–83). Seoul, 1961.

Lee, Man-gap. *The Social Structure of Korean Village and Its Changes* (Eng. summary, pp. 357–93). Seoul, 1973.

Lee, Sang-beck. "On the Ch'onja Sumo Classification of Status Relates to Slave in Inter-marriage between the 'Free' and the 'Slave.'" *CH*, 25–27 (1964), 155–83 (Eng. summary, pp. 482–85).

Lee, Sang-ok. "Society in the Middle Age of Koryo and Neo-Confucianism." *Woo Sok University Journal*, 1 (1967), 1–45 (Eng. summary, p. 46).

Lee, U-song. "A Study on Paik-song of the Koryŏ Dynasty." *YH*, no. 14, (1961), 25–44.

Lee, Woo-chul. "A Consideration on the Eunuch in the Koryeo Dynasty." *Sahak Yuenku*, no. 1 (1958), 18–44 (Eng. summary, pp. 140–41).

Min, Byong-ha. "On the Military Officials of Government during the Koryeo Dynasty." *Sahak Yuenku*, no. 6 (1959), 27–68 (Eng. summary, pp. 110–12).

Moon, Byong-jip. *A Study on Village in Korea* (Eng. summary, pp. 191–203). Seoul, 1973.

Park, Byeong-ho. *A Study on the Legal History of Korea* (Eng. summary, pp. 133–47). Seoul, 1960.

Park, Joon-hee. "A Brief View of the Educational Attitudes of Korean Parents in Rural Areas." *JKCRI*, 19 (1972), 101–16 (Eng. summary, p. 117).

Park, Won-sun. *Kaekju (Factors)* (Eng. résumé, pp. 317–57). Seoul, 1968.

———. *Pubosang, a Study on Native Korean Merchant* (Eng. résumé, pp. 1–22). Seoul, 1965.

Pyon, Tae-sup. *Studies in the Political System of Koryo Dynasty* (Eng. table of contents only, p. 10). Seoul, 1974.

Ree, Jong-ha. *Labour Legislation in Josun Dynasty* (Eng. summary, pp. 1–4). Seoul, 1969.

Roh, Chang-shub. *A Study of a Residential Community in Seoul* (Eng. résumé, pp. 173–89). Seoul, 1964.

Ryu, Kyo-song. "A Study of the Busang Guild during the Period of the Yi Dynasty." *YH*, 17–18 (1962), 385–412 (Eng. summary, pp. 710–11).

(as) Ryu, Kyo-sung. "A Study on Ryukichun in Seoul: The Character of City Commerce in Yi Dynasty." *YH*, no. 8 (1955), 377–434.

Suh, Il-kyo. *A Study on the Criminal Law and Procedure of the Chosun (Yi) Dynasty (1392–1910)* (Eng. summary, pp. 1–21). Seoul, 1968.

Wŏn, Yu-han. *A Study of the Monetary History of the Latter Period of the Chosŏn Dynasty* (Eng. résumé, pp. 1–4). Seoul, 1975.

Yang, Hoe-su. *A Study on the Structure of the Korean Farming Village* (Eng. résumé, pp. 609–16). Seoul, 1967.

Yi, Hi-dok. "A Study on the Development of the Thought of Filial Piety in the Koryo Dynasty." *YH*, no. 55 (1972), 37–70 (Eng. summary, pp. 71–72).

Yi, Tai-chin. "Discriminating System for the Descendants of Concubines in the Early Yi Dynasty." *YH*, no. 27 (1965), 65–104 (Eng. summary, p. 180).

Yoo, Won-dong. *History of Commerce and Industry in the Latter Period of the Yi Dynasty* (Eng. résumé, pp. 247–57). Seoul, 1968.

Yu, Hoon. "Perception of Villagers on Community Development Activities in Korea." *Korean Journal of Public Administration*, 9.2 (1971), 83–99.

Yu, Kyo-song. "Organization and Function of the Peddler Merchants in the Late Yi Dynasty, as Seen in Chung-chong U-do." *YH*, no. 10 (1958), 167–96.

*B—Works with Korean Titles*

Chŏn, Sŏktam. *Chosŏn Kyŏngjaesa.* Seoul, 1949.

———. *Ilcheha ŭi Chosŏn Sahoe Kyŏngjaesa.* Seoul, 1947.

———, Pak Kŭngch'ae, Pak Sihyŏng, and Kim Hanju. *Chosŏn Sahoe Kyŏngjaesa.* Seoul, 1946. Mimeo.

Ham, Sŏkhŏn. *Ttŭsŭro Bon Han'guk Yŏksa.* Seoul, 1975.

Han, Yong'un. *Chosŏn Bulgyo Yusin Non.* Seoul, 1973.

Hyŏn, Sang'yun. *Chosŏn Yugyosa.* Seoul, 1960.

In, Chŏngsik. *Chosŏn Nong'ŏp Kyŏngjaenon.* Seoul, 1949.

———. *Chosŏn Nong'ŏp Munje Sajŏn.* Seoul, 1948.

Kang, Man'gil. *Chosŏn Hugi Sang'ŏp Chabon ŭi Paltal.* Seoul, 1973.

Kim, Ch'ŏlchun. *Han'guk Kodae Kukka Paltalsa.* Seoul, 1975.

Kim, Chunbo. *Han'guk Chabonchu ŭi Sa Yŏn'gu.* 2 vols. Seoul, 1970, 1974.

Kim, Tuhŏn. *Kungmin Yulli.* Seoul, 1972.

Kim, Yongmo. *Han'guk Sahoehak.* Seoul, 1972.

Ko, Sŭngje. *Kunse Han'guk Sanŏpsa Yŏn'gu.* Seoul, 1959. (Reviewed in Eng. by Ki-zun Zo, *JSSH*, no. 15 [1961], 84–96.)

Minjok Munhwa Yŏn'gusa. *Han'guk Munhwasa Taegye.* Vol. 6. Seoul, 1970.

Mun, Chŏngch'ang. *Han'guk Nongch'on Tanch'esa.* Seoul, 1961.

Nongchi Kaehyŏksa. *Nongchi Kaehyŏksa Pyŏnch'an Wiwŏnhoe.* Seoul, 1970.

Paek Sŏn'guk Paksa Sŏngsu Kinyŏm Saŏp Wiwŏnhoe. *Paek Sŏn'guk Paksa Sŏngsu Kinyŏm Bulgyo Nonmunjip*. Seoul, 1959.

Pak, Sihyŏng. *Chosŏn T'oji Chedosa*. Vol. 1. P'yŏngyang, 1960.

Yi, Haenam. *Han'guk Hyŏndae Chŏngch'i Munhwasa*. Seoul, 1963.

Yi, Pyŏngdo. *Tugye Chapp'il*. Seoul, 1956.

Yi Pyŏngdo Paksa Hwan'gap Kinyŏm Saŏp Wiwŏnhoe. *Yi Pyŏngdo Paksa Hwan'gap Kinyŏm Nonch'ong*. Seoul, 1949.

Yi, Sangbaek. *Yijo Kŏn'guk ŭi Yŏn'gu*. Seoul, 1949.

Yongjae Paek Nakchun Paksa Hwan'gap Kinyŏm Nonmunjip Kanhaenghoe. *Yongjae Paek Nakchun Paksa Hwan'gap Kinyŏm: Kukhak Nonch'ong*. Seoul, 1955.

Yun, Paengnam. *Chosŏn Hyŏngjŏngsa*. Seoul, 1948.

Yun, T'aerim. *Han'gugin ŭi Songgyŏk*. Seoul, 1964.


**III—Books and Articles in Japanese**

*A—Works with English Titles*

Arii, Tomonori. "On the Census Registration Law in the Early Period of Yi Dynasty." *CG*, nos. 39–40 (1966), 42–93 (Eng. summary, p. 3).

———. "Statutory Labor in the Early Period of I Dynasty." *CG*, no. 30 (1964), 62–106 (Eng. summary, p. 2) and no. 31, 58–101.

Bag, Jong-gyn. "An Analysis of Jeng Jag-iong's Reformation on Land System." *CG*, 28 (1963), 75–111 (Eng. summary, p. 2).

Ebara, Masaaki. "A Study on the Provincial Army of Gorie Period." *CG*, no. 28 (1963), 35–74 (Eng. summary, pp. 1–2).

Gim, Jong-gug. "Inquiry into the Characteristics of the Military Government of the Goryeo." *CG*, no. 17 (1960), 51–80 (Eng. summary, pp. 1–2).

———. "A Study on the Contentions between the Warrior's Regime and the Buddhist Monks in the Goryeo Period." *CG*, nos. 21–22 (1961), 567–89 (Eng. summary, p. 20).

Hiraki, Makoto. "On the Standing of Slaves (Mean Class), Wives of Common People and Their Children in 17th and 18th Centuries." *CG*, no. 61 (1971), 45–76 (Eng. summary, pp. 2–3).

I, Dae-heui. "On the System of Water Transportation in the Period of Yi Dynasty." *CG*, no. 23 (1962), 83–102 (Eng. summary, pp. 3–4).

Kubo, Noritada. "Belief of Samsi Doctrine during Yi Dynasty." *CG*, nos. 37–38 (1966), 270–95 (Eng. summary, p. 8).

Kumagai, Osamu. "On Dong-je, the Festival Commemorating Community Gods." *CG*, no. 74 (1975), 97–110 (Eng. summary, pp. 1–2).

Miyahara, Toichi (listed in error as U.). "Employers and Labourers in Korea in 15th and 16th Centuries." *CG*, no. 11 (1957), 93–116.

———. "Local Markets in 15th and 16th Century Korea." *CG*, no. 9 (1956), 165–84.

———. "A Study on Formation of the Military Labor System of Yi Dynasty." *CG*, no. 28 (1963), 112–31 (Eng. summary, p. 2).

Morioka, Yasu. "A Study on the Law Prohibiting the Accusation of One's Superiors in the Reign of King Injo in the Yi Dynasty." CG, nos. 21–22 (1961), 817–43 (Eng. summary, p. 32).

Nakai, Masataka. "On the Organs for Controlling Buddhism in Silla." CG, no. 59 (1971), 1–22 (Eng. summary, pp. 1–2).

Niida, Noboru. "The Law of Succession to a Property of Gorye and I Dynasty and the Chinese Law." CG, no. 30 (1964), 1–10 (Eng. summary, p. 1).

Tagawa, Kōzō. A Study on the Tribute System of the Ri Dynasty (Eng. summary, pp. 1–9). Tokyo, 1964.

Takeda, Yukio. "Management of the Temple Estate in the Koryŏ Period." Tōyōshi Kenkyū, 251.1 (1966), 70–91 (Eng. summary, pp. 2–3).

Zenshō, Eisuke. "Merchants of Gaiseng and Their Business Customs." CG, no. 46 (1968), 105–24 (Eng. summary, p. 4).

———. "Traditional Commercial Customs of Korea." CG, no. 9 (1956), 185–216.

*B—Works with Japanese Titles*

(Korean authors are cited with the Korean readings of their names)

Akamatsu, Chijo, and Takashi Akiba. Chōsen Fuzoku no Kenkyū. 2 vols. Tokyo, 1938; rpt. Seoul, 1970.

Ch'oe, Hojin. Kindai Chōsen Keizaishi. Tokyo, 1943.

Ch'oe, Sil-song. "Shiragi ni okeru Jizen Sonrakusei-teki Kindensei." Rekishigaku Kenkyū, no. 237 (1960), 40–47.

Ehara, Masaaki. "Kopponsei-Shiragi no Jibunsei ni kansuru Oboegaki." Shicho, no. 92 (1965), 50–55.

Fujii, Tadajiro. Chōsen Musan-Kaikyū no Kenkyū. Tokyo, 1926.

Hatada, Takashi. Chōsen Chusei Shakaishi no Kenkyū. Tokyo, 1972.

Hishimoto, Nagatsugu. Chōsen Mai no Kenkyū. Tokyo, 1938.

In, Chŏngsik. Chōsen no Nōgyō Kiko. Toyko, 1940.

Keijō Teikoku Daigaki Hōbungakubu. Chōsen Shakai Keizaishi Kenkyū. Tokyo, 1933.

Kim, Sŏkhyŏng. Chōsen Hōken Jidai Nōmin no Kaikyū Kōsei. Tokyo, 1960.

Moritani, Katsumi. Tōyōteki Shakai no Rekishi to Shisō. Tokyo, 1948.

Mun, Chŏngch'ang. Chōsen no Shijō. Tokyo, 1941; rpt. Seoul, 1969.

Murayama, Chijun. Burakusai. Keijō, 1937; rpt. Seoul, 1971.

———. Chōsen no Fusai. Keijō, 1931; rpt. Seoul, 1971.

———. Chōsen no Gunshu. Keijō, 1926.

———. Chōsen no Kishin. Keijō, 1929; rpt. Seoul, 1971.

———. Chōsen no Ruiji Shūkyō. Keijō, 1935; rpt. Seoul, 1971.

———. Chōsen no Semboku to Yogen. Keijō, 1933; rpt. Seoul, 1971.

———. Shakuson, Kiu, Antaku. Keijō, 1938; rpt. Seoul, 1971.

Nakamura, Hidetaka. "Richō Jidai no Kirosho ni Tsuite." In Ichimura Hakase Koki Kinen Tōyōshi Ronsō. Tokyo, 1933.

Nakane, Chie, ed. Hankoku Nōson no Kazoku to Saigi. Tokyo, 1973.

Paek, Namun. Chōsen Hōken Shakai Keizaishi-Jōkan. Tokyo, 1937.

———. Chōsen Shakai Keizaishi. Tokyo, 1933.

Shikata, Hiroshi. "Chōsen ni Okeru Dai-Kazokusei to Dōzoku Buraku." *Chōsen*, 11 (1937), 26–42.

Sumiya, Mikio. "Hankoku no Rōdōchiba: Sono Kōzō to Kinō." *Ajai Keizai*, no. 16 (1975), 2–12, 47–62.

Suzuki, Eitarō. *Chōsen Nōson Shakai no Kenkyū*. Tokyo, 1973.

Takahashi, Kamekichi. *Gendai Chōsen Keizairon*. Tokyo, 1935.

Watanabe, Manabu. *Kinsei Chōsen Kyoiku Kenkyū*. Tokyo, 1972.

Yi, Ch'ŏngwon. *Chōsen Shakaishi Tokuhon*. Tokyo, 1936.

Zenshō, Eisuke. *Chōsen no Shijō*. Keijō, 1924.

———. *Chōsenjin no Shōgyō*. Keijō, 1925.

———. *Chōsen no Shuraku*. 3 vols. Keijō, 1935; rpt. Seoul, 1974.

# Index

# A Note on the Author

Norman Jacobs is a professor of sociology and Asian studies at the University of Illinois. He is the author of *Modernization without Development: Thailand as an Asian Case Study*, *The Origin of Modern Capitalism and Eastern Asia*, and *The Sociology of Development: Iran as an Asian Case Study*, as well as scholarly articles on development in Asia.